The Money Doctor in the Andes

THE MONEY DOCTOR IN THE ANDES

The Kemmerer Missions, 1923–1933

Paul W. Drake

Duke University Press   Durham and London 1989

© 1989 Duke University Press
All rights reserved
Printed in the United States of America
on acid-free paper ∞

Library of Congress Cataloging-in-Publication Data
Drake, Paul W., 1944–
The money doctor in the Andes: U.S. advisers, investors, and
economic reform during the Kemmerer missions, 1923–1933 / by Paul W.
Drake.
p. cm.
Bibliography: p.
Includes index.
ISBN 0-8223-0880-0
1. Finance—Andes Region—History—20th century. 2. Kemmerer,
Edwin Walter, 1875–1945. I. Title.
HG185.A5D73   1989
332.1'098—dc19 88-18045 CIP

For my wife, Susan

CONTENTS

TABLES

TABLES

PREFACE

When this project began in 1977, the consequences for Latin America of foreign bank lending—accompanied by international economic advisers, institutions, and models—loomed as a topic of rising importance. Today, the resulting debt crisis permeates hemispheric concerns. Many of the issues and debates evoke parallels with the previous boom and bust that occurred from World War I through the Great Depression.

The phenomenon of "money doctoring" has a long pedigree. Time and again, external economic consultants and supervisers have played a crucial role in Latin America's financial development. They have been particularly significant in the accumulation, management, and impact of foreign loans. Yesterday as today, money doctors have helped local political forces reform and restructure their economies to respond to foreign investments. As intermediaries, these advisers and monitors have also enhanced access and security for those foreign investors. A rare opportunity to explore the origins, patterns, and dynamics of those inter-American financial relations was presented by the missions of Edwin Walter Kemmerer to the Andean countries. The so-called "Money Doctor" supplied many of the services that were assigned to international agencies after World War II.

Following his footsteps took as long as the original missions. Although scant secondary studies existed, the primary materials turned out to be voluminous. The extensive paper trail stretched from Princeton through Washington, D.C., to the five Andean nations. In many cases, especially in Ecuador and Bolivia, very few scholarly analyses of the 1920s and 1930s were available. The historical context of the period had to be pieced together before the role of external forces could be assessed. Consequently, I learned a great deal not only about U.S. technocrats abroad but also about the Andean republics, as I hope my readers will.

ACKNOWLEDGMENTS

My journey through six countries in ten years accumulated enormous professional debts that not even the Money Doctor could help me repay.

For funding I am indebted to the Joint Committee on Latin American Studies of the Social Science Research Council and to the Latin American Program of the Woodrow Wilson International Center for Scholars. During my stay in the Castle, the Wilson Center staff was highly supportive, especially Abraham F. Lowenthal and Alexander Wilde. The University of Illinois, Urbana-Champaign, where I enjoyed thirteen years on the faculty, also financed part of this research, through a paid sabbatical and through grants from its Research Board and its Center for Latin American and Caribbean Studies. That center's secretary, Dorothy Osborne, gave me constant encouragement and typing assistance. My new home, the University of California at San Diego, supported the final stages, while Lee Dewey skillfully processed these words. Through these institutions I benefited from industrious and thoughtful research assistants: Mark E. Brewster, Orlando Pacheco, Baldomero Estrada, Marcus Joaquim Maciel de Carvalho, Gerardo Munck, and Wendy Prentice.

The research in the United States began in the University of Illinois library, where I received the guidance of Carl Deal, Nelly Gonzalez, and Sara de Mundo Lo. In Washington, D.C., extensive work was conducted in the National Archives and the Library of Congress. Even more important were the Edwin Walter Kemmerer Papers in Princeton University's Seeley G. Mudd Manuscript Library. There, Donald L. Kemmerer, Edwin's son, first granted me access, and the curator, Nancy Bressler, extended every courtesy.

Indeed, no one provided as much help with the overall project as did Don Kemmerer. In an extremely professional and generous manner he shared with me his father's papers, transcriptions from his diary, personal and bibliographic leads, and reminiscences of the man and the missions. Unlike some descendants of famous parents, Don never tried to restrict my investigation or influence my judgments. Although he may not agree with this book's interpretations, I hope he finds them scholarly and fair.

Other U.S. academics also gave me useful suggestions and comments on the general project and its conceptualization. Bruce R. Dalgaard introduced me to Don Kemmerer, eased my entry into the topic, and discussed freely his own studies of the missions to South Africa and Guatemala. My longtime colleague Joseph L. Love tirelessly criticized, and improved, draft after draft. I also gleaned insights from Brad Barham, John Coatsworth, Peter Cowhey, Richard Feinberg, Albert O. Hirschman, Miles Kahler, Charles Lipson, Emily S. Rosenberg, Barbara Stallings, and Rosemary Thorp.

For the Colombian chapter, Albert Berry, Charles Bergquist, Roger Findley, Juan Carlos Jaramillo, Mauricio Solaún, Steve Stein, José Torres, Eduardo Vélez, and Alex Wilde opened doors in that country. The Department of Political Science at the Universidad de los Andes was kind enough to make me a visiting research professor; my hosts there included Fernando Cepeda Ulloa, Francisco Leal Buitrago, Gabriel Murillo, and Dora Rothlisberger. I am also grateful for advice and comments from Antonio Alvarez Restrepo, Rodrigo Botero Montoya, Rudolff Hommes, Samuel Hoyos Arango, Rodrigo Losada, José Antonio Ocampo, Alfonso Palacio Rudas, Alfonso Patiño Roselli, Jaime Recaman, and Miguel Urrutia. My endeavors were also facilitated by the Banco de la República, the Biblioteca Luis Angel Arango, and the Biblioteca Nacional.

Exploring the Chilean case was made easier and more interesting by Jorge Barría, Pedro del Fierro, Marcos Duffau Urrutia, Ricardo Ffrench-Davis, Manuel Antonio Garretón, John P. Harrison, Alvaro Jara, Julio César Jobet, Rolando Mellafe, and Osvaldo Sunkel. The personnel of the Banco Central, the Biblioteca Nacional, the Biblioteca del Congreso, and the Dirección General de Estadística also deserve thanks. Frank W. Fetter clarified key points in an interview. Stephany Griffith-Jones, Markos Mamalakis, Thomas O'Brien, and William Sater provided comments on the draft chapter.

Marcelo Naranjo, Frank Salomon, and Norman Whitten established my initial contacts in Ecuador. While there, I profited from conversations with Paul Oquist and Rafael Quintero. My most important connections were with the following people and their institutions: Nick D. Mills, Jr., and the Andean Study and Research Center, Irving Iván Zapater and the Banco Central, Julián Bravo and the Biblioteca Ecuatoriana Aurelio Espinoza Polit, José Clemente Bognoli and the Biblioteca Municipal, and Juan Freile-Granizo and the Archivo Nacional de Historia. My graduate student, Cynthia Nichols, also merits recognition for her assistance.

My incursion into Bolivia was smoothed by Horencia Ballivián, Alberto Crespo R., Peter DeShazo, Nelly Gonzalez, Jack Harrison, and Antonio Ovando Rojas. I spent many fruitful hours in the repositories of the Biblioteca Central de la Universidad Mayor de San Andrés, the Biblioteca Municipal, the

Banco Central, and the Contraloría General. Graduate student Jayne Spencer also supplied bibliographic leads.

Finally, in Peru, my initiation began with Werner Baer, Tom Davies, Steve Stein, and the Llosa and Gavilano families. I received indispensable guidance from Heraclio Bonilla, Baltazar Caravedo Molinari, Julio Cotler, and Alberto Escobar at the Instituto de Estudios Peruanos. Also helpful was Adolfo Figueroa. I found the essential collections at the Biblioteca Nacional (with the able assistance of Graciela Sánchez Cerro) and the Banco Central de Reserva. David Wise, a graduate student, fleshed out my bibliography.

All the scholars and institutions mentioned above deserve credit for this study's virtues but not its shortcomings. Through that decade of traveling with the Money Doctor, my wife, Susan Bryant Drake, supported and enriched this investigation. To her this book is dedicated.

Political map of South America, 1904–1938. © 1969 John Wiley & Sons, adapted from Theodore R. Miller, *Graphic History of the Americas*, New York, 1969.

1 MONEY DOCTORING AND THE DIPLOMACY OF THE DOLLAR IN LATIN AMERICA: WORLD WAR I TO THE GREAT DEPRESSION

During and after World War I the United States extended its economic dominance from the Caribbean and Central America into South America. The Colossus of the North displaced Great Britain by establishing an "open door" for "the diplomacy of the dollar." In the 1920s the United States wove trading, investing, and political connections throughout the hemisphere, foreshadowing the crises of debt and hegemony of the 1980s. During the interwar years and thereafter, private and public financial institutions, practices, and interactions significantly influenced those relations and their impact on "dependency" and "development" in Latin America. Despite their importance those international and national financial mechanisms have, until recently, received little scholarly attention. Even more neglected have been the integral and intricate roles of foreign advisers and models in facilitating the evolution of those economic linkages.

A unique opportunity to examine the origins, operations, and ramifications of U.S. economic supremacy in South America is provided by the Kemmerer missions to the Andean countries. From 1923 through 1931 Dr. Edwin Walter Kemmerer, a professor of economics at Princeton University, carried out profound reforms of the monetary, banking, and fiscal systems of Colombia, Chile, Ecuador, Bolivia, and Peru. During the same era he performed similar surgery in Mexico, Guatemala, Germany, South Africa, Poland, China, and Turkey. This study uses his missions and their extensive documentation as a rare framework for comparative history. This book does not constitute a biography passing judgment on the man; his exceptional talents and stature speak for themselves.

It is possible to examine the effects of Kemmerer's missions in five countries because his ideas and recommendations—and the issues he addressed—varied little during a short, well-defined time period in a coherent region. Since virtually the same international forces enveloped the entire hemisphere, comparisons of how domestic interest groups related to the world economy will stand out among the Andean republics. Especially evident will be common economic and political patterns too often interpreted as intrinsically domestic phenomena. For example, it is quite unlikely that one country's local problems explain its creation of a central bank when all its neighbors were establishing exactly the same institution at precisely the same time. Examining five cases in depth, as well as others in passing, will yield generalizations about the politics of money doctoring, foreign investments, and economic reforms.

The economic changes fostered by Kemmerer were vast, but his influence should not be exaggerated. His reforms mainly reinforced and guided larger international and domestic forces that were already present and were the primary cause of the pace and character of transformations in the 1920s. Similar trends occurred in Latin American countries he did not visit. Nevertheless, an examination of his missions provides an unparalleled and concentrated focus on those forces and patterns, and shows how his policies acted to slant them in particular directions.

Above all, this analysis of such financial missions sheds light on the political economy of four key developments in the era. First, it examines the motives and methods of these types of foreign technical assistance; it asks how and why they experienced success, and for whom. Second, it assesses the influence of economic advisers and other factors on the growing dependence of these countries on the external market in general and on the United States in particular, and shows the shift from British to U.S. "hegemony." Third, it evaluates the impact of these external influences on the articulation of internal capitalist sectors, institutions, and operations, especially in the burgeoning cities of Latin America. A particular focus will be on the formation of coalitions which made—and unmade—the Kemmerer policies; those policymaking coalitions were both national and transnational, linking internal and external actors. They clashed as well as cooperated in their pursuit of advantageous positions in an increasingly internationalized economy. Fourth, this book explores how the state in the Andean countries became both more reliant on foreign forces and more capable of managing domestic affairs. In sum, although the economic history of these phenomena will be described, the overwhelming emphasis will be on the politics of these changes instead of on econometric measuring or testing of economic theories.

According to Kemmerer and most observers of his missions, he experienced his spectacular success mainly because of a particularly adept and valuable transfer of technology. In truth, although his hosts desired those new economic institutions and techniques, they turned to foreign advisers through ulterior motives. Above all, the Andean countries wanted to improve their access to U.S. financial and commodity markets in order to satisfy emergent urban groups and to enhance the state's capacity to cope with those rising foreign and domestic forces.

Before analyzing those broader economic and political motivations, it is valid to interpret the missions more narrowly, as transfers of technology and builders of institutions. For the growth of capitalism in Latin America, the adoption of more efficient foreign laws, agencies, and policies proved crucial. For example, improvements in the legal and institutional infrastructure narrowed the biggest gap between the market economies of Mexico and the United States in the late nineteenth century. Modernizing Mexico's economic superstructure, organization, and transportation reduced the major political and social obstacles to the mobility of entrepreneurs, capital, and labor. Mexico achieved that rationalization of the "rules of the game"—and thus growth—by embracing foreign models, investors, and traders.[1]

In similar fashion Kemmerer introduced monumental innovations in Andean economic regulations, practices, and underpinnings. In his most sweeping renovation he implanted twenty-six new laws and agencies in Ecuador, thoroughly revamping money, banking, government budgeting, taxation, customs, credit, public works, and railroads. The institutions he fostered—such as the central bank, the superintendency of banking, and the national comptroller—still dominate the government plazas and policy apparatuses in the Andean countries. Studying those accomplishments fills a void in Latin American research, where the origins and functions of public entities in the twentieth century (in contrast with the colonial period) have received little attention. The formation of these financial and fiscal foundations in the 1920s deserves more scrutiny.

The institutional approach, however, explains only a small part of the causes and consequences of utilizing foreign technical missions. Deeper research shows that these countries normally could and did design equivalent reforms without relying on advisers from abroad. For example, most of them had already hammered out adequate central bank projects before Kemmerer arrived. The authorship and intention of these innovations can only be understood in the context of more profound international and national processes dovetailing in the twentieth century.

More than channels for the diffusion of so-called "modernization," the primary significance of foreign missions was as a device for multiple actors in the United States and in the Andean countries. Although Kemmerer saw his primary goal as scientific enlightenment, his external and internal supporters entertained additional expectations. This type of foreign assistance provided a mechanism for three interrelated purposes, as it often still does.

First, private missions offered leverage for the United States to extend its hegemony from the Caribbean and Central America into South America. In accord with the "open door" policy, Kemmerer's reforms secured capitalist conformity without the counterproductive use of direct U.S. economic, diplomatic, or military pressures. His installation of economic principles and practices copied from U.S. blueprints reduced uncertainties for international investors and traders. Incorporating North American laws into the Andean countries compensated for the lack of enforceable international regulations for transactions. For the South Americans, Kemmerer's "good housekeeping seal" allowed them to take some advantage of U.S. predominance and resources without becoming virtual colonies like their brethren in the Caribbean Basin.[2]

Second, political and economic contenders within the Andean countries used these outside experts to further their own ambitions. In an era of growing cities and factories, emergent urban interests capitalized on foreign missions to improve their standing vis-à-vis traditional agricultural and export sectors. One partial exception was Bolivia, where the tin mine owners proved almost omnipotent. There as elsewhere, however, Kemmerer's reforms helped industrialists, financiers, and merchants to tap national and international sources for credit and infrastructural development. As a result of his legislation, producers for domestic consumption usually made gains on producers for foreign consumption. Through the lens of these advisory teams a seldom-studied facet of urban changes within Latin America in the 1920s comes into view.

Third, Andean central governments employed foreign commissions to expand their extractive and distributive capabilities. Those growing and increasingly activist bureaucracies became better managed and financed. The public sector enhanced its ability to mediate between foreign and national capitalists and between conflicting domestic groups, and responded to urban middle and working classes as well as to entrepreneurs. Kemmerer's visits reflected and facilitated significant growth of both the state and urban enterprises well before the Great Depression accelerated those trends.

Those structural patterns between external and internal forces become more obvious when the Kemmerer missions are placed in the context of broader interpretations of outside influences on Latin American economic history. Over the years, two fundamental and contradictory perspectives on his work took hold. Just as many Latin Americans did during the 1920s, most later analysts praised him as the pioneer of scientific financial and fiscal codes and operations. Kemmerer was lauded as the father of such public landmarks as the central bank and the national comptroller. These enthusiasts observed that the essential features of his reforms eventually spread from the Andean republics to nearly all of Latin America. In short, his admirers enshrined the Money Doctor as a catalyst of modernization and development.[3]

Like many Latin Americans during the Great Crash, however, a minority of later commentators condemned Kemmerer as the opening wedge for U.S. capitalist penetration and domination, the midwife of financial imperialism, the Trojan horse of dependency and underdevelopment. For example, Colombian critics of "scientific and cultural neo-colonialism" complained that "dependency is the economic missions of foreign experts which, from the Kemmerer Mission in 1923 up to our days, have planned for us banking, commerce, and above all the tax system, and which to boot have encased us within the economic programs of the U.S.A., with the . . . recommendation that that is the only way to escape from 'underdevelopment,' thereby stimulating the mentality of the false technocrats of developmentalism."[4]

Neither stereotypical "modernization" nor "dependency" perspectives capture all the subtleties and complexities of these missions and the accompanying changes in the Andean region. Contrary to any simplistic modernization theory, export and debt-led growth entailed high costs in terms of subservience to external powers, outflows of capital, and unequal distribution of gains. Although an open economic model brought significant benefits during the upswing of the world economy in the mid-1920s, it ushered in disaster during the collapse at the end of that decade. In contrast with any schematic theory of dependency, the national state and local urban industries grew not only after the Great Depression shattered ties to the international system but also during the period of massive U.S. penetration. In the 1920s the Latin Americans hoped to use their deepening reliance on North American goods, capital, companies, advisers, and technology to build up their domestic economic and political institutions as potential bulwarks of national development for the future. This study will show that the Andean countries were more dependent on the United States than many historians have realized. That "dependent development," however, took contradictory turns that were uncontrolled by U.S. interests.[5]

Following the opening of the Panama Canal and the devastation of Europe in World War I, the increasing integration of the Andean republics into commercial and financial systems dominated by the United States became virtually inevitable. Given those countries' historically subordinate place within the international economic order, the growth and contours of capitalism in the Andes were bound to be heavily influenced by external industrial giants. Nevertheless, these countries were not mere putty in the hands of the world system. Those outside forces filtered through elitist domestic sociopolitical structures and groups, who pursued their own agendas within the constraints and opportunities presented by the international arena. Those predominantly agrarian societies emphasized their comparative advantage in raw material production for export. In the prosperous 1920s Latin American leaders rarely deviated from the prevailing Western orthodoxy of economic ideas. Almost no one articulated alternative strategies to capitalist expansion through increasing interconnections with U.S. markets. In that era the question was not whether South America would deepen its dependence on the Colossus of the North, but rather how much, in what ways, and with what impacts within diverse countries and among their conflicting socioeconomic sectors. The key issue was through what mechanisms and to what extent might these small nations take some advantage of an inherently unequal relationship.

Andean political and economic elites brought in U.S. technocrats to smooth their countries' adjustment to seemingly unavoidable reliance on the emerging Western world leader. They used such missions to bring their economic techniques up-to-date with North American methods, to fortify indigenous money and banking institutions, and to bolster their states' financial and management capabilities. Although appreciating the intrinsic value of many of those imported reforms, these governments desired foreign advisers primarily to attract external investors and to consolidate political stability internally. While U.S. government and corporate representatives strongly encouraged the Latin Americans to invite and heed these experts, the hosts also exploited the technicians for their own purposes.

Although unique in some ways, the Kemmerer missions' techniques resembled three analogous reforms of Latin American finances generated from abroad. First, his advisory teams echoed some themes from the Spanish Bourbon reformers of the latter half of the eighteenth century. Both programs tried to stimulate a more open export economy, control credit, update economic techniques and management, and expand central state revenues, efficiency, and powers. The Spaniards brought legal, administrative, and technical innovations from the imperial center to the colonies to facilitate and channel economic growth. Besides causing rising colonial productivity, they helped the empire and local bureaucracies take advantage of it as well. In the short run the Bourbons tied Spanish-American satellites more closely into the metropolitan network. In the long run, however, they helped set in motion local forces and expectations which led to independence from the mother country in the opening decades of the nineteenth century. Thereafter, Latin Americans latched on to British, French (to a lesser extent), and later U.S. economic models.[6]

A second, much closer analogy with the Kemmerer reforms is seen in the policies of the United States in dealing with its informal empire in the Caribbean and Central America during the first three decades of the twentieth century. Private missions used persuasion in South America to replicate much of what U.S. officials had achieved through force of arms in Central America and the Caribbean: exchange stability, modern banking, fiscal order, more efficient customs administration, punctual debt payments, Anglo-Saxon commercial practices, and equal rights for foreign capitalists. Consequently, international loans and trade increased as the United States displaced European competitors.

After World War I, most U.S. government and business leaders realized that all they needed to exploit their intrinsic advantages over European and Latin American rivals was equal opportunity. They knew that they were more likely to obtain such an "open door" for trade and investments in South America without resorting to coercion. An advocate of laissez-faire, Kemmerer convinced his compliant hosts to reduce encumbrances to the free flow of goods and capital. Despite significant differences in political and economic autonomy between the Caribbean and the Andes, there evolved a structural similarity of increasing adoption of U.S. economic models accompanied by increasing reliance on U.S. exports, loans, companies, and entrepreneurs, which pulled the South American pattern closer to that of direct client states. This systemic parallel was personified by a few of the U.S. specialists hired by the Andean republics on Kemmerer's recommendation because they had gained experience in forced financial cleanups in the Caribbean and Central America.[7]

Although sending in experts achieved some of the same results as sending in marines, their roles differed significantly. The United States never exerted political-military power or official control of fiscal institutions in South America as it did in countries closer to its own borders. The Andean governments engaged Kemmerer's missions independently. Although his teams' members rotated in and out of U.S. banks and government agencies before and after their advisory work, they were contracted privately by Kemmerer. As a hired consultant for the Andean republics, he tried to maintain a professional distance from Washington as well as Wall Street. Whether formally linked or separated, these pluralistic U.S. advisers, financiers, and public officials in effect worked in harmony toward the same broad goals. However autonomously conceived, Kemmerer's reforms served the mutual desires of North American and South American elites for increased economic interaction.

Kemmerer's stabilization missions also prefigured later International Monetary Fund (IMF) operations. Neither the Money Doctor nor the IMF arrived as an official envoy from formal or informal imperial governments. Both claimed reputations as international, neutral experts, invited voluntarily by host countries. Critics attacked both agents, however, as tools the United States used to impose unpalatable formulas on weaker nations. In actuality, both Kemmerer and the IMF helped install economic policies usually desired by local elites as well as by North Americans, and transnational coalitions made these policy changes possible. Through those measures the host governments sought better access to foreign loans to favor selected domestic groups, although Kemmerer had less direct influence in that area than did the IMF. They both visited foreign governments to reorder finances and improve the balance of payments, thus facilitating future debt servicing. In many cases their prescriptions sounded similar: stabilized exchange rates, controlled currency emissions, restricted credit allocations, and economized and monitored government budgets.[8]

In contrast with the highly controversial IMF, Kemmerer's missions normally encountered a near-national consensus in favor of their recommendations. In almost every country he obtained stunningly easy acceptance of stabilization measures which would have been considered painful and conflictual in the decades following World War II. One reason for his success was that foreign loans were amply available in the 1920s to soothe the pain of adjustments; another was that Kemmerer's hosts sometimes carried out his strictures—especially those calling for austerity—on paper only. More important, in still highly agrarian societies, elitist governments could ignore many in the lower and even middle classes at minimal political cost. Low levels of social and political mobilization prevailed in the Andean countries prior to the 1930s. Therefore inflation and stabilization policies seldom became fierce battles over scarce resources among well-articulated interest groups and social classes. The range of political participation was especially narrow in Ecuador, Bolivia, and Peru, where over half the population were still defined as Indians tangential to the cash economy and national decisionmaking. For Kemmerer's suggestions to win acceptance, almost all he needed was agreement among the sectors of the upper class.

Also in contrast with the IMF, Kemmerer attracted a broad base of support because labor usually saw him as an ally. Trade unions hailed his efforts to stem a rising cost of living which benefited only the wealthy few. In the 1920s South American reformers normally viewed currency depreciation and price inflation as schemes by landed oligarchs, exporters, speculators, bankers, and/or the state to achieve an inequitable distribution of income. That politicosocial image of inflation changed from the 1930s onward. Henceforth champions of the working class denounced stabilization programs as plots by the rich to maintain an unfair distribution of income. Kemmerer's recommendations did not evoke labor hostility because they came prior to the days of strong unions, heavily protected industrialization, and government controls over wages and prices. Before organized labor acquired enough political muscle to become a significant actor in the inflationary spiral, stabilization seemed to mean belt tightening principally by the state, bankers, and producers. For example, in Chile and Ecuador a coalition of army and labor leaders spearheaded the campaign for Kemmerer—an alliance unlikely to act for the IMF.[9]

However imperfect, these IMF, U.S., and Bourbon analogies underscore the need to analyze foreign economic modeling as far more than merely technical assistance. The greatest importance of this imported technology lay within the contexts of broader international relations and of individual host country economic, social, and political configurations. Before examining the Kemmerer missions as an influence and a window on the development of the Andean countries in the 1920s, let us explore their origins within the United States.

Edwin Walter Kemmerer and His Missions

Kemmerer stood, for a historical moment, at the intersection of external and internal economic forces shaping the development of Latin America. He occupied a position and a vantage point rarely held by reasonably neutral agents or observers. Without being an official of any government or corporation, he enjoyed extraordinary access to all the key public and private actors—to presidents of countries as well as banks, to both Latin and North American policymakers. Moving in the interface between the international and national economies, his missions conditioned and revealed the political economy of intricate interactions among multiple foreign and domestic interests. He brought to that role a cluster of experiences and beliefs acquired as an academic economist.[10]

Edwin Walter Kemmerer (1875–1945) earned his Ph.D. at Cornell University in 1901. His relationship with the U.S. government began with his assignment to put the Philippines on the gold standard in 1903. He spent most of his career as a professor of economics and finance at Princeton University. He assisted in the organization of the U.S. Federal Reserve System in 1911, helped edit the *American Economic Bulletin* and the *American Economic Review*, and became president of the American Economic Association in 1926. After an unsuccessful stint as adviser to President Venustiano Carranza in Mexico in 1917, he accepted an invitation from the Guatemalan government, at the State Department's suggestion, in 1919. That effort also foundered on the shoals of local political and economic obstacles to his plans. When the State Department recommended him as an adviser to Colombia in 1923, Kemmerer launched his first full-scale, and highly successful, independent mission, replete with a team of experts and a complete overhaul of financial and fiscal institutions. Thereafter, his soaring reputation attracted invitations from numerous governments without any official U.S. mediation. The subsequent State Department role in arranging his missions usually consisted only in "good offices," for example proposing his name to governments or requesting his leave of absence from Princeton.

Although publishing extensively, he achieved more fame as an extraordinary international economic adviser than as a theorist.[11] Nevertheless, his writings and beliefs built the reputation that made him a desirable consultant. Kemmerer pioneered in the application of statistical methods to the study of money. Joining the debate over the quantity theory of money, he wrote widely on that topic as well as on banking and financial reforms. Kemmerer always argued that inflation posed a greater peril than deflation, especially to the working class. Even after the Great Depression he remained a true believer in the gold standard. Steadfast, he implemented the gold standard in the Philippines during 1903–6, recommended it as a hemispheric monetary unit to the Pan American Union in 1916, installed it around the globe in the 1920s, and bemoaned its abandonment in the 1930s, considering Keynesian economics impractical. After the Great Crash his fame and influence faded.[12]

A product of the Progressive Era, Kemmerer saw himself as a professional expert bringing universal, scientific advances to backward countries. In his view such technical enlightenment could create efficient institutions free from the corrupting influence of politics and privilege. He intended his reforms to improve opportunities for underdeveloped countries and their poorer citizens. During a tour of South America as a trade commissioner for the U.S. government in 1922, he was impressed by labor protests against inflation. The following year he got his first opportunity to apply his expertise to those problems when Colombia presented the first of a series of invitations to the Andean countries. Kemmerer realized that those solicitations came to him and to other North Americans largely because of the snowballing U.S. role in international trade and finance.[13]

Growing Dependence on the United States

Andean countries in the 1920s preferred North American over European advisers because they found themselves increasingly involved with international markets suddenly dominated by the United States. U.S. global expansion in the wake of World War I resulted from general domestic prosperity and relative European weakness, and was also a response to the international restoration of basic features of the prewar economic system, especially the gold standard and exchange stability. After an explosion of activity in South America during the war, the United States lost a little ground to renewed European competition in the early postwar years and then reaffirmed its supremacy during the remainder of the 1920s. In that decade U.S. overseas expansion concentrated on Latin America, and U.S. foreign policy sought the peaceful replacement of European business interests there.[14]

As a result of World War I and the economic tide from the United States, Great Britain lost its nearly century-old preeminent position in the Andes. Its share of exports and imports on the west coast of South America declined even more than its generally shrinking proportion of trade around the globe. From 1913 to 1929 England's share of world imports fell from 16 to 15 percent and of world exports from 14 to 11 percent.[15] Meanwhile, the value of U.S. total trade in South America rose approximately 300 percent, leaving Britain ahead only in Argentina, Uruguay, and Bolivia. Investment patterns followed trading trends.

In 1913 Britain had an estimated $532 million invested in the five Andean republics, while the United States had a mere $72 million. Sixteen years later, England's investments had increased by only 14 percent, while those of the United States had risen—according to enthusiasts—by over 1,200 percent, surpassing the British total by over $360 million. British direct and indirect investments were increasingly concentrated in Argentina, Brazil, and Mexico. South American governments could borrow at lower interest rates in New York than in London, where overseas investments plummeted from roughly 8 percent of national income in 1913 to 2 percent by 1929.[16] Previously powerful British banks within the Andean countries also faced challenges from U.S. competitors. Although the influx of U.S. dollars, goods, businessmen, and advisers weakened the position of those British institutions, they normally favored the stabilization of currency and banking instigated by Kemmerer.[17]

Because his visits improved Andean economic and political relations with the United States, the British and the French sometimes carped about the Kemmerer missions, urging South Americans to hire their experts instead. Despite heated rivalries over Latin American markets, England and the United States increasingly engaged in "cooperative competition" as the 1920s wore on. Their mutual desire for international order and security, for both business and diplomacy, motivated the two industrial giants to reach an informal entente on economic policies in Latin America. When South American leaders tried to play the two powers off against each other, it often turned out that British and U.S. government and business interests were in collaboration.[18]

The United States first displaced the British in trade. Following the opening of the Panama Canal at the start of World War I, all the Andean countries multiplied their commerce with the United States, peaking at the end of the 1920s. Even before the war North Americans had made significant inroads. Then, from 1913 to 1928, South America's exports to the United States rose from 19 to 25 percent, while exports to the United Kingdom fell from 25 to 21 percent. At the same time imports from the United States rose from 16 to 30 percent, while imports from the United Kingdom fell from 28 to 19 percent. While Latin American exports to the United States increased only slightly more proportionately than did total exports, imports from the United States almost tripled as the total value of imports nearly doubled. Of the total value of U.S. exports from 1910–14 to 1929, those going to South America ascended from 6 percent to 10 percent. During the same period U.S. imports from South America climbed from 12 percent to 14 percent of total U.S. imports. Table 1.1 shows the particularly dramatic U.S. gains over the British in the Andean countries. Prior to the Kemmerer missions, U.S. policymakers hoped that increasing investments south of the border would induce Latin Americans to buy more from

Table 1.1   Latin American Trade with the United States and the United Kingdom, 1913–1929 (in millions of U.S. dollars)

Imports

	Total		From United States		From United Kingdom	
	1913	1929	1913	1929	1913	1929
Latin America	1,453	2,415	357	931		
South America	1,157	1,868	196	581		
Colombia	28	122	7	56	6	18
Ecuador	9	17	3	7	3	3
Peru	29	76	8	32	8	11
Bolivia	21	26	2	9	4	4
Chile	120	197	20	63	36	35

Exports

	Total		To United States		To United Kindom	
	1913	1929	1913	1929	1913	1929
Latin America	1,588	2,920	472	994		
South America	1,204	2,222	201	557		
Columbia	33	123	15	92	5	6
Ecuador	16	17	4	8	2	1
Peru	44	134	15	47	16	25
Bolivia	37	51	0	7	30	39
Chile	143	279	30	71	56	37

Sources: Pan American Union, Division of Economic Research, *The Foreign Trade of Latin America since 1913* (Washington, D.C.:, 1952), pp. 25–49; J. R. McKey and H. S. Giusta, *United States Trade with Latin America in 1925.* II. *Southern Latin America* (Washington, D.C., 1926); Grace A. Witherow, *Foreign Trade of the United States in the Calendar Year 1930* (Washington, D.C., 1931); George J. Eder, *A New Measure of Our Latin American Trade* (Washington, D.C., 1930); Clyde W. Phelps, *The Foreign Expansion of American Banks* (New York, 1927), pp. 113, 123.

the United States and thus improve its unfavorable balance of trade with the region. Rising sales to South America in the latter half of the 1920s did brighten that trade picture.

Already leading in Colombian and Ecuadorean trade before the war, the United States thereafter surpassed England everywhere except in Bolivia. More isolated from the Pacific and closer to the Argentine pattern, Bolivia continued doing business primarily with Great Britain. This commercial relationship persisted even though U.S. capital outstripped British capital in Bolivia. Despite U.S. government and business hopes, trade did not always follow finance.[19]

The Kemmerer missions furthered soaring foreign trade in the Andes—especially U.S. exports there—by recommending exchange stabilization, negotiable instruments laws, and customs reforms. U.S. government officials and exporters believed that the "Iberian institutional heritage" and depreciating currencies had been major impediments to commercial expansion in Latin America. They expected Kemmerer's reforms, by removing those obstacles, to spur foreign loans and domestic growth in South America, thereby increasing purchases from the United States.[20]

U.S. investments as well as trade spiraled upward in the Andes in the 1920s. As a result, the United States caught up with Great Britain in total investments in Latin America, while shooting far ahead in the Andes. U.S. investments rose more rapidly in the five "Kemmererized" countries than anywhere else except Cuba and Venezuela. Between World War I and the Great Depression Latin America received more private U.S. capital than any other world area; total U.S. investments in the region roughly tripled. By the end of the 1920s, over one-third of all U.S. foreign investments were in Latin America. There, the biggest increases occurred in South America and in portfolio (indirect) investments. From 1914 to 1929 South America's share of total U.S. direct and indirect investments in Latin America spurted from 22 to 56 percent (see table 1.2). In the 1920s portfolio investments comprised 70 to 80 percent of the increase in total U.S. investments in Latin America. Latin American governments imposed virtually no restrictions on the entry or exit of foreign capital.[21]

Table 1.2.   United States Investments in Latin America, 1914–1930 (in millions of U.S. dollars)

	Direct investments		Indirect investments		Total investments	
	1914	1930	1914	1930	1914	1930
Latin America	1,281	3,634	368	1,610	1,649	5,244
South America	323	1,631	43	1,411	366	3,042
Colombia		130		172	22	302
Ecuador		12		0	9	12
Peru		125		75	63	200
Bolivia		62		54	11	116
Chile		441		260	181	701

Note: These figures, like much of the data in this book, represent reasonable agreement among approximations from several sources, all of which present slightly different numbers but concur on general magnitudes. More precise statistics and calculations were either impossible to establish or unnecessary for this book's argument. Unless stated otherwise, most values in this book are presented in nominal terms.

Sources: See note 21.

Most of the direct investments went into mining, petroleum, agriculture, railways, and public utilities. Kemmerer had little impact on these infusions of corporate capital. Although his reforms helped such investors by modernizing the general economic setting, his missions seldom served the interests of any particular U.S. enterprises. He did play a role in facilitating a 1930 U.S. bank loan that encouraged Colombian generosity to U.S. oil companies. He also clashed with U.S. firms, however, by recommending increased taxation on exporters of bananas in Colombia and copper in Chile. He intended those revenue measures to solidify government finances in order to protect the gold standard and service foreign debts. Some U.S. resident exporters and currency speculators within Latin America also bemoaned his exchange stabilization, which was welcomed by exporters and lenders within the United States.

Although normally complementary, the interests of U.S. corporations, banks, government officials, and advisers sometimes conflicted, especially on specific issues. Latin Americans frequently perceived diverse U.S. business and governmental groups as more intimately interconnected and unified than they actually were. South Americans mistakenly believed that friendly treatment of one set of U.S. concerns would necessarily help with others. Lack of coherent coordination among U.S. economic and political actors perplexed Andean leaders trying to juggle these multiple foreign forces.

The United States promoted worldwide adoption of the gold standard to guarantee order for its economic expansion, and sought to pull Latin American countries away from reliance on British sterling. Many of those nations even began having their money printed in the United States. U.S. business executives wanted predictable exchange rates. U.S. elites hoped that gold standards tied to the U.S. dollar and U.S. banks would increase U.S. exports and safeguard U.S. investments.[22]

Kemmerer's gold standard and central bank facilitated indirect more than direct foreign investments. His system, in turn, depended on foreign loans to help service previous external debts, to cover shortfalls in the balance of payments, and to convince Latin Americans of the value of exchange stability. In part the Andean countries received a flood of foreign loans because of the gold standard and to sustain the gold standard. In the 1920s Latin America received the greatest influx of U.S. private finance capital prior to the 1970s. It also obtained a rising share: after absorbing approximately 19 percent of all U.S. foreign loans from 1920 to 1924, Latin America took 32 percent from 1925 to 1929. Those dollars funded a great deal of domestic state activism because they went mainly to governments, as the estimates in table 1.3 show.

From the point of view of the United States, these loans were expected to generate more purchases of its exports and more return payments on interest and principal. It was widely believed that overseas outlets were needed for

Table 1.3.   United States Indirect Investments in Latin America, 1930
(in millions of U.S. dollars)

	National	Provincial	Municipal	Government-guaranteed corporate	Private corporate	Total
			Government			
Latin America	1,014	293	162	106	35	1,610
South America	830	293	158	99	31	1,411
Colombia	44	63	23	14	28	172
Ecuador	0	0	0	0	0	0
Peru	71	1	3	0	0	75
Bolivia	54	0	0	0	0	54
Chile	155	0	20	85	0	260

Sources: Paul D. Dickens, *American Underwriting of Foreign Securities in 1930* (Washington, D.C., 1931); P. D. Dickens, *A New Estimate of American Investments Abroad* (Washington, D.C., 1931); Eugene W. Chevreaux, *Financial Developments in Latin America during 1930* (Washington, D.C., 1931); Max Winkler, *Foreign Bonds; An Autopsy* (Philadelphia, 1933); M. Winkler, *Investment of United States Capital in Latin America* (Boston, 1928); Ilse Mintz, *Deterioration in the Quality of Foreign Bonds Issued in the United States, 1920–1930* (New York, 1951).

excess U.S. products and capital. Even before World War I the U.S. government encouraged initially timid U.S. bankers to lend in Latin America to facilitate the general growth of U.S. business there. By the 1920s, eager North American financiers were competing avidly with each other and with Europeans to arrange loans to equally voracious Latin American borrowers. At the start of the 1930s the U.S. assistant secretary of state for Latin American affairs concluded: "In the carnival days from 1922 to 1929, when money was easy, many American bankers forsook the dignified aloof attitude traditional of bankers and became, in reality, high pressure salesmen of money, carrying on a cutthroat competition against their fellow bankers, and once they obtained the business, endeavored to urge larger loans on the borrowing countries." Those bankers sometimes pressed imprudent loans because they were not extending their own money. Rather, they served as intermediaries who sold government bonds to individual U.S. investors. The bankers' profits came from commissions on the original contracts, not from eventual servicing of the debt. Some investment houses stooped to bribes to win those contracts. While greed caused some financial firms to ignore the creditworthiness of Latin American borrowers, other bankers went to great lengths to try to investigate, solidify, and even control Latin American finances. Those more responsible bankers hoped to establish long-term relationships with both the debtors in Latin America and the creditors in the United States. They sometimes relied on North American advisers to assess, shore up, and/or burnish the image of financial conditions in Latin America. Bankers hoped that Kemmerer's checkup of a country would improve the security, or at least the marketability, of its bonds.[23]

By the same token, South American governments employed such advisers to improve their access to loans at reasonable terms. They knew that a record and reputation for fiscal disorders and loan defaults dissuaded many North Americans, who were new to international finance, from placing their dollars in Latin American securities. They realized that Central American and Caribbean bonds sold at better terms in the New York market because of investor trust in direct U.S. supervision over those countries. After instilling similar confidence through inspections by U.S. economists, the Andean governments used the subsequent loans as a way to expand revenues without having to impose heavy taxes on local elites. By using foreign funds to enlarge the size and scope of state activities, they buttressed their political strength without having to engage in democratic mobilization of the masses.

The South Americans spent most of those dollars on administrative expenses, on previous debts, and, above all, on public works. Funding those construction programs often entailed payments to U.S. suppliers and builders. Railroad and highway projects particularly intensified dependence on external trade, the vigor of internal capitalism, and the reach of the central government. Although waste and extravagance characterized some usage of these loans, external financing also contributed to significant public transportation and utility improvements. Reliance on foreign capital made the Andean countries more generous to certain U.S. interests, but also paid for enormous governmental and infrastructural expansion, ultimately at the expense of U.S. bondholders.[24]

When the depression struck, the major beneficiaries of this lending extravaganza had been the Latin American governments and the U.S. bankers, exporters, shippers, and builders. The soaring relative burden of servicing the debts made default compelling. From 1925–29 to 1930–34, Latin America's exports declined 48 percent and its imports declined 56 percent. Governments rushed to impose import restrictions and exchange controls. They regulated remittances abroad and suspended foreign debt payments. Latin America defaulted on 85 percent of its dollar bonds, and only Argentina (under heavy British influence) and Haiti and the Dominican Republic (under direct U.S. control) continued servicing their external debts.[25]

Since governments which had contracted those debts were reluctant to declare bankruptcy, the first defaults transpired in the wake of overthrows of existing regimes. Thereafter, the contagion spread throughout Latin America and then to Europe. Bolivia set off the global chain reaction in January of 1931, followed by Peru in March and Chile in July. Other countries followed suit during 1932–34.[26]

No Latin American government, however, repudiated its foreign obligations. Very few voices called for cancellation on the grounds that many of these debts were pushed on the countries by overzealous bankers, consummated through bribes, and acquired by dictators. Such complaints surfaced more frequently in the United States, especially from aggrieved creditors. Associations of bondholders in New York and London eventually negotiated with most Latin American governments to settle those debts at reduced amounts by the early 1950s.[27]

In the 1920s the desire for foreign loans provided a crucial motivation for adopting Kemmerer-style reforms. For example, Colombia capitalized on the new creditworthiness bequeathed by Kemmerer to increase its total public foreign debt by nearly ten times between his first visit in 1923 and his second in 1930. Chile nearly tripled its foreign indebtedness following Kemmerer's 1925 mission. The Ecuadorean government hoped that his house call in 1926–27 would help it win recognition from the U.S. State Department and thus loans from U.S. bankers. Those financial hopes failed to materialize because of a miserable past debt record and a slump in cacao exports. Bolivia's minister of finance explicitly urged Congress to rush through Kemmerer's legislation in 1927–28 so that the nearly bankrupt government could obtain foreign capital. Passage of those laws helped Bolivia to secure immediate financing from Dillon, Read, and Company. In a desperate dash to get U.S. bankers to save the country from the depression, Peru enacted Kemmerer's central bank bill in 1931 in one day, without even reading it. When loan relief was not forthcoming, Peru shelved most of Kemmerer's proposals. Kemmerer himself steered clear of most of these loan transactions and counseled against unbridled indebtedness. His clients, however, frequently had less interest in his technical recipes than in the effect of his stamp of approval for attracting foreign funding.

To function successfully as an objective intermediary between lenders and borrowers, Kemmerer maintained an independent stance toward those banking operations. In most circumstances he avoided prescribing particular banks to his country clients or recommending particular bonds to investors. For example, when the president of Chemical National Bank asked Kemmerer to help the bank become the fiscal agent receiving deposits from the central banks established by Kemmerer, he responded that the banker would have to contact the directors of the central banks on his own. When U.S. financial firms requested confidential copies of his reports, Kemmerer rebuffed them by replying that those documents had to be released first by the host government. He declined an offer to become a director of the International Securities Trust of America because "such a connection might prejudice my reputation for impartiality in foreign work." He even resisted a bond-holding reverend seeking his "advice, which of course I could not give except by hints."[28]

Not surprisingly, total detachment and neutrality proved impossible for such a powerful international economic adviser. Just as bankers beseeched Kemmerer to help them collect information, clients, and loan payments, so governments hoped he would persuade U.S. financiers to be generous with their dollars and lenient with their demands. While some Latin Americans feared Kemmerer would reveal secrets to U.S. business and government leaders, others hoped he would lobby those decisionmakers on their behalf. His diary and personal papers are filled with encounters and consultations with the major U.S. bankers—before, during, and after his missions. Those financiers helped convince some foreign governments, including those of Colombia, Peru, and China, to extend invitations to Kemmerer. The investment bankers with whom he maintained the closest contact, and indeed a financial relationship, were Dillon, Read, and Company. That firm conducted extensive operations in many of the countries he advised, where they encouraged his missions and profited from his favorable impact on their investments (bonds from a Kemmererized country sold more readily and at higher prices). From 1924 to 1929 Dillon, Read paid him $3,000 per year as a consultant and, in 1928, contributed to his endowed chair at Princeton. Kemmerer stipulated that his affiliation with them lapsed during and for sixty days after his contract with any foreign government. Throughout his career as a money doctor Kemmerer kept this connection confidential to protect his reputation as an uncontaminated scientist. Latin Americans were correct when they worried that North American advisers were unlikely to be totally free of entanglements with U.S. interests. No evidence has surfaced, however, to indicate that such relationships influenced the general character or content of Kemmerer's missions. For example, Kemmerer always cautioned against excessive indebtedness. He even warned both Dillon, Read and Bolivia not to consummate too large a loan contract in the wake of his mission. With or without such direct ties, his financial house cleanings served the intrinsic interests of the world's bankers.[29]

Kemmerer's legislation for central and commercial banking encouraged the entry into Latin America of major foreign banks as well as loans. The North American laws he introduced into Latin America virtually prohibited foreign branch banking in the United States, but he amended those codes to give resident foreign banks the same rights as nationals in the Andean countries. He also put foreign bankers on the boards of directors of the South American central banks, which he advised to deposit a large percentage of their reserves overseas. Although these reforms cleared the way for significant gains by U.S.

banks in the 1920s, those institutions did not swamp their British or local rivals in the Andes.

Following the 1915–25 rush from the United States, the next great influx of foreign banks into Latin America did not occur until the 1960s. From 1920 to 1933 the number of U.S. bank branches abroad actually shrank from 181 to 132. By 1926, out of 107 foreign branches of U.S. banks and subsidiaries, 61 were in Latin America. In the 1920s some foreign banks there (especially those that had previously profited from exchange speculation) disapproved of Kemmerer's tight regulations, which made South America a world leader in government supervision over banks. Other U.S. bankers remained reluctant to establish or sustain numerous branches abroad, to the disappointment of the U.S. State and Commerce departments. Those government agencies shared the views of National City Bank of New York, which believed that its expanding involvement in branch banking and investments in public securities in the Andes increased South American purchases of surplus U.S. production.[30]

Kemmerer joined a parade of other foreign advisers arriving in Latin America at about the same time. From the 1890s through the 1920s, every country except Argentina and Brazil hosted U.S. financial consultants, though no other private experts carried out such sweeping reforms as Kemmerer. One contemporary observer brimmed over with enthusiasm in 1931: "It is true now that the United States practices financial sanitation as a business almost all over the world. She is a financial doctor through whose acquired relations, knowledge, and study American business as a whole will, of course, profit."[31]

Prior to World War II, Latin America led all world areas in bringing in U.S. technicians. That stream of experts followed the flow of U.S. economic and strategic interests. The U.S. government realized that all advisers dispatched abroad could further U.S. economic and diplomatic objectives. For example, health experts could induce foreigners to purchase U.S. pharmaceuticals, military trainers could induce them to buy U.S. arms and equipment, agronomists to favor U.S. seeds and tractors, engineers to hire U.S. construction firms, and educators to assign U.S. textbooks. The introduction of North American technologies and systems, whatever the purely scientific motives of the agents, encouraged the consumption of North American products. U.S. leaders also believed that these technical missions would generally improve economic growth and political stability in the Third World, thus reducing the dangers of disorder or, worse, revolution. From the 1890s through the 1920s the United States found it increasingly efficacious to achieve these goals through the export of private agents rather than government officials.[32]

To manage the institutions he created overseas, Kemmerer recommended not only laws but also administrators from the United States. Wealthier countries with better credit ratings, like Colombia and Chile, usually rejected these suggestions, choosing not to appoint foreign officials. Meanwhile weaker, poorer nations, like Bolivia, Ecuador, and Peru, hired North Americans to oversee customs, national accounting, and banking. Even Colombia succumbed to the pressures of the depression during Kemmerer's second visit in 1930, acceding to his suggestion to place U.S. technical advisers in charge of the national comptroller and the customs administration in order to get an emergency loan from New York bankers. The bankers had originally insisted on their own supervision of budgets and customs but, when Colombia rejected that demand, accepted the Kemmerer appointees to monitor public finances instead. More than Kemmerer and other visiting consultants, these regular employees from abroad encountered severe resistance to their authority from local nationalists and vested political and economic interests. In most cases their welcome lasted only as long as their presence helped attract U.S. investments.

Latin Americans contracted foreign experts of all kinds at least as much for their generally favorable impact on relations with external great powers as for their specific technical advice. While the industrial nations vied for those positions, the Latin Americans began hiring North Americans in the nineteenth century as a counterweight to the dominant Europeans. Although employing primarily U.S. citizens by the 1920s, the Andean governments continued bringing in British, French, German, Swiss, and Belgian technocrats to promote business in Europe as well as the United States. Thus, the South Americans also acquired a variety of technological expertise without totally relying on one country or foreign companies.

Despite seeking and obtaining improved relations with the United States in the 1920s, South Americans remained suspicious of that government's role in the relationship. Especially disturbing was its history of armed interventions in the Caribbean and Central America. From World War I on, U.S. policymakers tried to allay those fears while at the same time they sought to extend their geopolitical and economic sphere of influence from the Caribbean Basin throughout South America. On the west coast they helped North American entrepreneurs compete successfully for domination of trade, finance, investments, strategic natural resources, transportation, communications, and technology transfer. The U.S. government achieved these objectives despite eschewing military invasion or coercive diplomatic lobbying on behalf of U.S. businesses. Instead, it relied on the "open door" and the "diplomacy of the dollar."[33]

The "open door" assumed that equal opportunity and reciprocity in national economic policies were sufficient for U.S. businesses to prevail over European and local competitors in South America. It represented the external projection of domestic liberalism, pluralism, and division between private and public domains. In the 1920s the diplomacy of the dollar envisioned the U.S. government encouraging such laissez-faire practices abroad, generally promoting the overseas expansion of U.S. traders, companies, investors, and banks, and providing only minimal assistance to particular firms, except in rare instances affecting national security. In return, policymakers expected the cascade of dollars abroad to render the recipients more prosperous, stable, and reliable friends of the United States. After World War I it became increasingly evident that U.S. private interests needed little government help to assert themselves in Latin America. Therefore the State Department played an increasingly smaller role in those economic relations, realizing that meddling was not only unnecessary but also counterproductive. Avoiding entanglements with individual U.S. enterprises kept the department out of conflicts among those firms and above disputes between them and Latin American governments. Although deviated from at times, official policy stated that U.S. investors in Latin America took their own risks, with no guarantee of protection from their government.[34]

Applying those principles to foreign loans proved particularly delicate. In 1922 the State Department asked all investment bankers to notify it of contracts for foreign loans to be sold to the public. Although that procedure implied government approval to some investors, the department explicitly refused to judge the business merits of the loans or back them in any way. It merely told the bankers whether or not it had any objections on foreign policy grounds. The only guidance for investors came indirectly from country reports by the Commerce Department and by returning economic advisers. Whereas the U.S. government closely supervised lenders and borrowers in the Caribbean region, it seldom interfered with South American transactions in the 1920s and rendered fewer and fewer official comments on those deals as the decade progressed. Reluctantly, the State Department did sometimes try to facilitate an accommodation between North American bankers and South American governments, especially when the Great Depression arrived, but it sustained an essentially aloof position. By the early thirties the major complaint from U.S. bondholders and politicians was that the U.S. government had played too small a role in policing those foreign investments.[35]

The ostensibly passive U.S. government retained many methods for pursuing its economic objectives abroad. In the countries on its southern perimeter the United States sometimes acquired economic privileges through the use of troops and treaties. Those military methods enhanced the reputation of an emerging hegemonic power willing to use force. At the same time, landing the marines bore intrinsic costs for the United States, both domestically and internationally, and it would have been extremely expensive in more distant, stronger nations. Uncomfortable with classical colonialism and imperialism, the State Department refrained from employing such draconian tactics below the Caribbean Basin. Nevertheless, the specter of those options made a few South Americans resist U.S. economic penetration out of fear that the flag would follow the dollar. Many more, however, welcomed North American investments, in hopes that such receptivity would avert armed intimidation.

Other levers at the disposal of the U.S. government included recognition, control of arms shipments, and promotion of friendly political factions. The most commonly used device was formal and informal diplomatic pressure. More explicitly economic measures involved encouraging or discouraging U.S. investments in a particular country and supervising its finances.[36]

As suggested above, theories of hegemony help place such financial supervision within the broader context of the international political economy of U.S.– Latin American relations. Since no world government exists to enforce such laws as property rights, capitalist giants seek other safeguards. Great powers try to establish and maintain hegemony in the international system by using coercion and inducements to compel weaker states to comply with the "rules of the game." The hegemon hopes thereby to reduce uncertainty and enhance predictability and stability. Its power rests on superior control over productive capacity, raw materials, capital, markets, technology, information, and military might. A great power does not need to invade everywhere in its domain; a hegemon only has to punish a few of its underlings to extract obedience from the rest. Those examples in the Caribbean Basin demonstrated that the potential for violence lurked behind the U.S. quest for economic concessions.

As it brings more and more states into its orbit, the hegemon and its system of domination acquire a reputation and an allure which render the use of direct force or incentives less and less necessary to enroll new members. The subordinates have less information than the hegemon about the costs and benefits of membership and envision few alternatives. They will accept the superior power's lead, for example in international trade or monetary regulations, when they perceive—rightly or wrongly—significant gains from participation. At the same time they may bargain to try to maximize those gains and minimize their contributions to sustaining that international order. Conversely, they may reject the hegemon's direction when costs appear to exceed benefits. Those decisions within the subordinate state will depend on the perceptions and preferences of the local ruling elites and the governing coalition. Therefore the hegemon seeks to shape not only the international arena but also decisionmaking within the weaker countries.[37]

Kemmerer's economic missions to the Andean countries proved a low-cost method for extending U.S. hegemony in the hemisphere. In the absence of easily universalized and enforced international laws, he reduced risks for U.S. capitalists by introducing reforms which duplicated U.S. economic institutions, regulations, and procedures within the host countries. Like foreign corporations going behind tariff walls, these U.S. and international norms became internalized. Kemmerer's reports and his agencies' subsequent publication of data also improved U.S. information about those economies.

For the South Americans, Kemmerer eased their entry into a system wherein the United States appeared to guarantee stability and prosperity. Their inducement for compliance with U.S. rules came mainly in the form of foreign loans. Their entry fee consisted of accepting U.S. institutions and regulations, adopting the gold standard, opening their economies, and respecting foreign property and obligations. In that era such an accommodation was reached without requiring extensive bargaining or negotiations. Outside of Russia no clear alternative economic models or networks existed. Within the recipient countries, opposing social or ideological forces were poorly articulated. Although a few Latin Americans feared that the United States gained far more than they did from this hegemonic stability, most of the ruling elites believed in a compatibility of interests in the 1920s. They eagerly welcomed U.S. advisers, investors, and reforms. When the depression made the costs of compliance overwhelmingly outweigh the benefits, these countries disobeyed the hegemon, but they did not repudiate its system. In later years international institutions, especially the IMF, would perform the task of constraining uncertainties for international capital movements by imposing and monitoring similar economic reforms, reporting, and conformity.[38]

Prior to the era of multilateral agencies, the instrument of financial supervision evolved from public to private manifestations. At the turn of the century the U.S. government dispatched economists to replace Spanish with North American financial institutions in the colonies of Puerto Rico and the Philippines, where Kemmerer and many of his cohorts got their start. There they first enacted most of the same reforms later installed in the Andes. A second public device subsequently channeled U.S. economic administrators throughout the Caribbean and Central America under treaties signed with occupied countries such as the Dominican Republic, Haiti, and Nicaragua. From 1911 to 1923 a third, less public, semiofficial practice emerged, wherein private contracts between Latin American governments and U.S. investment bankers stipulated that loans would be safeguarded by placing the country's fiscal institutions under the control of a North American adviser, to be approved by the State Department. The U.S. government hoped that such "controlled loans" would convince those countries to adopt Kemmerer-style reforms, which would convert them into less unruly and risky outlets for U.S. business. This procedure allowed the State Department to avoid anti-interventionist criticisms at home and abroad, while still achieving both protection for loans and renovations in foreign fiscal policies. The State Department cooperated with U.S. bankers and advisers to implement such contractual arrangements in Guatemala, Honduras, El Salvador, Bolivia, and Peru, as North American financial influence spread into South America through the Andes.

From the early twenties onward, the U.S. government further shielded itself from any charges of complicity with lenders and advisers by favoring a fourth mechanism: independent missions hired voluntarily by loan-seeking governments. In most cases the State Department's only involvement consisted of helping the country find an adviser and quietly encouraging all parties from behind the scenes. As seen with Dillon, Read, and Company, bankers also backed away from direct responsibilities, but maintained insider ties with these financial emissaries. Kemmerer's 1923 commission to Colombia set the mold for the final privatization of this intricate relationship among governments, investors, and professional consultants. By shifting from the public to the private arena, these connections became less susceptible to political assault.[39]

The economic adviser of the Department of State, Arthur N. Young (a former Kemmerer student), summed up its position on this advising system in 1927:

> Also there has been considerable misunderstanding concerning the activities of American experts engaged by some governments. A better understanding of the invaluable services which capable and high-principled experts have rendered is, however, dissipating criticism based upon ignorance. Americans are proud of the services, which, for example, Professor Kemmerer has been able to render to many of the Latin American governments. These governments have engaged his services sometimes with and sometimes without the assistance of the Department of State. Americans also are proud of the services of other American financial advisors and customs experts, who have loyally served the governments by which they have been employed and who have not used their position to benefit in any exclusive or preferential manner American commercial or other interests. . . . Where American experts have been engaged in connection with loan agreements, it has ordinarily been at the instance of the borrowing government and the bankers concerned, who have joined in asking the good offices of the Secretary of State in procuring the appointment of a properly qualified and impartial person. The engagement of such a person has often permitted the flotation of a loan on terms which give the borrowing government a credit higher than that enjoyed by strong European nations. Expert and impartial handling of the service of the loan has created in all circles confidence that there will be no default.[40]

In a major speech in 1928 at Princeton University, Secretary of State Charles Evans Hughes rebutted anti-imperialist critiques with a similar defense of the process:

> Distinct from action authorized or required by treaties, from time to time eminent citizens of the United States are requested by Latin American governments to aid them by giving advice for the improvement of their fiscal systems. The services of such experts have at times been obtained without the assistance of our government and sometimes our government has been requested to suggest names. In not opposing the selection of advisers of this class and in suggesting competent men at the request of other governments, the United States has had no ulterior motive whatever and it has not had, and has not sought to exercise, control or authority of any sort over the advisers. If our government had refused either to give information or had objected to the selection of distinguished American economic experts for such services, it is hardly necessary to say that we would have assumed an attitude toward our neighbors which would naturally have been resented by them and would have offended public sentiment in this country. This University [Princeton] has repeatedly permitted a distinguished member of its staff, Professor Edwin W. Kemmerer, to assume these duties and he has rendered services of inestimable value in advising several of the Latin American governments.[41]

This form of exporting advice reflected the U.S. liberal conviction that private North Americans should spread their model of development throughout the world. In this view the government ought to promote and guide, but not control, technological and ideological diffusion. Since colonialism proved unpopular, U.S. elites looked to the private sector to lead cultural as well as economic expansion. Prior to the post–World War II reliance on multilateral agencies to effectuate such international conformity to U.S. principles, the U.S. government turned to "chosen instruments": private companies, institutions, or individuals who could help improve foreign climates for U.S. economic interests. In pursuit of international financial stabilization in the 1920s, those chosen instruments—which included private banks, the Federal Reserve Bank of New York, and financial commissions—were independent from but cooperated with the U.S. government. Without assuming any overt responsibilities, the State Department usually recommended these advisers to foreign governments and implied that their services would improve economic and political relations with the United States. This depoliticized mode of operation suited the U.S. effort to sell its beliefs in limited government and free enterprise. It also, however,

opened up the possibility that foreign hosts could utilize those private instru-
mentalities for their own purposes.[42]

Kemmerer walked a fine line between independence from and collaboration with the U.S. government. Even without any collusion they shared the
same views on proper economic policies. Both he and the State Department
realized that his missions would be more effective without any public involvement of U.S. officials. Anxious to see his recommendations adopted, the department usually instructed local embassies to stay in the background. They knew
that the same advice would be less acceptable from representatives of U.S.
government or businesses. They placed great confidence in Kemmerer's autonomous operation because of his long record of successful implantation of standard North American institutions and practices.

At times Kemmerer actually complained of lack of cooperation from U.S.
officials. In some cases, however, U.S. embassies unofficially continued lobbying governments to hire Kemmerer and abide by his prescriptions. Even as late
as 1931 the State Department assured New York bankers that "this government
was very instrumental in having the Peruvian government invite Professor
Kemmerer to go to Peru to make a survey of the financial situation and suggest
the best method of meeting it."[43]

Informally, Kemmerer maintained other ties with the U.S. government.
He kept in touch with close friends there, especially former student Arthur N.
Young, economic adviser in the State Department from 1922 to 1928. Another
confidant was fellow Republican Herbert Hoover, who claimed that Kemmerer
"is like a brother to me" and who, after his 1928 trip through Latin America,
raved about the "great differences between the Kemmererized countries and the
non-Kemmererized countries." He also regularly informed the State Department, particularly Assistant Secretary of State for Latin American Affairs Francis White, about his missions. And the department took his advice into account
on questions ranging from nonobjection to loans to recognition of governments.
Although some countries remained unaware of such connections and communications, others hoped Kemmerer would influence the U.S. government on their
behalf. During his missions Kemmerer overstated his total detachment from
U.S. officials and bankers. Nevertheless, he remained detached enough to serve
not only their interests but also those of powerful groups within the Andean
countries.[44]

Impact within the Andean Countries

Although it is important to understand the role of economic missions within the context of U.S. foreign relations, the primary concern of this study is the

ramifications of those international forces for equally complex domestic groups, power relations, and national developments within the recipient countries. The main focus of this book will be on the impact of these missions and accompanying U.S. influences on the governments and interest groups inside the Andean republics. We will examine the conflicts and alliances among those domestic actors vis-à-vis foreign forces and financial policies, and concentrate on their motives, reactions, and results.

Those predominantly internal events and issues will be traced in the ensuing five chapters by following the trail of the Kemmerer missions chronologically through the Andean nations. Each case study will be organized in the same comparative framework and will examine: (1) the roles of foreign and domestic economic and political factors and groups on the eve of the Kemmerer mission; (2) why and how the mission was invited and accomplished its tasks; (3) the implementation and consequences of its money and banking reforms; (4) the implementation and consequences of its fiscal reforms; and (5) the transformation of those reforms during the Great Depression. In the process of addressing those questions, lacunae in the historiography of those countries during the period will be, at least partially, filled. The concluding chapter will synthesize the functions of international economic advisers, the commonalities among the five countries' experiences in the era, and legacies for the future, including some parallels with the 1970s and 1980s.

The awesome growth of commercial, financial, and technological reliance on the United States aroused little resistance in the Andes in the 1920s. Although significant strikes erupted against North American companies, economic nationalism and leftist movements remained frail until the depression. Criticisms of subjection to U.S. tutelage usually sprang from partisan opportunism by the party out of power, not from profound ideological or programmatic differences. Andean elites generally accepted U.S. hegemony because domestic as well as foreign capitalists flourished under the propitious conditions and Kemmerer systems of the 1920s. Mainly in response to externally generated growth, twentieth-century capitalism expanded within South America.

Kemmerer's reforms promoted the ongoing concentration, urbanization, institutionalization, and, to a lesser extent, integration of each national economy. By fostering a uniform currency, a central bank, and a regulated commercial banking system, Kemmerer furthered a national monetary and credit network operating under more mobile and rationalized methods. His rigorous regulations accelerated the concentration of banking in a few hands, but also amplified overall credit availability, especially for more liquid commerce and industry. Enterprises and workers in the cities also gained from public works. The unfolding transportation lines not only facilitated foreign trade but also made the economy less fragmented and regionalized. At the same time Kem-

merer's enhancement of the size and efficiency of government's financial operations provided greater order and security for business. Andean capitalists responded to his innovations and to widening opportunities by improving their
accounting, management, and production methods. The increasing articulation
and specialization of the economy and the state encouraged by Kemmerer also
inspired the various economic sectors to develop more forceful interest group
organizations.

In every country Kemmerer's legislation gave preferential treatment to
urban bankers, merchants, and industrialists. These blueprints imported from
an industrial society to agrarian societies weakened the influence of large landowners over national financial decisions. Despite the historical domination of
rural barons, control over credit proved almost as crucial a source of power as
control over land. Surprisingly vulnerable, agriculturalists and agro-exporters
struggled for a larger share in Kemmerer's system.

In spite of his commitment to laissez-faire, Kemmerer also contributed to
notable growth of the state in the Andean countries. Fueled by external loans
and trade revenues, mounting state activism in the 1920s responded to rising
internal pressures for social control, welfare, and employment, as well as for
economic modernization. Public works projects met multiple needs by providing jobs for workers and infrastructure for producers. At the same time the state
took more interest in labor-industrial relations. The central government, the
bureaucracy, parastate agencies, the military, and other public institutions became more professional and influential. In particular, the Andean elites enlarged and rationalized public agencies and capacities for monitoring economic
activities intimately involved with foreigners: money, banking, credit, trade,
and government revenues. External assistance helped Andean elites adjust from
the predominantly rural nineteenth to the increasingly urban twentieth century
through state expansion to mollify new groups, rather than through any wrenching redistributions of power and income.[45]

Kemmerer aided that elaboration of the state, even though he tried to
check the government's influence in the quasi-private central bank and to hold
down its budget through fiscal restraints. Despite those intentions, his creation
of the central bank commenced modern national public management of currency and credit, over which the government gradually extended its influence.
The superintendency of banking established by Kemmerer broke new ground
in public regulation of private property. Kemmerer's policies fortified the government's ability to collect taxes and attract loans, and improved its data acquisition and management, administration of revenues and expenditures, and
budget planning. His missions also strengthened the executive over the legislative branch. Consequently, many South Americans saw Kemmerer as a daring
reformer on the side of progressive taxation and public supervision over the

private economy. Moreover, the Andean elites went far beyond Kemmerer's intentions by using his system to inflate the central government.

When the depression arrived, the overextended states had become heavily reliant on revenues from foreign trade, loans from foreign bankers, and advice and legitimation from foreign advisers. This dependence momentarily prompted acquiescence to U.S. government and business demands. Regardless of U.S. pressure, however, Andean leaders found it very difficult to reduce their bloated expenditures commensurate with plummeting income. If the strapped administration slashed public works, the bureaucracy, and the military, that endangered social and political stability. If it cut foreign debt payments, that destroyed any hope of being rescued by external creditors. The only guidance from the Kemmerer formula was to balance the budget, prune domestic outlays, meet foreign obligations, sustain the gold standard, and await the revival of the world economy.

Once it became apparent that international relief was not in the offing, the Andean governments suspended service on the foreign debt and jettisoned the gold standard. They refused to incur the economic and political costs of drastically adjusting the national budget and balance of payments through exacerbating domestic recessions. Instead, these states in the 1930s twisted Kemmerer's institutions to serve even greater government expansion, pumping up the internal supply of money and credit. By using revenues and advisers from abroad during the 1920s to stretch its scope and capacities, the state emerged from that decade as a more powerful instrument of national policy and integration, a potential counter to foreign penetration. Building on those foundations, the central government played a far more dynamic interventionist role from the depression onward.

Neither Kemmerer nor his clients had foreseen either the fundamental drawbacks to debt-led development or the coming severity of the Great Crash. He had escorted the Andean countries onto a roller coaster, zooming up with the U.S. economy in the 1920s and careening down with it in the 1930s. The depression then drove them to develop their economic systems in more statist, nationalistic, and protectionist directions than Kemmerer ever envisioned. From the 1930s to the 1970s they placed greater emphasis on elaborating the internal economy under insulation from external direction and shocks. Although Kemmerer's free-market policies lost sway, his institutions continued to serve as major instruments of economic planning, execution, and development. The Andean republics also maintained the trajectory of amplifying the central state, of articulating the latest Western capitalist modes and patterns, and of relying on U.S. markets and models. To understand those trends, it is necessary to examine their initiation, acceleration, and variation in each of the Andean countries.

2 COLOMBIA'S DANCE OF THE MILLIONS, 1923–1933

Edwin Kemmerer's first South American mission ushered in Colombia's "dance of the millions" in 1923, after that country contracted his team to synchronize and capitalize on its growing dependence on the United States. He was invited back in 1930, during the global depression, to rescue it from the disastrous consequences of that relationship.

From the turn of the century to the start of the 1920s, surging coffee exports had generated the need for more advanced capitalist laws, institutions, practices, and infrastructure, which were required to underpin, rationalize, and accelerate economic growth. To promote those developments in ever closer association with the United States, Kemmerer's first house call brought Colombia's legal and financial support system into line with that of its leading foreign trading and lending partners. Those reforms spurred foreign sales and investments, and economic growth per capita from 1923 to 1930 averaged 5.2 percent per year, a rate never equaled thereafter. Colombians came to label that decade of mounting reliance on U.S. markets as *prosperidad a debe* (prosperity through debt).[1]

Kemmerer's gold-standard system and U.S. capital undergirded an era of unparalleled prosperity from 1923 through 1928. While Colombia's total circulating medium nearly doubled, foreign trade, government budgets, and banking deposits and loans roughly tripled. Despite this boom, Colombia continued to lag behind the wealthier nations of South America.[2]

According to one rough and inflated estimate for the end of the 1920s, Colombian per capita income totaled approximately $500, reputedly nearly half that of Chile, double that of Peru, and even farther above that of Ecuador and Bolivia.[3] The U.S. Bureau of Foreign and Domestic Commerce in 1929 calculated Colombia's purchasing power as one-twentieth that of the United States and one-sixth that of Argentina. The bureau blamed Colombia's poverty on the depressed consumer capacity of the vast majority of the population, especially in the countryside. Rising prosperity seldom trickled much beneath the upper 10 percent of Colombian society. As one bureau official explained: "If we can bring the remaining 90 percent into the market we shall enormously increase our sales in those countries. That is why the United States, even for the most selfish commercial reasons, is desirous of helping the peoples of Latin America to attain a greater degree of prosperity. Our hopes for future increased trade with Latin America are based upon the rise of the masses, and not upon the purchases of the present wealthy ruling classes."[4]

It was appropriate that Kemmerer's first South American mission went to Colombia, which had switched economically from Great Britain to the United States earlier and more decisively than had its neighbors farther down the Andes. The United States surpassed England as a recipient of Colombian exports by the 1890s, as a supplier of imports by World War I, and as a source of investments after the Kemmerer mission. Geographically and economically, Colombia fell into the U.S. orbit in the Caribbean. As one of many North American boosters of U.S. economic expansion in Latin America boasted about Colombia in 1929: "Today it has by far the largest investment of American brains and American money of any territory washed by the Caribbean except Cuba."[5]

Foreign Factors in Colombian Economic Growth

Blessed with political stability, vast untapped resources, and rising prosperity, Colombia in the 1920s offered an ideal laboratory for the Kemmerer experiment. The period of greatest annual average growth in the total value of exports in its independent history took place from 1911 to 1929. From the inauguration of the Panama Canal in 1914 to the arrival of the depression in 1929, Colombia quadrupled its foreign trade, which grew faster than that of the other major South American countries. Nevertheless, it remained a late-blooming export economy. By 1924 foreign commerce accounted for roughly $20 per capita in Colombia compared to $30 in Peru, $100 in Chile, and $180 in Argentina. Since imports grew more than exports, the balance of trade was unfavorable during a majority of the years in the 1920s, especially 1926–29. Foreign loans and gold reserves covered those shortfalls. A trade deficit in 1923 underscored the urgency of Kemmerer's recommendations for exchange stabilization, customs reforms, and negotiable instruments laws.[6]

Kemmerer entered an economy that was becoming increasingly monocultural. Whereas Colombian coffee production averaged an annual growth rate of 4 percent from 1915 to 1972, it peaked at 10 percent per year during 1915–32. The 1920s constituted the decade of greatest dependence ever on coffee as a percentage of the value of total exports, rising from 49 to 61 percent. By the end of the 1920s over 90 percent of coffee exports went to the United States. In addition, North American firms dominated the export of the native-grown coffee to the United States and took many of the profits.[7]

Colombia led all of South America in increasing its commerce with the United States in the 1920s. From 1921–22 to 1926–27, U.S. exports to Colombia rose 213 percent, to Chile 147 percent, and to Peru 133 percent; U.S. imports from Colombia grew 163 percent, from Chile 64 percent, and from Peru 36 percent. During this period the United States consolidated a preeminent position never relinquished thereafter. Although pleased with this mushrooming exchange, the North American government saw the persistently unfavorable balance of trade as its major economic problem with Colombia on the eve of Kemmerer's visit. His reforms, however, failed to expand U.S. sales there as much as hoped. The United States purchased over 80 percent of Colombia's exports and furnished nearly 50 percent of its imports in the 1920s; Great Britain ranked second in both categories.[8]

In the 1920s total U.S. investments in Colombia reached well over $300 million, with the majority in public loans. Both indirect and direct North American investments increased most after the 1922 indemnity treaty and the 1923 Kemmerer visit, though he had little impact on direct investment. According to various estimates, U.S. direct investments in Colombia soared from roughly $24 million (2 percent of the U.S. total in Latin America) in 1914, to $45 million (2 percent of the U.S. total) in 1919, to $84 million (3 percent of the U.S. total) in 1924, to $133 million (5 percent of the U.S. total) in 1929. The United Fruit Company (UFCO) came to control roughly half of Colombia's banana lands and virtually all foreign sales—which led Latin America—and accounted for 6 percent of Colombian exports by the mid-1920s. At least half of U.S. direct investments in Colombia poured into petroleum, which made up 20 percent of exports before the end of the decade.[9]

President Pedro Nel Ospina, his minister in Washington, Enrique Olaya Herrera, and most Colombian businessmen hoped that Kemmerer's seal of approval would unleash U.S. loans, especially for public works. The existing tiny foreign public debt in 1922 had been mainly acquired prior to World War I and was overwhelmingly owed to the British. Thereafter, virtually all indirect investments emanated from North America. The U.S. government favored enlarging private loans to Colombia. Extending credits for public works induced Colombians to turn to U.S. rather than British know-how and materials for those projects.[10]

Installation of Kemmerer's gold-standard system was expected to meet Colombian desires for improved acquisition and management of foreign capital. That system, in turn, depended on foreign loans to cover shortfalls in the balance of payments and to convince Colombians of the value of exchange stability. Colombia invited Kemmerer in 1923 to advise the government on the disposition of the $25 million indemnity payment from the United States for the loss of Panama. That indemnification was supported by U.S. economic interests seeking greater access to Colombian resources, especially oil. Through 1926 the government depended on those installment payments to found the central bank and build public works, which required foreign loans thereafter to keep going. By the end of the 1920s Colombians had ignored most of Kemmerer's prudent advice on contracting foreign obligations. The total public foreign debt during the depression loomed nearly ten times as large as it had in 1923. From 1924 to 1931 the central government's external debt leapt from 19 to 81 million pesos, overwhelmingly owed to North Americans.

The desire for foreign loans as a motivation for adopting the Kemmerer reforms was crucial in Colombia, but it was obscured because the central government did not incur massive external debts until four years after his 1923 mission. The national government exerted restraint during 1923–26 because sufficient foreign capital arrived in the form of U.S. indemnity payments. It also found U.S. lenders more forthcoming after it reached generous agreements with U.S. oil companies. Moreover, the U.S. financial market became generally more willing to absorb Latin American national government bond issues in the latter half of the 1920s. Nevertheless, Colombian departments (provinces), municipalities, and banks immediately took advantage of the new creditworthiness bequeathed by Kemmerer in 1923 to acquire unprecedented foreign loans. Kemmerer's return visit in 1930 related directly to the central government's effort to get U.S. bankers to bail it out during the depression.

Colombian public administration at every level benefited from and became beholden to U.S. capital in the 1920s. Rather than the national government, it was departments, municipalities, and banks that incurred a majority of foreign obligations. Although national coffee growers (*cafeteros*) rather than foreign companies controlled the primary export commodity, they relied on credit from mortgage banks obtained through floating bonds in the U.S. market. In all the Andean countries, other apparently independent indigenous agriculturalists, urban property owners, and contractors also leaned on this indirect foreign capital.

When foreign credit sources abruptly closed down during the depression, economic elites turned to the state. Reliance on external capital initially motivated Colombia to make concessions to foreign investors. In 1930 Kemmerer was recalled in hopes of unleashing loans from U.S. bankers. When the central government could find few foreign lenders it expanded its own credit facilities in the 1930s, tapping the central bank and abandoning Kemmerer's monetary system. The collapse of the export sector and foreign investments also led Colombia to default on its external debts. In the final analysis, dependence on debt-led growth not only rendered Colombia more generous to some U.S. interests but also paid for the great expansion of the Colombian infrastructure.

Those foreign debts taken on by governmental units in the 1920s went mainly into public works, especially railroads. Colombia's woefully inadequate transportation and communications improved tremendously and came increasingly under state control. Despite Kemmerer's cautions, however, many expenditures were politically motivated, excessive, wasteful, and unproductive. This overspending spawned cumulative deficits and foreign borrowing. Foreigners often advised, built, and supplied these projects, but did not own them. These expanded railroads, roads, and ports wove Colombia's regional economies together, but mainly connected local markets to the export–import sector. While that stimulated domestic output for sale abroad, it also exposed previously isolated Colombian producers to foreign competition.

Kemmerer's 1923 legislation for central and commercial banking encouraged the influx of major foreign banks. In the 1920s, however, they did not achieve great prominence in Colombia compared to domestic institutions. Some foreign banks disapproved of Kemmerer's tight 1923 banking regulations, and all opposed his 1930 reduction of their rights. The U.S. State and Commerce departments remained disappointed in their efforts to prod timid U.S. bankers to establish more branches abroad. Consequently, older resident British banks remained stronger in Colombia than their North American rivals.

As the U.S. trade commissioner in Colombia noted at the start of the 1920s, contracting North American advisers for developmental projects also increased the likelihood of adopting U.S. models, capital, and goods. He urged more U.S. professionals to come to Colombia, not only to provide specific skills but also to improve general economic relations. By the same token, Colombians realized that employing foreign technicians enhanced their country's economic visibility and reputation abroad. They also perceived that borrowing technology by hiring experts, rather than admitting foreign companies, involved less risk of exploitation or diplomatic entanglements. As the U.S. embassy had hoped, Colombia responded to multiplying North American economic influences by importing U.S. advisers in increasing numbers.[11]

Kemmerer's mission also marked a significant improvement in general U.S.–Colombian relations. Colombia had closely observed and suffered from U.S. interventions in Central America and the Caribbean. Along with Peru, it exhibited the most anti-American attitudes of any country Kemmerer would advise. The Thomson-Urrutia indemnity treaty created a friendlier atmosphere, but strained relations persisted when Kemmerer arrived.[12]

Domestic Hindrances to Colombian Growth

Colombia invited Kemmerer to bring its banking, monetary, and fiscal systems up-to-date with the expanding needs of economic growth. When he arrived, national banks remained few in number, concentrated in the capital city of Bogotá, unstable, and poorly managed. Credit was scarce, capital mobility restricted, and interest rates astronomical (12 to 18 percent per year) for the era. No detailed banking legislation existed.[13]

Nevertheless, domestic banks far overshadowed foreign institutions in Colombia. Only two small British banks, the Banco Francés e Italiano, and the struggling U.S. Mercantile Bank of the Americas operated there in 1923. Foreign, especially British, branch banks established themselves more solidly after Kemmerer's reforms, but they never captured much of the market.[14] Prior to 1923 Colombia's slow economic growth and horrendous civil wars had doomed attempts to found a true central bank, the cornerstone of Kemmerer's system. During the 1890s the government had spewed forth paper money to cover deficits incurred in the throes of civil strife. Currency emissions snowballed from 9.4 million notes in 1887 to 850 million by 1902. This catastrophe convinced public opinion into the 1920s that any central bank stabilization would have to be firmly shielded against government meddling.

From 1905 on, the restoration of political peace facilitated improving monetary conditions. Opposition to inconvertible paper money became so fervent that a 1910 constitutional amendment prohibited any more government emissions of fiat currency. Exchange fluctuations of the Colombian peso in terms of U.S. dollars became minimal. The peso was worth 96 cents in both 1905 and in 1923. Although it fell to an unusual low of 86 cents during the 1920–22 recession, its value was rebounding when Kemmerer arrived. Most educated Colombians desired a central bank primarily to get on the gold standard.[15]

As throughout the Andean countries, the foundations for a central bank were already in place when Kemmerer reached Colombia. Economic dislocations caused by World War I had heightened desires for more stable money and banking. After several years of debate, Congress in 1922 passed central bank legislation that contained many of the provisions Kemmerer's 1923 reforms would have. Colombia invited him to fix any deficiencies in the law, persuade the public to accept its implementation, and add luster to it in foreign eyes.[16]

Colombians favored the gold standard to curb exchange and price instability, but these were not the burning concerns Kemmerer would later encounter in inflation-ridden Chile. The Colombians had invited him primarily to stabilize government finances rather than the currency. Agriculturalists, merchants, and government leaders wanted monetary reform mainly to facilitate the orderly expansion of currency and credit. They believed that excessive restrictions on currency emissions since 1905 had left the country with an insufficient and inelastic money supply. Regional shortages became particularly acute during the coffee harvest. Monetary circulation of 4.08 pesos per capita in Colombia in 1917 contrasted with paper money circulation per inhabitant of 45.76 pesos (or their equivalent) in Argentina, 43.45 in Brazil, and 15.66 in Chile in 1916. Colombians also desired a unified, regularized national currency to replace the polyglot types of money that had accumulated over the years among diverse regions.[17]

The Colombian government hoped Kemmerer could help it handle spiraling expenses and deficits. Especially following World War I, an urbanizing, growing economy and society increasingly called for expanded government services, employment, and contributions to infrastructure. The spreading state's antiquated fiscal methods produced perennial budgetary crises. Unstable customs duties generated roughly 75 percent of government revenues; the rest came mainly from small stamp and stamped-paper levies or from state monopolies.

The minuscule role of internal taxes on income, profits, or property revealed the low level of development of twentieth-century capitalism and of state extractive capabilities. Government leaders hoped that Kemmerer could fatten their coffers not only by improving internal taxation but also by attracting foreign lenders. Thus the state envisioned itself becoming more dependent on external economic factors in the short run, but stronger and more autonomous internally in the long run.[18]

Both major political parties in Colombia gradually accepted an enlarged role for the state. They went beyond Kemmerer's intentions by using his system to inflate the central government, as did the leaders of Chile, Ecuador, and Bolivia. Governments Kemmerer advised in the Andes eventually took advantage of his fiscal reforms, rising customs and tax revenues, and soaring foreign loans to expand their budgets, bureaucracies, and public works. The state in Colombia multiplied its ordinary revenues from 44 million pesos in 1923 to 75 million in 1928; extended its clientelistic political reach as a major employer of the urban middle and working classes; established wide influence over transportation; and took charge of the nation's railroads. During the depression the government moved for the first time into direct domestic credit operations, again advised by Kemmerer.

Conservative President Pedro Nel Ospina (1922–26) emerged as one of the first Colombian chief executives to view the government as an engine for economic development. Much like presidents Ibáñez in Chile, Ayora in Ecuador, Siles in Bolivia, and Leguía in Peru, Ospina cast himself as Colombia's first modern, technocratic leader. He vowed to solve problems through economic efficiency and expertise rather than partisan political wrangling. The founder of a textile factory in Antioquia, he brought to the presidency a businessman's belief in technology and financial responsibility, an army general's devotion to administrative order, an Antioquian *cafetero*'s commitment to economic growth, and a former University of California student's eagerness to link his country's future with the United States. As in the other Andean countries, Kemmerer encountered a fresh administration attuned to his vision of economic reform.[19]

The First Kemmerer Mission

In 1922 the Conservative president preceding Ospina asked Congress to authorize not only a central bank but also a commission of Colombian experts to overhaul the fiscal system. Instead, Liberal as well as Conservative congressmen approved contracting a foreign mission. They believed that foreigners could better overcome local opposition by guaranteeing that new banking, customs, and tax regulations were not designed primarily to serve narrow political, economic, or regional interest groups. As President Ospina told Congress in his 1923 message, the same reforms already under consideration by Colombians would have more chance of being carried through if recommended by foreigners, "whose prestige would not be haggled away as would happen with our own professionals in a backward environment like ours, in which nothing and no one escapes the objections and pettiness of politics." U.S. bankers also suggested to the Colombian government that foreign loans would be easier to acquire after employing an outside economic adviser recommended by the U.S. government.[20]

Although favoring and facilitating the private contracting of the Kemmerer mission by the Colombian government, the U.S. Department of State neither initiated nor controlled it. The U.S. government played a larger role in arranging this mission than the later ones, but all were independent. Under orders from the minister of the treasury, Colombia's ambassador in the United States, Enrique Olaya Herrera, obtained enthusiastic State Department assistance in procuring an economic adviser. The department did not want to recommend anyone formally tied to the government or previously connected with enforced financial refurbishings in Nicaragua or Panama. It suggested Kemmerer because of his writings on money and banking, his past advising experience in the Philippines, Mexico, and Guatemala, his working knowledge of Spanish, and his tact and judgment. Another reason was his service in 1922 as a special commissioner of the Department of Commerce to survey financial conditions in Argentina, Uruguay, Brazil, and Chile.[21]

The U.S. secretary of state recognized the significance of the Colombian mission and approved departmental assistance in arranging it. He also personally urged Princeton to grant Kemmerer the necessary leave of absence. Despite its lively interest in the success of Kemmerer's expedition, the State Department realized the importance of stressing that the "mission is an expert mission engaged by the Colombian government, and . . . is in no sense connected with the government of the United States."[22]

The mission included Howard M. Jefferson from the Federal Reserve Bank of New York as general banking expert. Fred R. Fairchild, a professor of political economy at Yale, advised on taxation for the mission, as he had previously done for the Connecticut legislature and the U.S. military regime in the Dominican Republic. Thomas R. Lill, a member of the New York accounting firm of Searle, Nicholson, Oakey, and Lill, provided accounting and financial expertise. He had earlier advised Mexico on fiscal reorganization, the Philippines and Cuba on accounting and auditing procedures, and U.S. municipal governments. While serving as chair of the mission, Kemmerer himself specialized in currency, banking, and public debt questions. Finally, Yale Professor of Spanish Frederick B. Luquiens went along as secretary and translator. Drawing on experts with some experience where the U.S. had intervened militarily to reorder finances in the Caribbean seemed logical, but it opened the mission to charges of imperialist connections; more important, it personalized the structural parallel between the financial recasting achieved under duress in the Caribbean and Central America and voluntarily in South America.[23]

Colombian government ministers and newspapers of all stripes received the mission warmly when it arrived on March 10, 1923.[24] The team's diligent operating methods contributed to its success. Prestigious former and future finance minister Esteban Jaramillo, an *Antioqueño* lawyer linked to manufacturing and coffee interests, furnished invaluable contemporary and later support for the Kemmerer reforms by serving as legal adviser to the U.S. experts. Liberals and others soon complained, however, that national participation in the mission's deliberations was too limited. They urged Kemmerer to involve more Colombians in his decisionmaking, so as to check the influence of the Conservative administration and to educate a new generation in modern economic techniques. They argued that the transfer of technology would be more effective if more Colombians gained firsthand experience with the mission. Thus they could implement Kemmerer's plans effectively after his departure and solve their own problems in the future. Not unlike U.S. corporations abroad in this era, however, the mission included very few nationals in the higher levels of its operations.[25]

The mission members knew little about Colombia, so they studied existing economic legislation, gathered data and opinions from government and economic leaders as well as U.S. bankers, and urged the public to send in suggestions. This information gathering refined their recommendations. It also helped convince skeptical Colombians that foreigners could adapt general economic principles and mechanisms to peculiar local needs.

The mission lacked the time to visit many of the provinces in the vast and regionalized country. To compensate, nearly all the departments sent special commissions of local economic and political leaders to meetings with the U.S. experts in Bogotá. As Kemmerer said, "If Mohammed could not go to the mountain, the mountain could come to Mohammed." A trip by Kemmerer to the major coffee and industrial zone of Antioquia, however, proved mandatory, at least as much to reassure those regional elites as to assess conditions there.[26]

As in some of the other Andean countries, a crisis during Kemmerer's visit contributed to rapid implementation and acceptance of his system. Three days after Congress passed his central bank bill, a fluke run on the banks in Bogotá threatened economic chaos and social upheaval. Kemmerer convinced the government to rush the central bank (Banco de la República) into operation in four days. He not only supervised that Caesarean birth but also obtained the support of U.S. banks for it. After declaring a special three-day national holiday, stock subscriptions were taken, directors elected, statutes and bylaws adopted, funds transferred from the government mint in Antioquia and from the indemnity account in the United States, and central bank notes and rediscount papers prepared. These lightning strokes provided instant rediscount privileges for beleaguered commercial banks. The panic stopped immediately.

At that same moment Colombia suddenly became the only South American republic on the gold standard. Remaining doubters, especially bankers, now applauded Kemmerer's system. It might have taken months for the bank to wrestle with debilitating arguments over its organization and exchange rate and years for it to earn public confidence. Instead, it fortuitously won high esteem in a matter of days. This emergency rescue burnished Kemmerer's international reputation as a miraculous financial savior.[27]

Kemmerer also helped establish his system by publicly exuding optimism—both in Colombia and back in the United States—about the reforms and about Colombia's consequently bright economic future. For example, he bought shares in the new central bank. Throughout the 1920s he kept himself informed on Colombia's economic progress and praised it to U.S. investors.[28]

During Kemmerer's visit most Colombians from both political parties enthusiastically supported the mission and its reforms. A few critics and skeptics, however, spoke out within both the Conservative and Liberal camps, usually to express concern about technical deficiencies in the Kemmerer laws or potential political or regional favoritism in their application.[29]

The most virulent attacks on Kemmerer came from a handful of nationalists. Former president Carlos E. Restrepo led a few Conservative dissidents in charging that the mission served as the vanguard for U.S. imperialism. A right-wing representative of the upper class, Restrepo feared U.S. cultural, economic, and even territorial absorption. In his view the mission designed its reforms to force Colombian "economic and fiscal dependence" on the United States. A few Liberal nationalists in Congress also lashed out at Kemmerer as an accomplice of foreign bankers enslaving Colombia in "chains of gold." They also worried that Kemmerer would reveal their national secrets to the U.S. government. Kemmerer's defenders retorted that his contributions to economic organization and prosperity would help Colombia resist foreign domination with a stronger central government and indigenous banking system. The mission itself simply ignored charges of being "paid agents for Wall Street." This minor debate illustrated a dilemma of the Kemmerer reforms: they made the Colombian economy and its key institutions both more open to external influences, especially in the short run, and more capable of managing internal developments, especially in the long run.[30]

By the end of their stay the missionaries had proposed revolutionary changes in Colombian finances. They presented their recommendations as exquisitely detailed laws ready to be enacted. An "exposition of motives" accompanied every bill to explain and defend its provisions. As a result, little discussion, revision, or repackaging by Colombians appeared necessary.

On money and banking affairs the mission proposed: a central bank of issue and rediscount modeled after the U.S. Federal Reserve system; the gold-exchange standard; general banking legislation with a national superintendent of banking, copied from the New York system; and adaptation of the North American uniform negotiable instruments law. On fiscal matters Kemmerer advocated: an organic budget law; reorganization of financial ministries; new procedures for collecting and administering government revenues; a fiscal accounting system centered around a national comptroller; new taxes on stamps, stamped paper, passenger transportation, and income; modernized customs administration; and policies on public loans and public works.[31]

After a six-month stay, the U.S. team left Colombia on August 20, 1923. Lill stayed behind as a technical adviser to the government. The minister of the treasury extolled the mission's recommendations as "happy and opportune adaptations of what is current in civilized countries to the exigencies of our progress and the idiosyncrasy of the Colombian people."[32]

Prior to Kemmerer's departure both the executive and legislative branches of the Colombian government rubber-stamped most of his recommendations. It had taken the mission only two months to submit the bulk of its reports to the chief executive; both Kemmerer and Ospina knew the major projects they favored before the mission arrived. All the laws—except those for taxes on passengers (tabled) and incomes (passed in watered-down form in 1927)—sailed through Congress in two weeks with only minor, principally stylistic, revisions.

According to the minister of finance, "Never before in the history of Colombia, and probably never before in the history of any other country, has there been realized in so brief a period of time a legislative labor so intense, so deep, and so transcendental in importance."[33]

Congress passed these monumental reforms with such celerity under great pressure from the president and the press. In his 1923 message to Congress Ospina undercut nationalistic critics by describing the projects as the embodiment of "the most advanced principles of science." Colombians bought Kemmerer's shrewd argument that all his projects and their components were delicately interdependent and therefore had to be adopted as an integrated, unadulterated, "scientific" package. Ospina also claimed the Kemmerer bills would elicit foreign loans, which would underwrite prosperity and thus social peace. He urged rapid passage before vested interests could emasculate or torpedo the reforms, as they had in the past. Congress responded swiftly because the president's party was in control, opponents were few, and some of the bills were only mild readjustments of existing or pending legislation.[34]

Newspapers affiliated with both parties admonished the government not to meddle with the reforms or delay their enactment. The Liberal press expressed the greatest urgency, because it had more faith in Kemmerer than in the Conservative administration.[35] One Liberal newspaper warned the president and Congress to make sure the mission succeeded because "its failure would be the failure of the credit of Colombia in the United States for many years."[36]

Despite the chorus of acclaim, a smattering of critics espoused alterations in the Kemmerer legislation. Some Liberals as well as Conservatives denounced legislators so smitten with modernization that they were eager to toss out centuries of their own jurisprudence in favor of poorly translated U.S. laws. Even the government admitted, by September of 1923, that some of the bills had been passed too hastily and were already in need of reforms.[37]

One Conservative congressman, especially upset about the exotic negotiable instruments law, brimmed over in defense of Latin against Anglo-Saxon culture: "We believed from the beginning . . . that the error consisted in bringing in the mission. Everyone knows the motives of sovereignty, of legitimate national pride, of recollections of the past and of preoccupations for the future which made us look poorly on this official immigration of the imperialist science of the United States." Quoting Uruguayan José Enrique Rodó on the dangers of Yankee cultural penetration, he asserted, "We must defend our juridical legacy like our race, religion, language, nationality." The Conservative went on to complain that "the historian of the future will doubtless explain the international fact that the United States pursued the acceptance of its civil and commercial legislation in Hispano-America, but he will not be able to give the justification for our passive and joyous acceptance of these strange and incomprehensible models." While conceding that North Americans were experts on economics and had brought generally sound recommendations, he insisted that Colombians were experts on laws and had to recast those recommendations. Even this unusually harsh attack on Kemmerer's legislation, then, constituted a largely legalistic criticism clothed in nationalism, rather than a fundamental assault on the new system.[38]

The top Colombian aide to the Kemmerer mission expressed the more typical view:

> Colombia has welcomed these missions of experts and has given them wholehearted and effective assistance, without feeling her independence in any way affected or her national dignity wounded because foreigners of great distinction and eminence have offered her their knowledge and experience with a view to the reorganization of the country. In addition to the prestige of distinguished attainments, these missions have enjoyed the moral authority which attaches to their impartiality and their freedom from the manifold influences which tend to warp the judgment of natives. These experts are looked upon with confidence, and this is in itself a guarantee of success.

After all, he pointed out, Europeans also hired U.S. financial wizards.[39]

In addition to bringing about legislation, the Kemmerer mission awakened Colombian interest in collecting and studying data on economic questions. Kemmerer, the institutions he fostered, the expanding government, and foreign investors needed better national statistics. Consequently, the quantity and quality of available economic indicators, information, and analyses greatly improved—both in Colombia and in the other Andean republics—and proved a great help in economic planning, precursing the influence of international organizations such as the United Nations on advancing data gathering in underdeveloped countries.[40]

Kemmerer's Money and Banking Reforms

The main result Colombians desired from the proposed central bank's sanitation of currency and stabilization of exchange was expanded availability of money and of domestic and foreign credits.[41] When Kemmerer arrived, the loudest outcry for loans came from agriculturalists, who employed over two-thirds of the active population. Like many urban producers, most Colombian rural elites really wanted a developmental bank dedicated to allocating credit more than a central bank consecrated to stabilizing exchange. Kemmerer dashed agriculturalist hopes that his project would be more favorable to them than the 1922 congressional bill. His belief in the high liquidity needs of the central bank and commercial banks militated against long-term loans tied to agricultural mortgages.[42]

During the debate over Kemmerer's central bank, some agriculturalists, coffee growers, and industrialists complained that it would benefit primarily bankers and merchants. One conservative farmer denounced the project as a takeover of the economy by domestic and North American bankers. Throughout the 1920s agriculturalists complained that exorbitant interest rates helped keep domestic food production costs high and therefore noncompetitive with U.S. imports, which rose along with the cost of living. Some critics drew the lesson that the central bank's short-term lending policies better suited the industrialized United States than underdeveloped Colombia, where agriculture, manufacturing, and transportation desperately needed long-term credits. The scarcity of such loans domestically made foreign credit sources increasingly important.[43]

From 1923 through 1929 the government and central bank encouraged mainly urban investments and public works. This reduced the supply of cheap labor in the countryside. Because bankers dominated its board of directors, the central bank did not make use of its right to deal directly with the public. Feeling slighted by Kemmerer's 1923 reforms, coffee growers belatedly forged a national federation in 1927. This sectoral organization allowed them to lobby the ever more powerful government more effectively. It also helped them capture a director's seat on the central bank in 1930, when agriculturalists bent every effort to get Kemmerer's second mission to favor them instead of urban bankers. Even when the Banco de la República began extending loans to agriculturalists at special low discount rates in 1930–31, it conducted those limited operations only with coffee and tobacco producers. Small agriculturalists and those producing for domestic consumption remained displeased with the banking system.[44]

In 1922–23 agriculturalist apprehension about banking reforms dovetailed with regionalist fears. Businessmen and bankers in Antioquia were wary of credit control by the central bank and government in Bogotá. Coastal provinces also voiced suspicions. Provincials, however, placed more faith in Kemmerer than they did in Bogotá politicians. His mission won over many regional elites, even though it promoted centralization and concentration of modern financial activities; banking expert Lill advised that "in Colombia it is necessary to think nationally."[45] Kemmerer favored centralism over regionalism, dropping the 1922 requirement that the Bank of the Republic establish a branch in every departmental capital, no matter how small.[46]

Compared to agriculturalists, the merchants and, to a lesser extent, the manufacturers became more avid backers of the central bank. By 1923 chambers of commerce and industrialists in provinces such as Antioquia and Cartagena joined their colleagues in Bogotá in support of the Kemmerer project. The bank's rapid expansion of currency and lower-interest urban loans confirmed their optimism. Merchants, especially importers, appreciated greater monetary uniformity.[47] Growth of domestic manufacturing in the 1920s paved the way for more rapid industrialization from the Great Depression onward. Expansion of credit, infrastructure, and urban labor and consumers helped Colombian industry's productive capacity grow more than 50 percent during 1925–29.[48]

Although initially divided and hesitant over creation of the central bank, Colombian bankers became its primary directors and beneficiaries. In his conferences with them Kemmerer discovered that most joined him in favoring a conservative central bank. He eased their worries about competition from the bank, excessive government participation, stringent requirements on their reserves and lending policies, bank inspections under both the central bank and general banking laws, and potential favoritism by the central bank for cronies, politicians, foreigners, or the national government. Smaller and provincial banks, for example in Antioquia, retained the most reservations about the Kemmerer projects. Larger and more solid institutions hoped his banking legislation would weed out adventurous smaller competitors. Most supported the 1922–23 legislation in order to get sound money and rediscount privileges.[49]

Most foreign bankers in Colombia also endorsed the central bank. Kemmerer gave foreign banks the same rights as Colombian banks, even including them as members and directors of the central bank. This stirred fears of a takeover by U.S. banks because they were more powerful and better able to meet the new requirements. Most Colombian commentators, however, argued that his regulations would expand contributions of foreign banks under better controls.[50]

Won over by Kemmerer's provisions and by patriotic public pressure, nineteen of the twenty-two major domestic commercial banks and all four foreign banks immediately subscribed the required 15 percent of their total paid-up capital and reserves to join the central bank in 1923. Throughout the 1920s the security and credit provided by the Banco de la República pleased the member banks.[51] As Kemmerer had feared, criticisms mounted against the commercial banks for controlling the central institution, monopolizing its credit facilities, and favoring urban economic elites.[52] The Banco de la República itself lamented the bankers' long-standing and continuing preference for making a few big loans at high interest rates instead of numerous smaller loans at lower rates, which might cumulatively bring in as great a profit.[53]

All these complaints focused on the bankers' dominance of the board of directors. Numerous interviews with Colombians had reinforced Kemmerer's conviction that government should have a minimal role in the central bank.

Colombians saw insulating the bank from government interference as the paramount consideration because of past inflationary abuses, because of monetary orthodoxy in the period, and because neither Liberals nor Conservatives trusted each other to manage money and banking for the general welfare.[54]

Therefore Kemmerer's bill established a board of ten directors: three chosen by the government; four chosen by Colombian banks (two of whom had to represent business, agriculture, and the professions outside banking); two by foreign banks (one of whom also had to represent nonbanking economic interests); and one chosen by general public shareholders. Kemmerer justified bankers selecting nonbanking board members because other economic sectors lacked well-developed interest organizations. Most Colombians praised the composition of his board. They even accepted inclusion of foreign bank representatives out of proportion to their weight in the domestic economy. Kemmerer insisted on seats for foreign bankers because they shielded the bank from local political influences; he also contended that "the prosperity of Colombia for many years in the future will depend in great part on its ability to attract foreign capital, and the success of the country in this regard will be more likely through strong foreign representation on the board of directors of the Bank." While stipulating that a majority of the central bank directors had to be Colombians, Kemmerer erased that 1922 requirement for the manager. A few Colombians agreed with him that a foreign manager would be more efficient and impartial, but nationalistic opponents scuttled the proposal.[55]

With these organizational issues temporarily resolved, the Banco de la República began operations in July 1923. During its opening months Kemmerer and Jefferson attended all meetings of the board of directors, which closely followed their advice. Kemmerer reported that "the board took action to the effect that they would adopt no measures while we were there to which we were opposed."[56] Thereafter, the bank from time to time solicited their opinions through correspondence, but basically ran its own affairs. Public confidence in the institution, which had always been high, grew so that, by 1927, congressmen were no longer discussing or attacking it.[57]

The bank's capital came mainly from abroad, and it deposited most of its reserves abroad. Playing a larger role than in the U.S. system, the Colombian government used the first North American indemnity installment to supply half the bank's initial capital. By 1927 50 percent of the bank's ten million pesos in capital came from government, 20 percent from national banks, 9 percent from foreign banks, and 20 percent from public shareholders.[58]

The central bank maintained higher reserves and kept more of them overseas than even Kemmerer had recommended (see table 2.1), and its officials became more extreme in their devotion to the system than were its foreign creators. To gain domestic and foreign confidence in the new institution, Kem-

Table 2.1   Central Bank Reserves and Monetary Circulation
(in rounded-off millions of pesos)

Year	Gold reserve in the central bank	Gold reserve in foreign banks	Total gold reserve of the central bank	Central bank notes in circulation	Total gold reserve as a percentage of the notes in circulation
1923	1.9	5.5	7.5	2.2	332%
1924	7.0	16.3	23.3	17.9	130
1925	15.0	21.3	36.3	29.8	122
1926	18.4	24.6	43.0	40.7	106
1927	20.5	23.7	44.2	46.4	95
1928	24.9	39.7	64.7	56.2	115
1929	22.4	15.4	37.8	39.1	97
1930	19.7	8.6	28.3	26.1	108

Note: These figures reflect December 31 of every year, except October 31, 1930.
Sources: Colombia, Banco de la República, *Revista del Banco de la República* (December 1930): 368; Guillermo Torres García, *Historia de la moneda en Colombia* (Bogotá, 1945), p. 347.

merer established the highest reserve requirement (60 percent of circulating notes and deposits) of any central bank in the world. To earn interest and facilitate exchange transactions, the bank stashed more than the Kemmerer limit of two-fifths of those reserves in major New York and London banks, which could prove risky in a crisis. Critics also complained that those high external deposits benefited foreign bankers at the expense of the domestic supply of money and credit: "The bank is the product of a law that North Americans sent us—the same ones who snatched Panama from us—in order to ruin us, debase us, and leave us under their control or dependence." The bank replied that location of the reserve made no difference in domestic monetary circulation under the gold exchange standard.[59]

Many Colombians expressed disappointment that the bank did not expand credit and lower interest rates more. Using quotes from Kemmerer, the bank constantly reiterated its inability to arbitrarily reduce interest rates. It pointed out that its discount rate was mainly determined by the balance of payments in defense of the gold standard. During its first year the central bank did slash its rate for member banks and the government from 12 to 7 percent, a rate that lasted until the depression. Consequently, private banks, partly because of the influx of foreign capital, dropped their rates from around 15 percent to around 10 percent, still double what borrowers had hoped for.[60]

Until the Great Depression, credits extended from the bank to the government stayed well within Kemmerer's 1923 limit of 30 percent of capital and reserves. Table 2.2 shows the absolute amounts of those allocations. Despite public fears, the government did not try to take advantage of the bank and maintained very harmonious relations with it from 1923 to 1929. The ample availability of trade revenues and foreign capital made bleeding the bank unnecessary. Even without providing hefty loans, the bank helped the government by handling service on the public debt, supervising currency, managing U.S. indemnity payments, and attracting foreign credits. In turn, the bank's solidity depended not only on the export economy but also on the fiscal and political stability of the government.[61]

The central bank hailed as its greatest success achieving its primary objective of stabilizing exchange rates by preserving the gold standard (see table 2.3). Colombians also applauded the increasingly reliable and ample domestic money supply.[62]

The bank stabilized exchange but not domestic prices. Although satisfactory statistics are unavailable, imperfect price indexes show basic agricultural goods going from a base of 100 in 1923, to a peak of 127 in 1928, to a low of 67 in 1932; average weekly prices of construction materials in Bogotá soared from a base of 100 in 1923, to 162 in 1928, and then fell to 78 in 1932; weekly cattle sale prices in Antioquia jumped from an index of 100 in 1923, to 152 in 1928, and then plummeted to 50 by 1932. The general cost of living in Bogotá increased an estimated 10 percent per year between 1923 and 1928.[63]

Colombians soon complained that Kemmerer's system aggravated inflation by attracting foreign investments, a situation his reforms had been expected to prevent. U.S. indemnity payments and loans during 1923–28 expanded the supply of money and credit.[64] The stream of foreign funds also helped pump up government budgets and public works projects, and this public spending raised demand for labor, consumer goods, and imports. Agriculturalists favored for-

Table 2.2 Central Bank Credits to the Government (in millions of pesos)

Year	Credits	Year	Credits
1923	3.8	1929	1.9
1924	2.8	1930	4.0
1925	3.6	1931	10.2
1926	2.0	1932	24.0
1927	2.1	1933	35.9
1928	2.4	1934	41.4

Sources: Robert Triffin, "La moneda y las instituciones bancarias en Colombia," *Revista del Banco de la República* (August 1944): 40.

Table 2.3   Exchange Rate of Colombian Peso in Terms of Current Dollars

Year	Value	Year	Value	Year	Value	Year	Value
1880	.836	1912	.982	1921	.855	1930	.966
1904	.424	1913	.966	1922	.915	1931	.966
1905	.961	1914	.959	1923	.960	1932	.952
1906	.943	1915	.929	1924	.933	1933	.803
1907	.971	1916	.961	1925	.984	1934	.645
1908	.943	1917	.990	1926	.983	1935	.561
1909	.980	1918	1.067	1927	.976	1936	.571
1910	1.042	1919	1.077	1928	.979	1937	.566
1911	.972	1920	.890	1929	.968	1938	.559

Source: Miguel Urrutia and Mario Arrubla, *Estadísticas históricas de Colombia* (Bogotá, 1970), p. 158.

eign-funded public works to improve transportation, but they subsequently protested that those projects increased competition for and costs of labor. Rural elites also blamed the paucity of domestic credit available through the Kemmerer system for their inability to keep the food supply on a par with spiraling demand. Rising domestic food prices led to increasing food imports from the United States, which threatened the balance-of-payments equilibrium. Despite increasing commercialization and modernization of agriculture in the 1920s, its output for domestic consumption lagged behind demand because of antiquated production methods and because the export boom pulled more lands into coffee cultivation. Although real wages and salaries apparently climbed, consumers lamented runaway inflation. In 1927 the minister of finance and public credit (a former aide to the Kemmerer mission) complained that "perhaps nowhere else is there such a monstrous disproportion between the incomes of the vast majority of citizens and the price of basic necessities." By the end of the decade Colombians increasingly blamed first inflation and then deflation on the Kemmerer system's excessive openness to external economic forces.[65]

Ironclad defense of the gold-exchange standard required tight regulations not only for the central bank but also for private banking and government financial operations. Much more than the central bank law, Kemmerer's general banking legislation established public control over private banks. He intended it to solidify all banking in order to facilitate domestic capitalism and reassure foreign investors. Paid for by quotas from the private banks, a banking superintendency under the minister of finance and public credit now would make sure that all banks were properly and securely managed.[66]

This law aroused resistance from many Colombian banks. In newspaper articles and a memorandum to Congress they excoriated the proposed superintendent of banks as dictatorial state interference in their private business. In particular, smaller provincial institutions feared they would not be able to survive government inspections, elevated reserve requirements, and restrictions on their multiple financial activities. Opponents unsuccessfully tried to discredit the bill by branding Kemmerer an "imperialist" who was imposing financial reforms on Colombia previously forced on Central America and the Caribbean at gunpoint. Supporters of the legislation replied that the Colombian masses trusted U.S. academics more than they did U.S. or domestic bankers. Even some bankers favored the law to help clean up their own operations, inspire greater public confidence in them, attract more foreign credits, and drive out shaky competitors. The bill zipped through Congress in four days with only meager modifications. This Kemmerer legislation worked so well that its essential framework endured for decades thereafter.[67]

Contrary to some fears and hopes, Kemmerer's law giving equal rights to foreign banks did not significantly increase their number or their operations in Colombia. Many foreign banks were not attracted by the new requirements in Kemmerer's central and general banking legislation, although the most lasting foreign institutions entered after his reforms. The British remained preeminent among foreign bankers. In 1925 the twenty-seven domestic banks had total paid-up capital and reserves of nearly 15 million pesos, while the four foreign banks had only 4.5 million pesos; by 1927 the remaining twenty-five domestic banks had increased their capital and reserves to 22 million pesos, while the four foreign institutions had only 4 million; by 1930 those figures were 33 million and 8 million, respectively. National banks retained their dominance in the 1920s, and no more foreign banks came in until the 1950s and 1960s.[68]

By making banking more specialized and secure, Kemmerer's legislation helped the system become more concentrated and centralized. Rather than encouraging creation of new banks and sources of credit, his law promoted absorption of smaller provincial institutions by larger entities in Bogotá and Antioquia. This followed the legal model in the United States, where there existed many more strong private banks that could satisfy stringent criteria. The percentage of total banking capital and reserves (not counting the central bank) in Bogotá's province of Cundinamarca and in Antioquia rose from slightly over 40 percent in 1924 to well over 60 percent by 1927. Regional and institutional concentration accentuated thereafter. The total number of private banks fell from thirty-five in 1924, to twenty-nine in 1927, to sixteen in 1930 (reaching fourteen by 1949); consequently, the four foreign banks loomed larger proportionately. While the total number of banks declined, the number of offices and size of deposits and operations increased overall as regional branches multiplied. Especially in outlying provinces, the public complained about this process of oligopolization, which left them more dependent on bigger banks in the richer departments. While the United States became more economically dominant over Colombia, the central regions (Cundinamarca and Antioquia) increased their supremacy over peripheral zones within the country.[69]

Merchants, businessmen, and surviving bankers applauded financial growth under the Kemmerer system. From 1923 to 1927 bank deposits soared 240 percent and commercial loans rose 255 percent. Not counting the central bank, all other banks from 1925 through 1929 increased their gold and exchange reserves from 14 million to 21 million pesos; and their loans, discounts, and investments from 67 million to 208 million pesos. Savings deposits in commercial and mortgage banks rose from an index of 100 in 1924 to 815 in 1929. Foreign credits of Colombian commercial banks jumped from 2 million pesos in 1925 to nearly 20 million by 1929. Total deposits in the central bank swelled from 1 million pesos in 1923 to 10 million in 1928. While many agriculturalists cried for more long-term credits at lower interest, other Colombians criticized domestic and foreign bankers for making too many easy loans in the 1920s.[70]

The superintendency to inspect all credit institutions constituted the centerpiece of Kemmerer's general banking system. It surprised Colombians that a North American champion of free enterprise should introduce state regulation of banking. Although a limited departure from laissez-faire, this reform provided the precedent and tools for later expanded state activism geared more to developmental planning of credit instead of just fiscalization. Congress calmed fears of a foreign (as Kemmerer recommended), politicized, or dictatorial superintendent. The final legislation required that he be a Colombian, supervised by the president and the minister of finance, and subject to an appeals process.[71] To undercut charges of "complete American control of finances" and to attract European in addition to U.S. capital, Ospina in 1924 ignored Kemmerer's suggestion for a North American technical adviser to the superintendent; instead he hired a German.[72]

Kemmerer complemented his banking laws with a roughly translated copy of North American negotiable instruments legislation. He intended for local lawyers to polish the language and details, but critics pounced on the bill for its lack of adjustment to existing Colombian legal and commercial codes and customs. Although the law passed, many sections remained unintelligible or inapplicable. Despite clarification in 1925, it continued to be controversial and never functioned properly.[73]

Kemmerer's Fiscal Reforms

Once Kemmerer established his money and banking laws to prop up the gold-exchange standard, he also had to prevent government financial operations from subverting the system. Colombia took his fiscal reforms more to heart than did those South American countries who sought Kemmerer's help simply because they were desperate to be bailed out by foreign lenders during 1927–31. In contrast with the other Andean republics, Colombia also had more time to make these fiscal innovations work before the depression upset all calculations. All his clients hoped that retooling government finances would attract foreign capital for state expansion, whereas he mainly urged economizing to avoid deficits, which could threaten exchange stability. As with all the Kemmerer reforms, these fiscal laws looked most successful at the general level of indicators of prosperity such as rising revenues; they looked less successful at the detailed level of specific measures such as estimating budgets.[74]

Kemmerer centralized, simplified, and tightened government budgeting processes. He reorganized financial ministries, streamlined revenues collection, consolidated government purchasing, and, most important, wrote a new organic budget law. Even more significant than Kemmerer's legislation in strengthening government resources and solvency in the 1920s, of course, was the flood of indemnity payments, loans, and coffee revenues from the United States.[75]

Although improving national budgeting, Kemmerer's reform, modeled after U.S. and British laws, did not work as well as planned. Problems arose partly because of deficient provisions poorly adapted to Colombian conditions and partly because of imperfect implementation. Highly automatic, routinized systems were unlikely to function properly in an underdeveloped, monocultural economy extremely dependent on oscillating international markets. Not only fluctuations in foreign trade and loans, but also Colombian eagerness to inflate the state's financial role undermined Kemmerer's delicate system.[76]

According to Kemmerer's law, budgetary projections now had to be based on the average of the three preceding years. Previously, wide miscalculations had resulted from projections based only on the preceding year. Kemmerer's method assumed a period of fairly regular economic growth. Consequently, it turned out to be too rigid to accommodate the spurting prosperity during the 1920s or the sudden crash at the end of that decade. Therefore the government fudged on the three-year rule to allow larger projections in the 1920s and smaller ones by 1930. However, neither Kemmerer's automaticity nor the government's flexibility produced very accurate budget forecasts (see table 2.4).[77] Kemmerer's reform generated more domestic and foreign confidence in Colombian budgeting procedures than greater actual efficiency. Until the depression, rising prosperity enabled the government to afford both budgetary inaccuracy and regular payments to creditors.

To fortify the economic strength and planning capabilities of the central state, Kemmerer assigned virtually all budgeting authority to the executive branch. Previously, Congress ran up deficits by adding budget items to reward

Table 2.4   Government Budget Projections and Results

	Percentage by which government revenues differed from government projection	Percentage by which government expenditures differed from government projection
1923	+ 50	+ 45
1924	+ 18	− 7
1925	+ 37	+ 23
1926	+ 38	+ 39
1927	+ 36	+ 51
1928	+ 31	+ 33
1929	+ 13	− 15
1930	− 30	− 12
1931	− 14	− 3

Source: Colombia, Contraloría General de la República, *Informe financiero del Contralor General de la República de Colombia correspondiente al año fiscal de 1931* (Bogotá, 1932), pp. xxii–xxiii.

electoral and regional clienteles. Kemmerer's law prohibited any congressional additions that lacked the approval of the executive branch or unbalanced the budget. Since the Colombian political system depended on payoffs to local supporters, congressmen circumvented Kemmerer's rules and continued expanding the budget through special yearly laws, through appropriations for congressional expenses, and through pressure on government ministers to approve additional regional outlays. With its enlarged budgetary powers, the executive branch also inflated government expenditures.[78]

Kemmerer tried in vain to discourage the long-standing government practice of opening up additional credits for additional expenditures after the budget was approved. In the years preceding 1923 this device had often accounted for as much as 25 percent of total expenditures. These additional credits not covered by budgeted revenues still equaled at least 20 percent of original budgetary appropriations during 1924–31. To better control public credit operations, Kemmerer instituted an extraordinary separate budget for indemnity payments and foreign loans. Those funds were to be used to invest in public works and to amortize the government's debt. Colombia expanded this extraordinary budget, and thus the state's economic scope, well beyond the boundaries intended by Kemmerer. As a result of budgetary excesses by both the legislative and executive branches, Colombia again incurred regular deficits, dependent on anticipated foreign credits, during the second half of the 1920s (see table 2.5).[79]

In the Andean countries the latter half of the 1920s brought huge foreign loans and public works which encouraged bulging budgets and deficits. In

Table 2.5   Central Government Ordinary Budgets (in rounded-off millions of pesos)

Year	Revenues	Expenditures	Deficit	Surplus
1913	14	14		
1914	17	20	2	
1915	21	18		3
1916	15	17	2	
1917	15	16	1	
1918	19	18		1
1919	14	16	3	
1920	24	28	4	
1921	26	35	9	
1922	24	28	4	
1923	44	39		5
1924	40	40		
1925	52	50		2
1926	61	67	7	
1927	63	69	6	
1928	75	79	4	
1929	75	83	8	
1930	49	62	12	
1931	44	52	9	

Note: Among varying budget figures these appear to be the best approximations. The data here do not include the extraordinary budget for foreign credits and public works.
Sources: Colombia, Contraloría, *Informe, 1931*, p. xxi; Eugenio J. Gómez, *Ideas económicas y fiscales de Colombia* (Bogotá, 1949), pp. 205–6; Torres García, *Historia de la moneda en Colombia* (Bogotá, 1945), p. 360; Esteban Jaramillo, *Exposición de motivos referente al proyecto de ley sobre presupuesto nacional* (Bogotá, 1927), pp. 6–7, 160–61; Diego Monsalve, *Colombia cafetera* (Barcelona, 1927), p. 102.

Colombia Kemmerer's fiscal system worked best under President Pedro Nel Ospina (1922–26). As the mission's advice grew more distant, President Miguel Abadía Mendez (1926–30) abandoned fiscal restraint. The first administration's budgetary caution made foreign lenders more willing to invest, which stimulated overspending by the succeeding administration. Rather than new and higher taxes, general prosperity and Kemmerer's methods for handling revenues accounted for the doubling of state income during the period 1922–25. Ospina's great success in raising revenues led his successor to hoist them still further, as expectations and obligations accumulated. When the Panama indemnity payments (1923–26) ended, Abadía replaced them with foreign credits. The state used those funds to employ rising urban middle- and working-class groups in the bureaucracy and public works. Since no true civil service existed, Liberals denounced Conservatives for trying to solidify their political hegemony through unparalleled budgetary expansion and clientelism that became ever more reliant on foreign credits, which jeopardized national sovereignty. An engorged bureaucracy, overextended public works commitments, and mushrooming reliance on foreign loans left the government extremely vulnerable to the Great Depression.[80]

Kemmerer's most important creation to guard the balancing of the budget was the national comptroller. This centralized authority over all government accounts became more powerful in Colombia than its models in the United States and England. The Colombian comptroller, however, never acquired the right to rule on the constitutionality of executive actions, as its Chilean counterpart would. After exerting prior legal and accounting control over all state financial operations, the comptroller in Bogotá filed monthly and annual fiscal reports. These analyses improved government economic knowledge, planning, and management. By the end of the 1920s Colombians were hailing this agency as the Kemmerer fiscal reform which had best fulfilled its duties and expectations.[81]

During the period 1923–25, Lill advised the comptroller and prepared most of the budgetary analyses and annual reports. He carried out many of the essential duties, despite the law requiring the comptroller to be a Colombian. Lill repeatedly urged Congress to tighten the budget. In 1924 he also tried in vain to help the U.S. embassy convince the Colombian government to select a North American rather than a British bank as its fiscal agent, which the embassy called the crucial "entering wedge" for North American capital and commercial expansion there. Although Colombians frequently criticized the comptroller as it began carrying out its mandate, Lill won their respect. Complaining of constant obstruction by the central government, however, Lill departed for the United States in 1925.[82]

The comptroller's initial years proved difficult because the government repeatedly resisted its jurisdiction and interference. In 1924 this conflict reached the Colombian Supreme Court, which admonished the comptroller to stick to purely fiscal rather than administrative functions. The comptroller also collided with ingrained practices and vested interests in the bureaucracy. U.S. indemnity payments and public credits complicated the task of estimating and controlling budgets. It proved hard to achieve speed and accuracy in managing revenues and expenditures among poorly interconnected regions. Clientelistic politics seeped into the new office at all levels. Rampant turnover of employees produced inefficient and erratic application of the law. Although Kemmerer recommended long-term comptrollers serving terms of at least four years, eight different men filled the post from 1923 through 1933. Such a powerful and expanding technical agency could not be removed from the spoils arena. Although never as smooth or authoritative a mechanism as Kemmerer envisioned, the comptroller nonetheless improved fiscal order.[83]

Kemmerer also recommended simplification, expansion, and better collection of taxes. Colombia needed to curtail widespread tax evasion. The government also desired to increase its regular revenue sources so as to be less reliant on oscillating customs receipts and more capable of extracting support domestically. In addition, business groups wanted less complicated taxes that were less inhibiting to commerce. U.S. interests naturally favored stiffer taxes on domestic elites to lighten the burden on U.S. corporations or exports to Colombia and to provide more reliable government resources to service foreign debts. Kemmerer, however, had little impact on these taxation problems.[84]

In 1925 government revenues still came 62 percent from customs, 12 percent from state railroads, 23 percent from myriad other special sources such as mail service, and only 2 percent each from the stamp and income taxes.[85] Meanwhile, taxes per inhabitant ascended from 3.9 pesos in 1923, to 5.3 in 1925, to 6.6 in 1929, and then fell back to 3.8 in 1930. Despite mildly rising internal impositions, the government still boasted to foreign investors in 1929 that Colombia had "the smallest taxation per capita and property in Latin America." The economic elites impeded domestic taxation and left the state reliant on income from foreign trade and loans. Such dependence resulted from internal class structure as well as external forces.[86]

The least well-received Kemmerer recommendations were those on taxes. Levies on passengers and incomes were his only bills not passed in 1923. Presidential, congressional, and press supporters of his progressive income tax argued that it would advance civic consciousness and national integration. They believed that everyone having to pay directly for the government would therefore identify with and demand accountability from it. Opponents blasted the bill as "a weapon of socialism against capitalism." Congress finally passed a mild upward reform of the 1918 income tax law in 1927, incorporating some technical improvements akin to those recommended by Kemmerer.[87]

Kemmerer also encountered frustration in his effort to lower tariffs. Colombian resistance to domestic taxation and support for mild protectionism convinced the mission merely to issue a report in favor of free trade rather than a concrete customs law. Criticizing "artificial industries," the mission recommended development through comparative advantage in primary material production. It also suggested hiring a foreign expert to revamp customs administration.[88]

The greatest debate over protectionism in the 1920s concerned domestic agriculture rather than manufacturing. As food prices rose, coffee growers, merchants, manufacturers, and labor groups blamed inefficient agriculturalists and their tariff protection. Quoting Kemmerer on the need for free trade, the government passed the "emergency law" of 1927 to slash duties on imported foods.

Coming mainly from the United States, these food imports soared from a volume index of 100 in 1922 to 573 by 1928. Once again traditional agriculturalists lost out to urban economic interests more attuned to the Kemmerer system.[89]

The Colombian government's primary motivation for adopting Kemmerer's reforms was to improve its credit rating abroad. The public debt (principally to cover deficits and railroad construction) stood at 39 million pesos (22 external and 17 internal) when he arrived in 1923. Because of the U.S. indemnity windfall and Kemmerer's recommendations for austerity, the Ospina administration amortized its public debt down to 24 million pesos (14 external and 10 internal) by 1926. Colombia became the only South American country during 1922–26 to reduce its national government debt per capita. The Colombian national debt fell by 66 percent while Argentina's rose 27 percent, Chile's rose 33 percent, Peru's rose 34 percent, and Bolivia's rose 54 percent.

Although the availability of U.S. and British loans improved immediately following Kemmerer's visit, the Colombian central government held back until the Abadía Mendez administration. Moreover, the U.S. government discouraged some loans to its Colombian counterpart until concessions were granted to Gulf Oil. Thereafter, its foreign debt skyrocketed. Public works loans arrived through U.S. financiers for a nominal $25 million in 1927 and $35 million in 1928. Thanks partly to the second Kemmerer mission, the Colombian government contracted its third major U.S. loan in 1930–31, for a face value of $20 million, to cover debts. These obligations propelled the total central government public debt to 119 million pesos (81 external and 38 internal) by 1931.[90]

In 1923 Kemmerer agreed with Colombians that they should take more advantage of foreign financing. He reasoned that the country was rich in resources but poor in capital and infrastructure. Moreover, interest rates were lower abroad. Upon returning home he praised Colombia's economic organization to U.S. bankers, who therefore became more willing to contract loans. Throughout the 1920s, however, he urged the central government to be circumspect in shouldering foreign debts and to control external borrowing by departments and municipalities. For most of the 1920s Colombia followed little of his advice on foreign indebtedness.[91]

The arrival of Kemmerer and the U.S. indemnity payments fulfilled Colombian hopes of improving their credit rating abroad. From 1923 to 1928 quotations in the London and New York markets rose on all Colombian bond issues, which did better than those of most of Latin America. Whereas national foreign debts prior to 1923 required specific guarantees and earmarked customs revenues, those thereafter did not.[92]

Until 1927, subnational entities in Colombia mainly capitalized on the new creditworthiness bestowed by the Kemmerer mission. After having virtually no foreign indebtedness in 1922, the leading departments, municipalities, and mortgage banks emitted bond issues for soaring amounts in the U.S. market from 1923 onward, especially during 1926–28. The coffee provinces became the biggest borrowers, mainly to improve transportation for exports. By June 1927, of 95 million pesos of foreign public debt, the departments (30 million), mortgage banks (20 million), and municipalities (13 million) accounted for 63 million. By June 1932, according to the minister of finance, Colombia's outstanding public foreign debt had reached $210 million, of which some $60 million was owed by the departments, $48 million by the mortgage banks, $22 million by the municipalities, and $80 million by the national government. The law required most of these subnational loans to be authorized and monitored by the central government, but it exerted no effective control. In the 1920s Colombians floated all but one of these subnational loans in the United States.[93]

Colombia's total public debt in 1932 weighed nearly ten times as much as it had in 1923. In those nine years the national government, departments, municipalities, and mortgage banks imported over $200 million from the United States, not counting the $25 million indemnity payments. By the end of the 1920s Colombia ranked second only to Chile among the Andean countries in total securities held in the United States. The first and richest South American countries Kemmerer advised succeeded best at tapping the U.S. financial market. Taking into account the North American shares in private banks and the loans floated by mining and oil companies added over $22 million more to the flood of U.S. finance capital into Colombia. Considering all direct investments as well pushed the total inflow of foreign capital for the decade well over $300 million, which accounted for nearly half of total capital formation in Colombia. In 1928, even before the depression, the U.S. State Department worried that the Colombian government's lack of control over its own deficits and over departmental and municipal borrowing endangered its ability to handle this galloping indebtedness.[94]

Throughout the 1920s most Colombians defended increasing foreign loans on the grounds that their country was relatively underindebted. Although comparative estimates varied widely, all agreed that Colombia's ballooning foreign debt remained small vis-à-vis the country's resources, population, and neighbors.[95] Even with indebtedness accumulating at full tilt by the end of 1928, one estimate published by the Banco de la República showed the South American national, provincial, and municipal foreign debts given in table 2.6. As a percentage of national wealth, it was reported that public debt accounted for only 2 percent in Colombia compared to 6 percent in Peru, 7 percent in Argentina, and 12 percent in Chile. According to another crude estimate for the end of the 1920s, Colombia and Peru bore an annual foreign debt service of less than 20 percent of their total national budget compared to roughly 25 percent in Chile and Argentina.[96]

Table 2.6   South American Foreign debts Owed in December 1928 (in millions of U.S. dollars)

	To Europe	To United States	Total	Per capita (in dollars)
Colombia	$10	$147	$157	$19.44
Chile	141	146	288	65.34
Ecuador	1	0	1	.40
Bolivia	0	61	61	17.03
Peru	106	47	153	17.01
Argentina	293	378	671	61.40

Source: Revista del Banco de la República (July 1930): 198–99.

Despite the seemingly low relative level of indebtedness, its rapid and massive accumulation in 1927–28 evoked more and more criticism from Colombians. Critics resurrected Kemmerer's 1923 sermons about overindulgence. By 1928 the U.S. ambassador warned that annual interest and amortization payments had risen to dangerous heights for such a poor and fragile export economy. He complained that loans made too easily available were spent to cover government deficits and to build wasteful public works. Once begun, those projects necessitated further loans for their continuation and failed to generate substantial revenues to repay the investment. Moreover, this construction extravaganza drew workers away from rural production of domestic foodstuffs and coffee, which jeopardized the balance of trade and thus Colombia's ability to meet its debt obligations. The ambassador scolded eager U.S. lenders for nudging equally reckless Colombian politicians to the brink of default: "The Legation has frequently in the past expressed its strong conviction that the various American banking houses who have during the past three years floated various Colombian national, departmental, and municipal foreign loans were not exercising due care in protecting the interests of the American bondholder and were not assuming that degree of moral responsibility towards their clients which is necessary to a sound policy of foreign financing."[97]

Colombian governments spent most of those foreign loans on the transportation network. One U.S. investment firm concluded in the mid-1920s that "there is no other country in Latin America so lacking in modern means of communication, and where the people labor under such incredible transport handicaps, as the Republic of Colombia." Kemmerer agreed that poor transportation constituted the major barrier to external trade, internal economic integration, and central government control. He suggested hiring U.S. engineers for these projects, both to obtain their expertise and to inspire confidence among U.S. lenders. By 1926 Colombia far exceeded the limited spending he recommended. The government showered pesos on widely scattered, technically inefficient, and politically motivated projects.[98]

Improving transportation facilities served North American as well as Colombian interests, but only as long as overindulgence did not imperil debt repayments. Better ports, roads, and railroads accelerated foreign trade. These projects created markets for U.S. construction firms, banking houses, transportation equipment suppliers, and automobile manufacturers. They also reduced the insulation of local producers from foreign competitors.[99]

Colombia invested approximately 50 percent of the foreign public debt during 1920–29 in transportation projects. From 1923 through 1931 the national government alone spent 210 million pesos on public works: 156 million on railroads and air cables, 33 million on roads, and 21 million on ports. During 1925–29 railroads claimed 54 percent of public transportation expenditures, roads 39 percent, and ports 7 percent. During 1926–28 extraordinary new public works construction consumed almost 40 percent of total government expenditures, causing mounting deficits that were covered by foreign loans.[100]

In 1923 a newspaper, praising Kemmerer's reforms as likely to attract foreign capital for transportation projects, observed that "every Colombian has a railroad in his heart."[101] Not only a majority of foreign loans for transportation construction, but also 60 percent of the U.S. indemnity payments went into railroads. The kilometers covered by those lines nearly doubled during the 1920s and came to account for over one-fourth of the national transportation network.[102] Still, Colombia's transportation infrastructure lagged behind other major Latin American republics. For every kilometer of railroads, Colombia possessed 4,100 inhabitants, Peru 1,500, and Argentina 250. By the end of the 1920s Peru still boasted nearly twice as many and Chile almost four times as many railroad kilometers as Colombia.[103]

Railroad construction simultaneously increased dependence on the external economy and central government control over transportation. As in the nineteenth century, railroads in the 1920s were designed primarily to channel exports to coastal outlets rather than to knit together domestic regions. Consequently, agriculturalists and others producing for internal consumption continued to complain about inadequate transportation at insufferable rates. The few foreign-owned lines, mainly in the hands of U.S. banana and oil companies, were especially geared to export-import traffic. In the 1920s national and departmental governments themselves usually built the new lines, rather than consigning them to foreign companies as in the past. The state acquired control over a majority of railroads and their fares in the 1920s, giving it stronger leverage over the national economy. Improving transportation also facilitated Colombia's change from 21 percent urban in 1918 to 26 percent by 1930.[104]

By the end of the 1920s Colombian enthusiasm for this public-works boom dimmed. Critics charged that railroad projects entailed "the naming of a manager for every kilometer." Agriculturalists blamed public works for labor shortages and inflation. When the depression struck, Colombia had to slash government budgets, curtail public works, lay off workers, revive domestic agriculture, and default on foreign debts. So long as that default formed part of a global crisis, however, it neither denied Colombia credits available to others nor incited U.S. intervention. From that perspective it could be argued that the country was fortunate to have enticed foreigners to pay for so much vital infrastructural development in the 1920s.[105]

The Great Depression

Ultimately, the Kemmerer system, and indeed the entire Colombian economy, rested on coffee sales abroad and on foreign credits to compensate for any balance-of-payments shortfall. As coffee prices fell and debt payments grew, the positive balance of trade conveyed a false sense of security at the end of the 1920s. According to National City Bank's estimate of the balance of payments for 1930, Colombia received from foreigners $81 million for its exports, $500,000 for miscellaneous transactions (freight, insurance, diplomatic service, etc.), and $9 million in new investments, for a total of $90.5 million; Colombia paid out to foreigners $62.8 million for imports, $14.3 million for miscellaneous transactions, $20 million for interest and amortization on national, departmental, municipal, and bank debts, and $2.5 million for interest and dividends on investments, for a total of $99.6 million; the deficit had to be covered by a gold outflow from the reserves of the central bank of $9.1 million. Colombia's ability to maintain the gold standard and service on foreign debts declined as the balance of payments worsened and customs receipts dwindled. From 1929 through 1932 the volume of exports fell by one-fourth and their value by one-half.[106]

Many Colombians had worried that a trade slump in a country heavily indebted and dependent on primary exports would break the gold standard, despite reassurances from Kemmerer that it could be sustained. Now they complained because his system maintained exchange stability and debt payments in gold at the expense of domestic credit and prosperity. Critics increasingly railed against economic openness as the degenerating balance of payments caused an exodus of gold, contracting domestic credit and thus further restricting export as well as import capacity. When the Kemmerer system transmitted the full ferocity of the Great Crash into Colombia, debt-led growth turned into debt-led disaster. "Prosperity through debt" became prostration through debt.[107]

An agricultural, monocultural, indebted economy found it extremely difficult to alter its exports or cut back its payments abroad. Colombia made extraordinary efforts to maintain the Kemmerer system and thus its credit standing, in vain hopes of being saved by U.S. financiers. Because of its reliance on foreign loans, the government held fast in the face of ever louder public complaints about budget reductions, debt services, and gold drains.[108]

The depression damaged all Colombian economic sectors and prompted them all to call for protection and credit from the government. At the 1931 convention of the National Federation of Coffee Growers, its manager stated the case for special government assistance for that crop:

> I am fiscal equilibrium, because customs revenues, which are the axis of our budgets, depend on coffee exports; I am the external credit of the nation and the departments, because with the exchange from coffee is serviced the external debts, public and private; I am the Bank of the Republic, because if coffee exports ceased in a given moment, the Bank of the Republic would break in less than three months; I represent and on me depends the sound monetary system based on the gold standard, the stability of exchange, the possibility of introducing into the country machinery, rails, scientific books, foreign professors, in a word, the civilization of Colombia from the material point of view.[109]

The federation convinced the government in 1931–32 to create—with the help of capital from the central bank—the Caja de Crédito Agrario and the Banco Central Hipotecario. *Cafeteros* resented charges that these extraordinary public credit institutions for agriculture undermined the central bank's ability to defend exchange stability.[110]

Agriculturalists producing for the domestic market joined coffee growers in persuading the government to provide unprecedented credit intervention on their behalf. In 1930 the Banco de la República finally exercised its right to deal directly with the public by offering preferential lending terms to agriculturalists, especially coffee growers. The government in 1931–32 founded not only special credit institutions for farmers but also the Ministry of Agriculture and Commerce. In 1931 the Society of Agriculturalists successfully pressured the government to repeal the 1927 low-tariff "emergency law" and hike protective duties on foodstuffs. The rural elites saw these measures as redress for the "indifference" and "hostility" displayed toward them by governments and banks in the 1920s. Now these landowners overturned many of the credit and trade policies advocated earlier by Kemmerer.[111]

Industrialists launched the National Federation of Manufacturers and Producers in 1930 to promote protection and purchase of domestic manufactured goods. Some labor unions backed these proposals. In reaction to scarcity of foreign exchange and jobs, the government also responded favorably to this protectionist industrialization program.[112]

Abrupt cancellation of credits from U.S. banks at the outset of the depression hurt Colombian banks, especially mortgage institutions and their *cafetero* clients. The conservative, restrictive policies of the central bank and its member institutions also caused credit to evaporate. Colombian banks shrank commercial loans from 95 million pesos in 1928 to 44 million in 1933 and mortgage loans from 85 million pesos in 1929 to 43 million in 1933. Banking deposits fell more than 50 percent during 1929–31. Bankers were roundly denounced for credit contraction. At this moment of political weakness they lost firm control over the board of directors of the central bank. In 1932 the government intervened to reduce the obligations of strapped commercial and mortgage borrowers, especially agriculturalists, to the bankers. Despite losses, the major banks survived the depression, largely thanks to Kemmerer's banking system and huge reserves accumulated in the 1920s.[113]

The depression devastated the central bank in Colombia earlier than the institutions in Chile and Ecuador. During 1929–30 the central bank's gold reserves and notes in circulation in Colombia fell 44 percent and 37 percent, respectively, while those in Chile dropped only 23 percent and 6 percent, and those in Ecuador 6 percent and 19 percent. By 1930–31 the depression had caught up with the other Andean countries; gold reserves and bank notes in circulation in Colombia decreased 32 and 22 percent, respectively, in Chile 42 and 20 percent, and in Ecuador 23 and 22 percent. Meanwhile Colombia's central bank maintained the lowest discount rate: 7 percent, compared to 9 percent in Chile and 10 percent in Ecuador. As the inexorable mechanics of the gold standard drained the Banco de la República, its orthodox policies exacerbated the domestic depression. Public outcries against its restrictions convinced the bank to offer slightly more credit and to lower its interest rate from 8 to 7 percent (6 percent for agricultural loans) in 1930 and then to 4 percent in 1933.[114]

Initially maintaining firm faith in Kemmerer's wisdom, the bank staunchly resisted mounting pressures to adopt more reflationary policies. Through 1931 it continued to hope that its defense of exchange stability, combined with the government's budget reductions and punctual debt payments, would bring salvation through foreign loans. Increasingly bucking public opinion, defense of Kemmerer's system by the central bank and government was bolstered by his return visit.[115]

When the depression arrived, the government was overextended from the spurt in spending and obligations during the latter 1920s. Ordinary revenues plunged by nearly 50 percent during 1929–31. The treasury fell into arrears on paying domestic obligations in 1929. According to the U.S. ambassador, "President Abadía had made application at the Banco de Colombia for a loan to be secured by the last month's salary due him which has not yet been paid." By March 1930 the national treasury bore a large placard announcing *"No hay dinero."* Having become heavily dependent on vanishing foreign revenue sources, the Abadía Mendez government tried to keep afloat by extracting advance tax payments from resident U.S. corporations.[116]

During the depression the Colombian government was torn between cutting foreign debt payments or domestic programs. Despite resistance, the government initially tried to cope with the budget crunch by paring down the payroll at the expense of the urban middle and working classes. The Ministry of War received only half its 1930 request. As opposed to the other Andean countries, Colombia demonstrated its dedication to civilian rule partly by responding to the depression through lower allocations to the armed forces, without igniting a coup d'etat. The government had to reassure the jittery U.S. ambassador that reductions in the military would not be so drastic as to impair its ability to control labor agitation against U.S. businesses. One reason for inviting Kemmerer back was to throw his weight behind government attempts to chop expenditures and thus attract foreign loans.[117]

Also in contrast to the other Andean countries, Colombia responded politically to the depression by peacefully transferring power to the opposition party. Enrique Olaya Herrera, a moderate Liberal, won the 1930 presidential election. Having served as ambassador to the United States in the 1920s, he was elected by Colombians for his ability to reconcile Conservatives and Liberals as well as to attract North American support. Inaugurated in August 1930, Olaya faced a staggering deficit of nearly thirty-two million pesos. He tried desperately to prune expenses, increase revenues, maintain the Kemmerer system, and thus save Colombia from the depression through U.S. relief. Olaya became the most pro–United States president in Colombian history.[118]

Like Ospina prior to the first Kemmerer mission, Olaya went courting capital in the United States between his election and inauguration. While there, Olaya vowed to erase remaining Colombian restrictions on foreign investments. He said that Colombia should have "a government that has a modern and ample concept—the concept of the open door—for foreign capital, so that when it arrives to submit itself to our laws it feels confident that the surrounding atmosphere is one of mutual cooperation and help, never one of hostility and suspicion."[119]

Once in office, Olaya cooperated closely with the U.S. embassy and U.S companies in hopes of attracting U.S capital. He tended to see the North American presence as an interrelated whole, wherein friendliness toward a U.S. corporation should have elicited reciprocal friendliness from a U.S. bank. The embassy tried to help all U.S. interests and get them to cooperate. It also endeavored to convince Olaya of the diversity and autonomy of multiple U.S. economic actors in Colombia.

During the depression the U.S. embassy became even more active on behalf of U.S. economic interests in Colombia than it had been during the 1920s. As a result of U.S. economic expansion there since 1923, the devastation of the depression, and the inauguration of Olaya, the embassy now found the Colombian government more receptive to its entreaties than ever before. In defiance of virulent Colombian protectionist reactions to the depression, the embassy convinced Olaya in 1930–33 to accept many of its recommendations for lower tariff duties on U.S. articles. Under pressure from the embassy, Olaya also agreed to give U.S. concerns preferential treatment under exchange controls. Throughout the Andean countries, increasing dependence on the United States in the 1920s rendered those governments exceptionally willing to grant concessions to U.S. interests during the initial shock of the depression.[120]

In 1933 the U.S. ambassador boasted of convincing Colombia to pursue numerous trade and other policies favorable to the United States: "I have the honor respectfully to point out that this Legation since the latter part of 1928 has been instrumental in assisting American business interests to the extent of some hundreds of millions of dollars." Another successful embassy effort, in opposition to widespread Colombian sentiment, was to convince Olaya to maintain payments on the central government's foreign debt into 1933, after most of Latin America had defaulted.[121]

Other examples of U.S. embassy success with Olaya included convincing him to not raise the export tax on platinum mined by U.S. corporations, to veto a bill promoting a native merchant marine to compete with U.S. shipping, to block legislation damaging to U.S. banks, to provide police protection to a U.S. emerald company, to defend U.S. electric companies from demonstrators protesting high rates and congressmen advocating increased taxes, and to favor North American telecommunications, aviation, and construction firms. Olaya also cooperated with the embassy by giving the United Fruit Company protection against labor demands for higher wages, against congressional and departmental proposals for new taxes, and against Colombian competitors' desires for greater domestic control over banana lands, irrigation, and railroad transportation. With encouragement from the embassy and at times Kemmerer, Olaya engaged North American experts for oil legislation, railroads, aviation, communications, customs, and the comptroller.[122]

Led by Conservative nationalists, several pundits and politicians began accusing Olaya of "converting Colombia into a Yankee colony." They denounced continuing payments on the foreign debt, granting concessions to foreign companies, and employing high-salaried foreign experts. Reviving deep-seated sentiments against U.S. "imperialist capitalism," these critics excoriated Olaya for having "the mentality of a colonial governor" in making "secret compromises with the masters of foreign capitalism called to our country to forge the chains of our economic slavery."[123]

The harshest criticism of Olaya centered on his generosity to U.S. oil interests. Conservative opponents bemoaned enactment of new petroleum legislation more favorable to U.S. companies and resolution of concessions satisfactory to those companies. They also attacked employment of a North American adviser in drafting that law and arranging those terms.[124]

Olaya hoped that improved relations with U.S. oil concerns would not only increase exploration and production but also brighten Colombia's credit standing with North American bankers. In particular, he believed that his petroleum deals would help consummate a short-term $20 million (face value) loan transaction with a group of financiers headed by the National City Bank of New York and the First National Bank of Boston. Indeed, that banking group released the final $4 million to Colombia in 1931, immediately after Olaya had generously settled outstanding concession disputes with the Gulf Oil Company. The State Department had urged the bankers to deliver the remainder of the loan, both to aid Olaya and to facilitate the favorable settlement of oil issues, which it helped arrange. The State Department did not want a last-minute collapse of that financial transaction to injure a broad range of other U.S. concerns in Colombia. Favorable terms for the oil companies, however, were not the primary condition for this emergency loan to go through; the bankers placed more emphasis on stern fiscal management, which Kemmerer helped Colombia carry out.[125]

Olaya made that loan agreement in June 1930 as a result of his visit to the United States. As the U.S. embassy noted, the new president "based his whole political program on friendship and cooperation with us." Many of his Colombian backers hoped Olaya could use the loan to revive credit and public works. That money, however, had to cover a huge floating debt and crushing deficit inherited from the Abadía Mendez administration.[126]

The bankers originally agreed to deliver the loan in installments if Olaya enacted tighter budget and comptroller laws to prevent overspending. They also demanded drastic cuts in expenditures to achieve balance, reorganized management for railroads and other public works to curb overruns, a ceiling on the public debt, acceptance of the new Kemmerer recommendations on these and other fiscal matters (such as customs administration), and appointment of the bankers as fiscal agents for the government. While negotiating that loan contract with National City Bank in New York, President-elect Olaya had conferred with Kemmerer about these burdensome demands for fiscal control. Except for desires for direct participation in supervising customs revenues and railroads, the bankers' fundamental conditions were met by the desperate government. U.S. financiers thus obtained broad powers to judge satisfactory fiscal performance by Colombia. Although favoring the loan, the State Department worried that these stipulations might constitute illegitimate interference in that country's sovereign affairs.[127]

As the depression worsened, the bankers' eagerness to make the loans cooled. They also lost interest in serving as Colombia's fiscal agents so as to have first option on future loans. Their escalating demands for severe budget cut-backs aroused opposition from Colombian bureaucrats, public opinion, and the U.S. State Department. The bankers' harsh terms also produced conflicts among U.S. interests. U.S. oil companies helped convince the bankers to hold back the final installment, pending more favorable action on petroleum legislation and the budget. Those corporations, however, did not want banker intransigence to turn Olaya against all U.S. concerns. The bankers' desires to see the Colombian treasury refilled led to new tax demands on U.S. companies, and recommendations to prune imports to improve the balance of payments clashed with the objectives of U.S. exporters to Colombia. Both the Colombian government and the U.S. embassy found it very difficult to juggle these multiple U.S. economic interests.[128]

Olaya's assumption of the amity and unity of U.S. economic and political interests was also upset when the North American bankers decided to spread the risk by bringing Lazard Brothers of London into the financial group. The State Department echoed Olaya's dismay at U.S. bankers aiding British interests. Olaya learned then that the U.S. government had little control over the bankers' behavior and that Colombia had little ability to play British and U.S. bankers against one another.[129]

When the bankers elevated their demands and delayed their payments, Colombian public opinion soured on U.S. banks. As Olaya tried to shove through more and more unpalatable legislation demanded by his creditors, one congressman charged that he had become "a prisoner of the bankers." When in March 1931 the final loan installment was held up, Olaya complained to the U.S. ambassador: "I have tried to play the game with the Americans; I have had the oil law they wanted passed, the Barco Contract signed [the Gulf Oil concession], have tried to protect American interests on tariff, etc., etc. It breaks my heart to have Americans let me down at the end." The lack of tightly unified U.S. policy toward Colombia or strong State Department control over U.S. capitalists left this ardent friend of the United States baffled and disappointed.[130]

The U.S. embassy tried to convince Olaya to expect less and the bankers to demand less. The exasperated ambassador complained that:

> the best efforts of the Department of State and our diplomatic missions abroad may be almost nullified by prejudicial activities of Ameri-

can business concerns. I have in mind especially the recent action of the group of American bankers, which has had such an unfortunate effect on our interests here in general in Colombia. . . . I do not believe that that hostility will cease until some way is found to have American business concerns understand that it is imperative for them to act towards the governments and peoples south of the Rio Grande in the same manner as they act towards people and concerns in the U.S.; and we are only deceiving ourselves if we pretend that the majority of American concerns act in these countries as they do at home.[131]

Kemmerer also took a hand in consummating this 1930–31 loan. He urged Olaya to listen to the oil companies and, more important, helped convince the Colombians to make the fiscal reforms the bankers wanted and helped persuade the bankers that Colombia was a good risk. The second Kemmerer mission's fiscal recommendations became part of the bankers' list of requisites to complete the loan. His reforms took the place of more direct banker supervision over government financial affairs. Coming from Kemmerer instead of just the bankers, those reforms appeared "scientifically" sound and less insulting to national pride. Congress passed that Kemmerer legislation, however, primarily because it satisfied the bankers' stipulations for the loan.[132] By the same token, the Money Doctor helped convince the U.S. bankers to have confidence in Olaya's presidency and budget-cutting efforts, to be less irritating in their demands, and to extend to Colombia the full amount of money promised. The government's hopes that Kemmerer would also be able to pry loose even further credits from North American investors during the depression, however, proved in vain, despite his best efforts.[133]

Kemmerer's missions also affected these loan negotiations in two more indirect ways. Colombians saw themselves as now finally following the advice of his 1923 mission to choose a single fiscal agent for their foreign market operations.[134] The bankers sent Howard Jefferson of the First National Bank of Boston to negotiate with Olaya in 1930, partly because of his prestige as a member of the 1923 Kemmerer mission. Members of the second mission helped Jefferson prepare fiscal information for his employer. Kemmerer advised Olaya on the terms of the loan contract and even cabled the president of National City Bank to protest the excessive and escalating demands. After returning home, Kemmerer continued pressing the bankers to cooperate with Colombia. He also tried to help arrange a monopoly contract and loan with the Swedish Match Company similar to its deal with Ecuador. Thus the second Kemmerer visit was much more directly related than the first to specific foreign loan transactions.[135]

The Second Kemmerer Mission

As the depression reverberated in Colombia in 1929, sentiment arose for reinviting Kemmerer. The central bank wanted the "skillful doctor of nations" to restore confidence in the bank, the gold standard, government fiscal restraint, the economy's future, and the country's creditworthiness. A newspaper columnist in 1929 averred that Kemmerer's influence with U.S. creditors could rescue Colombia from the depression:

> This does not mean intervention, nor penetration, nor renouncing rights and sovereignty, but looking for the one to counsel us and put us on the right track. We are incapable of increasing the value of our riches and of completing the most important public works. We do not understand finances, nor can we reach agreement on anything, nor can we succeed in economizing or putting order in our businesses . . . we dare to suggest the return of Mr. Kemmerer as the only remedy. We are a client and a debtor of the United States, and trained by foreign experts we will be a better client for commerce and banking, even more so if some money is furnished us, when it is calculated that our resources, well administered, and our revenues, well managed, provide a margin for that money. . . . Our financing by our principal creditor will benefit him and save us without sacrificing the prestige of our independent republic. Better said, we have an enormous estate in abandoned condition, and we lack a good majordomo who can start it up and administer it.[136]

One of Olaya's best-received campaign promises was to recall Kemmerer to get state finances back on track and thus rejuvenate Colombia's credit rating abroad.[137] Olaya had befriended Kemmerer while serving in the United States in the 1920s and had discussed the possibility of a second mission with him while visiting there after his election. At the request of the president-elect, the Abadía Mendez administration contracted the second mission. Kemmerer was reluctant to return because he believed that Colombia's current problems were mainly in the fiscal arena rather than in his field of money and banking. Being invited back constituted a tribute to both the success and the incompleteness of Kemmerer's first financial housecleaning.[138]

Kemmerer's arrival coincided with Olaya's inauguration in August 1930. The Money Doctor's return added prestige to a new party in power, facing a national crisis. Paid 100,000 gold pesos in U.S. currency, the mission stayed four months (August 4–November 29). Although Kemmerer himself departed on October 1, he reviewed the rest of his team's work at his office in Princeton. The mission's members—none repeaters from 1923—were Joseph T. Byrne (budget and accounting), W. W. Renwick (customs), Walter E. Lagerquist (public credit), Kossuth M. Williamson, a professor at Wesleyan (taxes and revenues), W. E. Dunn (general secretary), and J. C. Schaefer (assistant secretary). While in Colombia, Kemmerer met daily with Olaya, who said "he intended to back our recommendations to the limit."[139]

The second mission made nearly twice as many proposals as the first. Those 1930 reports treated the central bank, general banking, government budgeting, revenues collection and distribution, the comptroller, public credit, public debt, treasury certificates, public works, and customs; and taxes on banana exports, merchandise imports, stamps and consular rights, land, fixed property, municipal valorization, incomes, and inheritances and donations. Virtually all represented marginal modifications in legislation from 1923 and succeeding years. The Colombian ambassador to Bolivia belittled this return mission as "a redundancy." More important than specific bills was the mission's impact on general confidence in the Colombian economy and government, at home and abroad.[140]

Kemmerer's minor reforms in the central bank incorporated improvements he had developed in the other Andean countries since 1923. His 1930 changes also made the bank slightly more flexible and more responsive to the depression. These innovations pleased agriculturalists and coffee growers, who were determined to have the mission serve their interests rather than those of the bankers, as it had in 1923. Most of these adjustments in the bank had been advocated by Colombians for years. Nevertheless, it required a second visit by the institution's creator to put them through. Kemmerer's purpose was to shore up support for the central bank and the gold standard; their maintenance remained the guiding star of all his reforms, just as in 1923.[141]

Despite continued resistance from domestic and foreign bankers, Kemmerer's prestige made possible the recasting of the central bank's board of directors long desired by agriculturalists, especially coffee growers. As modified by Kemmerer and Congress, the board's composition changed from three chosen by the government, four by domestic banks, two by foreign banks, and one by public shareholders, to three named by the government, two by domestic banks, and one each by foreign banks, public shareholders, the Society of Agriculturalists, the National Federation of Coffee Growers, and the Chamber of Commerce. Kemmerer still left industry and labor off the board in Colombia, in contrast with his more representative directorate in more urbanized Chile. Whereas his 1923 reforms in Colombia favored urban economic activities, those in 1930 tilted more toward the rural sectors as the traditional elites reasserted themselves.[142]

Kemmerer and his disciples in the central bank would later be appalled at how the government would further relax that institution's reserve and lending policies. Nevertheless, his second visit initiated that greater flexibility. His moderately expansive reforms in 1930 broke the sacred untouchability of the bank's original charter. Although not going as far as many Colombians desired, Kemmerer lowered the bank's minimum reserve requirements from 60 to 50 percent of notes and deposits. He also raised the amount of credit available to the government from 30 to 45 percent of the bank's capital and reserves, prefiguring the even greater role for the state soon to come.[143]

The Banco de la República and Congress quickly approved Kemmerer's recommendations, only tinkering with a few provisions. Passage occurred after Kemmerer and Esteban Jaramillo, his Colombian aide, convinced Olaya to adopt the legislation despite banker opposition. As in the other Andean countries, Kemmerer believed his reforms were so vital that their implementation necessitated authoritarian means. The zeal for technical efficiency spawned impatience with democratic methods. According to the U.S. ambassador, Kemmerer urgued the president to override any opposition:

> Kemmerer went so far as to suggest that Olaya use "arbitrary action" to force the bill through Congress; said that, in his opinion, the project was so important that arbitrary measures would be justified. Dr. Olaya very much deprecates Kemmerer's attitude and hopes that the Colombian public will never know how much Kemmerer has been influenced by Jaramillo in his recommendations; for were it realized here that many of the ideas embodied in Kemmerer's reports are Jaramillo's and not Kemmerer's own, the Kemmerer bills would have little chance of ever appearing on the statute books of the Republic.[144]

Draping the mantle of a prestigious foreign mission around legislation made it more acceptable than if it bore the signature of a controversial local political leader.

Kemmerer's revision of his 1923 general banking law recognized the need for special credit systems for agriculture in a country with Colombia's economic structure. In conjunction with the congressional commission handling banking legislation, Kemmerer crafted regulations for government creation of a Caja de Crédito Agrario and a Caja Colombiana de Ahorros, both designed primarily to help credit-hungry agriculturalists. As in the other Andean republics, he also now established that Colombians and resident foreigners would have first claim on the active funds of foreign banks operating there. Since no banks failed during the crisis, however, Kemmerer concluded that the superintendency had worked splendidly.[145]

The major problem Olaya wanted Kemmerer's help with was the budget crisis. The comptroller complained that the Abadía Mendez government either had not understood how to follow Kemmerer's budgetary and fiscalization rules or had not wanted to. Therefore Kemmerer in 1930 tightened his 1923 budget regulations. His new methods for more efficient and centralized collection and management of revenues never functioned properly, however; they suffered from bureaucratic resistance and insufficient funds to hire additional trained personnel. The continuation of the depression and of clientelistic politics greased by the spoils of office—especially with Liberals eager to take their turn—undermined the effectiveness of budgetary reform. Congress passed Kemmerer's budget legislation with numerous modifications; it wanted to retain more of the 1923 provisions than he recommended. In general, Colombians proved less willing to approve blindly the mission's projects in 1930 than in 1923.[146]

Kemmerer also recommended modifications in the comptroller. He sought to fortify its controls for preventing deficits and to clarify its functions for avoiding administrative conflicts. Rather than running the congressional gauntlet, reforms of the comptroller—worked out between that office and the executive branch and adapting some of Kemmerer's recommendations—were decreed under extraordinary powers in 1931–32. While creating a weaker agency than Kemmerer desired, these reforms preserved his essential structure.[147]

Following suggestions from Kemmerer, Olaya hired North American technical advisers James Edwards for the comptroller and William Roddy for the customs administration, primarily to reassure U.S. bankers. Edwards helped the Colombian comptroller and executive branch prepare the 1931–32 reforms. He opposed, however, the new legal restraints Olaya slapped on the comptroller in 1932 to prevent it from inhibiting expanded state activism. The government's political adversaries charged that Olaya was attempting to disarm the comptroller just because the office was in Conservative hands.[148]

The two most significant Kemmerer tax proposals concerned income and bananas. Customs receipts as a percentage of ordinary national revenues declined from over 60 percent during 1923–27 to 43 percent by 1930, while the contribution of the income tax climbed from 2 to 7 percent. The mission mainly tried to eliminate loopholes and centralize collections. Congress passed an emasculated version of the income tax bill in 1931. Kemmerer's reform set the stage for the massive overhaul of 1935, when Colombia established the progressive income tax as a more important revenue source than customs duties, a rare achievement in Latin America.[149]

The tax on banana exports constituted a Kemmerer recommendation apparently directly favoring Colombian over U.S. interests. At the request of the United Fruit Company, the U.S. embassy asked Kemmerer if he was considering a banana tax. He replied in the negative but "added laughingly": "Thank the Fruit Company for the suggestion; we shall look into it at once, for we are looking for new means of taxation."[150]

United Fruit was not totally opposed to Kemmerer's project. Its contract with the government for exemption from special taxation was to expire at the end of 1930. When Kemmerer arrived, UFCO was already trying to use the squeeze of the depression to arrange a new tax deal with the government, in return for guarantees of a stable rate and protection of its interests. The company preferred steady taxation by the central government to avoid unpredictable impositions by provincial officials. Kemmerer also saw one of the benefits of a new tax program as elimination of uncertainties for the company as well as the government. The U.S. ambassador, however, informed the mission of his opposition to any export tax on United Fruit bananas. Kemmerer retorted that most Colombians favored the idea. He also pointed out that Colombia was the only Latin American country where UFCO operated without an export levy on its bananas.

In discussions with the company Kemmerer proposed a two-cents-per-bunch export tax. UFCO replied that it might be willing to acquiesce to a lower rate of one and one-half cents (not to be shifted to domestic banana producers), if the government would guarantee no alteration in those taxes for the next ten to twenty years. Kemmerer objected on the grounds that the company could not be trusted not to transfer the burden of the tax to local growers and that the government should not contract away to the company its sovereign right of taxation.[151]

When Congress approved Kemmerer's unconditional two-cents-per-bunch banana export tax and attached further articles opposed by UFCO, Olaya vetoed it. Instead, he persuaded the legislature to pass the bill the company wanted, which included twenty years' exemption from further taxation. In hopes of getting advance tax payments from United Fruit, he also helped them with other concerns, especially maintaining control over the railroad and irrigated lands which allowed them to dominate domestic producers for export. Although Kemmerer and the Colombian Congress would have been tougher on United Fruit, Olaya did approve the export tax, and even raised it from two to three cents per bunch.[152]

Kemmerer, U.S. bankers, and Colombian opinionmakers all urged reform of excessive dependence on unstable and poorly administered customs revenues. In 1931 Colombia implemented a diluted version of the mission's customs recommendations, mainly designed to improve administration. On their own, Colombians hiked protectionist tariffs.[153]

Of the eighteen Kemmerer projects, Olaya submitted eleven to Congress. The comptroller bill did not pass, but ten others did: central bank, general banking, budget, revenue collection and administration, and customs; and taxes on income, banana exports, merchandise imports, stamps and consular fees, and municipal valorization. The existing Kemmerer institutions, the central government, and the legislature modified these bills more extensively than the ones resulting from the 1923 mission. Many of these 1930 reforms functioned poorly.[154]

The Great Depression, and the new economic directions taken as a result, rendered many of Kemmerer's innovations undesirable or unworkable. The bureaucracy also hobbled many of the administrative changes. Once the emergency loan through National City Bank was consummated in 1931 and no more foreign credits were forthcoming, interest waned in Kemmerer's recommendations. Because of the timing and setting, his second mission constituted a hasty rescue operation that had far less impact than the expedition in 1923.

Collapse of the Kemmerer System

Colombia sustained essential features of the gold standard longer than Kemmerer's other advisees. Olaya heeded the urgings of U.S. bankers and embassy personnel despite ever louder domestic outcries against artificial exchange stability. During 1932–33 many coffee growers spearheaded public denunciations of the central bank for maintaining the gold-exchange standard to the benefit of foreign bankers and to the detriment of national producers. A rather typical congressional critic charged that the United States and England had saddled capital-shy, underdeveloped countries with the gold standard to leave them short on domestic money and credit and thus more dependent on foreign loans. Since foreign capital was no longer available, this congressman advocated expanding money and credit internally rather than clinging to the gold standard, "which was imposed on the country by the American mission and the creole financiers who serve the interests of commerce, the industry favored by this standard, against the larger interests of the other national industries, particularly those of agriculture."[155]

British abandonment of the gold standard in September 1931 intensified Colombian discontent with Kemmerer's system. England's action did not cause great losses because Colombia's central bank held almost all its foreign reserves in the United States. That British decision did, however, prompt Colombia to adopt immediate exchange controls. This supposedly temporary suspension of unlimited monetary convertibility and free commerce in gold was intended to defend Colombia's balance of payments and the central bank's gold reserves. The country thereby left the pure gold-exchange standard in 1931.[156]

Nevertheless, the Banco de la República maintained controlled gold outflows and official exchange stability until Peru invaded Colombian territory in Leticia. That border conflict in 1932–33 sparked defense expenditures to rebuild the military. Colombians now regretted having reduced the armed forces previously to channel resources to servicing the foreign debt. Consequently, the state drastically expanded its internal debt and its borrowings from the central bank, which forced total abandonment of exchange stability in 1933. Definitively scrapping the gold standard dealt a blow to laissez-faire. The state moved to control exchange and currency. To the dismay of U.S. banking and government representatives, but to the relief of many coffee exporters, exchange devaluation and monetary expansion finally commenced in 1933. Partly as a result, recovery from the depression reached full swing by 1934–35.[157]

Colombia also maintained payments on its foreign debts longer than the other South American countries visited by Kemmerer missions. During 1930–33 the U.S. State Department, embassy, banks, and Kemmerer convinced a president sympathetic and beholden to the United States to keep up payments. He held fast despite overwhelming Colombian opinion to the contrary. Critics contended that the government had taken on too many debts in the late 1920s and was now sacrificing too many domestic needs to make service payments, which exceeded 20 percent of the national budget. Hopes for future credits evaporated by 1932, as did fears of U.S. retaliation with import duties on coffee. Led by the departments and municipalities, Colombia gradually reduced servicing its external obligations. The need for defense expenditures to confront the Leticia conflict with Peru finally moved Olaya to default on national, departmental, municipal, and bank foreign debts by April 1933. The "dance of the millions" was officially over.[158]

From the depression onward, Colombia recast Kemmerer's money and banking system to serve more expansionist, nationalist, statist ends. The central bank's currency and credit policies became more determined by the national budget and domestic economic growth objectives and less by fluctuating international reserves. The volume of currency grew approximately 220 percent from 1932 through 1941. The exchange value of the peso fell by nearly 50 percent. Although prices rose, the government and central bank cooperated to keep inflation under far better control in Colombia than in Chile.[159]

The state progressively intervened in monetary and credit policies. As in Bolivia and Peru, a border conflict during the depression also provided a patriotic rationale for tying the central bank closer to the government and making its policies more expansionary; those border fights resulted largely from heightened desires to control peripheral resources and to distract public attention during the economic crisis. To defend itself against that Peruvian incursion, to save the treasury from bankruptcy, and to furnish credit to domestic producers, the government convinced the central bank to raise its quota for loans from 30 percent of capital and reserves in 1930, to 45 percent in 1931, and to 300 percent by 1935. The bank's loans to government became far more important than its loans to member banks in the 1930s. Its rediscount rate dropped from 7 to 4 percent. Also between 1930 and 1935, the Banco de la República's legal reserve requirement plummeted from 60 to 35 percent. It expanded credit to all sectors, especially agriculturalists and coffee growers. This occurred partly through direct public loans but mainly through support for new state credit institutions. Instead of merely a banker's bank to guard exchange stability, the Banco de la República became more of a developmental credit institution to promote growth.[160]

Despite the collapse of the gold standard, the restriction of free trade, and the rise of state activism, important legacies of the Kemmerer reforms and the 1920s survived the depression. Colombia's modern monetary management and policies evolved from the seeds he planted in the 1920s, and beneath multiple later revisions the foundations of Kemmerer's institutions endured. The structure and many of the functions of the central bank remained intact, and it never became a full-fledged state bank. Kemmerer began state control over banking under the superintendency, which continued to preserve a solid, orderly financial system attuned to his principles. His technical modernization of budgeting, fiscalization, and taxation procedures served later state economic activism. The comptroller, for example, flourished over the years.[161]

Although Kemmerer's orthodoxy was discarded, his offspring continued serving as major instruments of Colombian economic planning and development. Alongside myriad and profound changes, the larger trends that his reforms had accompanied and reinforced also continued to grow from their roots in the 1920s. For decades thereafter, Colombia still depended heavily on the external sector (especially the United States), elaborated more specialized and urban capitalist institutions and practices, and enlarged the role of the state in the economy and society. The interaction between internal and external economic actors continued to shape government policies, often designed with foreign consultants.

3 ECLIPSE OF THE CHILEAN *PAPELEROS*, 1925–1932

The Kemmerer mission to Chile confronted the most notorious case of currency depreciation in South America. For decades the so-called "*papeleros*" had sustained inconvertible paper money against repeated attempts to stabilize exchange. Then, in 1925, during the only period of overt military intervention in Chilean national politics prior to the 1970s, the Money Doctor miraculously put Chile on the gold standard overnight. Unlike later stabilization missions from the United States to Chile, Kemmerer did not clash with nationalists and leftists. Instead, he appeared as the champion of labor against nefarious aristocratic elites, who were allegedly debasing the currency and hoisting the cost of living to siphon income to themselves. In the process of exchange stabilization, Kemmerer also stimulated the growth of domestic urban capitalism, the central state, and dependence on foreign trade and capital, ever more emanating from the United States.

Foreign Factors in Chilean Economic Growth

In the 1920s Chile exported an estimated 40 percent of its measurable annual production of goods.[1] Another rough calculation showed that for every $100 per capita of domestic commerce there transpired $90 per capita of foreign commerce; the comparable figures in the United States were $750 and $75, respectively. In other words, the ratio between domestic and external trade in Chile registered 10 to 9, and in the United States 10 to 1.[2]

After the global slump of 1921–22, trade rebounded but remained unsteady. Chilean as well as U.S. and British businessmen hoped that Kemmerer's exchange stabilization would undergird more reliably expansive trade, which it did. In rounded-off millions of pounds sterling, the value of Chilean imports climbed from 25 million in 1913, to 31 million in 1925, to 40 million in 1929. In those same years export values soared from 30 million to 47 million to 57 million pounds. That 1929 peak value was not reached again until 1955. The post-

Kemmerer prosperity also boosted the domestic GNP by 24 percent in 1928 and 10 percent in 1929. The balance of trade during 1920–29 showed exports averaging 40 percent more than imports. Therefore most Chileans expressed confidence in their ability to adopt and maintain the gold standard. Chile's consistently favorable commercial balance also made North Americans exceptionally eager to sell and invest there.[3]

That mushrooming trade increased Chilean reliance on the United States, partly thanks to the opening of the Panama Canal and World War I.[4] After a precipitous decline during the war, British commerce with Chile revived to compete almost equally with the United States in 1920–21. By 1925 Chile remained England's third most important trading partner in South America, trailing only Argentina and Brazil. Following the Kemmerer mission, however, the United States surpassed Great Britain as a supplier of Chilean imports and solidified its supremacy for the future (see table 3.1).

Chile's trade with the United States exemplified the international division of labor. The United States purchased mainly copper, iron ore, nitrates, iodine, and wool. It then processed those raw materials to be sold back to Chile in the form of electrical equipment, steel, explosives, and textiles. In turn, explosives and capital equipment from the United States were used to extract further minerals to be sold to the United States. Moreover, most of that trade traveled on U.S. ships, often arranged by U.S. export-import houses. In a 1925 history of U.S. diplomatic and economic relations with Chile, William Sherman, a North American, prefaced his study with a typical explanation of the impor-

Table 3.1   Chilean Total Trade with Its Three Leading Partners, 1913–1929

Year	Chilean imports from			Chilean exports to		
	Great Britain	United States	Germany	Great Britain	United States	Germany
1913	35%	17%	25%	38%	21%	21%
1920	31	31	5	—	—	—
1923	27	27	13	31	45	5
1924	26	23	13	34	41	6
1925	27	27	11	36	40	7
1926	23	33	13	25	50	6
1927	25	31	13	37	32	11
1928	22	32	13	36	34	10
1929	21	32	15	21	38	13

Note: The figures for Great Britain include Australia, Canada, and India.
Sources: Great Britain, Department of Overseas Trade, *Report on the Industrial and Economic Conditions in Chile* (1923), p. 23; (1925), p. 8; (1928), pp. 76ff.; (1931) pp. 90–91.

tance of that commerce: "It is now well appreciated that the continued growth of American industrial production beyond the limits of domestic consumption creates the necessity of an expanding foreign market for this exportable surplus and that the most natural and promising field for the development of our foreign trade lies in the more progressive Latin American countries."[5]

Chile increasingly relied not only on imports from the United States but also on exports by resident U.S. companies, which came to dominate nitrate and copper mining and exports. This contrasted with domestic control of the key exports in Colombia, Ecuador, and Bolivia. As artificial substitutes drove down nitrate prices and sales, that commodity began losing its previous monocultural preeminence to copper (see table 3.2).

Determined by foreign demand and companies, the volatile prices and sales of these products held sway over Chile's economic destiny. An estimate for 1924 showed that mining accounted for 1,687,961,556 pesos (each equivalent to six pence) of the total value of national production, while industry generated 1,471,583,948 pesos and agriculture 747,553,829 pesos.[6] In the mid-1920s Chile's annual mineral production exceeded two-thirds of the total mining output in South America.[7]

By the 1920s the United States was taking control of nitrates from the

Table 3.2   Nitrates and Copper as Percentages of the Total Value of Chilean Exports, 1920–1937

Year	Nitrates	Copper	Combined percentage
1920	67%	12%	79%
1921	62	8	70
1922	51	26	77
1923	57	24	81
1924	53	22	75
1925	55	21	76
1926	43	27	70
1927	51	29	80
1928	48	32	80
1929	42	41	83
1937	18	55	73

Sources: Chile, Ministerio de Hacienda, Memoria de la hacienda pública correspondiente a los años 1928 y 1929 (Santiago, 1930), p. 25; Frederick M. Halsey and G. B. Sherwell, Investments in Latin America. III. Chile (Washington, D.C., 1926), pp. 59–61; Abraham Waissbluth R., La minería en la economía chilena (Santiago, 1941), pp. 49–51; Raúl Simón et al., El concepto de industria nacional y de protección del estado (Santiago, 1939), p. 26.

British, copper from the Chileans, and iron ore from the French, and these irreplaceable resources poured out of the nation. The end of the decade found North American capital making up over 90 percent of the total invested in Chilean mineral exporting enterprises. Chileans charged that at least one-third of the value of these exports actually departed the country each year, leaving the balance of trade far less positive than it looked. They further complained that depreciating currency helped foreign companies by boosting exports and reducing domestic production costs. Equally galling, copper and iron ore paid no export levies and virtually no direct taxes.[8] The United States also absorbed construction contracts and international communications. The slipping British expressed regret that "commerce follows finance."[9]

Total British investments in Chile peaked at around the time of Kemmerer's arrival, when they nearly doubled U.S. capital. Those British investments went primarily into national and municipal government bonds, railroads, public utilities, and nitrates. By the eve of the depression, however, North American investors had captured first place.[10]

The United States hoped that its capital injections would generate returns and sales which would eventually create a more favorable balance of payments with Chile. From just before World War I to 1930, North American investments there increased by a factor of ten, mainly in mining. By the end of the twenties Chile ranked first in South America as an importer of U.S. capital, though only fourth as an importer of U.S. goods. In all of Latin America only Cuba received more per capita U.S. investments in that decade. In addition to mining, U.S. capital became increasingly prominent in public utilities, cable traffic, merchandising, manufacturing, and banking. On the average, from 1925 through 1929, foreign investments accounted for 36 percent of Chile's existing capital.[11]

Although the United States dominated Chile's trade less than it did Colombia's, its investments in Chile, especially directly in the export sector, loomed far more important. Also in contrast to the Colombian case, the United States sank far more dollars into direct than indirect investments in Chile. The Chile-American Association, made up of the major U.S. companies active in Chile, hailed rising investments there in 1926 and observed that "Chile is 5,000 miles from New York measured in steamship distances, but in economic perspective it is at the door of the United States."[12]

Through 1920 Chile's foreign debt existed entirely in British pounds. From 1921 on, U.S. dollars became equally important. Measured in millions of pesos, Chile's external debt declined from 1,331 in 1914 to 1,253 at the time of Kemmerer's visit in 1925; thereafter it jumped to 3,597 by 1930. Chile boasted a long-standing excellent foreign credit rating because it had never defaulted on any external obligations. Kemmerer's mission made the country an even more attractive borrower.[13]

As in the other Andean republics, this flood of foreign finance capital accelerated the integration of Chile into the global economy and pulled the country from the British into the U.S. orbit. The financing encouraged more imports, particularly for infrastructural development, and more exports, particularly to pay for those imports and to service debts. This capital inflow also funded state expansion (while simultaneously giving the United States greater leverage over the Chilean government) and underwrote certain economic sectors, notably in the cities.

Increasing involvement with the international market prompted Chile to rely upon a rising number of foreign consultants, who came increasingly from the United States. North American military advisers reached Chile in 1912, nitrogen experts in 1923, and sanitary engineers in 1925.[14]

Chilean Domestic Economic Problems

Chile wanted Kemmerer to smooth its adjustment to an increasingly outward-oriented and urbanized economy. Agriculture's percentage of the active population slid from 38 percent in 1907, to 36 percent in 1920, to 35 percent in 1930.[15] The sector least penetrated by foreigners and most dominated by the traditional upper class allegedly benefited most from debased currency. Although paying few taxes, landowners enjoyed massive mortgage credits from the state-controlled Caja de Crédito Hipotecario, which welcomed foreign investors.[16] In 1925 alone that institution floated a $20 million bond issue in the New York market.[17]

Manufacturing still claimed only some 15 percent of the active labor force in the 1920s, contrasted with 36 percent each in agriculture and in commerce and services.[18] Numerous Chileans supported industrial growth in the name of economic nationalism, but that sector, too, was heavily beholden to foreigners. An economic nationalist in 1925 complained that 60 percent of the capital and 50 percent of the primary materials employed in manufacturing came from foreigners. Moreover, the number and size of foreign-dominated industries was growing more than that of domestic ones in the 1920s. According to an exaggerated British report later in the decade, "90 per cent of the so-called Chilean industries are conducted and owned by foreigners," doubtless referring to the large role of immigrants as well as foreign capitalists.[19]

The huge influx of foreign capital in the second half of the twenties led to expansion and denationalization of Chilean manufacturing. As tariff walls rose, foreign and immigrant manufacturers increasingly established branch factories or took over and built upon Chilean industries. Only a small percentage of foreign investments went into industry as compared to mining, bonds, transportation, and utilities. Nevertheless, those investments represented a large and rising percentage of the relatively small amount of total capital in Chilean manufacturing. Foreign capital also gained prominence in trading, commerce, banking, and insurance.[20]

While imploring the government to erect tariff barriers to protect national industry, the Society for Factory Development (SOFOFA) also desired more foreign direct and indirect capital to help fund industrialization. The significant role of foreign capital in Chilean industry was not a new feature in later years following concentrated import-substituting industrialization. Rather, it was always important and became increasingly so in the 1920s.[21]

When Kemmerer arrived, Chile had fifteen domestic and ten foreign (mainly British) commercial banks. The paid-up capital of those foreign institutions represented only 20 percent of all banking capital in Chile in 1913; it rose to 26 percent by 1922 and 30 percent by 1925.[22] Because of this rise nationalistic Chileans complained of inadequate government controls on banking.[23] At the start of the 1920s, Guillermo Subercaseaux, the president of Kemmerer's central bank, averred that foreign banks "did not serve as commercial channels for the conveyance of foreign capital into the country, but rather as commercial pumps which drained the country of a considerable sum per annum in the form of profits earned." He noted that countries like France and the United States did not welcome foreign banks. In his view the only allowable contribution of foreign banks should be facilitating international transactions. Consequently, Subercaseaux favored currency stabilization to entice foreign bankers to make investments as well as to acquire deposits. He also called for state regulation of banks to supervise their operations and ensure their maintenance of sufficient capital and reserves in Chile.[24] President Arturo Alessandri Palma echoed these widespread sentiments for new banking legislation in the early 1920s and urged Congress to prevent foreign banks from siphoning capital out of the country and thus worsening the balance of payments.[25]

Most Chilean as well as foreign observers cited currency depreciation as the country's gravest economic ill. After the first banks sprouted in the 1850s, French economist Jean Gustave Courcelle-Seneuil had accepted a government contract (1855–63) to organize the Ministry of Finance. He pushed through a very liberal banking and emissions law in 1860, which spawned excessive currency output by private banks and persistent depreciation. Another foreign adviser would be required in the next century to reverse that trend. The only intervening experiment with the gold standard, in 1895–98, unleashed unpopular deflation. Although Chileans consequently remained pessimistic about their ability to sustain such metallic-backed currency, the central government took over emissions from the private banks before the end of the nineteenth century. The protracted debate between the *oreros*, who favored the gold standard, and the *papeleros*, who preferred paper money, was dominated by the latter until the eve of World War I. By then the continuing fall in the exchange value of the peso (see table 3.3) had turned public opinion against inconvertible currency.[26]

Domestic price inflation reflected this declining value of the peso. Accord-

Table 3.3   Chilean Money and Exchange, 1890–1932

Year	Total paper money in circulation (millions of pesos)	Average annual exchange value in London (pence)
1890	39.4	25
1900	50.7	17
1910	150.3	11
1918	227.6	15
1920	302.8	12
1921	324.6	7
1922	301.9	7
1923	292.5	6
1924	336.2	6
1925	393.6	6
1926	450.0	6
1927	490.0	6
1928	450.0	6
1929	500.0	6
1930	392.8	6
1931	429.6	5
1932	788.3	3

Note: Sources vary on the precise estimates but not on the general trends of concern here.

Sources: Adolfo Ruffat, *La política monetaria y el sector externo en Chile entre las dos guerras mundiales* (Santiago, 1969), pp. 80–83; Roberto Soto Vera, *La inflación monetaria en Chile* (Santiago, 1943), pp. 124–25; Roberto Edwardson-Meeks Valdivieso, *El mundo y nosotros* (n.p., n.d.), p. 18. For further data on money and prices, see Markos J. Mamalakis, *Historical Statistics of Chile: Money, Prices, and Credit Services*, vol. 4 (Westport, 1983); *Historical Statistics of Chile: Money, Banking, and Financial Services*, vol. 5 (Westport, 1985); Dirk Holz Fay, *Algunos aspectos de la historia monetaria de Chile entre 1820 y 1925* (Santiago, 1974); Berta Prieto P., *Evolución del circulante en Chile, 1879–1957* (Santiago, 1959).

ing to one cost-of-living index for Santiago, annual average prices rose from a base of 100 in 1914 to 132 in 1919, 156 in 1920, 172 in 1924, and 187 in 1925. This inflation motivated political unrest and the invitation to the Kemmerer mission. Following his stabilization plan, the cost of living index declined until it hit 175 in 1931. After abandonment of the automatic gold standard, the index shot up to 243 by 1933.[27] Chileans credited Kemmerer's medicine for giving 1920–30 the lowest rate of price inflation in Chile in the hundred years from 1880 through 1980; that decade registered only a 30 percent increase, compared to 74 percent during 1910–20 and 94 percent during 1930–40.[28]

How did contemporaries explain the persistence of this currency depreciation and price inflation up to 1925? Chilean analysts normally indicted agriculturalists and, to a lesser extent, mineral exporters.[29] The most popular thesis pilloried the upper class for fanning inflation through their control of Congress so as to transfer income from laborers and savings depositors to themselves. Allegedly, those elites who had sales and investments abroad or owned real estate, especially indebted agriculturalists, preferred depreciation. Landowners also reputedly desired a weak currency to inhibit competitive food imports from the United States and Argentina. These charges reflected a broader negative image of affluent *latifundistas* exploiting the masses.[30]

Kemmerer agreed that the "debtor classes" corrupted the currency: "The big landed interests were for years the most powerful forces both in Congress and out favoring paper money, the device which enabled them to reap what others sowed."[31] The secretary of his Chile mission, Frank Whitson Fetter, elaborated the argument in a famous book, drawing the analogy of western farmers in the United States opposing the gold standard and championing cheaper money in the nineteenth century.[32]

Although many landed barons may have favored currency depreciation in the past, almost none argued for it publicly when Kemmerer arrived. Therefore, either the Fetter thesis was overblown, the agriculturalists were lying low, or the rural elites had transformed their position by 1925.[33] The landowners' National Society for Agriculture (SNA) welcomed Kemmerer enthusiastically and refuted the charge that most agriculturalists favored paper money. Despite desires for more abundant and flexible currency and credit supplies, the SNA officially hailed Kemmerer's monetary and banking laws.[34]

Since there was virtually no evidence of landowner opposition to monetary stabilization in 1925, who were the legendary *papeleros*? Some Chileans accused exporters. Monetary depreciation allowed them to increase sales and accumulate hard foreign currency while paying their workers declining real wages. Sometimes foreign export interests, like the nitrate and copper producers, conflicted with foreign import interests in Chile over stabilization policies and exchange rates. Although Chilean monetary authorities undoubtedly took the general needs of such foreign enterprises into account, there is little evidence of adherence to the specific desires of individual companies; policymakers had to respond to pressures from multiple foreign and domestic groups. Rather than a plot by agriculturalists or exporters, monetary depreciation, as Albert Hirschman has suggested, was more likely a result of international commercial difficulties and lax government policies.[35]

Some Chileans believed the government to be the real culprit behind inflation. Government policies were closely linked to the vagaries of nitrate sales not only because of the need to prop up that strategic industry, but also because export duties on nitrates furnished nearly half of government revenues in the early 1920s. Any dip in nitrate sales prompted currency expansion by the state both to help the mineral exporters and to meet its own expenses. For example, nitrate losses after World War I led that industry to tap the government for extraordinary loans, which inflated the money supply. In other words, dependence on monocultural exports paved the way to inflationary policies during slumping sales; some Chileans feared that the gold standard would cause unacceptable recessions during downward fluctuations in nitrates. For a weak government, printing money was an easier way to cover deficits than raising taxes on the rich and powerful.[36]

Since most state income came from export-import duties in the form of gold or hard currencies, the government profited temporarily when depreciation raised its yield in paper currency and allowed it to make domestic disbursements in devalued pesos. Conversely, currency depreciation hurt the government by reducing the value of domestic tax payments and raising the cost of foreign debt services. Both exporters and government officials thought that foreign loans attracted by the allure of a gold-standard system might compensate for the previous benefits of inflation. In short, a political economy of scarcity—given the constraints of monocultural export dependence and an elitist domestic social structure—usually left either inflationary government spending or reliance on foreign capital as the only viable fiscal alternatives.[37]

Kemmerer encountered more and more Chileans blaming government financial excesses for inflation, especially when the reformist administration of 1925 ballooned the size and salaries of the bureaucracy and the military. This inflationary spending further angered the very groups it was trying to appease, as their benefits eroded. Policymakers came to believe that the gold standard would help them acquire foreign loans to assuage the same credit and income demands without incurring price inflation.[38]

General lack of confidence in the government and the currency—which Kemmerer was expected to restore—also encouraged speculation, which further fueled depreciation. Some Chileans excoriated foreign and domestic banks, commercial houses, and merchants for profiting from exchange instability and deterioration.[39] Indeed, many speculators, agriculturalists, exporters, government officials, and bankers did profit from currency depreciation. These groups did not lead the fight for stabilization, but neither did they speak out strongly in favor of inflationary policies. While no group developed a vigorous case against the gold standard, some sectors became particularly conspicuous in their support for it. Most outspoken were importers, merchants, industrialists, the urban middle and working classes, and, most decisively, the armed forces.

Merchants, especially importers, spearheaded the campaign for stabilization. The primary import city of Valparaíso hosted prominent meetings in support of currency reform. The national Central Chamber of Commerce and the International Chamber of Commerce in Valparaíso, as well as the directors of the stock exchange and commercial exchange in the capital and port cities, denied any profiteering from currency speculation and in 1924–25 they called for exchange stabilization. These commercial elites argued that the gold standard would lower interest rates, attract foreign capital, and underpin general prosperity and "social peace." They attributed past depreciation to speculative and expansive bankers, indebted landowners, nitrate exporters, and the profligate government.[40]

Industrialists, represented by the Society for Factory Development, were equally vehement proponents of stabilization. Manufacturers exuded praise for Kemmerer's projects. They wanted a gold-based currency mainly to expand domestic and foreign credit supplies for manufacturing and infrastructure, and they pinned depreciation primarily on speculators and government spenders. One SOFOFA representative in 1924 admitted that paper money helped manufacturers by raising the price of competitive foreign goods and by cheapening wages. In his view, however, depreciation was more harmful than beneficial. It upped the cost of imported capital goods and raw materials, discouraged foreign investment, diverted bank loans into speculation, and distorted business calculations. Whereas a shrinking peso adversely affected all imports, industrialists preferred selective policies that would favor ingredients they needed and tack high tariffs on competing items. They believed currency reform would make Chilean manufacturing more modern through greater access to foreign capital, equipment, and materials.[41]

Industrialists also supported stabilization to defuse middle- and working-class discontent over the spiraling cost of living. Indeed, the salary and wage earners in the cities and mines generated the greatest enthusiasm for the gold standard. Their fervor and wage demands converted many rural as well as urban elites to their position in order to restore "social tranquillity." Usually stemming from complaints against price inflation, a wave of strikes rocked Chilean society from World War I to 1925. White-collar employees' associations joined blue-collar unions in 1924–25 in demanding stabilization. Many public employees found themselves in arrears on their salaries and sinking beneath the surging cost of living. Consequently, the government sought to stifle their raise demands by halting inflation. Exhibiting the same motive toward workers, manufacturers hoped that Kemmerer could achieve industrial peace by stabilizing both prices and wages. For the national Committee in Favor of Monetary Stabilization, the worst outcome of currency depreciation was its contribution to social unrest, fed upon by "agitators." The argument arose that monetary instability had opened the door to communism in Russia and would do the same in Chile: "The day that we have recovered money of stable value, we will have reestablished in Chile the principal factor of social peace." When Kemmerer landed in Valparaíso, the labor organizations invited him to a coliseum to celebrate his arrival and express their ardor for stabilization. These working-class protests were probably the single most decisive force convincing Chilean elites, even former *papeleros*, to adopt the gold standard.[42]

Partly in response to those mass pressures, most political and military leaders came to endorse stabilization. Since World War I, all Chile's presidents and major parties had sworn to end currency depreciation. Arturo Alessandri had switched from *papelero* to *orero* by the time he reached the presidency in 1920. This change coincided with his broader transformation into a reformer claiming to speak for the middle and working classes against the moneyed elites ensconced in Congress. Alessandri's inability to deliver on his stabilization promises left the salary and wage earners looking for fulfillment from the military juntas which replaced him in 1924–25.[43]

One of the military's central justifications for seizing power was curbing runaway inflation. It not only disrupted the economy and social harmony, it also eroded the standard of living and preparedness of the armed forces. The middle-class officers who sparked the takeover preferred to quiet worker discontent using currency and welfare reforms rather than troops. They also wanted increases in their own pay and benefits, as did the restless rank-and-file soldiers and sailors. Moreover, they did not want those gains erased by subsequent inflation. As the peso's value dwindled, the army and navy faced rising costs both domestically and, especially, overseas. They saw a sick currency as inimical to national security, both in terms of equipping the armed forces and preserving domestic tranquillity. The public beseeched the 1924 and 1925 juntas to carry out their vows of currency reform and avoid the political turmoil which had been sapping recent civilian administrations. Monetary stabilization had thus become a prerequisite for political stabilization. It also promised to restore order within the armed services. As in Ecuador (see chapter 4), Kemmerer arrived to deal with an authoritarian regime committed to currency reform. Indeed, Santiago's leading newspaper drew a strong analogy between the contemporaneous military revolts in Chile and Ecuador—it believed both were dedicated to economic modernization.[44]

Although public opinion had solidified in favor of stabilization prior to the 1924 coup, several obstacles remained. The cumbersome and quarrelsome parliamentary system had failed to settle on one concrete plan. As one Chilean economist explained in 1925: "The capital reason why the government of Chile came to engage the services of the Kemmerer Mission was not as it has been said, in order to find the causes and point to the defects in our monetary system. Causes as well as defects, and also the solutions, were too well known here. The reason was, precisely, in the excess of solutions which, aggravated by the parliamentary chaos, had rendered impossible the choice of a definite remedy."[45] Nagging worries persisted about the mechanisms and viability of stabilization under central bank auspices in an economy and fiscal system heavily dependent on external trade and loans. Above all, Chileans still lacked confidence in the financial integrity and capacity of the free-spending central government.[46]

The 1920s witnessed the birth of the modern interventionist state in Chile. The state intruded in banking, credit, social welfare, labor-industrial relations, and even agricultural colonization. The groundwork was laid for government activism to take a qualitative and quantitative leap forward during and after the Great Depression, especially in the 1940s. In response to the economic crisis after World War I, mounting urbanization and pressures from the middle and working classes, and new demands for modernization, the central government swelled in size and scope. Government revenues rose from 14 million pounds sterling in 1913 to 18 million in 1925, while expenditures climbed from 12 to 21 million.[47] National budgets rose an average of 5 percent per year from 1863 to 1927, but those increases jumped to 10 percent in 1925 and 36 percent in 1926.[48] From 1913 through 1927 ordinary government expenses rose 90 percent, while government outlays for salaries soared 132 percent; this expansion reflected rising salaries (especially during 1925) and multiplying numbers of bureaucrats.[49] The percentage of the active population employed by the government dropped from 5 to 4 percent between 1907 and 1920, and then doubled to 8 percent by 1930.[50] Whereas the government created only seventeen new administrative agencies from 1891 to 1925, it launched twenty-one more during 1925 alone and fifteen more during 1926–31.[51]

When Kemmerer arrived, complaints ran rampant about the bulging, cumbersome, costly bureaucracy. As Kemmerer himself noted about the government's policy of soaking up social discontent through state employment: "It is conceded on all sides that the Chilean public service is seriously over-manned."[52]

Despite his intentions, Kemmerer's reforms and the foreign loans they attracted contributed to further state growth during the remainder of the 1920s. Especially under President Carlos Ibáñez del Campo (1927–31), government expenditures, bureaucrats, and agencies continued to proliferate; most notable were Ibáñez's new credit departments for industry, mining, and agriculture.[53]

To fund this expansion the government relied heavily on foreign trade and loans. During 1922–25 indirect taxes (mainly export-import duties) furnished 53 percent of state revenues, while loans supplied 34 percent, diverse other sources 7 percent, and direct taxes only 6 percent.[54] From over 50 percent of ordinary government revenues during the war, nitrate export taxes fell to 37 percent by 1925.[55] To compensate, the junta hiked all existing domestic taxes; for example, on stamps and tobacco. The government wanted Kemmerer to improve its internal taxing capacity and its external borrowing power to fill in for plummeting nitrate receipts. Whereas Kemmerer entered economies becoming more monocultural in Colombia and Bolivia, those he encountered in Chile and Ecuador were becoming less monocultural and were in need of readaptation.[56]

Chileans bemoaned this unreliable, inefficient, and unfair tax structure. They scolded the upper class and foreign corporations for paying so little. National mining companies paid higher taxes on their capital than did foreigners, who declared fraudulently low assets according to the Bureau of Internal Taxes.[57]

Chileans also criticized chronic government deficit spending and consequent indebtedness. Therefore they proved very receptive to Kemmerer's recommendations for better revenues collection, budget procedures, fiscalization, and accounting.[58] In his electoral campaign and subsequent presidential messages, Alessandri had vowed to enact most of the money, banking, and fiscal reforms soon to be implanted by the U.S. mission.[59]

Frustrated by Congress, Alessandri fell victim to a rightist military coup in 1924. Reformist officers led by Carlos Ibáñez then replaced that junta in 1925. One of their top demands was monetary stabilization. Similar to their Ecuadorean counterparts, these juntas issued decree laws to raise taxes, boost pay to the bureaucracy and military, and expand central government economic and social responsibilities. They rammed through Alessandri's promised reforms—a new labor code, revised tax laws, a stronger chief executive, the government's right to infringe on private property for the public good, and separation of church and state—embodied in the Constitution of 1925. Although the second junta returned Alessandri to the presidency, Ibáñez and the armed forces dominated behind the scenes. Consequently, Kemmerer encountered an authoritarian government dedicated to overhauling the basic administrative and financial system of the nation.[60]

The Kemmerer Mission

Alessandri had explored inviting Kemmerer in 1923 because of the Money Doctor's success in Colombia and his previous visit to Chile in 1922. Congress, however, blocked all financial reform initiatives. Immediately after ousting Alessandri, the military junta in late 1924 had the Chilean ambassador in Washington contact Kemmerer to arrange a mission patterned after his Colombian expedition. Although Kemmerer kept the Department of State informed, the new mission was an entirely private arrangement between him and the Chilean government.[61]

While Kemmerer presided over the commission and concentrated on the design of the central bank and gold standard, Howard M. Jefferson specialized on general banking questions. He was an officer of the Federal Reserve Bank of New York and the only carryover from Kemmerer's 1923 Colombian team. Harley L. Lutz, a Stanford professor, supplied expertise on taxation. Joseph T. Bryne had served previously with a public accounting firm in New York and as a member of a U.S. financial mission in 1922–23 to Peru, where he became collector general of customs. He provided accounting and fiscal control advice for the Kemmerer mission in Chile and again in Colombia in 1930. William W. Renwick, an agent for National City Bank in many Latin American countries and currently fiscal representative for El Salvador, handled problems of customs administration for the mission in Chile in 1925 and later in Colombia in 1930. Henry H. West, who had served with North American financial advisers in Peru and with U.S. firms making loans to Bolivia, came along as general secretary to the mission. Frank Whitson Fetter functioned as Kemmerer's secretary. Once in Chile the mission also employed G. Van Zandt, a professor of engineering from the University of Southern California, to advise on railroads. Moreover, the host government supplied them with a large staff of Chilean lawyers, accountants, translators, and clerks.[62]

Visiting Chile during July–October 1925, the mission was received euphorically. Led by the army, a stellar contingent of military, political, banking, and business leaders greeted the commission, as did representatives from the U.S. embassy. Moreover, a huge crowd organized by the Committee in Favor of Monetary Stabilization staged a public demonstration to cheer the Money Doctor. Both public opinion and armed force obviously stood behind the recommendations Kemmerer was expected to make.[63]

During its stay the mission received warm support from all political and social sectors. Even Chileans dubious about the mission held criticisms in check, hoping that Kemmerer's blessing would open foreign credit lines. Liberal as well as Conservative publications lauded its members and their recommendations, mainly out of the belief that these visitors would expand sales to and loans from the United States. Politicians and columnists warned the government not to revise the Kemmerer proposals, so as not to damage Chile's foreign credit rating. They exhibited more confidence in Kemmerer than in their own government, calling for publication of his original reports to make sure there had been no alterations in the decreed versions. The Democrat party, representing many employees, artisans, and workers, urged the implementation of Kemmerer's legislation over the opposition of "speculators."[64]

The Academy of Economic Sciences toasted Kemmerer and his work as "a ray of hope, a dawn that announces a new day full of happiness and peace . . . a brilliant page in our republican life."[65] Chileans believed this "financial messiah" would cure "our poor anemic and wrinkled peso."[66] Even street crowds greeted Kemmerer as "the second savior of Chile." No one openly opposed the mission, although many bankers, big landowners, and British seemed unenthusiastic.[67]

Most opponents as well as supporters of the current regime backed the mission. Indeed, in the eyes of some Chileans, one of the only justifications for the abnormal dictatorship was to put through the Kemmerer reforms and the new constitution. As in Ecuador, they argued that a return to civilian, constitutional, stable government was necessary as soon as those tasks were completed and, moreover, was the only way those reforms could really be consummated. These critics claimed that the Kemmerer innovations would only be fully accepted and successful if they were carried out by an orderly, representative government, rather than arbitrarily decreed by a nonelected government. Thus Kemmerer's reforms were used to plead for a restoration of democracy. This argument came mainly from conservatives, who feared that military reformers would continue to decree social welfare legislation along with higher taxes and expenditures for the government, unless Kemmerer could impose restraint.[68]

The mission's operating methods reinforced existing propensities to welcome their recommendations. Alessandri was so pleased with the mission's work that he persuaded Kemmerer to stay on longer than originally intended.[69] Some Chileans expressed awe at their working hours (from eight in the morning until eight at night) and hoped this would serve as an example to "lazy" government bureaucrats.[70] As in the other countries, Kemmerer was very reluctant to say anything of substance to the press. This both shielded the mission from public debate and created an aura of technical superiority above the usual political squabbling.[71]

Meanwhile, wide consultation with all principal interest groups made Chileans feel that their ideas were being adopted. Actually, Kemmerer only incorporated those proposals which coincided with the plans he already had before reaching Chile. Kemmerer usually spoke in Spanish, which increased local confidence that he was tailoring solutions to local conditions.[72]

Kemmerer's excellent working relations with government officials left no doubt about the passage of his projects. Immediately upon the team's arrival in Chile Alessandri promised to sign whatever central bank and monetary laws were drafted by Kemmerer. The government knew the mission was likely to propose a carbon copy of the Colombian reforms, and Kemmerer did not try to offer anything unexpected or undesirable to the Chilean administration. These U.S. advisers realized that the real key to the implementation of their proposals was the unified backing of the armed forces, which "notified the government that every measure recommended by the Kemmerer Mission must be accepted without amendment." As one newspaper observed when the troops greeted Kemmerer's train: "The presence of all those military in the station is like a warning to the entire country that they will not allow obstruction of the progress of the great financier."[73]

While establishing rapport with Chilean elites, Kemmerer purposely maintained distance between his mission and the U.S. embassy, stressing that he was working for the Chilean rather than the U.S. government. In turn, the embassy scrupulously avoided implying any connection with the missionaries, though the ambassador was pleased with Kemmerer's contribution to better U.S. economic and political relations with Chile.[74]

The mission succeeded also because most Chileans saw these outsiders as more objective and skilled than nationals. In the eyes of the press and government, a foreign expert "found himself free from any local and perturbing interest of creole criteria."[75] These commentators argued that Kemmerer was neutral between U.S. and Chilean interests, despite the fears of some Chilean producers that he would favor North Americans over themselves. Kemmerer enjoyed a reputation as a scientific, dispassionate mediator between conflicting government and private economic interests.[76] As Kemmerer himself told his hosts:

> The laws of economic science are eternal and universal. In their application to the problems of the moment, nevertheless, one must always leave room for the special conditions which reign in the country where they're applied and for the national psychology and the traditions of its inhabitants. The members of the Mission do not pretend to have presented anything essentially new in the various measures which they have recommended to the government of Chile. What we have done is to take the fundamental scientific principles, which the experience of other countries has demonstrated to be solid, and we have applied them to the conditions we encountered in Chile. Many of the fundamental characteristics of our reforms have already been proposed by Chilean economists. But in Chile, as occurs in other countries, the proverb is very certain that "a prophet is without honor in his own

land," and many of the economists in Chile will have seen accepted and promulgated in the laws we have presented to the government the same ideas which had been rejected when they were proposed by them. A man from outside, and who therefore finds himself free from family ties and from the interests of cliques, and free at the same time from prejudices against himself, many times can obtain acceptance of his recommendations, when the same recommendations, presented even with the same words by men of the nation, would be rejected. We are fully aware of how little we could have accomplished in Chile without the fact that the ground had been so well prepared by the many studies and investigations of Chilean economists.[77]

Kemmerer's recommendations were also well received because most of them merely added nuances, adjustments, and prestige to existing or pending legislation. Also, as in the other countries he advised, his preparation of detailed laws rather than just general recommendations facilitated rapid adoption. Moreover, implementation proceeded smoothly because Byrne stayed on for a while to advise the government on new accounting methods, as did Jefferson to advise on organization of the central bank.[78]

After less than two months in Chile, Kemmerer had delivered his principal recommendations to the government. The mission submitted proposals on a central bank, the gold exchange standard, general banking, and negotiable instruments and mercantile securities. It also suggested alterations for the commercial, mining, and civil codes. For fiscal reforms, the mission presented projects on the budget, a national comptroller and government accounting, state railroads, public debts, the Bureau of Internal Taxation; and taxes on incomes, real property, stamps and stamped paper, tobacco, public spectacles and hippodromes, club memberships, and iron ore exports. Such sweeping economic remodeling also led Kemmerer to advise minor modifications in the financial sections of the new constitution being drafted in 1925.[79] Before the mission departed, Chile enacted virtually all of this legislation without serious revisions.[80]

As soon as Kemmerer completed his work, Alessandri resigned and a conciliatory but lackluster president was elected. He served from 1925 until 1927, when the real power behind the throne, Ibáñez, took charge directly. He presided over a boom in foreign loans and domestic prosperity until capsized by the Great Depression in 1931.

Kemmerer's Money and Banking Reforms

Kemmerer's central bank bill encountered ideal conditions for acceptance. The official exchange rate had already stabilized at six pence, and the government's accumulated conversion fund easily underwrote the new institution.[81] After submission to the government on August 12, the plan became law almost verbatim on August 21, 1925.[82] Nearly unanimous praise greeted the reform, partly because it differed little from previous Chilean proposals.[83]

As in Colombia, the economic elites—especially landowners—expected the new central bank to expand credit availability. Kemmerer's system, however, favored short-term loans—mainly just for commerce—because of the need for high liquidity. Agriculturalists thus remained dissatisfied with the bank throughout the 1920s. In contrast to Colombia, Chile's central institution always exercised its right to deal directly with rural borrowers. Even the exceptionally high ceiling of six months for agricultural loans, however, was still so low that few farmers ever tapped the bank. The government compensated them in 1928 by founding the Caja de Crédito Agrario, which received special rediscounts from the central bank.[84]

Compared to landowners, merchants and manufacturers were always more pleased with the central bank and its credit policies.[85] They voiced satisfaction even during 1926–27, when the new bank's attainment of stable currency accompanied falling prices in a recession that caused all economic sectors to readjust and cut losses.[86] At the same time commercial and industrial groups pressed the bank to lower interest charges even more than already obtained by its reduction of the discount rate from 9 percent in 1925 to 7 percent in 1927.[87]

Although leading the opposition to a central bank in previous years, private bankers became the main beneficiaries of Kemmerer's brainchild in the latter 1920s.[88] Many commercial banks had long feared a competing central institution. Others had opposed the gold standard because they profited from making loans to the government and politicians and from speculating in exchange.[89] Indeed, President Alessandri had denounced the "improper marriage" between the treasury and banks as the cause of Chile's "economic slavery" to paper money. He criticized repeated loan contracts between the government and private banks that helped the banks keep afloat by inflating the money supply. Time and again overextended banks had been rescued by the government to the detriment of monetary stability. Now, however, the bankers believed that discount privileges through the central bank could give them similar security and access to expanded credits without entailing currency depreciation. They also muffled their resistance to Kemmerer's project because the dictatorship had silenced their friends in Congress.[90]

During Kemmerer's interviews with Chilean bankers he found the smaller institutions more favorable to a central bank. The larger ones felt less need for the services of a central bank and already performed some of the tasks it would assume. The domestic banks also preferred a central bank without foreign or government participation and without direct dealings with the public. Resistance by the largest domestic bank (Banco de Chile) to foreign bank participation revealed conflict between national and foreign capitalists.[91] Conversely, some Chileans were more suspicious of bankers than foreigners and did not want any bankers dominating the new institution.[92] Under Kemmerer's law all domestic and foreign banks in Chile had to subscribe 10 percent of their capital and reserves to the central bank, which thereafter offered them liberal discounts.[93]

Most Chileans shared the domestic bankers' animosity toward foreign banks. Whereas Kemmerer's project granted foreign banks a director's seat as well as membership in the central bank, previous Chilean proposals had barred them altogether. While Kemmerer was preparing his recommendation, Chile's leading newspaper endorsed exclusion of foreigners because "in general they have no connection with the interests of the national economy. This opinion is strongly rooted and must be taken into consideration by the North American Mission as the expression of a very respectable nationalist sentiment which is justified by the same reasons which inspire the laws of the United States and of other countries, which go so far as to prohibit the functioning of foreign banks or agencies."[94]

Kemmerer's legislation allayed two long-standing Chilean grievances against foreign banks. First, the gold standard eliminated the past problem of foreign institutions reaping huge profits by speculating in the mercurial value of Chilean currency. Indeed, some foreign banks closed down in Chile and other countries Kemmerer advised because they could no longer manipulate exchange.[95]

Second, Kemmerer prevented foreign banks from declaring a disproportionately small capital and reserve in their Chilean branch. The new law stipulated that the 10 percent contribution of foreign banks to the central bank had to be calculated on "a quantity of capital and reserve which is in just relationship with the business they develop within the country, with the capital and reserve of competing national banks, and with the business they carry on in other countries where they operate." The proportion between the capital and reserve held in Chile and the total capital and reserve of the foreign bank had to be equal to the ratio existing between the assets of the Chilean branch of the foreign bank and the total assets of the foreign bank. In other words, foreign banks had to be suppliers of capital as well as absorbers of deposits and profits.[96]

Most foreign banks themselves favored Kemmerer's legislation because it placed them on an equal footing with domestic banks. It ended discriminatory taxes against foreign banks and gave them a voice in monetary policy they had never had with the government. Since they preferred commercial transactions while domestic banks leaned toward agricultural business, the foreign entities applauded Kemmerer's highly liquid short-term lending regulations. Their anxiety about being subjected to Chilean laws and institutions calmed because these reforms were designed by a North American from predictable U.S. blueprints.[97]

Kemmerer's transfer of technology to Chile was minimal. Far more important was his provision of the final political impetus to legitimize the central bank in domestic and foreign eyes. Prior to his arrival Chileans had already hammered out essential decisions about the bank, including its strong powers, its sole right of currency emission, and its ability to maintain reserves abroad. They had also concluded that its viability required complementary legislation on general banking and fiscal procedures. Such thorny issues as the government's role in the bank had led Chilean planners to rule out a state bank; Kemmerer merely resolved the precise percentage of government participation and borrowing rights in the central bank. While Chilean proposals included rediscount privileges for member banks, the mission added direct dealings with the public. Whereas earlier recommendations had called for the gold-exchange standard, the North American advisers settled the lesser issue of stabilizing exchange at the average existing rate. Chilean reformers had already suggested representation of economic sectors (including labor) in the bank's directorate to avoid domination by politicians or bankers; Kemmerer's only innovation was the inclusion of foreign bankers.[98]

On the sensitive issue of the central bank's board of directors, Kemmerer created ten seats: three were to be filled by appointees of the president of the country, two by the national banks, one by the foreign banks, one by the stockholders at large, one jointly by the SNA and SOFOFA, one jointly by the Association of Nitrate Producers of Chile and the Central Chamber of Commerce, and one by labor unions.[99] Although this plan deviated little from previous Chilean proposals, representation for foreign banks and for labor evoked spirited discussion.[100]

Kemmerer argued that inclusion of a foreign representative further insulated the central bank from local politicians and bankers, increased domestic and foreign confidence in the new institution and in the economy generally, provided technical expertise and external connections, and added to the bank's capital. After all, a foreigner could exert no control with only one vote. Virtually all Chileans interviewed by the mission had accepted its idea of resident foreign banks selecting a member of the board.[101]

Nevertheless, Chile's leading newspapers and banks opposed inclusion of foreign bankers.[102] Critics pointed out that few other countries allowed foreign directors in their central banks. The only European institutions with foreign executives—those in Germany and Austria—had had them imposed as a result of losing World War I. The Dawes Commission, on which Kemmerer had served, had forced that arrangement on the Reichsbank in 1924. Consequently, some Chileans charged that Kemmerer had inserted foreign directors to help U.S. bankers make Chile "economically dependent on the United States of North America, a semi-colony, disputed over by English and Yankee imperialisms." A Spanish professor of public finance visiting Chile in 1928 expressed shock that the central bank admitted a foreign director and deposited most of its reserves abroad. During ensuing decades Chileans increasingly shared that discontent and later removed the seat for foreign banks.[103]

Believing that he was the champion of the common people against inflationary elites, Kemmerer exuded pride over the director's seat for labor. Impressed with the strength of unions in Chile, he included them, whereas they had been left out in less urbanized and politicized Colombia. He argued that laborers had a special interest in the central bank's maintenance of currency stability. In turn, participation in the bank was intended to be a valuable education for workers in the mechanisms and virtues of the capitalist system. The mission convinced the few opponents, for example, some industrialists, that inclusion of a labor representative and stabilization of the currency would reduce worker unrest and demands. Although Kemmerer's central bank legislation differed little from country to country, this trade union seat is an example of one slight modification made to fit local conditions. He was more pleased with his diverse directorate in Chile than with the banker-dominated board in Colombia.[104]

Labor leaders saw their inclusion as further proof that Kemmerer and his stabilization served working-class interests. Even conservative Chilean elites generally hailed worker participation to integrate laborers into capitalism and teach them the folly of socialist ideas. Chilean rightists also urged workers to buy shares in the bank so that "they will abandon many prejudices against the capitalist classes, having their interests linked to theirs."[105]

There arose, however, a serious dispute over how labor's representative would be chosen. Communists controlled the largest union organization, the Federation of Chilean Workers (FOCH), which Kemmerer assumed would make the selection. Some supportive commentators contended that participation by FOCH leaders in the bank would promote "harmony between capital and labor." In response to complaints from the Right, however, Kemmerer and Alessandri replaced the stipulation of the FOCH with a complicated formula for broader union representation.[106] This modified process neither assured an authentic representative from the organized working class nor included private white-collar employees. Despite flaws, this provision did make Chile one of the only countries in the world to have a central bank director representing, however indirectly, the working class.[107]

To the disappointment of the mission, politics intruded in the first general election of bank directors. Ex-president Alessandri successfully campaigned for the seat representing the public shareholders. His reported desire to deliver control of the bank to certain Chilean and European bankers, however, did not bear fruit.[108]

Jefferson prodded the Chileans to speed up the opening of the central bank, which debuted in January 1926.[109] During its first two years the bank performed well, despite falling nitrate revenues, and followed Kemmerer's advice by hiring North American banker Walter M. Van Deusen as ongoing technical adviser. As the bank gained experience and confidence, it refined some sections of the original law, often in consultation with Kemmerer.[110]

To generate public confidence in the new bank, Kemmerer's 1925 legislation made it acquire capital and reserves larger than most comparable institutions. Most of its capital came from commercial banks—approximately three-fourths from domestics and one-fourth from foreigners.[111] By the end of the 1920s the bank maintained legal reserves at over 100 percent of currency in circulation and deposits, far above Kemmerer's requirement of 50 percent. Some Chileans urged the bank to expand the money and credit supply instead of padding its reserve account. Others criticized the bank for going overboard with Kemmerer's advice by placing a majority of its reserve in foreign institutions; few central banks in the world risked such a large proportion of their reserves abroad. Critics complained that foreign depositories profited from lending those funds and could refuse to release them in an emergency. Such fears were realized when England's declaration of inconvertibility in September 1931 caused Chile to suffer severe reserve losses. Charges that Kemmerer had recommended such external deposits to ensure Chile's "vasallage to Yankee imperialism" resurfaced when U.S. banks resisted the socialist republic of 1932. During the 1920s, however, most Chileans defended holding reserves overseas because those accounts earned interest and also facilitated exchange stabilization, international transactions, and credit acquisitions, all of which linked Chile closer to the world economy.[112]

The greatest purpose and success of the central bank was exchange stabilization.[113] The new system proved its mettle in 1926, when a breakdown in border negotiations with Peru unleashed a speculative assault on the Chilean peso that the bank withstood. Despite fears of failure, both the exchange rate and domestic prices stayed under control in the latter half of the 1920s.[114]

As Chileans had hoped, foreign capital flowed in and interest rates fell. The bank reduced its discount charges from 9 percent in 1926 to 6 percent by 1928. By the end of the 1920s, however, commercial interest rates had not fallen as far as agriculturalists and manufacturers had expected. They still had to borrow privately at rates of 10–12 percent.[115]

Like Kemmerer's other creations, his Chilean central bank adopted policies mainly favorable to urban interests. Its statutes mandated only short-term loans to the public: ninety days normally, or six months for those with agricultural products as collateral. During 1927–29 almost 90 percent of the central bank's rediscounts went to national rather than foreign banks; their expanding loans went mainly to urban enterprises. As in the other Kemmererized countries, agriculturalists spearheaded complaints that this system was not furnishing enough low-interest, long-term credit to producers.[116]

To meet this problem the bank extended short-term credits to newly established government lending agencies for the various economic sectors. These institutions were created when President Ibáñez announced in 1927 that the central bank could not make enough direct loans to agriculture and industry to expand production sufficiently. He feared that resulting government or trade deficits might undermine the gold standard.[117] Like Leguía in Peru, Ibáñez responded to low export receipts, poor agricultural output, rising industrialization, mounting urbanization, and middle- and working-class discontent by channeling domestic and foreign capital into the more modern sector. He founded the Caja de Crédito Agrario and the Caja de Crédito Minero, but his main initiative came through the Instituto de Crédito Industrial. He complemented it with new import duties to protect domestic manufacturing. In response, factories adopted more modern technology, expanded in size, and drove out smaller competitors.[118]

The greatest Chilean worry about the central bank was that it would become a political plaything. To avoid that problem Kemmerer established a governmental credit quota from the bank even lower than that in Colombia or in most past Chilean proposals. During the 1920s the government did not seek loans in excess of the statutory ceiling of 20 percent of the bank's paid capital and reserves.[119]

Synchronized with the central bank legislation was Kemmerer's monetary law, which placed Chile on a gold standard the same year as Great Britain. In accord with prevailing local opinion, the mission stabilized the peso at its average recent value of six British pence. Despite the eruption of U.S. influence, Kemmerer chose a British standard because Britain's historic and continuing economic importance made pounds still Chile's principal means of international exchange. Except for some minor fiddling with coinage, the government passed this monetary law verbatim.[120] Kemmerer argued that this stabilization would increase foreign trade and investment to the benefit of both Chile and the United States: "To America, Chile's return to the gold standard is a matter of great importance because of our interests in the prosperity of our sister republics and because of our large investments in that country and of our large and growing foreign trade with it."[121]

The mission's third major financial law replicated the Colombian general banking bill. Chile's extremely liberal banking law of 1860 had provided ample privileges and virtually no regulations. The only government inspections were cursory ones for tax purposes. As capitalism became more expansive and complicated in the twentieth century, demands rose for supervision of the inflationary, unstable, and mismanaged banking sector. Bankers typically doled out extravagant long-term credits at ridiculously low interest rates to their directors, employees, relatives, business friends, political patrons, and cronies. Consequently, credit-hungry producers complained, and overextended banks collapsed. Amidst the general political and economic instability, foreign and domestic confidence in the banks had reached low ebb when Kemmerer arrived. Bank deposits decreased in 1924–25 as jittery funds fled abroad.[122]

Kemmerer's legislation followed the outlines of the New York banking law and the U.S. Comptroller of the Currency. After only three days of study the Chilean government enacted the bill essentially intact. It created a national superintendent of banking to inspect, regulate, and certify all private and public banks. He mandated modernized accounting procedures, raised minimum reserve requirements from 10 percent to 20 percent, and encouraged scientific and short-term lending practices. Despite this commitment to high liquidity, Kemmerer recognized the importance of agriculture in Chile and also recommended slightly more liberal powers for banks to grant loans guaranteed by real estate. The law gave foreign banks the same rights and obligations as domestics. It also recommended that a North American bank inspector serve as the superintendent or as his assistant in the beginning years. Both foreigners and Chileans viewed this regulatory legislation as a sharp departure from prevailing laissez-faire beliefs and practices.[123]

Chileans who had long been advocating similar legislation applauded this banking bill. Particularly pleased were industrialists, discontented for years with bankers' preferences for lending to speculators and agriculturalists.[124] Vigorous opposition, especially from bankers, might have torpedoed the law if criticism had not been cowed by the dictatorship. According to opponents, the superintendency violated the sanctity of private enterprise. Critics also chided the legislation for sloppy terminology and translations. Others, including industrialists, fumed about the "open door" for foreign banks.[125]

Like some of Kemmerer's institutions in other countries, the superintendent vanquished the opposition by dramatically solving a crisis in its opening days. In December 1925 the second-largest Chilean bank suddenly closed its doors, nearly precipitating a general financial panic. Like so many banks, it was poorly managed, overly committed to loans to its own directors, and heavily involved in exchange speculation. In the past the government would likely have inflated the money supply to save the overextended institution. Instead, the superintendent took charge of the ailing bank. He reviewed and revised all its operations, protected its creditors, and soon had it back on its feet.[126]

The superintendency did not function as merely a derivative of foreign models. During its initial years the institution evolved through practice, interaction with the banks, and adjustments to local customs. It also consulted with Kemmerer on interpretations and revisions of the original law. Two years after its birth, the superintendency, the banks, and big borrowers convinced the government to modify the general banking legislation. That reform lowered reserve requirements and allowed smaller provincial banks to charge slightly higher interest rates.[127]

As was usual under the Kemmerer system, the number of banks shrank while banking operations grew. One foreign bank departed because it could no longer profit from exchange speculation; this pruned the total from eight in 1926 to seven in 1929. Some smaller Chilean banks also folded, reducing their ranks from seventeen to fifteen. Approximately 40 percent of the commercial banking headquarters and 20 percent of the branches remained concentrated in Santiago and Valparaíso. Although to a lesser extent than in Colombia, such regional imbalance evoked resentments. Meanwhile, capital and reserves of the banks mounted along with confidence in them, thanks to the superintendency and general economic well-being. Bank deposits per inhabitant also increased during 1926–29. The Kemmerer bill did not usher in any invasion by foreign banks. Domestic institutions continued accounting for at least 75 percent of total capital and reserves in Chile, although only 60 percent of all deposits and loans.[128]

In response to complaints about parasitic foreign banks, Kemmerer pointed out that at least his legislation imposed some controls.[129] The system made foreign banks obey all the same laws as Chileans, submit all disputes to Chilean courts without recourse to foreign citizen rights, maintain an amount of capital in their Chilean branches equivalent to that required of domestic banks, give residents of Chile preferential rights to their assets in the country, and pay a slightly higher tax on their capital. Under the superintendency it also became easier for a national bank to increase its capital.[130]

Nevertheless, the U.S. banker hired as an assessor by the central bank, on Kemmerer's recommendation, soon came to agree with Chilean critics of foreign banks. Van Deusen concluded that foreign banks engaged in shady exchange speculation, took business away from domestic institutions, and deceived the superintendency about their capital input:

> The policy of most foreign banks is to force the local managers to finance their branch by means of deposits obtained locally, and if possible to get enough deposits to aid branches in other countries where for the time being the deposits are not sufficient . . . the foreign banks operating here have not brought even their capital into the country . . . a close study of their loans and investments would show that they, taken as a whole, have less than their capital here . . . there are too many here in Chile. They all compete for the most liquid business and get most of it. . . . There is a lot of business that is

necessary for the country, such as agricultural loans and loans to small merchants and manufacturers . . . the foreign banks do not want this and the result is that the local banks take all they can of it, and on account of the competition and low rates, do not go after their proper proportion of the liquid business. . . . As a general thing I do not think that the foreign banks in Chile are a benefit to the country.[131]

Kemmerer also modernized Chilean financial transactions by putting through a new negotiable instruments law that smoothed the handling of checks, drafts, and bills of exchange. As the North American copper companies informed the mission, U.S. exporters and importers desired these improvements as much as Chilean merchants.[132]

Kemmerer's Fiscal Reforms

To inhibit the state from sabotaging monetary stability, Kemmerer also recast fiscal procedures. Chilean governments had been encountering mounting difficulties achieving budgetary equilibrium because of declining nitrate incomes and multiplying obligations. Fluctuating export returns upset revenue predictions. Total expenditures routinely exceeded the original figures authorized by Congress.[133] Pushed upward by both the executive and legislative branches, government receipts per inhabitant rose from 46 pesos in 1910 to 59 in 1920, to 74 in 1923; in those same years expenditures per inhabitant climbed even further, from 49 to 70 to 89 pesos.[134]

Many Chileans warned Kemmerer that bureaucratic *empleomanía* (mania for government employment) and greed would subvert his efforts to restrain these government expenditures.[135] While most letter writers urged him to chop away at government excesses, others pleaded with him to support their needs. For example, many provincials wrote in favor of funding for local projects, and the Veterans of the War of the Pacific (1879–83) sought his backing for better pensions.[136] The Association of Accountants of Chile lauded his fiscal reforms, which would place the government in further need of their skills.[137]

Chile's leading newspaper cautioned that the widespread desire to put the government on a diet clashed with the need for more and higher-paid bureaucrats to provide expanded services:

The Chilean State, like all the States of the world, has in recent years entered onto the path of socialization. The State has acquired new obligations and new necessities corresponding to them. It has become a Providence which reaches into the smallest details of the individual's existence and attends to his well being, or that which it believes to be his well being, like a grand family father. The notion of the State reduced to a police function, to preserve order and prevent conflicts between two individual rights, has long been lost in the night of history. And the socialist State is expensive, very expensive.[138]

Another newspaper expressed equal pessimism about a foreigner's ability to curtail government profligacy: "When Mr. Kemmerer says that ten thousand useless employees must be cut out, that less must be spent on luxuries and automobiles, when he puts a tourniquet on our life of Nabob, we will smile and say that this man is crazy, and we will bid him goodbye with music."[139]

One month after it was submitted, the government decreed Kemmerer's "organic budget bill" with very few modifications. It set strict limits on the government's abilities to misrepresent probable revenues and expenditures, to go beyond original authorizations, and to incur new debts.[140] The new law tried to eliminate budgetary errors by requiring that projected receipts be calculated using the average of the three preceding years. Like many Chileans before him, Kemmerer also advised that nitrate revenues be estimated separately because of their high variability and recommended that their projection should not exceed their lowest return in the previous five years. Since Chile had become too dependent on those nitrate earnings not to count them in with ordinary revenues, that Kemmerer proposal became one of the few discarded; the government found it too automatic and rigid, especially when revenues rose and expansionist policies got under way in 1927–28.[141]

Although restricting the chief executive's ability to violate the budget, Kemmerer greatly increased his fiscal powers over those of legislators. He left Congress with the authority only to trim, not fatten, projected expenditures. Kemmerer's support for weakening the legislature helped the 1925 constitution writers transform a parliamentary into a presidential republic.[142]

In 1926 Chile did not adhere to Kemmerer's budget law. The government, faced with continuing economic hard times, still intentionally overestimated income and underestimated outgo. This resulted in massive deficit spending and borrowing abroad.[143] President Ibáñez significantly reshuffled the state's finances and bureaucracy in 1927. As nitrate sales rose along with revenues from Kemmerer's tax reforms, the mission's fiscal prescriptions also took hold. Better managed and balanced budgets resulted. From 1927 to 1929 government revenues rose from 21 to 32 million pounds sterling equivalent, and expenditures from 20 to 30 million. Renewed prosperity shifted public opinion from austerity to expansion. Responding to increasing exports and especially foreign loans, Ibáñez circumvented Kemmerer's budgetary restraints in order to pump up the central government. Alongside the ordinary budget, Ibáñez introduced an extraordinary budget for foreign loans and public works.[144]

The state expanded its foreign and domestic revenue sources, mainly to take care of the rising numbers and incomes of bureaucrats from the middle class. When the junta hiked compensation for public employees, government salaries leapt from 26 percent of the ordinary budget in 1925 to 41 percent in 1926 and stayed in that range thereafter. During 1921–31 the cost of civilian public administration escalated 70 percent.[145]

Just as Kemmerer created the superintendency to monitor the central bank, so he founded the national comptroller, or contraloría, to safeguard his budget law. Previously in Chile several uncoordinated institutions with overlapping functions and jurisdictions had exercised tardy and haphazard fiscal control. To improve its economic planning and accounting the government was already designing a single, powerful fiscalizing agency before Kemmerer arrived. It then used his mission to consummate the project.[146]

The contraloría amalgamated Chilean practices stretching back into the colonial period, accounting procedures of large corporations, and fiscalizing methods in the United States and England. In short, Kemmerer photocopied his Colombian creation. Named by the president, the comptroller general became an independent official exerting prior control over all government transactions. Kemmerer noted that the comptroller's statistical-financial reports would help the government plan and execute economic policies. Those data were also intended to attract foreign investors, who were eager to ascertain the exact state of the government's accounts and thus its creditworthiness.[147] Chileans gave the new institution high marks for making state expansion and modernization more orderly and efficient.[148]

Despite widespread public support, the comptroller, of all Kemmerer's projects, took the longest to come into being. An elected president and Congress bottled it up during 1925–26. Only in 1927, when Ibáñez reasserted his authority, first behind a weak president and then as president himself, did the comptroller become a functioning legal entity.[149]

After the mission's departure the North American assessor whom Kemmerer had recommended for the central bank helped adapt the comptroller project to Chilean jurisprudence. Since the original English version of the project had been lost, Van Deusen and a Chilean commission had to work from a clumsy Spanish copy. Then Ibáñez imposed their revamped law in 1927. As Van Deusen explained to Kemmerer:

> The translation was so poor that some parts none of us could understand. I have heard that the poor translation was intentional to make more difficult the passage and putting into effect the law, as many of the government officials were very much opposed to the law. It would have been impossible to have passed the law through Congress. For-

tunately the present government wants to clean house, and they can dictate this project under the authority of a law recently passed by Congress authorizing the consolidation of offices. Most of the provisions of the law regarding inspection and penalties are in old laws that have never been enforced.[150]

Also in 1927, the government, following Kemmerer's advice, contracted U.S. public accountant Thomas Lill to help set the comptroller in motion. After fighting in the Spanish-American War, Lill had helped defeat the rebellion in the Philippines, where he became examiner of accounts. Then he assisted the national comptrollers in Mexico and Colombia, serving in that latter country for three years prior to the Chilean assignment. Now his reorganizing efforts in Chile resulted in a second decree, which gave the comptroller its final form by the end of 1927.[151]

It took another year for the comptroller to overcome accounting deficiencies and bureaucratic resistance in existing government agencies.[152] Meanwhile, some commentators and government officials called for a return to the old fiscalizing system. Critics complained that the comptroller was too powerful, complicated, and unwieldy.[153]

Nevertheless, Ibáñez went further than even Kemmerer had envisioned by transforming the comptroller into a virtual fourth branch of government. In line with his technocratic approach to government, Ibáñez gave the comptroller the authority to rule not only on the fiscal propriety of government expenditures but also on their constitutionality. At the same time he further centralized its powers in accord with the unitary Chilean system by scrapping Kemmerer's provision for provincial accounts inspectors, which was implemented in more regionalistic Colombia, Ecuador, and Bolivia.[154]

As President Alessandri and many Chileans had been urging for years, Kemmerer also revamped the tax system.[155] Complaints about inequities and inefficiency mounted in 1924–25, as the juntas decreed a rash of new domestic taxes on the middle and upper classes. Furthermore, foreign merchants and bankers hoped Kemmerer could dampen enthusiasm for heavier taxation or nationalization of foreign enterprises. Domestic industrialists also wanted lower income taxes and smaller compulsory contributions to worker welfare than those enacted by the juntas; manufacturers preferred to see the government raise tariffs. Most critics, however, argued for reduced reliance on customs receipts. Nitrate producers, of course, advised Kemmerer to pare down their export tax burden, but other commentators questioned whether a foreigner should rule on a tax ultimately paid mainly by foreigners.[156]

Kemmerer tendered a series of recommendations to make taxation simpler and more effective. He reorganized the Bureau of Internal Taxes to give the government more centralized, extensive, and precise powers to investigate and regulate economic activities. The new system required the private sector to adopt more rigorous and detailed business methods, accounting practices, and appraisals, with stiff penalties for violations of the reporting regulations. Some Chileans bemoaned this intrusion into the privacy and independence of free enterprise. Kemmerer also tried to improve tax valuations, assessments, and collections and to increase revenues from stamps, real estate, tobacco, club memberships, public spectacles, iron ore exports, and incomes. To offset the regressive character of Chile's revenue system, most of these tax hikes were aimed at wealthier groups and luxury consumption. Existing taxes also became less burdensome to commercial transactions; for example, by eliminating nuisance stamp fees on checks and sales receipts.[157] The Kemmerer reforms worked well, as total tax revenues rose 10 percent during 1927–28 and 20 percent during 1928–29.[158]

The mission's most important recommendation in this field concerned the income tax. Some businessmen feared it would discourage the capital formation so direly needed in an underdeveloped country. By the early 1920s, however, most Chilean opinionmakers supported a mildly progressive income tax. They believed its universality and fairness would increase "social solidarity" behind government collections and expenditures, thus furthering national integration. President Alessandri had criticized the law Congress passed in 1924 for being too regressive and bringing in too little in revenues. Some upper-class Chileans hoped such legislation would relieve them from property taxes, which were harder to avoid or underpay. The junta later made the income levy more progressive, but not in any planned or scientific manner.[159]

Kemmerer removed many of the exemptions for the wealthy and tightened collection procedures. He included a 6 percent tax on the income from nearly all commerce, industry, and mining, as well as an additional 6 percent levy on the copper mines.[160] After minor government alterations in his law, most Chileans praised its provisions and its generation of rising revenues during the remainder of the 1920s.[161]

Like the banana tax in Colombia, Kemmerer's iron ore and copper taxes in Chile displayed notable service to the host country at the expense of U.S. enterprises.[162] U.S. copper companies all urged Kemmerer to ignore nationalistic demands for increased Chilean taxation and control, denying charges that they were looting the country's wealth and leaving nothing behind. Although the companies were displeased that Kemmerer established a higher income tax on them, they were relieved that he spurned Chilean recommendations for an export duty as well. They might be able to deduct payments of a Chilean income tax from their U.S. income tax, but not payments of a Chilean export levy. Although small, Kemmerer's tax on the copper mines represented significant state encroachment on that foreign enclave.[163]

Kemmerer also looked at Chile's poorly administered customs system. The mission ignored strong pleas from industrialists and agriculturalists for higher hurdles against foreign competitors. Instead it endorsed free trade, to the applause of Chilean and U.S. merchants. Nevertheless, Ibáñez hiked many tariffs in 1928, especially those on manufactured goods.[164] Accompanying administrative reforms proposed by Kemmerer were also thwarted, mainly by customs employees. The government did, however, adopt his suggestion to hire a North American expert to help reorganize the customs offices.[165]

The government hoped that improved customs collections would allow it to use foreign loans less to cover deficits and more to fund productive projects. Of the mounting public debt under President Alessandri, Chile owed approximately three-fourths to foreigners and one-fourth to nationals.[166] The public debt per inhabitant had risen from 223 pesos in 1875 to 245 in 1895, 333 in 1905, and 505 in 1925, a factor of 2.26; during those same years, external commerce per inhabitant increased by a factor of 2.94; from 268 to 336 to 440 to 783. Consequently, some Chileans contended that the country could and should afford to take on even more foreign debts.[167] Others worried about the rising burden, however, since over one-third of total budget expenditures was going to service the public debt when Kemmerer arrived.[168]

In the early 1920s Alessandri contracted more and more loans to cover deficits and pay for public works. The state also guaranteed foreign loans made to the government-owned railroads and the Caja de Crédito Hipotecario. Some Chileans complained that mushrooming indebtedness was being used unproductively to expand public works and government employment just to pacify the lower and middle classes.[169]

Kemmerer realized that the national and municipal governments, many economic elites, and foreign lenders were overly eager to expand Chile's external indebtedness.[170] In accord with the bulk of Chilean opinion, his report to the government recommended using foreign capital for national development but with prudent loan contracts for productive projects which would repay themselves:

> For many years in the future Chile will be a borrower of money in foreign markets. A country so rich in natural resources needs large amounts of capital for its economic development and, for some time, it will be wise public policy to obtain much of this capital by foreign borrowing. Chile is passing through the same stage of economic development that the United States passed through during the last century, and that Canada, Australia, South Africa, and all countries of Latin

America are passing through today. It is to the advantage of any country with great undeveloped resources to obtain capital in those countries where the rate of interest, due to the great accumulations of capital, is substantially lower than it is in the borrowing country.

He thought Chile would have excellent access to foreign funds because of its exemplary past debt record and because of his recent banking, monetary, and fiscal reforms: "In particular will these reforms stimulate the interest of foreign investors in the possibilities of investments in Chile, both in private enterprises and in government securities." Kemmerer also warned Chile to plan and accumulate debts gradually, to monitor borrowing by subnational units, and to acquire its external loans through a single reputable banking house. In addition, he cautioned his hosts to demand fair and honorable terms; for example, not pledging any specific revenues as collateral and not promising to spend the loan in the lender country.[171]

The mission not only gave Chile advice on its public debts, but also became involved in that foreign borrowing. Immediately after leaving Chile, Kemmerer tried to ensure that all its government loan contracts in the United States would be placed with the most esteemed financial houses. For example, when Dillon, Read, and Company asked him in December 1925 about his mission and the advisability of handling a loan that Chile wanted to float, Kemmerer encouraged the firm. He also offered to introduce the Chilean ambassador in Washington to Dillon, Read or other top banking establishments where he had influential friends, including Morgan, National City Bank, Guaranty Trust Company, Blair and Company, and Kuhn, Loeb, and Company.[172] In 1927 former mission member Jefferson returned to Santiago as a representative of the First National Bank of Boston to look into possible loans to the Chilean government.[173]

During the 1920s foreign loans to the Chilean government averaged over $42 million per year.[174] In the years following Kemmerer's visit, and especially under Ibáñez's presidency, that indebtedness exploded. From 1925 to 1930 the total external public debt in dollars mushroomed from 18 million to 257 million and in pounds sterling from 26 million to 33 million. In those same years Chile obtained 110 million Swiss francs. As a result, its total foreign debt, measured in gold pesos of six pence, leapt from 1,253 million in 1925 to 3,597 million in 1930.[175]

This total foreign debt included both direct obligations of the central government and those it guaranteed for municipalities, state railroads, and credit agencies. Some cities also floated loans abroad that were not guaranteed by the central administration. By 1930 the internal public debt had reached 507,760,000 pesos. Consequently, out of a total public debt of 4,105,009,000 pesos on December 31, 1930, Chile owed 2,177,373,000 to the United States; 1,198,319,000 to Great Britain; 197,604,000 to Switzerland; 26,953,000 to Germany; and 507,760,000 to its own citizens.[176] In 1929 the total Chilean national, municipal, and public corporation external loans floated in the United States exceeded any other Latin American government issues publicly offered.[177]

Despite these staggering figures, Chilean officials felt, prior to the depression, that the country was pursuing a wise debt policy. One reason was improving terms. Whereas pre-1925 foreign loans had been contracted at interest rates of 7–8 percent, post-1925 obligations carried rates of only 6–7 percent, with lighter amortization and service charges. The country did not have to pledge any specific revenues to secure these loans. Moreover, its annual foreign debt payments declined from one-third of ordinary government expenditures in 1925 to one-fourth in 1928 and 1929. As a percentage of ordinary government revenues, service on the direct public debt of the central government dropped from 30 to 20 percent during 1926–29; while the state's ordinary revenues increased 68 percent, its direct public debt increased only 48 percent.[178]

Ibáñez's minister of finance pointed out that returns (taxes, salaries, and purchases) from the rising copper industry alone totaled some 250 million pesos in 1928, which exceeded the 231 million due on the public debt. In his opinion Chile could therefore take on more foreign loans, in effect to be paid back by foreign capitalists. He believed that increasing dependence on foreign investments in the short run would make Chile more prosperous and self-sufficient in the long run.[179] The mood remained buoyant in 1929, when the minister claimed that Chile's total public debt was merely 2.3 times as large as its total government expenditures, compared to 4.9 times in the United States, 3.3 in Argentina, 2.6 in Peru, and 1.6 in Colombia.[180]

England lost the competition with the United States to place most of these loans for the Chilean government. The U.S. ambassador worried that ferocious competition among U.S. banks would help British competitors, but U.S. financial prowess left the British far behind, although in the late 1920s some Chilean loans were handled jointly by U.S. and British concerns. The strong Chilean desire to balance the U.S. financial and commercial surge with British capitalists went unrealized. Most of these foreign loans in the latter twenties went into public works, social welfare programs, and budgetary deficits, infusing capital mainly into the modern urban and industrial sectors.[181]

As these debts multiplied, criticism mounted, finally erupting during the depression. In the latter part of the 1920s a few Chileans worried that debt-led growth was becoming a vicious circle. The country needed a yearly trade surplus of almost one-third more exports than imports to meet its debt obligations. Those figures, however, did not take into account "invisible" financial movements, which reduced the real surplus; thus more foreign loans had to be shouldered to maintain payments on the old ones.[182]

Other critics feared that spiraling external indebtedness would endanger monetary stability and national sovereignty.[183] By 1930 nationalists were complaining that these loans had been overseen by the State Department and had gone into roads and bridges to increase Chilean consumption of U.S. cars and tires, into railroads to facilitate transportation for U.S. export companies in Chile, into urban buildings erected by U.S. construction firms, and into payment and consolidation of earlier debts owed to North Americans, all of which were "always favorable to the interests of imperialism" and served "to prolong dependency."[184]

Ibáñez funneled most of these foreign loans into public works. The central government's public works expenditures soared from 89 million pesos in 1928, to 202 in 1929, and 288 in 1930. Spending fell to 181 million pesos in 1931 and dropped further thereafter.[185]

Most Chileans were dazzled by the construction and progress in 1928–29. A few, however, cautioned that these projects might not be productive enough to pay back the foreign loans behind them. In Colombia public works that helped domestic producers also boosted exports (mainly coffee) that earned hard currency to repay foreign debts. Since foreigners dominated Chile's export sector, however, public works improvements for domestic producers seldom generated foreign exchange to meet external debt obligations. Instead of indebting the country to foreign lenders to help local foreign companies expand exports, Ibáñez emphasized the riskier course of using foreign loans to underwrite industry, agriculture, and, above all, the bureaucracy in central Chile.[186] When the depression arrived, criticism reached a crescendo against excessive reliance on foreign finances for poorly planned projects to serve the central elites, Santiago, and the *empleomanía* desires of the middle and working classes.[187]

When Kemmerer arrived, the loudest outcry for public works improvements concerned railroads. The costly and inefficient public rail service ran up deficits which accounted for more than half the government's debt in the mid-twenties. Private, principally British lines served the profitable, foreign-owned mines, while the state franchises subsidized domestic agriculturalists. Since a majority of Chile's railroads already belonged to the government, nationalization was not a key issue as it had been in Colombia. Neither was there the same degree of railroad fever for additional routes and trackage. Rather, Chilean landowners and mine owners primarily wanted streamlined management, modernized equipment, and lower fares.[188]

Kemmerer recommended reorganizing and economizing in state railroad management, and proposed control by a board of experts rather than political appointees. Following some of these suggestions, Ibáñez created a new superior inspector of railroads. Thereafter the public lines ran more efficiently and stopped bleeding the treasury. Rather than economizing, however, the government used foreign loans to continue subsidizing railroad growth and employment. For example, in 1927 the 4,600 kilometers of state railways employed 24,000 workers, compared to only 8,500 for the 4,000 kilometers of private railroads. Typically, the government implemented some of Kemmerer's ideas but did not obey his recommendations for austerity.[189]

Results of Kemmerer's Reforms, 1926-29

Chileans lauded the 1925 government for presiding over "the financial and administrative kemmerization" of the nation. Newspapers gushed that henceforth "the history of this country would be divided in two epochs, in two very well defined eras: Before Kemmerer, After Kemmerer."[190] U.S. and British observers echoed their enthusiasm for Kemmerer's reforms and Chile's consequent attractiveness for foreign investors.[191]

Mainly because of the nitrate and copper mines, Chile already exhibited a very high level of direct foreign investments. Both direct and indirect investments increased substantially after Kemmerer, as shown in table 3.4. Table 3.5 shows estimates of the size of those foreign investments within sectors in 1928, excluding agricultural real estate, which was overwhelmingly in domestic hands.

Chilean debates about the impact of foreign investments in the 1920s rested on inadequate data; the government did not keep proper track of outflows for amortization, interest, or profits.[192] Balance-of-payments calculations did not accurately reflect service payments or the sizable funds sent abroad by wealthy

Table 3.4 Accumulation of Value of Foreign Investments in Chile, 1925–1932 (in millions of dollars)

Years	Indirect investments	Direct investments	Total investments
1925	188	535	723
1926	282	581	863
1927	316	609	925
1928	376	641	1,017
1929	407	649	1,056
1930	457	646	1,103
1931	446	786	1,232
1932	404	702	1,106

Source: See note 192.

Table 3.5 Capital Investments in Chile, 1928 (in millions of pesos of six pence)

	Total capital	National capital	Foreign capital
Commerce	89	50	39
Manufacturing	2,200	1,000	1,200
Mining	10,500	4,500	6,000
Agriculture	2,000	1,360	640
Transportation	1,925	1,247	678
Fixed property	12,636	10,396	2,240
Direct public debt	1,863	106	1,758
Cuaranteed public debt	899	48	851
Totals	32,112	18,706	13,406

Source: Aníbal Jara Letelier and Manuel G. Muirhead, *Chile en Sevilla* (Santiago, 1929), pp. 209–10.

Chileans and resident foreigners.[193] The U.S. ambassador claimed that many of the gains registered from foreign-controlled exports actually leaked abroad. Heavy smuggling, as throughout Latin America, brought in many unrecorded imports. Because official statistics in the era only showed the favorable balance of trade, most Chileans could not really assess the precariousness of their ability to meet their foreign obligations.[194]

In general, Chileans waxed enthusiastic about the flood of Yankee dollars. Ibáñez's ambassador to the United States celebrated that country's switch from negative, militaristic imperialism to "commercial, technical, scientific, cultural, and moral penetration," labeling it "a new form of legitimate imperialism, which is that of cooperation."[195] Nevertheless, a minority of Chileans expressed reservations about the heavy role of foreign capital in the late 1920s. Some feared that the United States would follow its investments with interventions, as it had done in the Caribbean.[196] Influenced by the American Popular Revolutionary Alliance in Peru (see chapter 6), these critics viewed foreign capital at best as a necessary evil for the short run. One unusually hostile and prescient nationalist complained in 1930 about U.S. dominance over mines and loans: "The export enterprise . . . with the simple suspension or dimunition of its productivity can create worker unemployment, budgetary deficits, the consequent need to contract loans, the fall of exchange, and finally, if it persists, the most absolute crisis and bankruptcy." He protested that the bulging bureaucracy was growing fat off imperialism: "Credit, the banking system, finances, all find themselves under the direct control of imperialism . . . the Public Debt, the heavy mortgages on all the budgetary sources, the control of the technical organisms of the public administration, complete the picture of the economic domination of imperialism, by direct reason of which is established and develops political domination."[197]

Chile continued relying on foreign advisers and investors in the latter 1920s, contracting outside consultants for public finance offices, the statistical department, the postal and telegraph services, state credit institutions, and schools. Most of these experts came from the United States and Germany. The British worried that their absence, except for a naval mission, would harm Great Britain's influence and sales in Chile.[198]

At the invitation of the government, Kemmerer himself returned in 1927 for a brief checkup on his handiwork, after his Bolivian mission. He heaped praise on the performance of the institutions he had sired in Chile, especially the central bank. Forecasting what would happen three years hence, Chileans pressed him about whether the bank could sustain the gold standard even in the face of a general export collapse. Kemmerer reaffirmed that the standard could and should be upheld even if nitrate sales evaporated. He reprimanded those Chileans who looked on the gold reserve as a "sacred and untouchable" commodity to be preserved even at the expense of the gold standard. He reminded them that the reserve was supposed to rise and fall to protect exchange stability. Other Chileans, especially agriculturalists, complained that the bank was not serving as a developmental institution by providing extensive long-term credits. Kemmerer retorted that the bank had to emphasize high liquidity in order to guarantee exchange stability, which was its primary purpose. His second visit helped fortify Chilean determination to perpetuate his system.[199]

Prospering foreign trade also solidified support for the Kemmerer formula (see table 3.6). During 1925–29 exports represented an average of 43 percent of the total value of goods (not counting services) produced in the country; imports accounted for an average of 50 percent of the goods available in Chile. In those same years primary products made up an average of 96 percent of all Chilean exports. On the import side, manufactured consumer goods accounted for 41 percent, capital goods for 38 percent, primary materials for 14 percent, and combustibles for 7 percent. Because of domestic industrialization, imports of capital goods rose more than consumer items by the end of the twenties. In the first two decades of the twentieth century, customs revenues from that external trade had furnished over 70 percent of government revenues. Declining nitrate sales in the face of competition from artificial substitutes, however, drove that figure down to an average of 49 percent during 1920–29. While export taxes—principally on nitrates—dropped from 26 to 24 percent of total fiscal revenues from 1925 to 1929, rising duties lifted the contribution of import taxes from 19 to 32 percent. Given the huge reliance of the economy and the government on the external sector, exchange stability seemed crucial to many Chileans. The consequent strong public support for relatively free trade and Kemmerer's gold

Table 3.6   Chilean Exports, Imports, and Customs Receipts, 1920–1933

Year	Index of constant dollar value of external commerce (average for 1920–21–22 equal to a base of 100)		Export and import receipts as a percentage of fiscal revenues
	Exports	Imports	
1920	151	127	68%
1921	84	107	39%
1922	64	66	39%
1923	106	92	48%
1924	118	102	44%
1925	122	114	44%
1926	107	120	57%
1927	110	100	57%
1928	127	112	42%
1929	149	151	56%
1930	87	134	47%
1931	54	68	29%
1932	18	20	29%
1933	22	18	40%

Sources: See note 200.

standard convinced Ibáñez to stick to those policies into mid-1931.[200] Although deepening Chilean dependence on the external sector in general and the United States in particular, Ibáñez also promoted the development of national capitalism and the central government.[201]

As in most of the Andean countries, agriculturalists in Chile felt slighted by the Kemmerer system and the modernizing regime presiding over it. They complained about labor and credit shortages caused by urban expansion.[202] Although it was the major economic activity in domestic hands, agriculture also relied heavily on the foreign sector. Taxes on foreign-owned mineral exports and duties on imports kept the fiscal burden on farmers microscopic. Meanwhile, they obtained generous credits from the Caja de Crédito Hipotecario and the new Caja de Crédito Agrario, which floated bonds guaranteed by the central government on the New York market. Since the landed elites could not repay their obligations with cheapened currency, soaring indebtedness rendered agriculturalists highly vulnerable to the Great Depression.[203]

Industry grew very rapidly in the latter 1920s. Out of 8,585 total manufacturing establishments in Chile in 1928, nearly 3,000 were founded during 1924–

28. By contrast, only 859 had been launched during 1919–23, 510 during 1914–18, and 377 during 1909–13. Furthermore, over one-fourth of all the workers employed in industry were located in those factories established during 1924–28. According to the 1928 industrial census, 7,178 of the owners, partners, and tenants were Chilean and 2,165 were foreign. Commercial establishments also boomed. Out of 33,241 total in Chile in 1928, 14,677 were founded during 1924–28; 28,957 of their owners, partners, and tenants were Chilean, 9,141 were foreign. As foreign capital became more predominant in mining, domestic capital increasingly went into manufacturing. Industrial capital from both foreign and domestic sources increased some 70 percent during 1925–30. That growing industry became concentrated in a few oligopolistic enterprises. Partly through reliance on foreign capital, parts, materials, and models, the modern, urban sector of the Chilean economy flourished.[204]

It was in the 1920s that the state began encouraging the development of the urban interests of the upper class. Ibáñez's tariff, credit, tax, and administrative policies promoting industrialization foreshadowed national economic planning and state capitalism after the Great Depression. To the pleasure of manufacturers, it laid the groundwork for the more aggressive import substituting industrialization of later years.[205]

Like the economic elites, the urban middle class also made gains in the second half of the 1920s. They enjoyed expanding government employment and social security protection. They also benefited from the growth of commerce and industry, but resented protective tariffs on imported consumer goods.[206]

To a much lesser extent, some urban workers—if not their rural counterparts—also experienced economic improvements under Ibáñez. Prosperity in the 1920s tightened the labor market, which would have benefited workers more if the government had not suppressed their independent unions. To smooth the path of industrialization, the dictator trampled autonomous unions and tried to supplant them with government surrogates. His oppression and monetary stabilization reduced the number of strikes from 160 in 1925 to 63 in 1926, and to 0 in 1927 and 1928.[207] Despite their displeasure with the brutal attacks against the labor movement, urban workers welcomed expanding employment in industry and public works. Whereas their real incomes had declined in the early years of the decade, average daily wages rose roughly 66 percent from 1927 through 1929.[208]

Therefore the most influential economic groups, especially in the cities, were reasonably satisfied with prosperity under Ibáñez. His authority rested on the mystique of efficient management of a modernizing economy, undergirded by foreign capital. When those foreign buttresses cracked, however, Ibáñez fell, along with the Kemmerer system.

The Great Depression, 1930–32

Chile's foreign trade felt the full force of the global depression in 1930. The gold value of Chile's international commerce fell proportionately more than that of any other country in the world, according to the League of Nations. By 1932 exports had plunged to 12 percent of their value in 1929. In response the government gradually hiked tariff duties, imposed import quotas and licenses, and established exchange controls and multiple exchange rates, administered by the central bank. By 1933 the depression had demolished the free trade and exchange system upon which Kemmerer's structure had been built.[209]

Of all Chile's economic sectors, the depression struck mining earliest and hardest. Even though comprising only 6 percent of the active population, miners came to account for over half the workers unemployed by the depression. The index of mineral production, with the 1927–29 average equal to 100, fell from a peak of 118 in 1929, to 83 in 1930, to 57 in 1931. The value of copper and nitrate exports dropped 89 percent from 1927–29 to 1932. Some U.S. nitrate and copper exporters came to favor monetary depreciation. Then the government placed discriminatory exchange controls on the earnings of these two foreign-owned sectors. Thus the state, in effect, increased its intervention in and taxation of nitrates and copper.[210] The U.S. companies and the State Department protested these impositions.[211]

As world prices for farm goods fell and consumption of food from central Chile by the northern mining provinces dwindled, the depression reverberated from the mineral into the agricultural sector. After rising from 1927 to 1929, prices for farm products in Chile tumbled by nearly 50 percent by 1931. Consequently landowners and their National Society of Agriculture denounced the central bank's deflationary policies. They also lambasted the government for continuing payments on the foreign debt. After the ejection of Ibáñez and financial orthodoxy in mid-1931, agriculturalists welcomed monetary expansion; they hailed the rising prices for their produce and the shrinking burden of their debts.[212]

As the U.S. ambassador noted, these inflationary demands from many landed elites created countervailing pressures on the government that followed Ibáñez, which tried to maintain an official rate of exchange for controlled convertibility. Whereas monetary expansion had been championed by agrarian populists in the United States,

> in Chile the reverse is the case. The advocates of cheap money are the conservative and aristocratic elements who are interested chiefly in agriculture. The advocates of sound money are the laborers and the

Army. Alessandri, at the present time, takes great pride in the fact he brought Kemmerer to Chile and established the present monetary system. The Ibañistas also feel that they had a part in establishing the present system, particularly in view of the fact that Ibáñez, who was in Alessandri's cabinet, insisted by the threat of force that Alessandri sign on the dotted line the laws prepared by Kemmerer. Before the time of Kemmerer both the laborers and the Army had many sad experiences with cheap and depreciated currencies and those experiences have been reduced to a political conviction that their interests are in line with sound and stable money measures. This sentiment is now being availed of by both the Alessandristas and the Ibañistas, and the moment the Government declares the peso inconvertible they will start a political agitation which will not only embarrass the present government but may result in its overthrow.[213]

Manufacturing suffered from the depression only belatedly and briefly.[214] The index of Chilean industrial production during the depression years is shown in table 3.7. Industrialists were less eager than agriculturalists to unhitch from the gold standard, but they also promoted protectionist, expansionary policies which ultimately undermined the Kemmerer system. The Society for Factory Development argued that higher tariffs on competing imports would reduce gold outflows and thus preserve exchange stability. The rural elites, also desiring stiff duties on agricultural imports, backed this protectionist campaign by the manufacturers. So did many U.S. firms established in Chile, to the dismay of U.S. exporters to Chile and the U.S. embassy.[215]

SOFOFA also called for expanded industrial loans from the central bank and the state credit agencies. This opposition by manufacturers to credit restrictions as a means of defending the gold standard soon led them to favor exchange controls and monetary devaluation. Although currency depreciation would impede imports of vital raw materials and capital equipment, it would also block

Table 3.7   Index of Chilean Industrial
Production, 1927–1936 (1927–29 = 100)

Year	Index	Year	Index
1927	87	1932	99
1928	96	1933	109
1929	117	1934	119
1930	117	1935	137
1931	87	1936	145

Sources: See note 214.

competitive consumer imports. The industrialists, like the agriculturalists, justified these programs in the name of economic nationalism.[216] In 1931–32 the government supported protected industrialization mainly to conserve foreign exchange.[217]

Only one foreign and two domestic commercial banks collapsed during the depths of the depression. From 1926 to 1932 the total number of commercial banks in Chile dropped from twenty-five to eighteen.[218] Amidst vociferous complaints from agriculturalists, manufacturers, and merchants, commercial bank reserves, deposits, and loans shrank until mid-1931. After disengagement from the gold standard, bank holdings, operations, and investments revived.[219]

Far more than the capitalist elites, workers suffered severely from the depression, especially in the mines and cities. Those officially seeking new jobs crested in 1932 at 129,000; the total number unemployed was probably double that figure. Devastated first by Ibáñez and then by the depression, unions floundered. Nevertheless, workers protested unemployment and wage reductions. Their outcries frightened the elites and generated political ferment. In the turmoil, worker demands for relief also helped undercut the Kemmerer system they had previously supported.[220]

As the depression deepened, so did the fiscal and political crisis. During 1929–32 total government revenues fell by 60 percent. While receipts from foreign trade plummeted by 72 percent, income from domestic sources dropped by only 25 percent. Whereas all internal taxes supplied only 15 percent of government revenues in 1924, they furnished 24 percent in 1927, 38 percent in 1929, and 63 percent of the ordinary budget in 1932. Domestic taxpayers opposed new impositions during the depression. At the same time the bureaucracy and the armed forces, who had been the major beneficiaries of state expansion under Ibáñez, resisted budget cuts. As revenues fell faster than expenditures, the kaleidoscope of administrations following Ibáñez incurred mounting deficits. There was no Keynesian vision behind this departure from financial orthodoxy; for example, the strapped government slashed public works during 1931–33. Nevertheless, by inducing greater reliance on national production, taxation, and government intervention, the depression served as a salutary shock.[221]

The drain on government finances and on the central bank's gold reserves compelled Chile to suspend payments on its external debt in July 1931 (see table 3.8). In addition to foreign obligations, the government more than tripled its internal debt from 1929 to 1932; that additional one billion gold pesos made the total public debt approximately five billion pesos in 1932, compared to some three billion in 1927.[222]

His model of debt-led growth bankrupt, Ibáñez resigned ten days after declaring the moratorium on foreign payments. Despite those drastic changes, the balance of payments remained unfavorable and central bank reserves con-

Table 3.8   Chilean Public Foreign Debt, 1932

	U.S. dollars	British pounds	Swiss francs	Equivalent in gold pesos of six pence
Direct central government debt	139,551,286	28,677,762	83,546,000	2,430,829,002
Railway, municipal, and credit bank debts guaranteed by the central government	126,908,714	1,193,509	36,311,500	1,155,460,978
Floating debt	24,865,819	3,310,000		337,543,009
Discountable treasury notes	4,049,895	153,000		39,406,087
Totals	295,375,714	33,334,271	119,857,500	3,963,239,076

Sources: See note 222.

tinued to fall into 1932. The interim government succeeding Ibáñez mandated exchange controls two weeks after the suspension of debt payments. Many domestic and foreign business interests expressed grave doubts about both measures. When the fiscal and banking crisis continued, full, official inconvertibility was decreed in April 1932.[223]

While Chile agonized over these issues in 1930–32, the U.S. State Department remained more reluctant than U.S. bankers or even its own embassy to get involved in these financial questions. The embassy complained about suspension of debt payments, about discrimination against U.S. companies in the allocation of foreign exchange, and about rhetorical assaults on U.S. property. The State Department, however, adhered to the policy that debt problems were to be resolved privately between the Chilean government and the U.S. bondholders. Therefore it encouraged formation of the U.S. Council of Foreign Bondholders and enlisted Kemmerer as one of the architects of that group. One reason the State Department did not want to coerce Chile to repay its debts was to avoid creating hostility toward other North American interests in that country. The United States believed that its large trade and direct investments were more important, as State Department estimates shown in table 3.9 indicate. The combined U.S. direct and indirect investment in Chile at that time came to roughly $1.3 billion.[224]

That U.S. policy of avoiding overt intervention was sorely tested during the economic tensions of the depression. Most North American policymakers and bankers, however, kept in mind broader, long-range interests in Chile. For example, W. W. Lancaster, a representative of National City Bank, asked the

Table 3.9   Major U.S. Direct Investments in Chile, 1932

Copper	
Guggenheim	$ 168,950,000
Anaconda	214,050,000
Nitrates	
Guggenheim	141,000,000
W. R. Grace	8,000,000
Dupont	1,720,000
Iron	
Bethlehem Steel	13,000,000
U.S. Steel Products	1,720,000
Public Utilities	
International Telephone and Telegraph	60,000,000
American and Foreign Power	190,811,000
All American Cables	1,000,000
Miscellaneous	
Grace National Bank	15,000,000
National City Bank	3,100,000
Ford Motor Co.	1,000,000
Approximate Total	1,000,000,000

Source: U.S. State Department, Francis White Papers, Box 40, "United States and Latin America, 1929–1933," vol. 2, "Recent Problems in the Protection of American Interests in Chile."

head of the State Department's Latin American division about the possibility of using military force to protect U.S. properties in Chile. That government official replied:

> that the properties in Chile were inland, the copper properties at least being high up in the Andes, and that a battleship could not climb mountains. He [Lancaster] said that he had told this to his associates in New York but they had insisted that he discuss the matter with us. I pointed out that we had never done anything of this sort before and had not landed troops in any country south of the canal. I told him it was my personal opinion that if we did so we could not accomplish what he wanted and our action would be such that there would be no benefits in Chile itself, and still less in the rest of South America. I said I thought it would be the end of our trade in South America for some time. Mr. Lancaster said he agreed with me.[225]

After the loss of firm ally Ibáñez, the United States was pleased to find the interim and subsequently elected government of Juan Esteban Montero (1931–

32) also favorable to North American interests. The U.S. ambassador discovered Montero's cabinet in agreement with him "when I said that Chile has no economic future except in cooperation with foreign business leaders and capital."[226] Relations deteriorated, however, when military and civilian conspirators overthrew Montero and inaugurated the so-called Socialist Republic, which lasted twelve days in June 1932.

The Socialist Republic's commitment to economic nationalism and social reform frightened domestic and foreign elites. U.S. residents began stockpiling food and arms. In order to solve its fiscal crisis and provide services to the poor, the junta requested a fifty-million-peso loan from the central bank. When its conservative directors rebuffed the request, the socialists tried to convert the central bank into a state bank run by government directors. They also announced nationalization of all gold and foreign currency deposits in the central bank and all commercial banks, and vowed to take control of money and banking away from the oligarchy and imperialists.[227]

Fearing loss of their deposits in the central bank, U.S. bankers—and the State Department—worked jointly with British banking and governmental representatives to foil the junta's plans. The United States withheld recognition of the government and delayed oil shipments. The ambassador warned the junta that U.S. banks would not pay out drafts from the central bank and that the country's trade might be stifled by the withholding of international credit. He also worried, however, that overly belligerent reactions by U.S. banks might incite retaliation against foreign companies by the junta. The State Department reassured nervous U.S. business interests that "we had done about everything we could short of sending military forces." The British went even further by dispatching a battleship to nearby Peruvian waters to warn the junta against any assaults on their money or property. Faced with these external threats and the refusal by foreign banks to honor withdrawals, the junta shelved its banking reforms.[228]

The United States found the junta's successor far more palatable. Ibáñez's former ambassador to the United States governed from June until September, when new elections returned Alessandri to the presidency (1932–38). That three-month government also claimed to be a socialist republic, but it followed models of corporatism and state capitalism without attacking foreign interests. Nevertheless, the second socialist republic blamed the restrictive policies of the central bank for the severity of the depression. Its leaders denounced the institution for having done "everything to maintain the flame burning in the altar of the doctrines of Sr. Kemmerer, who, in turn, appears convinced that men should sacrifice everything to metallic reserves." They believed that the solution to the depression was to expand, rather than contract, the supply of money and credit. Therefore they required the central bank to open credit lines for government lending agencies. Their inflationary policies bailed out indebted agriculturalists and other credit-starved property owners at the expense of workers, who suffered from the soaring cost of living. This transformation of the central bank from a passive guardian of exchange rates into an active developmental credit institution continued for decades thereafter. This monetary expansion helped initiate Chile's recovery from the depression, which reached full swing by 1933. The *papeleros* had returned.[229]

Demise of the Kemmerer System

Throughout the crises of the depression, the central bank was the focal point of controversy. Under Ibáñez the bank clung to Kemmerer's system too long, in the opinion of most Chilean commentators.[230] Until mid-1931 both Ibáñez and the bank, referring to Kemmerer's teachings, ardently defended their procyclical policies. The bank's most outspoken public defender was its U.S. adviser, Walter M. Van Deusen.[231] Kemmerer reinforced that resolve in a 1931 letter to Van Deusen, urging Chile to uphold the gold standard "at any sacrifice." Kemmerer recommended elevation of high discount rates, severe contraction of the money supply, absolute maintenance of full convertibility, and deposit of practically all the gold reserve in New York. He sympathized with temporary suspension of foreign debt payments but not with any relaxation of the gold standard.[232]

The central bank followed Kemmerer's advice. From 1929 to mid-1931 it hiked the rediscount rate to member banks (which had dipped from 9 percent in 1926 to 6 percent in 1928 and would fall to 4 percent by 1933) from 6 to 9 percent. The bank presided over a 42 percent reduction of the circulating medium in eighteen months. During the extraordinary depression, however, this gold-standard remedy for reducing imports failed to keep pace with even faster falling exports, causing rising gold outflows and diminishing resources to service the foreign debt. Even more addicted to Kemmerer's system than its creator, the Chilean government and central bank suspended foreign debt payments and introduced exchange controls in July 1931 with great reluctance, hoping it would be merely a temporary lapse from virtue.[233] When Great Britain declared inconvertibility thereafter, in September 1931, the gold reserve in the Bank of England had fallen by only 20 percent, compared to over 50 percent in Chile's central bank, which proved even more willing to tolerate adversity to defend the gold standard than were its British promoters.[234]

The central bank and Van Deusen expressed dismay over the installation of selective exchange controls, but they hoped this interference with laissez-faire would salvage the beleaguered gold standard, which was formally retained until April 1932. Because gold reserves were still falling and the depression still worsening by 1932, Van Deusen later concluded it would have been wiser to have completely dumped the gold standard back in 1931.[235] Whereas the depression caused England to devalue its money by 42 percent, the United States by 40 percent, and Japan by 60 percent, Chile shattered world records with a devaluation of approximately 400 percent.[236]

Following the declaration of full inconvertibility and the expansionary programs of the socialist republics, inflation replaced deflation. The central bank now became an agent of monetary and credit expansion, as rising numbers of Chileans, especially agriculturalists, had been urging. It reduced its legal reserve requirement from 50 percent to 35 percent in 1931 and to 25 percent in 1932. One reason for that reduction was the loss in reserves held in pounds sterling in London when England left the gold standard before Chile. The central bank also lowered its rediscount rate from 9 to 4 percent and raised the amount of its capital and reserves that could be extended to the government from 20 to 80 percent. Central bank loans to the government then vaulted from 25 million pesos in early 1931 to 555 million by the end of 1932, not counting some 82 million pesos extended to state credit institutions. Concomitantly, loans to the private sector shriveled in importance. Currency circulating from the bank had shrunk from 500 million pesos in 1929 to 340 million in mid-1931, but then rebounded up to 445 million by the end of the year, and shot up to 825 million by the close of 1932. By late 1932 the peso had fallen to one-fifth its 1929 value. The index of wholesale prices, which had slumped from 100 in 1928 to 80 in 1931, jumped to 178 by the end of 1932. From 1931 through 1932 the prices of imports rose an estimated 265 percent, agricultural goods rose 117 percent, and national industrial products rose 78 percent.[237] Despite attempts by the Alessandri government to roll back these trends during 1932–38, the inflationary operations of the central bank had become established practice.[238]

More than any fundamental change in economic thought, the rush of events during 1930–32 prompted Chilean elites to discard Kemmerer's commandments. A few commentators during the depression called for definitive abandonment of any gold standard so that the domestic money supply would never again be tied to the external sector. Even those who lost faith, however, failed to articulate a coherent alternative model of national capitalism, let alone socialism. Rather, most economic and political leaders in the early thirties still admired Kemmerer's principles, regretted their neglect, and hoped to reinstate them as soon as possible. At the same time they came to believe that any future reconstruction of monetary stability would require more state intervention and more insulation from external forces than in the past.[239]

Exchange controls, protective tariffs, and credit allocations from the government and the central bank for industrialization keynoted a new era of state capitalism from the 1930s through the 1950s.[240] As elsewhere in the Andes, the central bank in Chile increasingly became a subordinate partner in government policies. It served as a source of developmental credits for the state and the private sector at least as much as a regulator of currency and exchange. The bank now tried to design its monetary policies mainly to preserve the internal purchasing power of the peso, not merely to adjust to oscillations in the balance of payments. As the bank and the government cooperated to strike a balance between growth and stability, recovery and virtually full employment solidified by 1934–35. Inflation slowed down after the explosion in 1932, but there was no return to the monetary and price levels of the Kemmerer years.[241] The circulating medium more than doubled from 1933 to 1940. During 1931–41 the index of prices rose almost 100 percent in Chile, 14 percent in Peru, 45 percent in Colombia, and 690 percent in Bolivia.[242] As agriculturalists, industrialists, workers, and all social groups looked to the public sector for credit and relief, inflation again became a permanent, structural feature of Chile's political economy.

Throughout the ensuing decades, Kemmerer's institutions—fiscal as well as financial—endured. The role of the central government, urban capitalism, and foreign, mainly U.S. economic forces also continued growing. Over time, leftist reformers came to blame chronic inflation on inadequate supply. They lashed out at monopolistic domestic and foreign elites for diverting income to themselves through currency depreciation, or for freezing that inequitable distribution through harsh stabilization measures. Rightist groups, by contrast, blamed endemic inflation on excessive demand. They criticized the workers and reformist governments for trying to extract exaggerated benefits from an economy of scarcity. In large part inflation persisted from the 1930s through the 1960s because all socioeconomic sectors came to have a vested interest in government subsidies; consequently, perennial, albeit unequal, increases for all groups became an imbedded feature of political bargaining.

In 1970–73 the massive redistributive programs of the socialist government of Popular Unity spurred triple-digit inflation. In response, the second major military regime in Chile's twentieth-century history marched into power—not unlike the soldiers of the 1920s—partly to halt runaway inflation. This time, however, the workers and leftists were seen as *papeleros*, the armed forces and rightists as *oreros*. The military clamped down on the working class and opened the door to U.S. banks. Chile's dictatorship in the 1970s and 1980s tried to resurrect the essential monetary, central banking, and foreign borrowing policies which had reigned prior to the Great Depression. Some central bank officials claimed they were returning to the fundamentals of the Kemmerer system.[243]

Chile had gone overboard with paper money prior to 1925, with the gold standard in 1926–31, and with inflation in 1971–73. In the latter half of the 1970s it again engaged in monetary extremism. The new military rulers converted the country into an extraordinary showcase of neocapitalist, conservative, monetarist theories, once again imported from U.S. economists. And, once more, that free-market model of debt-led growth resulted in temporary prosperity followed by a great crash. As in the thirties, the depression of the early eighties ignited protests against the dictatorship and its economic ideology.

4 REVOLUTION AND REGIONALISM IN ECUADOR, 1925–1933

In his 1926–27 Ecuadorean mission Edwin W. Kemmerer found power held by young military officers and a technocratic president similar to their counterparts in Chile. In both cases the governments were dedicated to sweeping modernization of their nations' financial and fiscal structures. The Ecuadorean rulers believed that Kemmerer's reforms could also help them reaffirm the supremacy of the central government in highland Quito over the banking and commercial bourgeoisie of the port of Guayaquil. Thereby they hoped the entire nation, not just the coastal elites, might catch up with more advanced Western economies. The so-called "July Revolution" entangled the Money Doctor in domestic political intrigue. The revolutionaries used his recommendations to further the ambitions of emergent socioeconomic sectors. Thus his Ecuadorean expedition had more impact on evolving domestic structures than on the external economic relations of a country more isolated and impoverished than either Colombia or Chile.

Foreign Factors in Ecuadorean Economic Development

Kemmerer discovered a poorly articulated export economy wherein the primary commodity had plunged into decline. The sharp falloff in foreign trade in 1925–26 lent special urgency to his mission (see table 4.1). In 1926, a typical year, manufactured goods accounted for over 70 percent of imports but only 12 percent of exports (mainly Panama hats). Conversely, food and drink products comprised only 19 percent of imports but 63 percent (mainly cacao, coffee, and ivory nuts) of exports. Although less monocultural than Colombia, Chile, or Bolivia, Ecuador remained an exporter of primary materials (nearly 90 percent of total exports) and an importer of processed items (over 80 percent of imports).[1]

Since official statistics only showed commercial transactions in goods, the enormously favorable balance of trade proved deceptive. Capital outflows, re-

Table 4.1   Ecuadorean Trade, 1914–1934 (in rounded-off millions of dollars)

Year	Imports	Exports
1914	8	12
1915	8	12
1916	8	16
1917	8	12
1918	6	9
1919	11	20
1920	18	20
1921	7	9
1922	8	11
1923	8	8
1924	11	12
1925	13	16
1926	9	12
1927	12	14
1928	17	15
1929	17	13
1930	13	11
1931	9	7
1932	6	5
1933	5	4
1934	8	9

Sources: Luis Alberto Carbó, *Historia monetaria y cambiaria del Ecuador desde la época colonial* (Quito, 1953), pp. 447–48; Eduardo Larrea S., *Ensayo sobre la moneda* (Quito, 1933), pp. 297–98; Ecuador, Ministerio de Hacienda, *Intercambio comercial del Ecuador* (Quito, 1926, 1927); Ecuador, Dirección General de Estadística, *Comercio exterior de la república del Ecuador en la década 1916 a 1925* (Quito, 1927).

mittances by foreign corporations and export-import firms, smuggling, and payments abroad for transportation, insurance, and other "invisible" costs normally exceeded the excess from exports. Therefore, gold and hard currency had to be paid out to cover the difference. The few Ecuadoreans who realized this precarious situation feared that their fragile foreign sector could not sustain a gold-exchange standard.[2]

Ecuador's leading economic thinker in the 1920s, Víctor Emilio Estrada, a Guayaquil banker, warned that this negative balance of payments was likely to continue and get worse. Anticipating later arguments by the United Nations' Economic Commission for Latin America, Estrada saw the deteriorating terms of trade as Ecuador's fundamental problem. He blamed the rising cost of imports in terms of exports on spiraling wages for labor in the industrial nations. From World War I through the mid-twenties the prices for Ecuador's raw material exports were rising more slowly than those for its manufactured imports, and Estrada worried that the gold standard would only further place his country at the mercy of an unequal international exchange system. Those dangers were compounded, in his view, as Ecuador's principal export, cacao, fell on hard times.[3]

The decline of cacao awakened many Ecuadoreans to the perils of monocultural dependence. At the start of the 1920s, "witches'-broom" disease swept through the plantations. It devastated production at the same time as world prices for the commodity slumped. New Brazilian and African output also undercut Ecuadorean sales. It became a classic example of a Latin American export bonanza gone bust. After rising from 60 percent of the total value of all exports in 1910 to 71 percent in 1920, cacao fell to 42 percent in 1926. Compared to 1925, the value of cacao exports was down 22 percent when Kemmerer arrived in 1926.[4] By 1929 Ecuador exported only one-third as much cacao as it had in 1914.[5]

Most of these exports went to the United States, as Ecuador's trading patterns became less diversified. Even before World War I the United States had supplanted England and France as Ecuador's primary trading partner. That supremacy soared during World War I and resisted challenges thereafter (see table 4.2).

These trading linkages tied Ecuador closely to the United States and made advisers from there more attractive. U.S. trade with Ecuador multiplied because of general economic growth in Latin America, the opening of the Panama Canal, World War I, and the decline of Europe. That commerce was also boosted when U.S. experts helped to eradicate yellow fever in Guayaquil and assisted in building the vital railroad link from there to Quito. Now both countries hoped that financial stabilization under U.S. guidance would further expand trade.[6]

Just as Ecuador's external commerce was not as robust as that of Colombia or Chile, so did external capital play a minor role. In the mid-1920s direct foreign investments remained small. The only noteworthy foreign enterprises operating in Ecuador were British and U.S. petroleum companies, U.S. gold and silver mines, a few British and U.S. urban public transportation and utilities ventures, export-import houses, and a handful of mixed industries. The value of total U.S. investments in Ecuador rose from approximately $10 million in 1913, to $20 million in 1920, to $25 million by 1928. Those small amounts left existing foreign capital and ownership insignificant issues, despite some resent-

Table 4.2   Ecuadorean Total Trade with Its Four Leading Partners, 1913–1926
(by percentage)

Year	Ecuadorean imports from			
	United States	Great Britain	Germany	France
1913	31	29	18	5
1919	71	23	2	—
1920	58	26	9	—
1921	39	24	9	—
1922	47	24	14	—
1923	41	25	15	5
1924	40	25	12	4
1925	45	22	10	4
1926	43	21	11	—
	Ecuadorean exports to			
1913	24	10	17	34
1919	49	6	2	21
1920	56	18	4	4
1921	32	3	29	9
1922	39	7	13	9
1923	45	8	7	9
1924	31	8	13	9
1925	42	6	11	9
1926	39	5	6	9

Sources: See note 6.

ments. In 1926–27 most Ecuadorean leaders worried about how to attract, not control, foreign capital.[7]

Ecuador's foreign debt was correspondingly tiny. Existing obligations stemmed from the war for independence and from railroad construction. Those debts rested mainly in British and, to a lesser extent, French and U.S. hands. Repeated defaults and disputes on payments rendered Ecuador a very unattractive borrower in foreign eyes. In rounded-off figures, the total external debt increased due to arrears of interest from 31 million sucres in 1914 to 39 million ($19 million) in 1925. Meanwhile, the internal public debt had ballooned from 15 million to 49 million sucres, mainly owed to domestic commercial banks.[8]

Many Ecuadoreans hoped that Kemmerer's financial reorganization would improve their creditworthiness. They desired foreign capital to pay off past obligations, to expand transportation among poorly connected regions, and to accelerate exploitation of natural resources. In contrast to the other Andean countries, however, Ecuador did not receive any rush of foreign loans as a result of Kemmerer's reforms, partly because that nation's economy stayed in the doldrums.[9]

Ecuadorean Domestic Economic Problems

Regionalism defined the Ecuadorean economy. Agriculture for export dominated the coast (costa)—the engine of the economy—and agriculture for domestic consumption the highland interior (sierra). The coastal zone produced over 90 percent of Ecuador's exports, which paid for the imports consumed there and in the interior. The sierra bought more from the costa than it sold there. The citizens of Quito (Quiteños) complained about their shortage of currency and credit and their dependence on banks in the port. Over 70 percent of all exports and over 90 percent of all imports flowed through the city of Guayaquil alone. By the eve of Kemmerer's visit that export percentage was down from earlier years, thanks to the slump in cacao. As the coast's sales abroad dipped, so did its food and textile purchases from the highlands. Consequently, declining foreign trade ushered in a severe recession and unemployment throughout Ecuador prior to Kemmerer's arrival.[10]

Many coastal and highland agriculturalists, not unlike their counterparts elsewhere in the Andes, averred that their greatest problem was the scarcity of money and credit. They denounced the banks for maintaining high interest rates (at least 12 percent) and apportioning most of their loans to merchants and to the government. Heavily indebted, desperately in need of diversification and modernization, bereft of adequate transportation, and angry at government neglect, many costeño and serrano agriculturalists expected the Kemmerer mission to give them special attention.

Some of the most outspoken landowners, however, preferred expansion of the money supply in accord with domestic production needs rather than establishment of the gold standard to adhere to international trade fluctuations. These inflationary policies proved especially attractive to coastal farmers. They needed cheap credit to convert to crops other than cacao, and they received hard foreign currencies for their exports. Other rural elites, especially in the sierra, clamored for monetary stabilization. The National Society of Agriculturalists in Quito called in 1926 for monetary convertibility in gold, accompanied by balanced government budgets and more productive allocation of bank credits. The president of the society, N. Clemente Ponce, urged the distrusted government to leave the solution of the problem of agricultural credit up to Kemmerer.[11]

The few industrialists—themselves often landowners as well—also demanded expanded long-term credit availability. Mainly consisting of highland textile mills, manufacturing received some protection from exchange controls and tariffs during 1921–25, especially under the July Revolutionaries. This government assistance responded to foreign exchange shortages occasioned by the decline in cacao. Some Ecuadoreans, however, opposed protection for national industry. These critics complained that most of the factories relied heavily on imported ingredients. For that reason many manufacturers advocated currency stabilization, higher tariffs on competitive imports, and lower domestic taxes. Industrialists also became willing to give up the natural protection afforded by currency depreciation because they hoped that Kemmerer would cap the rising cost of living. They believed that stabilization would reduce their costs and dampen working-class discontent. No concentrated industrialization policy emerged until the 1930s, however. When Kemmerer arrived, manufacturing remained a frail sector with scant influence on national financial policies.[12]

Merchants, especially in the import business, spearheaded demands for an end to monetary depreciation. As U.S. export-import agencies multiplied along with trade with the United States in the early 1920s, this Ecuadorean commercial sector acquired a natural interest in monetary and financial reform modeled after and designed by the United States. These merchants also increasingly allied themselves with the importing interests in the *sierra*, as opposed to the exporting interests in the *costa*.[13]

The villain blamed for Ecuador's financial woes was the banking community centered in Guayaquil. The most powerful banks grew up in the latter half of the nineteenth century and early years of the twentieth. Their financing came from the wealth accumulated by the cacao growers and the merchants of Guayaquil. By 1925 there were six domestic commercial banks and five minor credit institutions.[14] The only foreign operation was the small Anglo South American Bank, which later expired during the depression. Ecuador, Bolivia, and Paraguay remained the only South American countries devoid of U.S. banks by the end of the 1920s. Kemmerer's legislation in Ecuador inspired no more an influx of foreign bankers than it did of loans.[15] Despite their insignificant presence, foreign bankers and merchant financiers evoked denunciations by Ecuadoreans for speculating on exchange rates, absorbing capital, avoiding taxes, and undercutting national competitors.[16]

In the years preceding Kemmerer's arrival, vehement protests erupted against the domestic banks' management of the supply of credit and money. In the nineteenth century the government authorized private banks to emit currency. Their profits from doing so and their mounting loans to the government led these banks of emission to spew forth increasing amounts of currency with little legal or gold backing. Their spiraling emissions responded to demands for more cash and credit as the growth of Ecuadorean capitalism and concomitant government activities strained the archaic monetary and banking system. The government reacted in 1914 with the Moratorium Law of Inconvertibility, which prohibited the export of gold or its exchange for paper money. This legislation also opened the door to further currency and credit extensions from the banks to the government.

As sucres depreciated in value, however, the banks and the government received the blame for the paucity of sound money and credit and for the mushrooming cost of living. By the mid-twenties Ecuadorean elites came to agree that the only cure for their inadequate supply of stable money was a gold standard sustained by a central bank of issue. The draconian attacks on the financial sector by the July Revolutionaries further shrank the availability of reliable cash and credit. Consequently, Ecuadorean private-sector leaders looked to the Kemmerer mission to furnish them with a healthy monetary system.[17]

Prior to Kemmerer's visit critics accused the government of allowing such cheap currency emissions because of its snowballing indebtedness to the banks. Successive administrations incurred those obligations to cover deficits, which rose along with state employment. Whereas other Andean governments rolled up foreign debts to underwrite new jobs and public works for the expanding urban middle class, Ecuadorean administrations turned to local bankers, especially as export revenues dwindled. Thus governments in Quito became dependent on domestic banks to keep them afloat by inflating the money supply. The private sector complained that this vicious circle debased the currency and left producers starved for reliable cash and credit. The spokesman of the 1925 July Revolution, Luis Napoleon Dillon (president of Quito's chamber of commerce), excoriated "inept, immoral governments, that were always on their knees before the clay idols of the port city bankocracy."[18]

As the U.S. embassy observed in 1926, "practically all banking institutions of Ecuador have been in the past and are still in favor of a policy of inflation."[19] It was risky to generalize, however, about the fiercely competitive banks. Those not involved in excessive emissions hoped Kemmerer would stabilize the currency to reduce economic uncertainties and ensure that debts were repaid at full value.[20]

The leading source of currency and controversy was the powerful Banco Comercial y Agrícola of Guayaquil, which accounted for 50 percent of the circulating medium by 1925. Its emissions exceeded the legal limit of double its gold reserve.[21] It also served as the largest creditor for the government, which allowed the bank to issue additional currency in return for those loans. Public opinion, stoked by populist reformers, came to believe that a wicked conspiracy between the Banco Comercial y Agrícola, cacao growers (represented by the

Association of Agriculturalists), and government officials underlay the economic crisis. Dillon and others chastised the bank for uninhibited and unbacked currency emissions, credit abuses, exchange speculation, and political manipulation.[22] These critics deplored the falling value of the sucre, which they blamed for the rising cost of living (see table 4.3).

Highland agriculturalists, salaried bureaucrats, military officers, and urban workers especially protested against rising prices. The Association of Employees, for example, complained about government paychecks falling behind the skyrocketing cost of basic necessities. In 1922 in Guayaquil, riots against soaring prices had to be quashed by the army. As in Chile, monetary reform came to be seen partly as a response to working-class discontent, even though the Ecuadorean proletariat remained very small and unorganized.[23]

Severe disagreements arose over the causes and cures of this monetary malaise. The most vociferous critics blamed monetary depreciation and price inflation on excessive emissions of paper money and easy credit by greedy banks. Allegedly, coastal agro-exporters and financiers purposely debased the currency to compensate themselves for sagging cacao sales at the expense of import merchants, highland landowners, and the middle and working classes. Those charges weakened confidence in the sucre and drove its value down further. Other experts claimed, to the contrary, that the money supply was inadequate, as evidenced by usurious interest rates. They said that the key problem was not excessive emissions but rather the misuse of currency and credit by the government, which ran up inflationary deficits for unproductive purposes. Another common theory pointed to low productivity and exports, charging that escalating domestic demand and imports fueled price inflation. Others blamed exchange speculation, capital flight, rising wages and taxes, and burdensome import duties. Whoever the culprit, most commentators by the mid-twenties recommended a gold-exchange standard managed by a central bank of issue as the minimal solution.[24]

Ecuadoreans still worried that any such attempt at monetary stabilization would be sabotaged by government expenditures and deficits (see table 4.4). Up to 1926 those mounting deficits were caused mainly by falling trade, since customs duties constituted the primary source of government income. Unbalanced budgets also resulted from inflation, inadequate domestic taxation, fiscal mismanagement, and rising expenditures to mollify emergent capitalists and urban groups. Currency depreciation eroded the real value of government revenues. For example, the intake from fixed import duties in dollars fell from $4 million in 1913 to $2 million in 1923.[25] Small internal taxes on consumption generated few revenues and left large properties and incomes unscathed. The state farmed out these tax collections, as well as its monopolies on tobacco,

Table 4.3   Ecuadorean Exchange and Prices, 1914–1935

Years	Sucres to the U.S. dollar	Index of prices
1913		100
1914	2.10	100
1915	2.16	130
1916	2.27	170
1917	2.44	204
1918	2.35	238
1919	2.11	214
1920	2.38	192
1921	4.14	194
1922	4.55	215
1923	4.00	208
1924	5.41	242
1925	4.41	245
1926	4.69	309
1927	5.00	300
1928	5.02	248
1929	5.06	—
1930	5.05	—
1931	5.06	216
1932	6.00	—
1933	6.00	—
1934	12.00	—
1935	10.50	—

Note: This partial price index measures domestically produced and consumed commodities.

Sources: Eduardo Ríofrío Villagomez, *Manual de ciencia de hacienda*, 2 vols. (Quito, 1936, 1938), 1:62–65; Ríofrío, "El problema monetario y el problema fiscal en el Ecuador," *Anales de la Universidad Central* 37, no. 257 (July–September 1926): 138–58; Ríofrío, "La circulación, los precios y el cambio en el Ecuador de 1913 a 1927," *Anales de la Universidad Central* 39, no. 261 (July–September 1927): 94–124; Eduardo Larrea S., *Ensayo sobre la moneda* (Quito, 1933), pp. 294–96; Luis E. Laso, *Contribución al estudio de la economía política ecuatoriana* (Quito, 1930), pp. 13–15; United Nations, *Public Debt, 1914–1946* (Lake Success, 1948), p. 56.

alcohol, and explosives, to private concessionaires (often banks), who delivered small returns to the government. No rigorous budgeting process existed. Instead, both the executive and legislative branches purposely and consistently overestimated inputs and underestimated outputs. This legerdemain permitted excessive payoffs to their provincial and personal clienteles. For example, rather than calculate a realistic new schedule of revenues and expenditures, the government simply maintained the 1920 budget for five years.[26]

Government outlays increased dramatically to cope with mounting capitalist complexities and social articulation. The state expanded the bureaucracy, raised payments to the military, and launched poorly planned public works to satisfy regional demands and occupy workers. Public employees hoped that Kemmerer's fiscal reforms would raise additional revenues for their salaries.[27] Covering the resulting deficits with loans from the Guayaquil banks, the growing government tripled its internal public debt from 1914 through 1925. Thereafter the government wanted to get out from under the high annual service payments on that domestic debt and the political sway of the bankers. Accordingly, it hoped Kemmerer could improve its internal taxing and external borrowing capacity.[28]

Table 4.4   Ecuadorean Government Revenues and Expenditures, 1920–1931 (in rounded-off millions of sucres)

Years	Revenues	Expenditures
1920	21	23
1921	21	21
1922	25	27
1923	25	29
1924	30	35
1925	39	44
1926	45	39
1927	75	72
1928	75	71
1929	64	63
1930	61	60
1931	45	45

Sources: Ríofrío, *Manual,* 1:52, 71–74; Carlos Rolando, *Obras públicas ecuatorianas* (Guayaquil, 1930), p. 343; Ecuador, Dirección del Tesoro, *Informe de la Dirección del Tesoro* (Quito, 1931), pp. 10–11.

The July Revolution

Twelve years of unusual political stability under civilian elites—dominated by Liberals from their power base on the coast—ended with the coup d'etat of July 1925. Highland landowners and salary and wage earners throughout Ecuador supported that uprising, in which younger military officers overthrew an ailing president loyal to the coastal agro-exporters and bankers. That revolt against the "bankocracy" of Guayaquil and its political allies launched the twentieth-century technocratic modernization of the national economy under state auspices. To carry out those transformations the revolutionaries contracted the Kemmerer mission.[29]

Economic grievances and regionalism underlay the July Revolution. The rebels blamed "the plutocratic oligarchy" clustered around the Guayaquil banks for the depreciation of the sucre, the rising cost of living, the scarcity of foreign exchange, and the fiscal penury, indebtedness, and disorder. Export prosperity at the end of the nineteenth century had elevated the economic and political power of the coastal elites, but then the decline of cacao sapped their strength, rendering them vulnerable to retribution by the *serranos*. Now the *Quiteños* captured control, through the national government, of money, banking, credit, taxes, customs, and public works—all previously very decentralized or monopolized by the *costeños*.[30] Discontent with the corrupt and ineffective political system also motivated the *Revolución Juliana*. The rebels wanted a more powerful and efficient central government, and they expected it to collect taxes, build public works, and design all economic policies with national, not regional or partisan, objectives in mind.[31]

Because the Liberals centered in Guayaquil had dominated since 1895, the Conservatives, rooted among highland landowners and proclericals, hoped the July Revolution would favor them. They expressed disappointment when the rebels declared that the Liberals had not been liberal enough. After the junta took office, the ousted Liberals were divided in their attitudes toward its policies, whereas the excluded Conservatives mounted implacable opposition.[32]

The military, backed by left-wing Liberals, captained the bloodless revolution. An army faction, known as the Military League and concentrated among younger, middle-class officers in Quito, had absorbed the antibanker propaganda of Dillon and other reformers. They believed that the financial claque in Guayaquil bore responsibility for the economic crisis and their own deteriorating standard of living and preparedness. The armed forces were also demoralized because corrupt politicians used them to steal elections and prop up unpopular and ineffective governments. Beginning in 1922, an Italian training mission, along with some education abroad, had helped convince many of these soldiers that Ecuador needed a more technically modern, professional, and scientific army as well as government. They also admired the concurrent seizure of power by officers in Chile.[33]

The coup was initially greeted warmly in nearly all circles. The middle and working classes in Guayaquil and elsewhere embraced the military takeover. The League of Students at the Universidad Central, the Workers' Confederation of Guayas, the fledgling Socialist party, and other white-collar and blue-collar groups publicly backed the revolution, hailing the promise of stable money and new labor laws. In turn, employers hoped that these financial reforms would curb labor's unrest and flirtation with socialism. Even Guayaquil banker Estrada broke ranks with his brethren and initially wired support for the junta and its program.[34]

In their declarations and first months in office, the rebels emphasized modernization of the state and of the money and banking sector. Their fiscal and financial reforms prefigured almost all the recommendations of Kemmerer.[35] To professionalize and energize an activist government the July Revolutionaries decreed a scientific budget law to eliminate waste and deficits. They swiftly centralized and systematized state collection and disbursement of public monies. They cashiered many provincial tax collectors, contractors for government monopolies, and other public servants. They also introduced strict national accounting procedures. To further ensure balanced budgets the junta tried to reduce reliance on customs duties and domestic bank loans by raising internal taxes on the wealthy. Higher levies on long-undervalued rural properties, on inheritances and gifts, and on municipal and stamp taxes provoked outcries from the Ecuadorean upper class. The rebels also tried to consolidate and begin paying off the government's domestic and foreign debts, so as to burnish its external credit rating. They used their new revenues to hike the salaries of the armed forces and the bureaucracy. They also planned to launch a fresh program of national public works—especially railroads and highways—to replace the scattered local projects designed to serve petty provincial and political desires. The July Revolutionaries expected Kemmerer to perfect their rapid fiscal innovations, whereas their opponents hoped he would tone them down.[36]

The heart of the rebels' economic program was the reconstruction of money and banking institutions. In its first act the mixed military-civilian junta arrested the president of the Banco Comercial y Agrícola: "We attended to the collapse of the oligarchic banking policy, personified by the one who was accustomed to making the chief of the Ecuadorian State his stock-broker," boasted the minister of the interior.[37] While closing that bank, the revolutionaries also temporarily shut down three others in Guayaquil. Leading the charge, Finance Minister Dillon denounced the commercial banks as "the criminal exploiters which had ruined the nation." In the first week of the July Revolution he created a fiscalizing commission to review all government and banking accounts; although concentrating on an investigation of the Banco Comercial y Agrícola, that commission also undertook the first thorough inspection of banks in Ecuadorean history, thus setting the stage for Kemmerer's banking superintendency. While lashing the banks rhetorically, the junta imposed fines for currency outputs beyond legal limits. It also refused to pay interest on some of the government's debts to those *costeño* institutions.[38]

After bringing to heel the private banks, the junta tried to reassign many of their functions to a central bank modeled after the systems Kemmerer had installed in Colombia and Chile. The rebels intended the new institution to reorganize and manage all public funds and indebtedness, to emit and stabilize all currency on a convertible gold-exchange standard, and to expand credit availability by lowering interest rates to 8 percent. They expected to acquire the bank's assets mainly from enforced gold subscriptions by the private banks.

Following the junta's announcement of its most ambitious project, in October 1925 the banks and coastal regionalists mobilized opposition. They denounced the government's enlargement of the public payroll, attacks on commercial banks, and incitement of regional animosities. Those deeds had prompted a currency and credit shortage, a run on the banks, a deepening recession, and a swelling tide of resistance. The officials of the army retaliated against opponents with a declaration that "by the blade of the sword and over the heads of everyone the Central Bank will be made." When few people rallied to support the initiative, however, the junta backed off. To calm the frightened public, the fiery Dillon left the government. He complained that Ecuadoreans should have taken pride in these financial reforms by their fellow citizens instead of placing more confidence in the upcoming Kemmerer mission, and he lambasted that preference for foreigners as "patriotism in reverse."[39]

A second junta, less committed to radical confrontations with the banks, took over in January of 1926. This more moderate government tried to win the bankers over to the central bank project through a blend of cooptation and coercion. The new minister of finance disarmed the opposition by calling a conference of bankers during February and March of 1926. He appealed to the bankers' desire for central bank credits and for repayment of their government loans, to their patriotism during an economic crisis, and to their fear of more radical proposals from Dillon, the public, the government, and the military. Most of the bankers reluctantly endorsed the concept of a central bank. The conference foundered, however, on the issues of the transfer of and reimbursement for the private banks' gold reserves to fund the proposed institution, the establishment of the new exchange value for the currency, the solution for the apparent scarcity of currency and credit, the participation of the government in the central bank, the repayment of the government's domestic debts, and the control of government profligacy. Even more vexing was the debate over whether the new bank should install its main office in Quito or Guayaquil. Neverthe-less, the bankers did agree, as a first step, to the creation of the Central Office of Issue and Redemption (Caja Central de Emisión y Amortización), which imme-diately began negotiating the transfer of private-bank gold reserves to a central depository. It also started unifying and controlling the currency, encouraging its convertibility. To begin seeking foreign loans, it set about consolidating and clearing up the government's debt to the domestic banks. All these measures helped lay the foundation for a central bank.[40]

As a result, most of Kemmerer's work had already been accomplished be-fore his arrival. Nevertheless, everyone looked to the Money Doctor to resolve the remaining issues and consummate the crusade for a central bank. In particular the private bankers placed more trust in him than in the revolutionary govern-ment. To shore up public confidence in the administration and its reforms, the second junta named a civilian provisional president, Isidro Ayora, in April 1926, who would take office in March and bring in the Kemmerer mission.

Throughout the July Revolution's first year it had aroused fervent opposi-tion as well as support. Naturally, most of the Guayaquil banks—as well as some in Quito—resisted the first and second juntas. Many also remained unre-conciled to the Ayora presidency. These bankers berated the revolutionaries for economic incompetence, fiscal mismanagement, socialist intervention, and re-gionalistic vindictiveness. They saw the scaling down of government debt pay-ments and the transfer of their gold reserves as extortion. Above all, the bankers tried to broaden their base of support by appealing to provincial resentments against Quito.

Some other coastal residents became convinced that the juntas were siphon-ing resources to the highlands by expanding the central government, inflating salaries for public employees, building public works in the mountains, and strengthening *sierra* banks at the expense of *costeño* competitors. They called instead for junta assistance with the coast's export malaise. A few *Guayaquileños* even formed a civic guard and plotted to overthrow the revolutionaries, accusing them—especially Dillon—of bolshevism. These dissidents attracted support from politicians, primarily Conservatives, desiring a return to constitutional government.

Even the banks, however, were not solidly opposed to the July Revolution. Although appalled by the juntas' antibanker rhetoric, attacks, and projects, many of the smaller banks in Guayaquil and those in Quito concurred with some of the criticisms directed against the large banks of emission. They also shared many of the juntas' objectives, such as a central bank of banks, a stable curren-cy, and a rationalized fiscal system. Therefore most bankers came to endorse these reforms during the bankers' conference and the subsequent Kemmerer mission. Moreover, the recalcitrant bankers never succeeded in rallying wide-spread opposition to the juntas. From the beginning many workers and other revolutionary sympathizers in Guayaquil denounced the bankers' regionalistic ploy and called for national unity behind the reformist governments. Indeed, most *Guayaquileños*, like most Ecuadoreans, were neither separatist nor ada-mantly opposed to the July Revolution and its program.[41]

Nevertheless, Ayora still had to defuse significant hostility in 1926 from a powerful minority of bankers and *costeños*. His own credentials reassured critics of the July Revolutionaries. A middle-class Quito physician and former rector of the Universidad Central, Ayora formally belonged to no party. He could thus claim to be devising intellectual, rational solutions above petty politics. Like his counterparts elsewhere in the Andes, he projected the image of a new, modern type of president, a twentieth-century man of science committed to technology and expertise. In his view remaining resistance to the government and its eco-nomic reforms could be overcome by a team of foreign specialists because of their universally recognized "neutrality and competence." Coastal elites looked upon Ayora as closer to the moderate mainstream of liberalism, which they had long supported. The July Revolutionaries applauded his continued, albeit less zealous pursuit of their goals.

By clearly isolating the proclerical Conservatives and the Banco Comercial y Agrícola as his enemies, Ayora broadened the government's base of support for fundamental financial reforms. He also dealt harshly with unrepentant Guayaquil banks, ordering five of them closed temporarily and some of their officers arrested. This broke their resistance, discredited regional protests as a ruse by the bankers, and curtailed the distribution of bad money. Thus an authoritarian regime was cowing its opposition and consolidating its hold when Kemmerer arrived. His visit helped authenticate the government's tenure and push through its program.[42]

The Kemmerer Mission

In sum, most Ecuadoreans looked forward to Kemmerer's arrival, as one newspaper put it, "like the Israelites awaited impatiently the clear principles of their Moses." They exhibited, however, mixed motives for welcoming his mis-sion. The proponents of the July Revolution—especially Dillon and the army—expected Kemmerer to remedy the nation's economic ills, particularly the flaws in the money and banking system. *Quiteño* partisans hoped that Kemmerer's fortification of the central government and its control over national financial affairs would strengthen their position vis-à-vis their rivals in Guayaquil. The shaky Ayora administration envisioned Kemmerer's visit as a legitimating mechanism both domestically and internationally. It could justify the prolongation of authoritarianism until his reforms were fully carried out, help persuade the U.S. State Department to stop withholding recognition from an unconstitutional regime, and attract foreign loans.

The government's opponents, especially the bankers, shared the hope that Kemmerer's certification would unleash foreign investments. But they wanted him to encourage government austerity rather than expansion. Since the military insisted on completion of the financial reforms before any return to constitutional civilian rule, party leaders and the U.S. embassy counted on Kemmerer to hasten that process. Conservatives, bankers, and *costeños* at least preferred whatever Kemmerer recommended to the lightning strokes of the juntas. Businessmen urged workers to have faith in Kemmerer, rather than socialism, to solve their economic problems. These elites warned laborers to cease agitation so as not to upset his reforms or foreign investors. Finally, U.S. government and business representatives thought that the mission would improve Ecuadorean political stability and economic growth, thus making the country more fertile ground for U.S. trade and investments.[43]

Actually, the idea of solving Ecuador's problems through hiring a U.S. savant was scarcely new. In 1922 U.S. government officials, bankers, and railroad managers had urged Ecuador to hire a North American financial adviser to revamp its monetary and fiscal systems, hoping the country would redeem its outstanding debts and thus become attractive to foreign lenders. The Ecuadorean government followed that advice in 1923 by hiring John Hord, who boasted previous experience in financial sanitation in the Philippines, Puerto Rico, Mexico, Cuba, and Haiti. Those connections aroused some fears of "American imperialism" and some calls for contracting a European expert instead. Despite such doubts, Ecuadoreans generally expressed satisfaction with Hord's appointment.

Nevertheless, the U.S. embassy realized that most officials of the government of President José Luis Tamayo (1920–24):

> did not want a financial adviser, but they felt the great need of obtaining a loan, and no loan could be obtained except from or with the consent of various interests in the United States. Those concerned had made it clear that before a loan could be granted many financial reforms must be instituted and amongst other things Ecuador must obtain the services of a reliable financial adviser. No doubt President Tamayo never intended carrying out the necessary reforms, but he felt that if he presented a bold front and hired a financial adviser the loan might be forthcoming, hence Mr. Hord was engaged at a salary which, with the rates of exchange which have since obtained, amounts to

more than twice as much as the regular salary of the President combined with all the perquisites which pertain to his office.

Under those conditions Hord encountered constant frustrations in his reform efforts. He did get legislation passed for a sales tax and for centralization of some revenues, but Congress drastically transformed his budgets. He proved no more successful at stabilizing the currency. Although newspapers called for cancellation of his contract in 1925, the July Revolutionaries initially enlisted Hord in their campaign to reorganize banking practices. As part of the clean sweep of the past, however, Dillon fired Hord. Thus Kemmerer was not the first U.S. expert taken on by the Ecuadorean government for ulterior motives.[44]

Nor was Kemmerer's visit the brainchild of the July Revolutionaries. When Hord's appointment had failed to elicit foreign loans, the Tamayo government had had its ambassador approach Kemmerer in 1924 concerning a possible mission for 1925. A month before the July Revolution, Víctor Emilio Estrada, who had admired Kemmerer's writings and accomplishments since 1923, had convinced the coast's leading merchants and bankers (including the Banco Comercial y Agrícola) that the Kemmerer mission to Chile should also be invited to stabilize and regularize the money of Ecuador. Impressed by his achievements in Colombia and South Africa, those *Guayaquileños* had urged the government to bring in Kemmerer. They even offered to help pay for the mission. Thus any interpretation of the call to Kemmerer as a blow by Quito against the coastal plutocracy should not be overdrawn.

Immediately after the July Revolution the first junta had issued an invitation to Kemmerer through the Ecuadorean embassy in Washington. According to the U.S. ambassador in Quito, "the Provisional Government, in extending an invitation to Professor Kemmerer, has taken the only possible means to escape from an almost impossible position which it had created in attempting to overcome the opposition of the banking and commercial interests by the use of force." Knowing the high regard in which the financial elites held Kemmerer, the revolutionaries wanted him to act as an "arbitrator between the Junta . . . and the bankers of Guayaquil." Kemmerer simultaneously received an identical inquiry from the Bolivian embassy. He delayed both those offers because he was already committed to a similar venture in Poland.

Then the second junta, increasingly buffeted by domestic opposition, urged the State Department in 1926 to convince Kemmerer to come to Ecuador immediately. The U.S. embassy in Quito cabled the following support for that plea: "Most urgent that Kemmerer come to Ecuador at once even though he cannot remain. . . . His coming may save the country from political chaos and hasten return of constitutionality. . . . I recommend most earnestly the support of the Department in the matter for the sake of Ecuador and further beneficial relations." Kemmerer promised to visit as soon as he completed his Polish expedition, at a cost of $70,000 plus expenses for his mission. Announcing their support for this venture, Ecuadorean banks, especially in Quito, agreed to help the government pay those costs.[45]

Kemmerer's Ecuadorean team mixed government, private, and academic economists. Mainly drawn from his previous expeditions, they were all (except railway engineer B. B. Milner) slated to advise Bolivia thereafter as well. Howard M. Jefferson, from the Federal Reserve Bank of New York and Kemmerer's Chilean and Colombian missions, provided banking expertise. New York accountant Joseph T. Byrne, who had served in the Dominican Republic, Chile, and Peru as collector general of customs, took charge of fiscal and accounting questions. From the U.S. Tariff Commission in Washington, D.C., came Captain Robert Vorfeld; he had previously helped the U.S. government reorganize customs offices in the Dominican Republic and Paraguay, and would now do the same for Ecuador. Oliver C. Lockhart of the University of Buffalo came along as a tax expert. Edward Feely, for many years the U.S. commercial attaché in Argentina, enlisted as general secretary for the mission. Frank Whitson Fetter served as Kemmerer's secretary, as he had in Guatemala and Chile. As usual, they spent the weeks before the visit and the long journey en route studying the Ecuadorean language and conditions, since their knowledge of the country was nil. Also along the way, Kemmerer met with the president of Panama, who asked him to plan a similar future mission there, which came to naught.[46]

Upon its arrival in Guayaquil on October 18, 1926, the mission encountered an enthusiastic welcome from all segments of the Ecuadorean elite. The team was hailed by Conservatives as well as Liberals, partisans as well as opponents of the government, bankers as well as agriculturalists, and *Guayaquileños* as well as *Quiteños*. Despite sharp divisions along party, regional, and sectoral lines, there existed a general upper-class agreement on the need for more efficient state regulation and stimulation of the private economy.[47]

Ecuadorean elites also united in the ardent belief that Kemmerer's reforms and prestige would attract foreign capital. The day the mission landed in Guayaquil, newspapers in Quito reported—allegedly from sources in New York—that several Wall Street millionaires had suddenly decided to loan millions of dollars to Ecuador and Bolivia, simply because those countries had contracted Kemmerer.[48] One welcoming editorial described in fractured English the obstacles to foreign lenders that Kemmerer was expected to remove: "Beside the lacks of fiscal legislation and administration, we have suffered for the erroneous concepts they have abroad, of our Country, considering it uninhabitable, mistaken it with the Equinoctial Line and erroneously judging that their national population is a remainder of inculture: the mutual dependence of the white race countries, the universal corporation induced by the encouragement of interesting prospects, are an essential factor for the flourishing of the new Countries."[49]

Ecuadoreans believed that Kemmerer could work such wonders where domestic leaders could not because he represented an "indisputable moral authority." He enjoyed greater national and international respect due to his "scientific" credentials. Rather than being wary of foreign advisers, these commentators preferred them to domestic leaders, whom they scolded for seldom reaching agreement on technical or institutional solutions. Neopositivist enthusiasts argued that the "prestige" of foreigners "gives the stamp of the definitive, of the well-finished, of the relatively indisputable, in a way in which disdains everything, and everything is put under mature consideration."[50]

Kemmerer's supporters urged all public and private interests to refrain from interfering with or modifying his projects. They warned the mission members to beware of provincial partisans trying to capture their attention or bleed the national treasury for local boondoggles; economic pressure groups attempting to curry their favor; bureaucrats seeking to inflate the national budget and impede reforms; military officers demanding excessive shares of government outlays; zealous patriots attacking their recommendations as foreign impositions; and local economists and politicians introducing ill-advised revisions. They also cautioned against any confidence in notoriously inaccurate national statistics. Indeed, newspapers in Quito said they had so much faith in the technical skills of the mission, as opposed to the incompetence of the government, that they totally supported whatever Kemmerer recommended even without seeing the content. They only wanted to read the Kemmerer laws before their implementation, not to debate them, but to make sure that the government did not alter what the mission proposed.[51]

Kemmerer's ability to sustain such a broad national consensus behind his work was threatened by conflicts among sectoral and regional interest groups and by nationalistic hostility to foreign penetration. For example, a pamphlet prepared for Kemmerer by the Banco de Descuento de Guayaquil, entitled *Facts about Ecuador*, enraged *Quiteños* when it asserted that, "Guayaquil . . . is the seat of a sectional government whose ideas and suggestions are generally adopted by the central government." The mission members had to visit Guayaquil and several other provinces to avoid any hint of regional favoritism.[52]

Although anti-imperialist attacks on the mission were rare at the time, that perspective gained adherents in later years. The strongest nationalistic salvo against Kemmerer in 1927 came from José Peralta, an upper-class Liberal leader, formerly minister of foreign affairs and rector of the University of Cuenca. While echoing Colombian critiques stemming from cultural pride, Peralta also lashed out at the mission on the grounds of economic nationalism, drawing analogies from U.S. intervention in the Caribbean. He condemned U.S. "dollar imperialism," "like an octopus, like a colossal and insatiable vampire who sucks up to the last drop of blood from the people." He warned his fellow citizens that the United States now preferred financial over military means for conquering Latin America:

> And the sappers at the service of the *Dollar* are the *Financial Missions*, learned groups of confidence men which offer marvels and wonders to the ignorant multitudes; they are the *Experts* in banks and tariffs, the *Comptrollers* and *Technical Assessors* which the imbecilic and blind *yankeephiles* rent and pay splendidly in order to enslave their nation; they are the *Philanthropic Lenders* which deliver their millions to starving or thieving governments over the invaluable security of national independence; they are the *Contractors* of public works, the mining, agricultural, commercial, and industrial companies, implanted in the nation, which, according to the program of conquest, create those *American interests* that the White House has the *duty to protect* with force, subjugating the nation in which they have put down roots.

Peralta specifically complained that "the sappers of the conqueror are now within the house. Mr. Kemmerer always works *pro domo suo*—says a Colombian writer—and he will not have forgotten the interests of his homeland, the watchword of his government, the imperialist program of Coolidge, upon completing his obligations with Ecuador." Peralta worried about these foreigners learning so much about Ecuadorean public and private finances. He also sounded the alarm against excessive loans and investments from the United States, preferring small foreign indebtedness, ideally contracted in less belligerent European countries. Since Kemmerer suggested that his financial reforms would work best if supervised by North Americans and if accompanied by foreign loans, Peralta concluded that Kemmerer's proposals were "scientific-economic charlantry," unsuited to Ecuador. He felt that Ecuadoreans could have done a better job designing new laws and institutions for the nation, since Kemmerer's team knew so little about the country's history, customs, and structure. He was especially dismayed that these foreign experts were consulted on matters outside their supposed expertise, such as the new constitution and penal code. He was enraged that they were even asked about the possibility of selling the Galapagos Islands to the United States to raise funds for the government. Peralta concluded that the incompetent and traitorous dictatorship, by bowing down to foreign advisers, was making Ecuadoreans look like "a tribe of Hottentots."[53]

Although Peralta provided a lonely voice of dissent in the mid-1920s, nationalistic resentments against the mission mounted after its departure.[54] The Socialist Party of Ecuador, formed in 1926, criticized the Kemmerer commission in 1929 as a "group of servants of the bourgeoisie and of the government of the United States."[55] That view became the standard perspective of Ecuadorean Marxists. In later years they accused the mission of establishing a monetary value which helped U.S. exporters to Ecuador at the expense of Ecuadorean consumers, of lowering tariff barriers to the benefit of U.S. sales and the detriment of national producers, and of imposing U.S. advisers on the nation as though it were a direct colony.[56]

To guard against such nationalistic suspicions Kemmerer maintained his usual distance from U.S. government officials. The State Department urged Kemmerer to work with the U.S. embassy and even dispatched a special agent, Waldemar J. Gallman, to watch over and assist the mission: "The Department particularly wants Mr. Gallman to gain a thorough knowledge of your work and your plans for the reorganization of Ecuadorean finances in order that after your departure he may be able to observe intelligently the way in which your recommendations are carried out, and offer advice and suggestions to the Ecuadorean authorities in an informal manner if they seem to be straying from the right path."[57] By the same token, Washington instructed the embassy to render Kemmerer all possible assistance, because "his mission presents great possibilities for the betterment of the economic and financial condition of Ecuador and . . . commercial and other relations between this country and Ecuador may be substantially augmented and improved as a result therefrom."[58]

Despite diligent efforts the embassy proved unable to carry out its instructions. Kemmerer insisted that he was working only for the Ecuadorean government. He rebuffed all embassy attempts to acquire any information from him or to influence his operations. Representatives from the British, German, French, and Italian embassies told the U.S. legation their fears about Kemmerer's rumored customs recommendations and urged a formal protest from the diplomatic corps, but the U.S. representatives failed to extract the slightest information or concessions from the mission.[59]

Kemmerer would allow his proposals to be released to the U.S. embassy only after they were enacted or otherwise made public by the Ecuadorean government. Although he refused to leak information to the U.S. ambassador, he did find Gallman and other embassy officials helpful. However, he criticized the ambassador to the State Department for being too aggressive with the commission and not realizing that his interference "would have jeopardized the success of our work by being seen with him very much." Kemmerer told the department that the ambassador did not understand that their work would be most effective—both intrinsically and for U.S. interests—if the embassy were not closely involved with the mission. He was surprised that the ambassador pressed for a more obtrusive role, "as we tried 'to play the game' with the American Legation in Ecuador the same way that we did in Colombia, Chile, and Poland." Kemmerer expressed shock that the ambassador demanded previews of their recommendations, since "it would have been immoral and a breach of trust to have given him such information in advance." The ambassador became especially upset when the German, Italian, and British embassies managed to purloin some preliminary copies of the central bank law from one of the mission's Ecuadorean employees. Relations grew so sour between the mission and the U.S. embassy that the ambassador refused to attend the farewell ceremonies for Kemmerer. Nevertheless, Kemmerer gave the State Department a full account of the mission after it was over.[60]

Prior to his arrival Kemmerer had notified the Ecuadorean government that his commission would need a collection of all the principal financial laws and administrative regulations, a compilation of financial statistics for both the public and private sectors with especially detailed information on banking, and a team of local legal, technical, and clerical assistants.[61] In response, the government in Quito founded the Central Office of Issue and Redemption, which studied Kemmerer's previous projects in Colombia and Chile. The government tried to fill the huge void in official economic data; for example, on exchange rates and foreign trade. This effort resulted in lasting improvements in national statistical recording and reporting, as well as rising interest in economic studies.

Committees of leading citizens in Quito and Guayaquil also organized to advise the mission. At the same time Kemmerer received scores of offers of and requests for information from Ecuadorean individuals and businesses, as well as U.S. firms. He shunned such involvements, however, so as not to compromise his role as a confidential adviser to the host government. Before, during, and after his visit, Kemmerer also consulted frequently with several Ecuadorean economic leaders he respected, notably Víctor Emilio Estrada and Minister of Finance Pedro Leopoldo Núñez. Despite this intensive effort by Ecuadoreans to inform the mission about a country with which it was totally unfamiliar, Kemmerer's recommendations mainly replicated his work from Colombia and Chile.[62]

He also followed the same operating methods as before. Essentially, Kemmerer worked behind closed doors with the government in order to avoid any public debate on his proposals. The mission also kept discussion within the administration to a minimum by delivering all its recommendations just before departing, rather than handing them over bit by bit.[63] According to the mission, the major justification for accepting Kemmerer's exalted authority without question was that he was a scientist and an outsider and thus above political biases.[64]

Kemmerer's desire to speed his reforms through the government without public discussion, however, called into question his political neutrality. Ecuadorean civilian politicians hoped that his visit and the passage of his recommendations would accelerate a return to democratic rule. But Kemmerer himself preferred the maintenance of the dictatorship so that his laws could be imposed by decree without prior debate. He also wanted them implemented "with a strong hand."

In one of Kemmerer's conversations with the U.S. ambassador, "he likewise stated that in his opinion it would not be wise to reestablish constitutionality until such time as would enable the provisional government to fully reorganize its various departments and by enforcing the decrees covering the recommendations of the commission firmly establish the new order of procedure regardless of opposition that might develop." Pleased that each one of his recommendations had "teeth in it," Kemmerer urged the U.S. State Department to support the regime as "one of the best that Ecuador had had for a long time."[65] He defended the regime's authoritarian methods because "the government seems anxious to put through in a thoroughgoing manner all of our measures and, inasmuch as they could get little or nothing done in this connection if they had to pass them through an Ecuadorean Congress, they are naturally postponing the return to constitutional government until these projects can be enacted into law and fairly well clinched in an administrative way under the supervision of the five American experts which they have appointed."[66]

This technocratic support for continuation of the dictatorship leaked to the press, which denounced Kemmerer's interference in Ecuadorean politics. The newspapers questioned his claims to a purely scientific approach, arguing that no one, especially an economist, could avoid the political aspects of government work. In response, Kemmerer and the administration vehemently denied his involvement in local politics and his having expressed any support for the unconstitutional regime.[67]

After that tempest blew over, Kemmerer presented his projects to the government. Those recommendations went much farther in number and scope than his previous proposals in other countries. In the area of banking and finance the mission submitted laws and reports for: a central bank, a monetary system, general banking, a mortgage bank, agricultural security contracts, and negotiable instruments. On fiscal matters the North Americans proposed legislation on: the budget, government accounting and a national comptroller, tax administration, the income tax, the stamp tax, the tax on rural property, the government alcohol monopoly, customs administration, customs import tariffs, customs documents originating abroad, export duties on ivory nuts, public credit, loan contracts for reorganizing and refunding the public debt, public works, railroads, and municipal finances.

These advisers also went beyond strictly economic matters to render recommendations on: functional organization and activities of the administrative branch of the government, reforms of certain articles of the new constitution, amendments to the code of civil procedure and the organic law of the judiciary, and even amendments to the penal code. The Ayora administration was so pleased with Kemmerer's work that it convinced him to stay on an extra twenty days to look into further fiscal matters. Ecuador adopted more of Kemmerer's legal and personnel recommendations than did any other country he visited, primarily because it had the poorest financial and diplomatic relations with the United States and thus felt most compelled to demonstrate the sincerity of this reform effort.[68]

At the farewell ceremonies in March 1927 the government bestowed the National Order of Merit on all the mission members. The Universidad Central also awarded Kemmerer an honorary doctorate, an honor previously conferred only on the eradicator of yellow fever in Guayaquil. The minister of finance, Kemmerer supporter Pedro Núñez, toasted the commission's work, saying: "Never before, in the history of the republic, has there been accomplished a study so extensive and so profound of the national economy." Exuding pleasure with the achievements of Kemmerer, he explained that the government had assigned these tasks to foreign rather than national experts "in order to attain a scientific basis of recognized prestige which would give vitality to that reform, in order to assure the success of the constructive economic policy, and in order to obtain confidence in the interior and the exterior of the republic for the seriousness with which this work was being undertaken." He praised the mission as "one of the most prestigious commissions of economic wise men traveling around the world today, like new apostles."

Kemmerer replied with encomiums for the Ecuadorean government: "In none of the countries which the Mission has visited has the government demonstrated a more open reception to our recommendations and in no country has the government responded so fully to the suggestions that expert foreign administrators and assessors be named to inaugurate the reforms that we have recommended and to help carry them out during the difficult first days in effect." He added, however, that the long-term proper administration of his institutions was more important than the laws or their initial implementation, and that only Ecuadoreans themselves could ultimately make the reforms a success.[69]

Immediately after receiving Kemmerer's recommendations and even before his departure for Bolivia, the government passed the central bank and customs proposals. The other bills followed in quick succession.[70] Most newspapers applauded this rapid government action to avoid resistance and to reactivate the economy, which had been virtually suspended awaiting completion of the mission's work. Other commentators, however, argued that democracy should have been restored before the projects were approved. In their view Ecuador should have given those laws the same airing as had Colombia, so that they would have had greater legitimacy afterward.[71]

Critics of the dictatorship, especially in Guayaquil, welcomed the legislation but not the process: "The country . . . today expects everything from the work of the Kemmerer Mission, which has been accepted without any discussion, without any observation, and even with the prohibition against anyone making repairs in the act, on pain of falling under the strong sanctions of the dictatorship." They pointed out that the Bolivian government had wisely established a national commission to review Kemmerer's recommendations and adapt them to local needs and customs, rather than assuming the "infallibility," universality, and neutrality of the mission's laws.[72]

Kemmerer's Money and Banking Reforms

As soon as Kemmerer left, an organizing commission of government officials and private bankers began setting up the central bank. From March through May of 1927 they enrolled all Ecuadorean banks—none of whom balked at joining—as members of the central bank. The commission was guided by two of the North American experts Kemmerer had recommended hiring for his agencies: Earl B. Schwulst (from the Federal Reserve Bank of Dallas), assessor of the central bank, and Harry L. Tompkins, superintendent of banks.[73]

Thereafter the board of directors of the central bank applied the finishing touches. They elected Neptalí Bonifaz, a wealthy highlands landowner appointed by the government, as first president of the bank. During these months of organization the bank's popularity was demonstrated by the rapid sale of shares in the new institution. That display of confidence had been initiated by Kemmerer himself, who bought fifty shares. Perhaps most noteworthy was the number of shares purchased in Guayaquil—by far the largest number—seen as evidence of both the port province's economic preeminence and its conversion to the central bank project. A lack of accurate economic statistics and infighting among the directors delayed bank decisions. Nevertheless, they managed to have the institution ready for full operations by August 10, 1927.[74]

According to Schwulst, he actually did most of the work and set most of the policies to get the bank functioning. He complained that the directors wrangled over petty details, haggled over personal and provincial prerogatives, and voted themselves extravagant salaries. Like Kemmerer's other appointees, Schwulst tried unsuccessfully to carry out his technical duties without getting mired in political conflicts among Ecuadoreans. Their reliance on him was so great that they even offered this North American the presidency of the bank, which Schwulst diplomatically declined. He saw his major task as keeping the board bound to conservative policies, so as not to succumb to public desires for the bank to become a fountain of easy credit.[75]

When the crowning achievement of the July Revolution commenced operations, dissenting voices were few. As soon as the law had been issued an attempted rebellion had erupted, inspired by some *Guayaquileños* and politicians opposed to the Ayora regime, but the government easily snuffed it out. Moreover, the leader of that uprising explained a few days later that one of his objectives was the immediate imposition of all the Kemmerer laws.[76]

The agricultural sector had the greatest hopes that the new bank would serve primarily as a developmental credit institution rather than simply a regulator of exchange.[77] Now landowners complained that Kemmerer's creation discouraged extensive loans to them, favoring urban interests instead. Nevertheless, they hoped its stabilization of exchange rates would attract external capital for farmers. To accomplish that, Ecuadorean agriculturalists, like their counterparts elsewhere in the Andes, persuaded the government immediately thereafter to launch the Mortgage Bank of Ecuador. It was designed to dole out domestic capital and, above all, to float bonds abroad for long-term loans to production sectors, especially landowners. The rural elites were also mollified because the National Society of Agriculture obtained a permanent seat on the central bank's board of directors. Moreover, both the president (N. Clemente Ponce) and the vice president (Neptalí Bonifaz) of that society won election to the first bank board.[78]

Given the weakness of urban enterprises and their interest-group organizations, those sectors had minimal impact on the Kemmerer legislation. Merchants and manufacturers supported the central bank more than agriculturalists. Since industry remained in its infancy, however, businessmen expressed more concern about the need for government protection and tax breaks to encourage their growth. The major actors in the development of the bank, then, were the bankers and the government.[79]

As in Chile and Peru, not only persuasion but also the threat of force ensured virtually unanimous cooperation with this new institution. After the regime proclaimed the Kemmerer project, the armed forces publicly reiterated their unflagging support for the ideals of the July Revolution, for the provisional government, and for the financial reforms, in particular the Banco Central del Ecuador. Military commanders in Guayaquil as well as Quito announced that no rebellions or resistance would be tolerated. To underscore their commitment and their advice to all patriotic citizens, the general staff of the armed forces and the minister of war officially urged all army units to subscribe to public shares in the bank.[80]

In populist tones, the officers saw themselves speaking for the middle and working classes in this campaign. Labor unions in both Quito and Guayaquil denounced the old "bancocracia." The Comité Obrero Pro Banco Central in Quito echoed the enthusiasm of the Confederación Obrera del Guayas for the central bank and its expected resuscitation of the economy.[81]

Another reason Kemmerer's creation won such easy acceptance was that it closely resembled prior Ecuadorean projects. After all, they had been heavily informed by his Colombian and Chilean laws. Although they differed in details, emphases, and exchange-rate recommendations, earlier local proposals—which had been appearing before Congress since 1890—had generally concurred in fearing excessive control of the central institution by the government. Therefore previous Ecuadorean plans had given most seats on the board of directors to bankers. Now Kemmerer reassured those who feared domination by either group. He created a ruling body with significant economic sectoral representation alongside small allotments for government and banking representatives.[82]

His only problem in adapting his Chilean directorate model to the Ecuadorean situation was the lack of strong interest groups. Kemmerer hoped that representation in the central bank for sectoral groups would not only bring them into the premier financial institution but also encourage them to improve their functional organizations for agriculture, industry, commerce, and labor. In contrast with his Colombian and Chilean creations, Kemmerer allocated no seats to foreign banks because those institutions remained so irrelevant in Ecuador. He did, however, give foreigners the right to be included in the two representatives elected by all banks operating in the country. Some Ecuadoreans complained that Kemmerer's exclusion of government officials, congressmen, and bank employees from the board of directors better suited a more developed country with more abundant trained personnel. Critics also continued to fear that political considerations would influence the selection and behavior of bank directors, despite Kemmerer's safeguards. Most Ecuadoreans, however, believed that he had drafted the best possible formula: nine directors, with two chosen by the president of the nation, two by member banks, one by the Chamber of Commerce and Agriculture of Guayaquil, one by the Chamber of Commerce, Agriculture, and Industries of Quito, one by the National Society of Agriculture, one by the labor organizations, and one by the public shareholders.[83]

The Ecuadorean elites, like their Chilean counterparts, responded positively to Kemmerer's designation of a seat for organized labor, which they had suggested prior to his arrival. They believed it would encourage the workers to adhere to the existing system and maintain discipline within it. The leading newspapers urged blue-collar and white-collar wage and salary earners to get properly organized so that they could elect a bank director as the law stipulated. That legislation required participating unions to have a minimum of two hundred active members and legal existence for three years; those prerequisites seemed reasonable to an outsider but, in fact, proved inapplicable in an agrarian country with a low level of unionization. Counting all 183 legal unions of either blue-collar laborers or white-collar employees, only five met Kemmerer's criteria. Even those five could not agree among themselves on a bank director, although some wanted to name Luis Napoleon Dillon. Consequently, the minister of labor simply appointed a bank director to represent the working class. Since economic organization along regional lines remained far in advance of any along sectoral or class lines, the government eliminated the seat for labor one year later, replacing it with one for coastal agriculturalists. Those landowners had been pressing for a stronger voice, even though they and their highland counterparts already had the largest block of directors.[84]

The rural elites of Guayaquil as well as Quito also wielded influence through the selection of *sierra* landowner Bonifaz as president of the bank. Many Ecuadoreans in 1927 believed that office to have "as much or more importance than the presidency of the republic." Some observers also thought the bank post might serve as a stepping-stone to running the country, which indeed it became for Bonifaz, who was elected president of Ecuador in 1932. During the bank's opening years he symbolized its domination by *Quiteños*, to the ire of Guayaquil bankers.[85]

The other key organizational issue Kemmerer had to solve concerned the location of the bank's headquarters. *Guayaquileños* argued for their city on the grounds of commercial supremacy. *Quiteños*, meanwhile, lobbied for their city because it was the political capital. Kemmerer sided with the latter but compensated the former by immediately having the first branch, which rapidly became the largest and most active office of the bank, installed in Guayaquil. He also stipulated that the board of directors would have to alternate its meetings between the two cities, causing the Ecuadoreans to dub the board "the Directorate on wheels."[86]

Kemmerer established the same 50 percent reserve requirement he had in Chile (10 percent less than in Colombia) for the Central Bank of Ecuador. Kemmerer argued that such a high reserve was needed for insulation in a country so dependent on fluctuating exchange demands from the agricultural and foreign trade sectors. In contrast to Colombia and Chile, the government of Ecuador made no contribution to that reserve; it lacked a special fund to call upon and still owed enormous debts to the private banks. Therefore the reserve came from subscriptions from the private banks (15 percent of their capital and reserves) and from shares purchased by the general public.[87]

After overcoming resistance from the private banks, the central bank began building up its reserve. It rapidly escalated far beyond Kemmerer's stipulation of 50 percent of currency in circulation. It opened with a reserve of 66 percent, 47 percent of which, following Kemmerer's advice, it deposited abroad. During the bank's first four years its total reserves exceeded 70 percent. Increasingly, many Ecuadoreans argued that such excessive inactive reserves harmed an underdeveloped country desperately in need of currency and credit expansion.[88]

Although Kemmerer had recommended, per usual, storing part of the bank's gold reserves overseas, he had not urged placing them in the United States as opposed to England.[89] From December 1927 through December 1929 the Central Bank of Ecuador kept over three-fourths of its reserve in foreign banks, consistently depositing more in London than in New York.[90]

Many Ecuadoreans hoped that the new institution, above all else, would lower lending charges and thus enhance credit availability.[91] During 1927–29 the bank reduced interest rates for member banks from 10 to 8 percent and for the public from 11 to 9 percent, but raised them back to the 1927 levels in response to the depression. Regardless of the discount rate during 1927–30, neither the commercial banks nor the public took much advantage of central bank loans. Resenting the rigid requirements and inspections, they preferred traditional informal arrangements between borrowers and lenders based on personal trust.[92]

From the beginning the bank's rigid lending policies aroused discontent. During 1927–30 the money and credit supply actually shrank. While the bank augmented its reserve percentage, the commercial banks retrenched to adjust to the new, strict regulations imposed by the central institution and by the banking superintendency. At the same time the government paid off some of its domestic and foreign debts, elites sent their capital abroad, foreign companies remitted profits, and foreign investors stayed away. When the central bank tightened its policies even further during the depression, the situation worsened drastically and the drumbeat of criticism grew louder.[93]

Although previous Ecuadorean plans had prohibited all central bank loans to the government, Kemmerer's bill allowed credit extensions of up to 20 percent of the bank's paid-up capital and reserves. From 1927 to 1930 government finances did well, which enabled the state to amortize its internal debt and even repay some of its old external obligations; its debt to the bank fell steadily from 1927 through 1929. Despite widespread fears, the government exerted no pressures on the central bank until the depression.[94]

Within the rules of the Kemmerer system the bank performed admirably, even though it did not live up to public expectations that it would spark general prosperity. The national economy not only had to adjust to the new legal system but also, and more important, had to recoup from the devastation of the earlier 1920s. Agricultural production and exports fell further, exacerbating unemployment. The general recession was reflected in the drop in the index of internal prices from 100 in 1927, to 92 in 1928, to 83 in 1929, while the index of import prices slumped from 100 to 89 to 80. Accordingly, the total active account of the bank shrank from 63 million sucres in 1927 to 59 million in 1928 and 55 million in 1929.[95]

Rather than generating credit directly, stabilizing, unifying, and regularizing the currency was the major objective of the central bank. Kemmerer's monetary law encountered a warm welcome. Ecuadoreans believed that the gold exchange standard would indirectly generate a rise in general prosperity, exports, and foreign capital inflows, especially from the United States.[96]

Widespread agreement existed on the need for exchange stabilization in general and a gold standard in particular. Ecuadorean elites, however, remained divided over the precise new value of the currency. The groundwork for consensus was laid prior to Kemmerer's arrival by the economic conferences for bankers and other opinion leaders in 1926. At those meetings the government established that everyone favored stabilization and most wanted a new value reflecting the existing depreciated worth of the sucre.

Those preferring revaluation to the old, pre–World War I figure of ten sucres to the British pound included some creditors, many importers (though they were willing to accept devaluation to get stabilization), and most worker and employee groups. Joining them were U.S.-owned firms, such as the Quito Electric and Power Company and the Quito Tramways Company, which were stuck with contracts and fares set at the outdated sucre level. The proponents of official devaluation to the current market level of approximately twenty sucres to the pound agreed with Kemmerer that it was more realistic and less disruptive. The banks championed that solution. Equally vehement in favor of devaluation were exporters, represented mainly by the leaders of Guayaquil and its chamber of commerce. Agriculturalists, especially agro-exporters and mortgage debtors, also backed the new, lower exchange rate, as evidenced by the statements of the Chamber of Commerce, Agriculture, and Industries of Quito and the National Society of Agriculture. Industrialists, particularly those competing with foreign producers (as were farmers producing for domestic consumption), took the same position.

The government remained torn. On one hand, it preferred the lower value to reduce its domestic debts and, it was hoped, revive the economy. On the other hand, it leaned toward the higher value to help pay off its external debts and to benefit its middle- and working-class constituents on relatively fixed incomes. Consequently, when Kemmerer submitted his recommendation for the depreciated value, the administration asked him to reconsider. After he explained more extensively the difficulties of trying to resurrect the old sucre and the simplicity of accepting the real existing rate of five to the U.S. dollar, the government went along.[97]

However, even some of those who endorsed devaluing the official rate to match the actual rate, including Estrada and Núñez, criticized Kemmerer for having pegged it too low, arguing that the sucre had been stabilizing and recovering its worth during 1925–26. In their view Ecuador's monetary valuation looked pretty healthy by the time Kemmerer arrived. They complained because he did not make an in-depth study of the true existing value of the sucre, a study for which evidence was sparse and contradictory. Therefore, his contributions to financial and fiscal institution building overshadowed his stabilization per se. Of all his missions, only in Chile was the monetary reform the most dramatic of his actions. Elsewhere his impact on banking and government financial practices proved more significant. Of course, Ecuador's major problem after the stabilization was not the precise rate, but rather the continuing poor performance of production.[98]

Upon implementation of the Kemmerer law, a negative balance of payments continued to prevail. The central bank accordingly contracted the money supply. Since the gold standard did not elicit the expected foreign investments, external resources did not compensate for the tightening of domestic finances. As a result, complaints against the Kemmerer system, except for its exchange stability, had risen to a crescendo by the time of the Great Depression.[99]

After the central bank and monetary laws, Kemmerer's most important financial creation was his standard general banking legislation. That innovation was more desired in Ecuador than anywhere else he visited because of the prior criticisms and closures of the banks. Now the public and the bankers wanted the state to help those financial institutions reorganize and reopen. They believed that such reforms would revive credit availability and foreign as well as domestic confidence in the banks.[100]

Although no general banking law existed in Ecuador prior to 1927, a consensus had already been reached prior to Kemmerer's arrival; his visit provided the final impetus and stamp of approval.[101] Since the July Revolutionaries had already established that the state was going to police the banks, government officials and bankers agreed at their conference preceding Kemmerer's visit that his Colombian and Chilean laws provided the best models. The bankers, however, preferred lesser powers for the superintendency and minor technical adjustments to compensate for Ecuadorean circumstances.[102]

After Kemmerer's general banking law was implemented, some Ecuadorean economic analysts excoriated it as a foreign concoction unsuited to local conditions and needs. Discontent mounted as the expectations of foreign loans and rising prosperity remained unfulfilled. Dissatisfied Ecuadoreans denounced the system for encouraging short-term commercial loans in an underdeveloped country. They contended that long-term credits to producers, especially agriculturalists, were far more necessary. For example, the Banco del Pichincha, the largest private bank in Quito, responded to the Kemmerer law's emphasis on security and liquidity by trying to turn over funds more rapidly through commercial transactions instead of granting mortgage loans to highland agriculturalists. In 1930 a study by the Superintendency of Banks showed that all the credit extended from all the banking institutions in Ecuador went to just 0.2 percent of the population (2,000,000 people). Whereas 14.0 percent of the 9,963 merchants received such credits, only 4.8 percent of the 2,667 industrialists and only 2.4 percent of the 56,241 agriculturalists obtained loans.

Critics now argued that the private banks previously had been very prudent in their lending practices, yet at the same time quite generous to rural borrowers, especially agro-exporters. They saw this law as a blow against the elites of Guayaquil in favor of new urban interests, especially in Quito. The opponents of the superintendency also noted that it proved unable to salvage those banks which succumbed to the crises of 1925–27, including the Banco Comercial y Agrícola. Out of ignorance of Ecuadorean conditions, Kemmerer allegedly made the system of banking and credit worse, as revealed by the continuing recession and subsequent depression. Lending also shrank because borrowers did not like the new regulations demanding detailed information for the banks on how they were going to invest their loans. Some nationalists also accused Kemmerer of deepening the nation's dependency. By constricting credit available to domestic producers and channeling it into commerce, his system encouraged imports while undercutting export capacity. Even Kemmerer supporters like Estrada expressed disappointment that his legislation afforded equal rights to foreign banks, since their international connections gave them intrinsic advantages over domestic institutions.[103]

Another target was Harry L. Tompkins, the North American recommended by Kemmerer to serve for the initial three years as superintendent of banks. He had previously worked in Latin America for the Mercantile Bank of the Americas and for the Guarantee Trust Company. Although many Ecuadoreans preferred a U.S. expert as more impartial and efficient than their own countrymen, a foreigner proved especially susceptible to charges of trying to be too independent and dictatorial. In 1929 the National Assembly accepted Tompkins's report accusing the government of injecting political considerations into his decisions and appointments. The minister of finance denounced him for insubordination and incompetence. This fight illustrated the difficulty anywhere of constructing autonomous, technocratic agencies immune from domestic political pressures. A foreign manager was unable to shield a foreign-born institution from local interference.[104]

Despite complaints, the Superintendency of Banks did carry out its assigned tasks effectively. It liquidated shaky banks—most notably the Banco Comercial y Agrícola—and kept the remainder solvent and solid until the depression. As in the other countries Kemmerer advised, his law reduced the number of banking institutions by driving out smaller, weaker entities; four quickly went out of business in Ecuador. In accord with the intentions of the July Revolutionaries, the establishment of control by the central government in Quito drastically diminished the political power of the banks in Guayaquil.[105]

In addition to these major financial reforms, Kemmerer recommended some minor improvements. He tried to take into account the special needs of agriculture in Ecuador, and suggested the creation of a national mortgage bank that would follow the example of some other South American countries by floating bonds in foreign financial markets. To aid agro-exporters and to reward *sierra* landowners for their support of the July Revolution, the government carried out that proposal in 1928.[106] Kemmerer also submitted a law to give agriculturalists increased access to bank loans by allowing them to pledge farm property as collateral.[107] Finally, his new negotiable instruments law made check transactions more secure and fluid. Nevertheless, Ecuador, like Colombia, subsequently found it necessary to recast that U.S. blueprint to comport with Roman rather than Anglo-Saxon jurisprudence.[108]

Kemmerer's Fiscal Reforms

Through both financial and fiscal reforms, the Kemmerer mission helped the Ayora government add enormous powers to the public sector. State or parastate institutions took charge of money and banking as well as taxation. At the same time the central government improved its ability to plan and manage those resources. It also acquired better information on the economy and its role in it.

One sign of the expanding role of the central government was the plethora of major new offices created by the Ayora administration, mainly as a result of Kemmerer's recommendations: assessor of the central bank, general superintendent of banks, director of the mortgage bank, general director of the treasury, general director of the budget, director of revenues, general director of supplies, comptroller, general director of government monopolies, general director of customs, general director of public works, and general director of the navy. This bureaucratic explosion provided numerous new jobs for technical personnel and the growing middle class.[109]

To improve the government's fiscal stability and reputation, Kemmerer recommended more efficient and controlled budgetary procedures. During the fifteen years from 1911 to 1925, expenditures exceeded the budgeted amount in every year but four. The government avoided or curtailed deficit spending only by postponing payments on the public debt, which ballooned in the hands of domestic banks. According to the Ayora administration, previous budgetary practices conformed only to "the personal fantasy of the Ministers of Finance." Collections of revenues were as decentralized as disbursements. Private agents in the provinces served as tax collectors for the government. They became notorious for failing to obtain many taxes due, for collecting others slowly, for investing those funds for their own profit, for turning in unpredictable amounts, and for often charging the government more than they delivered. Naturally, these local vested interests resisted Kemmerer's reform, as did tax evaders. Also trepidatious were the beneficiaries of government largesse, notably the armed forces, who consumed almost one-third of the national budget. In the face of such entrenched interests, Kemmerer could not significantly reduce expenditures or massively hike taxes. Nevertheless, he did convince the government to adopt his budgetary procedures. He argued that no regime could manage national affairs that could control neither the collection nor the allocation of its own revenues.[110]

Prior to Kemmerer's legislation no separate budget law existed. Ecuadoreans realized the need to fill that gap, but previous attempts—most recently in 1924—died in Congress. The July Revolutionaries began centralizing government financial affairs in 1925, but they issued no coherent set of regulations until Kemmerer's recommendation.[111]

His Ecuadorean bill duplicated the mechanisms for automatic budgeting stability, restraint, and control previously implanted in Colombia, Chile, and Poland. It centralized budgetary authority in the hands of the national government and the executive branch. After receiving this law from Kemmerer in March 1927, the government enacted it and most of his others with celerity in April. Then, in November 1927, it completed the fiscal overhaul by weaving other Kemmerer recommendations on public finances, taxes, and fiscalization into its own new code for the Ministry of Finance, replacing the previous charter of 1863. Following modifications in 1928, that budget system endured for five decades.[112]

The government touted this financial refurbishing as a major triumph. A few critics, however, complained that the panoply of new offices and intricate regulations constituted an excessively complicated, burdensome, and expensive import from an incomparably larger, wealthier country. Allegedly, the government also harbored reservations about this package but rushed it into law so as not to break up the interrelated Kemmerer system.[113]

In the constitution drafted in 1928, opponents of the dictatorship altered Kemmerer's law, striking a more even balance between the budgetary powers of the congressional and executive branches. Both governing bodies still found ways to circumvent the rules and inflate expenditures beyond Kemmerer's prescriptions. Politics, favoritism, regionalism, and clientelism continued to distort the budget-making process. As elsewhere in the Andes, President Ayora used Kemmerer's fiscal tools to expand, rather than contract, government spending and employment. Critics bemoaned the creation of "a rich government in a poor country." The upper class also complained about increasing taxes. Meanwhile, the middle sectors appreciated expanded government employment and salaries, improved conditions for the armed forces, elevated outlays for education, better circulation of currency and credit, and lower import levies on consumer goods. Both the middle and working classes also benefited from new public works projects.[114]

Despite imperfections, Kemmerer's reforms did make government financial operations more effective and orderly. Although it took time to adjust to the new procedures, the Ayora administration did follow some of Kemmerer's budgetary recipes from 1928 on. Improved collection methods produced mounting receipts. Expenditures also grew, but not as inordinately as critics charged. Whereas every year from 1920 through 1925 registered a deficit, every year from 1926 through 1929 showed a surplus. That improved fiscal management allowed the government to reduce its internal debt from 49 million sucres in 1925 to 11 million by 1930.[115]

As elsewhere in the Andes, Kemmerer installed a national comptroller as a watchdog over fiscal propriety. Previously, separate Tribunals of Accounts in Guayaquil and Quito had provided the only regular overseers of fiscal movements. Displeased with such slow, erratic, and often corrupt management of national accounting, the Ecuadorean Congress had begun considering establishment of a comptroller in 1922. Although the legislators admired Kemmerer's Colombian and Chilean projects, those models did not become law in Ecuador until his initiative in 1927.[116]

Kemmerer's bill created an independent, centralized agency to ensure that government financial operations conformed with budgetary laws and authorizations. The comptroller was also supposed to provide the government with regular and reliable fiscal data, and those reports were expected to win favor with local businessmen and foreign investors. As Kemmerer pointed out, "The standing of a country among financial men abroad depends in no small degree upon the character of its financial publications."[117]

As in his other South American missions, this Kemmerer institution collided with unusual resistance both before and after its implementation. The minister of finance, the officials of the outgoing Tribunals of Accounts, and other bureaucrats fearful of losing authority balked at the comptroller's dominant role. The Ecuadorean director of the treasury wrote Kemmerer that launching the comptroller was comparable to "the preparation, equipping and organization of an army in full battle." Some newspapers complained that making a technocrat into a dictator over fiscal policy seemed especially ill-advised when that official was a foreigner.[118]

Based on Kemmerer's recommendation, Ecuador hired North American James H. Edwards as the first comptroller general. He had banking experience in Cuba, Puerto Rico, and Bolivia, and had worked with the U.S. government to oversee customs collections in the Philippines and to reorganize finances in the Dominican Republic. After helping overcome the Ecuadorean government's doubts about creating the office, Edwards encountered severe difficulties carrying out the law. He found numerous errors in the government's budget, many departments unwilling to follow the new accounting rules or allow the comptroller to monitor their expenditures, and personnel decisions made by clientelism rather than merit. The heart of the Kemmerer system was supposed to be prior fiscalization of all government outlays. However, bureaucratic inexperience, long distances and slow communications across Ecuador, and the anger of those waiting to be paid led Edwards to abandon that procedure in favor of posterior fiscalization. Like the other U.S. appointees to Kemmerer institutions, Edwards ended his sojourn frustrated at trying to bend reality to preconceived organizational blueprints.[119]

From 1929 on, obeying the new Constitution, the government replaced the North American superintendent of banks and comptroller with Ecuadoreans. Thereafter, those national authorities modified the offices to better fit domestic conditions. From the 1920s into the 1970s, however, the comptroller improved fiscal accounting and control while retaining the fundamental design laid down by Kemmerer.

Kemmerer also responded to widespread Ecuadorean desires for tax reform. Especially given the decline of cacao, most observers called for less reliance on customs revenues and other indirect taxes. The July Revolutionaries began the task of simplifying, unifying, and centralizing taxation in 1925. They eliminated numerous nuisance taxes which impeded commerce, started an income tax, slashed export levies, and reduced imposts on those least able to pay. They also brought the whole system of taxation and state monopolies under central government control. The revolutionaries sought to make taxation less of an obstacle to modern capitalist development and to foreign trade, less of an unfair burden on the poor, and less of an unreliable and corrupt source of revenue. While the government wanted Kemmerer to refine and consolidate these tax reforms, many wealthy Ecuadoreans hoped he would dilute their impact.[120]

The mission recommended thorough reorganization of tax administration to make it more hierarchical, rigorous, and efficient. Since direct taxes only averaged about 7 percent of total revenues, the advisers emphasized boosting that category.[121] They simplified the 1925 progressive income tax, which aroused little resistance since it had already been endorsed by Conservatives as well as Liberals.[122] The mission members also improved administration of the stamp tax, as they had in Colombia and Chile.[123] They put their seal of approval on the 1925 government takeover of public alcohol and tobacco monopolies from private concessionaires.[124] And they implanted U.S. methods for basing the rural property tax on fair assessed valuations, on progressive rates, and on actual collections from the large landowners.[125] Here, too, the mission was endorsing a reform begun by the July Revolutionaries. The landed elites expressed equal displeasure with Kemmerer's law, and they managed to reduce the rate on large properties following his departure.[126]

After overcoming resistance from wealthy Ecuadoreans and incorporating minor adjustments in the laws, the new tax system worked smoothly. From 1925 to 1929 tax receipts, measured in U.S. dollars, climbed from $9 million to $12 million.[127] In 1928 and 1929, however, over 40 percent of government revenues still came from customs, 25 percent from the monopolies on alcohol, salt, tobacco, and matches, and only 2–3 percent from the income tax (see table 4.5).

To further enhance government revenues as well as foreign trade, the Kemmerer mission also revamped the customs administration and laws. This legislation aimed to reduce errors, corruption, and tariffs. It rebuffed the protectionist desires of many Ecuadorean industrialists and called for customs duties only for limited revenue purposes.[128]

The government also heeded Kemmerer's recommendation to name a North American, William F. Roddy, as director general of customs. He drew upon his previous customs management experience in the United States, the Philippines, and in Nicaragua during the U.S. occupation (1918–27). Like the other U.S. appointees in Ecuador, Roddy initially stumbled on problems with poor data and unqualified personnel protected by political connections. Despite obstructionist merchants, he installed the new system and increased customs revenues. From 1925 to 1930 receipts from import duties rose from 19 percent to 25 percent of the total value of imports. The government lavished praise on

Table 4.5   Ordinary Government Revenues from Customs Receipts, 1919–1934 (by percentage)

Year	Percentage	Year	Percentage
1919	63	1927	45
1920	78	1928	43
1921	79	1929	43
1922	54	1930	38
1923	54	1931	39
1924	55	1932	30
1925	55	1933	30
1926	42	1934	42

Sources: Ecuador, Banco Central del Ecuador, *Boletín* 3, no. 29 (December 1929): 22–25; no. 35 (June 1930): 23–26; Linda Alexander Rodríguez, "Ecuador's National Development: Government Finances and the Search for Public Policy, 1830–1940" (Ph.D. diss., University of California at Los Angeles, 1981), p. 342.

his achievements, concluding that only a foreigner could have broken though the network of vested interests which vitiated previous customs administration. The U.S. ambassador also credited Roddy, who kept him confidentially informed, for sharply improving customs operations. In spite of such acclaim, the government canceled his contract at the start of 1930, along with those of the other Kemmerer appointees. After replacing him with an Ecuadorean, however, the government retained Roddy's services by contracting him to be technical assessor of customs.[129]

Most complaints about the customs law originated in Guayaquil. Merchants denounced the complicated regulations and strict enforcement for slowing their business and raising their costs. They charged that the legislation had been written with little knowledge of Ecuadorean conditions and needs. Robert Vorfeld, the mission member who authored the bill, simply copied his previous work in Paraguay. Since external commerce moved on an international river there, this transcription inadvertently led to the application of customs regulations to Ecuador's internal waterway traffic, thus inhibiting domestic commerce. Critics quickly convinced the government to stop treating Kemmerer's code as sacred and to weed out these minor defects.[130]

A more substantive criticism was that Kemmerer's dedication to free trade committed customs policies to fiscal rather than protectionist purposes. Having lost the indirect insulation provided by depreciating currency, domestic producers now faced rising imports. Some Ecuadoreans feared that Kemmerer's open system condemned their nation to agrarian backwardness while industrial countries grew wealthier. Influenced by Kemmerer's advice, the government essentially clung to laissez-faire until 1932, despite the more vigorous protectionist positions of many domestic producers and other nations, including the United States.[131]

The government also hoped that Kemmerer would increase its financial resources by facilitating the acquisition of foreign loans. Ecuadorean opinion leaders agreed that the government should renegotiate, reduce, and redeem its existing foreign obligations. Thereby they expected to improve its credit rating and attract new outside capital for both the private and public sectors. Some newspapers, however, worried that excessive new government indebtedness to the United States would lead to "gilded slavery" and military invasion.[132]

Kemmerer agreed with his hosts that Ecuador needed foreign capital and that his recommendations would help turn on the spigot. He also cautioned prudence and patience, especially since Ecuador's past nonpayments gave its external bonds the lowest ratings of any in South America. During at least seventy-two of the ninety-three years from 1834 to 1927, the Ecuadorean government had been in default on its debts. Its current lack of diplomatic recognition by the United States further discouraged investors. Kemmerer also warned the Ecuadoreans that, because of their lowly credit standing, they could probably obtain foreign loans only by paying high interest rates and by pledging customs revenues to be collected by the bondholders. Therefore the mission proposed consolidation, readjustment, and settlement of all existing public obligations, followed by a comprehensive and conservative plan for borrowing abroad.[133]

After returning home Kemmerer tried to convince U.S. government officials and private bankers that Ecuador's enactment of his reforms merited diplomatic recognition and financial assistance. At the State Department, "he said that Ecuador has now probably the best and the most honest Government it has ever had and that he hoped the U.S. would find some way of recognizing it as soon as possible. He pointed out that such a step would give great encouragement to the people and to the authorities who have demonstrated their good faith in employing American experts and in giving them great power over the customs, in banking matters, and in the control of public funds." Kemmerer also informed the department that his discussions with U.S. banking firms had revealed that diplomatic recognition would reinforce their intentions to extend financing to Ecuador. Those financiers were willing to arrange loans to retire Ecuador's outstanding debts so long as any new obligations were secured by customs collections by Roddy. At the same time, however, the long-neglected previous bondholders pressured the department to withhold recognition until their repayment. Kemmerer countered that this position created an insoluble dilemma for Ecuador. On one hand, that country could not reimburse the old bondholders until it negotiated a settlement with them to be fulfilled by a new loan from New York. On the other hand, it could not float a fresh loan through U.S. banks until it obtained recognition from the U.S. government, which refused to normalize relations before Ecuador settled the claims of the bondholders and restored constitutional rule. Moreover, in Kemmerer's view, Ecuador could not renegotiate with the bondholders except through the provisional dictatorship. He warned that "a Latin American Congressional debating society" would never approve a reasonable settlement. Despite these arguments, the State Department maintained nonrecognition until August 1928, officially discouraging any U.S. bank loans to Ecuador.[134]

State Department approval of loans, however, was not legally required. Therefore Kemmerer helped President Ayora try to convince Dillon, Read, and Company and other U.S. financial houses to arrange financing regardless. Kemmerer involved himself more than normal in such negotiations because of Ecuador's dismal credit rating. In conversations with bank officers, he "made as strong a case for Ecuador as I honestly could." He "agreed to help if I could do so consistently with my principle that I would recommend and support nothing that I did not believe was 100% in favor of Ecuador, and that my name should be kept in the background and not used for publicity." In early 1928 those New York bankers dispatched Edward Feely, former general secretary of the Kemmerer mission, to Quito to discuss a loan with the government. Those negotiations angered the U.S. embassy, which complained that the Ecuadorean regime not only lacked recognition but also was preparing to cancel the contracts of the Kemmerer appointees at the Central Bank of Ecuador and the Superintendency of Banks. Ironically, some Ecuadorean leaders thought that the State Department was pressuring them to take a loan with a U.S. bank and would grant them recognition if they did so.

Even after Kemmerer's good offices finally led to improved diplomatic and financial relations with the United States at the end of 1928, problems remained. North Americans still pressed claims for past railroad debts and for losses suffered during the 1926 bank closures. The persistence of antibanker, antiforeign attitudes—exemplified by the 1929–30 removal of the Kemmerer appointees—also dissuaded foreign investors. At the same time some Ecuadoreans campaigned against external borrowing; they feared that their country's poor past debt record would prompt U.S. lenders to impose onerous terms. Most Ecuadoreans, however, expressed regret that their shaky financial and political situation still prevented the government from floating any loans in the United States in the 1920s.[135]

Ecuador's only public foreign loan in the period arrived immediately after the conclusion of the Kemmerer mission. In November 1927 the Swedish Match Company, after conferring with Kemmerer in the United States, extended the government eight million sucres in return for a twenty-five-year monopoly on the importation and manufacture of matches in Ecuador. The government used those funds in January of 1928 to found the Mortgage Bank of Ecuador to assist agriculturalists; it sold shares abroad worth five million sucres. Foreigners also made a few new direct investments in Ecuador, as shown in the figures given in table 4.6.

Above all, Ecuador desired foreign credits to meet its desperate need for infrastructural improvements. Upon his arrival the provinces besieged Kemmerer with demands for the government to allot them more revenues and public works projects, especially railroads.[136] However, he concluded, as had most Ecuadorean critics, that the government had been undertaking too much. As a result, "the country finds itself scattered with half-finished public works." The government was pouring over 20 percent of total expenditures into those endeavors. The wastage of funds on politically inspired, nonproductive construction caused the treasury to incur deficits and postpone foreign debt payments. Therefore Kemmerer called for fewer, better-planned projects. The mission also suggested getting funding, engineers, and companies from abroad.[137]

Thereafter, President Ayora improved centralized management, technical

Table 4.6   U.S. Investments in Ecuador, 1930

Public utilities	$ 5,350,000
Mining	1,750,000
Manufacturing	1,000,000
Trading	200,000
Real estate	3,780,000
Agriculture	25,000
Lumbering	60,000
Railway and government bonds	8,701,628
Total	$20,087,408

Sources: Charles Cunningham, *Economic and Financial Conditions in Ecuador* (Washington, D.C., 1931), p. 12; Great Britain, Department of Overseas Trade, *Economic and Financial Conditions in Ecuador* (London, 1928), pp. 8–12.

planning, and fiscal control. The budgetary allocation to public works remained around 20 percent. Although he found it impossible to cancel numerous projects already under way, Ayora did concentrate his resources on railroads and highways. He intended those links to boost national integration and governmental authority as well as economic growth. Most of the railroads were designed, however, to transport regional products to the coast for export, rather than to knit the national economy together. Ayora's building program alleviated regionalist suspicions by launching new endeavors in Guayaquil as well as Quito. The government failed to enlist foreign capital, but it did hire a few U.S. and British construction firms.[138]

Ecuadoreans did not heed Kemmerer's caution against building too many costly, inefficient railroads. For example, his mission suggested that a highway would be a cheaper and more reasonable link between Quito and Esmeraldas. The government declined to publish that report, so as not to arouse the wrath of municipalities hungry for modernization.[139] Kemmerer expressed disappointment that Ecuador ignored his railroad expert's advice, dismissed him as a subsequent government consultant after a few months, and continued employing political rather than economic criteria in construction decisions.[140]

To round out their financial remodeling, the mission members added some minor recommendations. They suggested streamlining the entire executive branch of the government to reduce overlapping functions among ministries and to eliminate some unnecessary offices. As in most of the other countries he visited, Kemmerer arrived when a new constitution was being prepared, so he proposed financial sections to take into account his other reforms. After consulting with businessmen and the Ecuadorean Academy of Lawyers, he also recommended a speedier judicial system, with the goal of expediting urban business cases such as disputes between creditors and debtors. He advocated stiffer penalties for counterfeiting money, falsifying checks, or engaging in bank fraud. He also suggested improvements in the anemic finances of municipalities. Although those entities were not borrowing abroad and were unlikely to be able to do so soon, he advised the national government to oversee all municipal credit operations.[141] Finally, the Ecuadorean government emphatically denied the rumor that it had asked Kemmerer about selling the Galapagos islands to the United States.[142]

Results of Kemmerer's Reforms, 1927–29

Although Ecuador rushed Kemmerer's recommendations into law and preserved the essence of most of his institutions thereafter, it quickly turned against their management by his North American appointees. Some Ecuadoreans initially defended the hiring of foreigners on the grounds that their country lacked sufficiently qualified technicians. They also hoped that these officials would reassure U.S. investors.[143] Most public opinion, however, denounced these outsiders. Ecuadoreans resented their high salaries, extensive powers, and foreign origins.[144]

The undiplomatic behavior of these foreign experts also embroiled them in trouble with the government and the private sector. Not understanding the Ecuadorean milieu, they endeavored to enforce the letter of the law even more strictly than they could have at home. Thus the North Americans constrained the flexibility of personalistic public officials and collided with powerful vested interests. They tried to run like clockwork offices which existed partly to provide employment and clientelistic rewards. According to Ecuadoreans, these imported officials failed because: "The 'technocrats' did not know . . . that the laws in Ecuador are generally dictated in order to remain written and enrich the republican and democratic literature, not in order to be a hindrance. . . . They believed, without a doubt, that the 'vested interests' here were fewer or weaker than in the rest of the world, and that one could be strict, fiercely legalistic and energetic without receiving immediately total disapproval or without producing complete blunders."[145]

In response to this spreading discontent, the Constituent Assembly drafted a new national constitution which ruled that foreigners could serve the government of Ecuador only as advisers, not as administrators. As the government's commitment to Kemmerer's reforms had waned, it had begun hampering the work of these appointees until it achieved its objective of pushing them out.[146] The first U.S. expert to go was the railway specialist, Milner, in 1927. Next, Assessor Schwulst clashed with the central bank president over minor decisions.

In response, the government repudiated his contract, to the relief of the bank directors. At the start of 1928 Kemmerer cautioned the State Department not to intervene on Schwulst's behalf; he did not want to tarnish the other appointees, and indeed his entire mission, as handmaidens of the U.S. government.[147]

According to the U.S. ambassador, Tompkins proved a complete failure as superintendent of banks and soiled the reputation of all U.S. experts. After dismissing Schwulst, the Ecuadorean government became eager to remove Tompkins as well because he was seen as arrogant, aggressive, and authoritarian. He repeatedly quarreled with the presidents of the country and the central bank. The minister of the treasury resented an independent superintendent of banks running the office the way Kemmerer intended, exposing irregularities in the management of banks and government finances.[148] Leaving his post in 1929, Tompkins bitterly criticized the Ecuadorean government for lack of cooperation:

> While the Kemmerer Mission needs no defense, nevertheless, if it is to be judged by the results alone it might be claimed that its visit to Ecuador was a complete fiasco. As a matter of fact it was, but through no fault of the Mission. . . . In the light of subsequent developments it is obvious that the whole matter of the employing of the Kemmerer Mission and of the several advisers contracted for was only a beautiful gesture. One object was, of course, to influence public opinion within the country. The other and more important one was for the sake of propaganda in the exterior and the obtaining of a loan.

Since loans were not forthcoming, the Ecuadorean regime circumvented some of the new laws and dismissed all of the U.S. experts.[149]

The Ecuadorean government displayed more satisfaction with Edwards as comptroller and especially with Roddy as director of customs. Nevertheless, Edwards also encountered friction. Just as Tompkins reported that the general banking law had not really been carried out properly, so Edwards concluded that the comptroller and other fiscal legislation had not been implemented as intended. Rather than following Kemmerer's budget law, the government vitiated it and the comptroller's control over it through decrees, deception, and interference by, among other things, blocking Edwards's investigation of financial affairs such as debts. When he discovered mismanagement of the state monopolies, which supplied 26 percent of public revenues, the government did not want to correct those mistakes but instead wanted Edwards to stop intruding. His attempts to curb mushrooming expenditures also proved futile. Not surprisingly, the government adamantly resisted control over its finances by an independent foreigner. In 1929 Edwards, too, found his contract terminated by the new Constitution.[150]

The last U.S. appointee, Roddy in customs, pleased the government, but import merchants opposed his administration as "the inflexible discipline of yankee legalism trying to impose itself in a country of distinctive peculiarities." Therefore Ayora demoted him to a customs adviser. Undoubtedly such U.S. appointees had found it easier to impose their will and their economic models in countries that were totally dominated by the United States, like Nicaragua and the Dominican Republic.[151]

The Great Depression, 1929-33

Unavoidably, Kemmerer's institutions also disappointed Ecuador because they could not rekindle prosperity before they were inundated by the Great Depression. During 1927 and 1928 Ecuadorean importers and exporters complained that Kemmerer's reforms did little to expand credit or commerce. Although external trade revived slightly, cacao still suffered from low production and prices, the value of ivory nuts fell, and the new customs and tax impositions restrained growth. Petroleum and mineral products rose to account for almost 15 percent of export value. The central bank claimed, however, that those returns from trade should have been subtracted from the balance of payments because they mainly accrued to foreign companies, chiefly British. In any case the balance of trade turned unfavorable by 1928.[152]

External trade overall declined from 1929 until 1934. Cacao led the plunge, as its international price fell even further than did the amount sold abroad. After tumbling from 66 percent of exports in 1919 to 45 percent by 1927, cacao sank to 24 percent by 1929. As the depression grew worse, so did government receipts from foreign commercial transactions. Those revenues plummeted from $30 million in 1929 to $25 million in 1930, and then to $19 million in 1931.[153] To conserve gold reserves and foreign exchange and to boost local industry, the government finally introduced higher tariffs and foreign exchange restrictions in 1931-32.[154]

The global calamity hit agriculturalists producing for export earlier and harder than it did those producing for domestic consumption. That was an especially severe blow to the coastal landowners, who had already been discriminated against in favor of their highland counterparts by the July Revolutionaries. Nevertheless, those in the *sierra* joined their lowland brethren in calling for increased credits and government support, also adding demands for higher tariffs on competitive foreign goods and for lower railroad fares.[155]

Quiteño manufacturers shared the protectionist desires of *serrano* agriculturalists. Thus the same regional groups that had helped install the Kemmerer system now undermined it. The mild protective measures enacted by the Ayora government both before and after the 1929 upward tariff legislation mainly benefited highland industrialists—especially textile producers—at the expense of Guayaquil import interests.[156]

As the Great Depression coursed through the domestic economy, some bankers continued defending the Kemmerer system. Most, however, complained of strangulation from the central bank's tight money and credit policies. Because of lax management in those banks and monitoring by the superintendent of banks, two banks in Guayaquil and one each in Quito and Ibarra collapsed in 1931.[157]

Responding to the balance of payments crisis and Kemmerer's advice, the central bank dutifully cut back the money supply from sixty-five million sucres in circulation in 1928 to thirty-seven million in 1931. It also maintained a reserve ratio against circulation and deposits much higher than the law required. The bank tried to fend off critics by quoting Kemmerer and by showing that his other institutions remained even more conservative (see table 4.7). Public and governmental pressure soon drove the Ecuadorean central bank to reduce its reserve to 78 percent in 1931, 50 percent in 1932, and even less subsequently. While monetary circulation and prices fell, the official exchange rate held steady until nearly the end of 1932. Meanwhile the U.S. dollar became worth nearly twice as many sucres in the black market. After devaluation the money supply and prices soared.[158]

As the Great Depression wreaked havoc in Ecuador, the central bank and the government again turned to Kemmerer. They needed him to reinforce their authority and policies in the face of spreading criticisms. First, they invited him to send copies of the reports resulting from his return expedition to Colombia in 1930 and, then, to spend a day in Guayaquil on his way to Peru in January of 1931. The minister of finance and other officials met Kemmerer there with a series of questions about the continuing applicability of his principles to the collapsing economy.

Table 4.7 Central Bank Reserve Ratios, 1928–1930 (percentages)

	1928	1929	1930
Colombia	102	95	84
Chile	111	97	88
Bolivia	95	96	—
Ecuador	77	80	81

Source: Ecuador, Banco Central del Ecuador, Boletín 4, no. 38 (September 1930): 5–26.

Kemmerer responded that the central bank's automatic adjustment of the money supply guaranteed the proper amount in circulation and should not be tampered with, despite outcries. He denied that Ecuador was undergoing deflation or a currency shortage and urged his hosts to maintain the gold standard and high discount rates. Kemmerer also observed that the global decline was injuring Ecuador less than many of its neighbors and would probably be over within a year. Therefore he recommended continued payments on the foreign debt. Pleased with his defense of their actions, the bank and the government reaffirmed their steady course. They publicized these pronouncements of this "high scientific authority" to refute their critics.[159]

In 1931 a few Ecuadoreans welcomed the administration's reaffirmation of the Kemmerer creed. Most, however, assailed the government for prostrating itself before the Money Doctor and his dicta a second time while the depression deepened.[160] They called for currency and credit expansion. Even the superintendent of banks opined that Kemmerer did not understand the devastating shrinkage of money and prices, and that the central bank should disregard his recommendation to continue squeezing currency and credit.[161]

As the country's supply of cash and reserves dwindled in 1930–31, it received an additional shock when Great Britain abandoned the gold standard in September 1931. Since most of Ecuador's gold reserve had been deposited in England, this depreciation of its sterling holdings cost over two million sucres. This disaster prompted the central bank to transfer its gold deposits to the United States. In response, public opinion mounted against the gold standard. While the 1931 Congress debated its suspension, the president who replaced Ayora that same year urged its abandonment. Then, in February of 1932, the government issued a decree temporarily suspending the gold standard to save the nation's metallic reserves. Since the drainage continued, that moratorium became a permanent declaration of inconvertibility in November of 1932. With the support of all economic sectors, including the working class, Ecuador then embarked on countercyclical inflationary programs.[162]

In a 1933 response to a letter from the Ecuadorean director of the treasury recounting his country's fall from grace, Kemmerer consoled his followers:

The conditions leading to the breakdown of the gold standard in Ecuador seemed to be very similar to those which led to its breakdown in many other countries. Of course, I am very sorry that it had to break, but it held for a long time, longer than in many other financially stronger countries, and the fact that it did not go down until after the avalanche of world crisis carried away the gold standard in many of the most advanced countries in the world, like Great Britain, Norway, Denmark, and Canada, is very commendable. I am proud of the fact that not one of my countries in South America broke from the gold standard until after Great Britain and Scandinavia broke.

At the present time, it seems to me to be very important for Ecuador to balance its budget. . . . It seems to me that inflation should be kept at its lowest possible point. . . . the ideal is for the Central Bank to function in times like these in a normal, liberal way. I still believe that the broad economic and financial philosophy upon which the monetary and banking structure was built in 1927 is sound; that it probably stood the test of this world crisis as well as any banking structure could have stood it in a country like Ecuador; and that reconstruction, when it comes, will probably need to be along the same general lines as those upon which the original structure was built.[163]

As Kemmerer noted, the Central Bank of Ecuador had exerted every effort to remain loyal to his legislation. During 1929–31 it wrote to him for advice and publishable quotes, referred to his teachings in its bulletin, took comfort in the equal steadfastness of his other South American central banks, and bolstered its case with the resolutions of the conference of central banks in 1931 in Peru.[164] After lowering its credit discount rate for member banks from 10 percent in 1927 to 8 percent in 1929, the central bank raised it back to 10 percent by 1932. The bank's faith, however, ultimately could not withstand the harsh reality of shrinking reserves, deposits, and monetary circulation.[165]

Mounting pressure from the economic elites and the government finally overturned the bank's tight-money policies. The agro-exporting and banking magnates of Guayaquil led the protests. Having suffered since 1925, and now seeing exports falling faster than imports, they cried out for monetary devaluation and expansion. These seaboard capitalists blamed the severity of the catastrophe on the management of the central bank by highlanders. They tried to recapture power from the *sierra* landowners by ejecting President Ayora in August 1931 and replacing him with a fellow *costeño* and inflationist, Alfredo Baquerizo Moreno. The *Guayaquileños* then got the gold standard scrapped, central bank loans expanded to the government, and full devaluation enacted in 1932.

Abandonment of the gold standard was also welcomed by most highlands industrial and agricultural producers for domestic consumption. Resenting foreign imports, they also received some tariff protection from the government, to the ire of the *costeños*. The *serranos* also lashed back politically, first with the presidential election of former central bank president Neptalí Bonifaz in 1932, and second, after the annulment of his victory, with the election of President José María Velasco Ibarra at the end of 1933. These political-economic battles among the regional and sectoral factions of the Ecuadorean upper class did nothing for the principal victims of the depression—the Ecuadorean workers, especially the growing number of unemployed. The political infighting did, however, destroy the government and the central bank as they had existed since 1927.[166]

The central bank had been able to defend its Kemmererian policies only so long as it had the backing of the executive branch of government. For example, the legislature in 1929 and 1930 had tried to reduce the number of central bank directors to strengthen the hand of agriculturalists and politicians, but the bank had marshalled Kemmerer and other loyalists to defeat that proposal. Presidential support for the bank had remained firm until 1931, when Ayora's constant conflicts with the Congress over bank policies culminated in his resignation. Following the loss of its champion, the bank engaged in a running battle with the government, until the new regime managed to enforce its will in 1932.[167]

After taking over from the Ayora administration, President Alfredo Baquerizo Moreno told the Congress in late 1931 that, unless restrictive economic policies were changed, "The money will be healthy but everything else will be sick." In response, Congress passed an emergency law in December 1931 to prevent the central bank from maintaining a legal reserve above 50 percent. At the start of 1932 the government convened a conference of bankers—much as in 1926—to try to resolve the crisis. President Baquerizo Moreno exchanged angry words with the central bank over its refusal to extend credits to the government for public works and agriculture.

Then, in February 1932, Baquerizo Moreno ordered the central bank to suspend the gold standard, lower its legal reserve requirement, bring all its overseas reserves home, and expand its credits to the national government. The president of the bank resigned in protest against this government takeover of his institution and scuttling of the Kemmerer system. Exchange controls requiring all foreign currency transactions to be handled by the central bank were added in May 1932. Longer terms were established for loans to the public. Also in 1932–33, the government began a recurring policy of reorganizing the directorate of the bank when it was unable to get all the loans it wanted. As Kemmerer had always feared, his offspring became an inflationary instrument of national politics.[168]

From 1932 on, the government continued resorting to central bank credits to maintain public works and thus reduce unemployment, to extend assistance to agriculture, and, above all, to cover its fiscal shortfall.[169] After barely beginning to implement Kemmerer's budgetary system in 1928, the government had found his rules for calculating next year's flow unworkable. Plummeting customs and tax revenues depleted the coffers and upset all expectations during 1929–32 (see table 4.8). For example, receipts for 1931 fell 26 percent short of predictions. During 1930–31 the government had tried vainly to balance the

Table 4.8   Government Budgeted versus Actual Ordinary Revenues, 1927–1934 (in millions of sucres)

Year	Budgeted revenues	Actual revenues
1927	42	65
1928	60	62
1929	65	64
1930	64	61
1931	61	45
1932	49	42
1933	49	42
1934	51	48

Sources: See note 170.

books by cutting back on public works expenditures and on funds set aside for foreign debt service. When that proved to no avail, it began tapping the central bank in 1932.

The depression also compelled the government to abandon its fruitless attempt to improve its foreign credit rating by following Kemmerer's advice. Immediately after his mission, Ayora had made some token payments on the foreign debt—mainly outstanding railroad obligations owed to British and, to a lesser extent, U.S. bondholders. In 1929 and 1930 the government began setting aside deposits in the central bank to redeem those external debts once a settlement was reached with the foreign bondholders. During those same years it regularly serviced the Swedish Match Company loan and the internal debt. From 1924 to 1931 the accumulating foreign debt rose from 39 million to 47 million sucres. Meanwhile the government slashed its domestic debt from 39 to 11 million sucres.[170]

As the depression drained government revenues, public opinion railed against any allocations for foreign bondholders. When those creditors demanded full payments before discussing any settlement, negotiations broke down in 1931. Consequently no further deposits were made and none were paid out. Also in 1931 the government canceled the Swedish match monopoly and then, in 1932, suspended payments on that loan. From 1931 to 1933 its internal debt rebounded from 11 to 37 million sucres, mainly thanks to loans from the central bank. Its unattended foreign debt inched up from 47 to 49 million sucres. After the depression abated, Ecuador struck a deal with its bondholders, resuming partial service of the foreign and domestic debt in 1936.[171]

By 1932–33 the Great Depression had laid waste to the political and economic models, policies, and policymakers put in place by the July Revolutionaries and the Money Doctor. Nevertheless, their far-reaching financial and fiscal institutions survived, and flourished thereafter. Despite disappointments and deviations, a revolution against regionalism—abetted by U.S. advisers—had indeed launched the continuing twentieth-century capitalist modernization of Ecuador.[172]

Initially, Kemmerer's reforms had deepened Ecuador's dependence on the United States. To an extraordinary degree Ecuadorean officials relied on him and his appointees. Following Kemmerer's advice when it matched their own inclinations, Ecuador's rulers adopted the gold standard and sought foreign loans. While channeling credit to import merchants more than to export agriculturalists, they also floated mortgage bank bonds in New York. In accord with the orthodoxy of the age, they promoted free trade. To connect more provinces to the ports they built railroads, often under contract to foreign construction firms. Although economic and diplomatic relations with the United States improved, the continuing poor performance of the Ecuadorean economy restrained U.S. financial penetration.

Rather than ushering in a parade of foreign capital and companies, the Kemmerer mission and the July Revolutionaries mainly benefited highland urban and rural producers for domestic consumption over the coastal agro-exporters and financiers. Following the reassertion of conservative highlanders behind the victory of Velasco Ibarra in 1933, *costeños* continued to resent *serrano* dominance over fiscal and financial policies through the central government and the central bank. Although Kemmerer viewed his reforms primarily as a neutral transfer of technology, Ecuadoreans exploited those innovations for their own political purposes.[173]

Also as a result of the Kemmerer mission and the July Revolution, politicians—whether Conservatives or Liberals, *Quiteños* or *Guayaquileños*, soldiers or civilians—now fought over a central government with greatly enhanced capabilities. In the twenties, and even more so in the thirties, the expanding state extended its control over money, banking, revenues, transportation and other public works. It improved its ability to manage economic information, planning, and resources. Consequently, the increasingly legitimate central state acquired greater authority over regional forces, greater capacity to cope with and substitute for foreign economic and political influences, and greater potential to guide national development. At the same time the conflicts which had produced those changes in the 1920s remained unresolved. In ensuing decades the tensions and dilemmas would persist between regional elites, and between nationalist and internationalist patterns of development.

5 EXPORTING TIN, GOLD, AND LAWS FROM BOLIVIA, 1927–1932

Immediately after his Ecuadorean mission, Professor Kemmerer turned his attention to Bolivia, the poorest and most overly indebted country he was to advise in South America. It possessed a relatively simple enclave export economy grafted onto an overwhelmingly agrarian society. In that revolving-door economy, exports and imports passed through the customs house without disturbing the vast majority of Indian peasants. Nevertheless, Bolivia presented Kemmerer with complex relationships among domestic elites and foreign bankers, mediated by the state.

Given the low level of urban development, the key interest groups affecting policymaking were tiny coteries of mine owners and merchants, accompanied by a handful of bankers. Bolivia relied on tin exporters for foreign exchange and on import houses for daily necessities for the emerging urban population. Both business groups kept the state afloat with customs revenues. The inflow of foreign capital and advisers benefited elites in the most modernized sectors but hardly touched the rural owners and workers. Except for disputes over exchange rates between the dominant tin barons and the subordinate import merchants, Kemmerer did not encounter severe conflicts among interest groups over his policies. Unlike Ecuadoreans, most Bolivians did not use his mission as a pawn in internal power plays. Rather, nearly everyone frankly sought his advice almost solely to satisfy external creditors.[1]

The state contracted foreign loans to avoid levying heavier taxes on exporters and importers. From a very narrow domestic tax base the fragile central government was trying to extend its ability to provide order, employment, and infrastructure for economic growth. Outside funds helped pay the costs of administering and enlarging the bureaucracy, expanding the transportation network, and servicing the pyramiding external debt.

Bolivia acquired credits abroad by exporting the tin, "gold" (hard currency), and laws that lenders saw as necessary for their repayment. To obtain loans for such an extremely underdeveloped and risky economy, Bolivia had to surrender exceptional sovereignty to foreign financial houses and inspectors. The country not only adopted the economic regulations and practices desired by its creditors, it also allowed North Americans to oversee its adherence to those rules. Beneath the surface, however, Bolivians often paid only lip service to these foreign codes and proctors, which did more to make their bonds marketable than secure. The precarious economy made it difficult for the government, even with the best intentions, to obey those strictures, and rendered new foreign loans mandatory.

Bolivia thus had to be certified repeatedly by a succession of outside experts in order to keep opening up fresh lines of credit. Its strategy resembled countries today that go back time and again to the International Monetary Fund with vows of good behavior to regain their creditworthiness. The Bolivian episode in the 1920s provides a graphic illustration of the process of privatization. Direct supervision began under U.S. bankers, with marginal intrusion by the U.S. government. That interference became insulting to Bolivia, burdensome to the bankers, and uncomfortable to the U.S. government, which increasingly adopted a public "hands-off" policy toward these financial arrangements. Consequently, those advising and monitoring functions were reassigned to the Kemmerer mission.

Bolivia also provides the most striking case of U.S. bankers willing to follow a Kemmerer mission by placing huge bond issues far beyond the country's capacity. Despite Kemmerer's gloomy prognosis, his retainer, Dillon, Read, and Company, handled that mammoth portfolio investment. Those securities lost their value when the Great Depression choked off exports of tin and imports of foreign capital. In response, Bolivia stopped sending gold (or its equivalent) overseas and no longer copied foreign financial laws to please U.S. investors. Debt payments and the gold standard fell by the wayside as inflation became the alternative to economic and political collapse. In the 1930s Bolivia turned away from the U.S. models and mentors which had spelled prosperity after World War I.

Foreign Factors in Bolivian Economic Development

Kemmerer encountered a growing export economy in which commercial exports far exceeded imports (see table 5.1). He also found the only Andean nation where Great Britain still dominated trade, even though the United States had become the principal supplier of imports (see table 5.2). England retained its preeminence by purchasing nearly 99 percent of Bolivia's tin. During 1925–29 minerals accounted for 93 percent of Bolivia's exports, and tin alone for 74 percent, rising from 63 percent in 1916–20 and 71 percent in 1921–25. As world prices for that commodity climbed until 1927, Bolivia became increasingly mono-

Table 5.1   Bolivian Trade, 1925–1935 (in rounded-off thousands of U.S. 1950 dollars)

Year	Exports	Imports
1925	$93,000	$54,000
1926	90,000	55,000
1927	98,000	53,000
1928	102,000	57,000
1929	113,000	64,000
1930	95,000	54,000
1931	78,000	28,000
1932	55,000	24,000
1933	45,000	31,000
1934	62,000	44,000
1935	67,000	50,000

Sources: See note 2.

Table 5.2   Bolivian Total Trade with Great Britain and the United States, 1913–1929 (by percentage)

Year	Exports to		Imports from	
	Great Britain	United States	Great Britain	United States
1913	81	1	20	7
1920	45	46	21	30
1921	53	24	—	—
1922	52	22	—	—
1923	59	35	22	27
1924	71	22	21	28
1925	81	8	20	27
1926	78	9	22	29
1927	80	9	19	29
1928	83	17	—	—
1929	77	14	17	34

Sources: Bolivia Económica e Industrial 1, no. 4 (July 1931): 308; Jorge Palenque, *Estadística boliviana. Primera y segunda parte* (La Paz, 1933), pp. 94–97; J. L. Tejada S., *Report on the Development of Commercial Relations between the United States and Bolivia* (Washington, D.C., 1920), pp. 7–21; Gustavo Adolfo Otero, *Notas sobre el comercio bolviano* (Barcelona, 1929), pp. 47–49, 113; J. R. McKey and H. S. Giusta, *United States Trade with Latin America in 1925. II. Southern Latin America* (Washington, D.C., 1926), p. 20; Clarence F. Jones, *Commerce of South America* (Boston, 1928), pp. 409–12.

cultural. The government also became more and more dependent on taxes on tin, which jumped from 8 percent of national revenues in 1921 to 21 percent by 1927, though falling thereafter to 16 percent in 1928 and 13 percent in 1929. When Kemmerer arrived Bolivians expressed fears about descending international tin prices, about their shrinking share of the world market, and about their heavy economic and fiscal reliance on sales of that item to one customer.[2]

In contrast with Chile, the mining companies were owned by Bolivian nationals. Nevertheless, the owners normally resided, incorporated, and invested their profits outside the country, behaving like foreign capitalists. That flow of capital abroad swelled with unregistered payments overseas for debts, transportation, insurance, and other invisibles. The positive balance of trade in the 1920s masked a negative balance of payments. Thus the need for foreign loans mounted.[3]

Data on foreign investments—like all economic statistics for Bolivia—varied widely according to source. Nevertheless, every compilation agreed that U.S. capital there had increased roughly tenfold from 1912 to 1927, far surpassing the previously dominant Europeans. From some $10 million in 1912, U.S. investments rose to approximately $15 million in 1920, $70 million in 1925, and at least $100 million in 1927, at the time of Kemmerer's arrival. Those dollars divided almost evenly between indirect investments in government bonds and direct investments in minerals, petroleum, and a few industries. That capital influx boosted U.S. sales to Bolivia, for the mining and oil companies purchased U.S. equipment, as did the railway firms funded by the government bond loans. From 1920 to 1927 British investments climbed from about $18 to $50 million, while others—principally French and Chilean—hovered around $30–$35 million. Those non-U.S. investments concentrated in mines, oil, railroads, public utilities, and, to a lesser extent, merchandising and manufacturing. Thus the United States accounted for over half the total foreign capital and increased its share with new loans to the government after the Kemmerer visit. By 1928 Bolivia hosted approximately $160 million worth of direct foreign investments, including roughly $70 million each from the United States and Great Britain. Most significant, virtually all the public debt rested in North American hands.[4]

From 1908 to 1931 Bolivia's foreign debt soared from zero to over $60 million. Measured in millions of bolivianos, the total public debt from 1920 through 1930 ascended from 63 (11 foreign, 52 domestic) to 208 (171 foreign, 37 domestic). The government increasingly relied on loans to cover its deficit spending, since fiscal outputs exceeded inputs during twenty-four of the thirty years from 1901 through 1930. From 1911 to 1931 the government's ordinary expenditures outpaced revenues by 117 million bolivianos. It also accumulated foreign debts to launch public works—especially railroads—and financial institutions. By the time Kemmerer arrived Bolivia was seeking more loans from

New York to meet the payments on its previous debts. The shaky government depended for its sustenance on the vagaries of mineral sales abroad by companies dominated by, in effect, foreigners, in order to attract and repay loans from foreigners, and now sought foreign advisers to keep the rickety machinery running.

Those loans proved particularly burdensome in a country where the vast majority of the population generated almost no resources to back up those external obligations. The highly unequal distribution of wealth and income rendered per capita national debt figures quite deceptive, placing Bolivia at the start of 1927 at only $14 per inhabitant. Realizing that only a tiny oligarchy benefited from and vouched for those credits in Bolivia, foreign bankers imposed high interest rates (7–8 percent) and strict controls over public finances. By 1927 the government was falling behind in its normal administrative payments and in its service of the internal debt because its external obligations absorbed around 50 percent of its revenues. Contractually, nearly 80 percent of those revenues were pledged to the service of outside loans. Since the government believed that this spiraling debt dependence was necessary to finance the growth of infrastructure and the state, it sought Kemmerer's counsel to elicit more foreign loans. It also expected him to facilitate their repayment by stabilizing the peso, augmenting tax revenues, and improving fiscal management.[5]

The most important foreign loan to Bolivia prior to the Money Doctor's house call came from New York in 1922. Floated mainly by the Stifel-Nicolaus Investment Company of St. Louis, it was dubbed the "Nicolaus loan." The U.S. embassy advised the Bolivian government to sign the contract. This twenty-five-year refunding loan in gold bonds at 8 percent (known as "Bolivian 8s") for a face value of $33 million (real value $29 million) hypothecated over half the national revenues as security. The most important pledge tagged all customs receipts, which made up around 45 percent of government income.

To ensure proper collection and disbursement of those revenues, the contract established the Permanent Fiscal Commission, comprising one member appointed by the government and two by the U.S. bankers. For the life of the loan they would supervise the collection of all national and departmental taxes, oversee government accounts, serve as director general of customs, function as inspector general of banks and monopolies, and provide one director of the Bank of the Bolivian Nation. The commission reported to the minister of finance and to the Equitable Trust Company of New York, which served as fiduciary agent for the debt. Bolivia rejected the bankers' suggestion that one member of the commission be named by the U.S. State Department, denouncing that condition as an infringement of sovereignty. The Permanent Fiscal Commission's powers resembled those conferred on North Americans by Kemmerer in Ecuador, and he would build upon the work of this agency in Bolivia to implant his own institutions. From its inception the commission praised Kemmerer's Colombian legislation and recommended similar changes in Bolivia, including his central bank, gold standard, and budgetary system.

After consummating the loan agreement, the government was deluged with domestic criticisms of the terms. It reacted by refusing to sign some of the permanent bonds unless the bankers modified the original contract. The State Department, however, made "strong representations" to convince the Bolivian government to adhere to all stipulations. Internally, State Department officials had concluded that this loan's conditions were exceptionally onerous and untenable, but they felt compelled to support the U.S. bankers; this imbroglio helped convince the State Department to maintain more distance from future South American financial transactions. Although this loan saturated Bolivia's capacity for foreign debt, it neither satisfied all its needs for foreign capital nor cured the government of deficit spending. This unusual arrangement did, however, set the stage for the acceptance of the Kemmerer reforms in order to obtain another New York loan in 1928.[6]

Opponents of the 1922 transaction criticized the size, terms, and guarantees. A special board appointed to review the contract in 1923 excoriated the Permanent Fiscal Commission as "an alienation of Bolivia's economic sovereignty, which imposes upon our institutions and upon the popular will the absolute discretion of a group of foreign bankers whose actions do not and cannot have any other guide than profit. . . . Such regulations try to impose on this part of America the imperialist sentiments of some bankers." Fearing that this subservience to the United States might lead to incursions like those in the Caribbean and Central America, some Bolivians urged the government to maintain countervailing ties with European capitalists. Other observers, however, praised the commission for its efforts to stabilize government finances. Most Bolivian elites hoped to continue attracting North American investments, albeit under less galling conditions than those in 1922.[7]

One way to woo foreign capital less slavishly was to invite Kemmerer, rather than U.S. bankers, to verify the country's creditworthiness. Bolivians believed that the preeminent position of the United States in international financial markets made it wise to import economic advisers, models, and loans from there instead of Europe. Admiring the Colombian and Chilean examples, one author urged in 1925:

> the contracting of a financial mission recommended by the Department of State or Commerce in Washington, which carries prestige in the United States. . . . It appears that only the authorized word of some Kemmerer will be able to attract the . . . capital for industrial development and the solidification of our economic edifice. Such a

mission has the following advantages: (1) the impartiality from any partisan political preoccupation or regional chauvinism; (2) the guarantee of probity and moral authority in the money market; (3) the decisive and frank solution of some problems of economic organization in an integral form; (4) the recognition of the exploitable resources of the country. . . ; (5) the elevation of the prestige of the country as a nation which tries to assure its solvency by establishing order in the management of its finances. . . . the successes of a . . . Kemmerer, far from being a threat to anyone, constitute a hope for sanity and improvement, a contact for mutual understanding and the attainment of reciprocal advantages, suggesting that American cooperation and its influence are precursors of world peace, with as much effectiveness as the very League of Nations.[8]

Bolivian Domestic Economic Forces

In the dominant mining sector Patiño Mines and Enterprises produced a majority of the nation's tin. Most of the rest came from the Hochschild and Aramayo companies. Since the Bolivian owners of these companies lived, incorporated, and received most of their profits and dividends overseas, Bolivian law treated their firms as foreign entities. Patiño established his corporation in Delaware in 1924, forming partnerships with U.S. companies and selling stock to North Americans. By 1926 an estimated two-thirds of the total capital invested in Bolivian mining was foreign, principally North American. The mine owners sent almost all their tin to England, which smelted most of it for sale to U.S. factories. Thus the tin barons had an enormous influence on and stake in Bolivia's international credit rating.[9]

The mine owners expected Kemmerer's visit to heighten the willingness of foreigners to invest in their enterprises. They wanted him to encourage foreign loans, unrestricted movement of foreign exchange, and free trade. The tin magnates also hoped that Kemmerer would recommend fiscal austerity and probity, enhanced tax collection from other sectors, and reductions in their customs duties and profits taxes. They complained that the government increasingly encroached on mining because it was the only lucrative enterprise. The general hike in taxes in 1923–24 especially affected the mines, which were also required to turn over to the state a portion of their foreign exchange earnings. As tin prices fell in 1927, smaller operations particularly felt squeezed: "The desire of almost every mineowner . . . is to sell his business to foreign capitalists."[10]

Although endorsing the gold standard to entice foreign investors, the big mine owners remained divided on the exchange issue. Previously they had benefited from the deteriorating value of the boliviano, which increased their sales and slashed their real wage and tax bills. Because of their stranglehold on the economy, the tin tycoons got from the Kemmerer mission an acceptable official currency value, an exemption from foreign exchange consignments to the central bank, and a reduction of their tax burden. Displaying similar leverage, they would also be the economic interests most successful at influencing government policies during the subsequent depression.[11]

Minimally articulated, the other production sectors exerted little impact on the government or the Kemmerer mission. According to the U.S. embassy in 1927, "The tin mines of Bolivia . . . produce 85% of the revenue [for government], whereas 80% of the other wealth of the country is invested in farms or haciendas by Bolivians who reside in the city in ease and idleness and live upon the products of the farm cultivated by Indians in a semi-state of slavery, because there is little inclination among the property-owning class of Bolivians to engage in industry." The agricultural and industrial elites shared the mining magnates' desires for lower taxes, improved transportation, sectoral credit banks subsidized by the government, and expanded foreign investments. As elsewhere in the Andes in the 1920s, the tiny group who owned most of the farmlands exhibited surprisingly little national political power, despite their control over most of the work force. They complained that most bank loans went to other sectors and urged Kemmerer to channel more credits in their direction. Both agriculturalists and industrialists also called for protection against competitive imports.

Although manufacturing began to emerge in the 1920s, significant growth did not really commence until the 1930s. The few industrialists agonized over the dilemma that depreciating currency discouraged the importation of not only consumer goods but also capital equipment. The minister of finance underscored their political weakness in his welcoming speech to Kemmerer: "Our few manufacturing industries are, in large part, artificial, since they have to import raw materials and try to live at the expense of customs protection, which, although favorable for the manufacturers, is onerous for the taxpayers, who are obligated to buy products often deficient and expensive." Neglected by the government and the banks, the agricultural and industrial sectors believed that any help from the Kemmerer mission would constitute a valuable improvement.[12]

After polling its constituents, the Chamber of Commerce of La Paz informed the Kemmerer mission of their need for greater access to foreign exchange, for which they depended on the tin producers and the state. Merchants hoped that Kemmerer would side with them against the mine owners on the issues of the availability of foreign currency, the high and stable value of the boliviano, and the burden of taxation. These importers also urged Kemmerer to revamp customs administration, especially to prevent fraud and contraband.[13]

All business groups hoped that Kemmerer's reforms would expand their supply of currency and credit from the banking system. Following the government's creation of a single bank of emission (the Bank of the Bolivian Nation) in 1914, the larger institutions consumed the smaller competitors. The remaining commercial banks mainly made loans to merchants and industrialists, usually at rates of 9 percent. They maintained branches throughout the republic, although poorer provinces and towns complained of inadequate service. These banks were supplemented by three small mortgage banks and by credit operations by a few commercial houses. Because of the very limited volume of transactions in Bolivia, the only foreign institution was the minuscule Transatlantic German Bank. From 1910 to 1926 the number of foreign banks had shrunk from three to one, while the number of domestics had dropped from six to three. These banks were solid and thriving when Kemmerer arrived, but their small number rendered the system intrinsically precarious. Consequently, Bolivians looked to his legislation to guarantee their security.[14]

Just as Bolivians had already consolidated and stabilized their private banks prior to Kemmerer's visit, so they had previously created the first central bank of issue in South America. For both commercial and central banking, his major task was merely to provide fine tuning and legitimation. After founding the Bank of the Bolivian Nation in 1911, the government turned it into a semipublic central bank, with the exclusive right to emit currency, in 1914. It maintained an obligatory gold reserve at 40 percent of notes in circulation. The sole depository of public funds, the bank's loans to the government could not exceed 20 percent of its capital. It was also supposed to extend credits and discounts to the private banks. Created by elites in La Paz partly to wrest financial dominance away from institutions in the judicial capital of Sucre, the bank quickly established branches in all the provincial capitals.[15]

Although the nucleus of the Kemmerer system existed prior to his arrival, critics believed that his reforms remained necessary to correct the deficiencies of the Bank of the Bolivian Nation, including government encroachment on the bank. The government had changed the bank's board from seven directors— with three chosen by the government and four by the other stockholders—to five directors, with three selected by the government and two by the other stockholders. Politicians also tapped credits beyond the 20-percent limit and channeled other bank loans to cronies and electoral supporters. Policymakers were further criticized for ceding control over the majority shares in the bank to the North American bankers in the Permanent Fiscal Commission, as collateral for the 1922 refunding loans. This central bank also angered the private bankers by appropriating their right to issue currency while failing to provide promised rediscounts. It drove many smaller foreign and domestic institutions out of business with its competitive lending and its high capital requirements for any legal bank. For example, although the law prohibited mortgage operations by the bank, its extensive activities in that field undercut private institutions.

Industrialists and merchants also complained about insufficient credits from the central bank and lamented its low level of currency emissions. Allegedly those outputs were not keeping pace with economic growth because they were determined by the bank's supply of capital and gold reserves. Nevertheless, from 1923 through 1927 the bank increased the money supply while holding its capital and reserves fairly constant. Many commentators still preferred a gold-exchange system tied to the balance of payments, which they knew Kemmerer would recommend.[16]

The Bolivians made Kemmerer's job easy because they had already stabilized not only the banking system but also the official exchange value of the boliviano. Despite repeated attempts to get on the gold standard, the currency remained inconvertible. To reduce oscillations and to ensure a regular supply for the government and for importers, the Commission of Exchange Control was established in 1924. It set the exchange rate and required all exporters to sell to the treasury foreign exchange up to 25 percent of the value of their sales abroad. Under those conditions the previously mercurial value of the peso to the dollar leveled off (see table 5.3). Within the commission, mine owners repeatedly lobbied for a lower exchange value, while merchants pressed for a higher or fixed value and for larger mandatory foreign exchange contributions from the tin exporters. While hoping to avoid that debate, the government also favored the gold standard. Policymakers believed that it would lure foreign capital and stabilize the public sector's debt payments and tax receipts.[17]

Table 5.3   Value of Bolivianos per $1 U.S., 1914–1935

Year	Value	Year	Value
1914	2.99	1925	2.90
1915	3.44	1926	2.96
1916	2.81	1927	2.87
1917	2.71	1928	2.74
1918	2.43	1929	2.78
1919	2.90	1930	2.71
1920	3.22	1931	3.94
1921	4.85	1932	5.46
1922	3.91	1933	3.92
1923	3.17	1934	4.17
1924	3.45	1935	4.24

Sources: See note 17.

Although revenues for the growing state doubled from 1921 through 1929, they lagged behind spiraling expenditures (see tables 5.4 and 5.5). The government desperately wanted Kemmerer to systematize, diversify, and amplify its budget. Prior to Kemmerer's visit the Bolivians themselves had pumped up the income from customs duties and domestic sources with the sweeping tax reforms of 1923–24, thus reducing the deficits. Coming after those changes and on the eve of the Great Depression, his recommendations had little positive impact. Instead, those suggestions coincided with a resurgence of uncontrollable deficits. The decline of international trade proved especially damaging because import and export taxes had come to supply a rising percentage of government revenues: 42 percent in 1921, 43 percent in 1925, 53 percent in 1926, and 57 percent in 1929. The government's budget projections never approached accuracy before or after Kemmerer. Nevertheless, they were nor-

Table 5.4   Bolivian Government Ordinary Revenues, 1911–1931
(in rounded-off millions of Bolivian pesos)

Year	Import taxes Budgeted	Actual	Export taxes Budgeted	Actual	Income taxes Budgeted	Actual	Other revenues Actual	Total revenues Budgeted	Actual
1911	6	9	3	4	—	—	4	13	17
1912	8	10	4	4	—	1	5	17	20
1913	11	10	5	5	—	—	7	22	22
1914	10	6	5	3	—	1	6	22	16
1915	6	4	3	3	—	1	5	17	13
1916	4	6	3	3	—	1	6	15	16
1917	5	7	4	6	—	1	5	17	19
1918	9	7	6	8	—	1	14	33	30
1919	8	7	7	7	—	1	10	31	25
1920	11	9	9	7	—	3	11	49	30
1921	6	8	2	2	—	2	12	32	24
1922	8	8	3	4	—	1	10	36	23
1923	8	10	4	5	—	3	11	25	29
1924	11	11	6	7	6	6	17	39	41
1925	13	13	7	9	8	6	14	50	42
1926	14	14	9	9	8	4	16	48	43
1927	15	17	9	10	8	5	14	49	46
1928	19	19	8	8	10	4	14	52	45
1929	20	21	7	7	8	5	16	62	49
1930	19	18	7	3	6	2	13	53	36
1931	12	10	1	2	2	1	10	28	23

Sources: See note 18.

Table 5.5   Bolivian Government Ordinary Revenues and Expenditures, 1911–1931 (in rounded-off millions of Bolivian pesos)

Year	Revenues			Expenditures			Deficit		Surplus
	Budgeted	Actual	Difference	Budgeted	Actual	Difference	Budgeted	Actual	Actual
1911	13	17	+4	18	17	−1	5	0	0
1912	17	20	+3	17	19	+2	0	0	1
1913	22	22	0	22	24	+2	0	2	0
1914	22	16	−6	25	19	−6	3	3	0
1915	17	13	−4	22	15	−7	5	2	0
1916	15	16	+1	23	20	−3	8	4	0
1917	17	19	+2	26	24	−2	9	5	0
1918	33	30	−3	36	33	−3	4	3	0
1919	31	25	−6	38	35	−3	7	10	0
1920	49	30	−19	54	36	−18	4	6	0
1921	32	24	−8	47	34	−13	15	10	0
1922	36	23	−13	40	37	−3	4	14	0
1923	25	29	+4	38	35	−3	13	6	0
1924	39	41	+2	45	45	0	6	4	0
1925	50	42	−8	50	48	−2	0	6	0
1926	48	43	−6	48	42	−6	0	0	1
1927	49	46	−3	50	47	−3	1	1	0
1928	52	45	−7	56	61	+5	4	16	0
1929	62	49	−13	61	53	−8	0	4	0
1930	53	36	−16	53	49	−4	0	13	0
1931	28	23	−5	32	32	0	4	9	0

Sources: See note 18.

mally rather prudent and, surprisingly, better calculated for customs receipts than for domestic taxes. Although rising, those internal revenues remained poorly collected, reported, and tabulated. Premature Keynesians, the Bolivians tried to build up a woefully underdeveloped economy through intentional, albeit undisciplined and atheoretical deficit spending.[18]

Besides customs duties, government domestic receipts came from a plethora of small taxes on income, profits, transactions, and sales. They also emanated from returns on government lands, monopolies, and services. The state had to rely mainly on revenues from foreign trade and foreign loans because of the resistance of local elites and the incapacity of the rest of the population to pay more significant levies. In the mid-1920s estimates indicated that the impoverished Indians (who made up at least 50 percent of the population) contributed only 1.94 bolivianos per person per year in taxes, the mestizos (35 percent of the population) contributed 11.89 bolivianos per capita, and the whites (15 percent of the population) 43.25 bolivianos each. Because of the extreme mal-distribution of income, even those highly unequal tax burdens left the under-privileged majority donating a disproportionate share of their livelihood to state coffers. According to one calculation at the start of the 1920s, those internal taxes—mainly indirect—took 19 percent of disposable income from the poor majority but only 4 percent from the tiny upper class. Following the increase in all taxes in 1924, Kemmerer seemed unlikely to be able to recast significantly a fiscal system with so little room for maneuver.[19]

The government confronted agonizing fiscal dilemmas. The state possessed few ways to increase resources without incurring additional foreign obligations, and almost no way to decrease expenditures without suspending debt payments. At the same time it could not cut back on essential infrastructural improvements or public employees, especially with scant job opportunities in the growing cities. The resulting temptation to resort to central bank credits jeopardized exchange stability, which in turn endangered the government's ability to meet its external obligations.

The executive branch controlled budget making, often disregarding legal or accounting restraints. As one critic noted, "It is sensible to recognize that the National Budget in Bolivia is a document of very little seriousness which represents a numbers game intended to show a false situation. They are not calculations based on the reality of revenues. To the contrary, in a desire not to alarm the public and to give it proof of fiscal economic solidity, the tendency is to present budgets with a surplus, balanced, or with small deficits." Not only the president but also the Congress inflated expenditures to reward political clienteles. Politicians frequently hired more bureaucrats and launched new transportation projects whose continuation required future budgetary expansion. External and internal borrowing became increasingly necessary to subsidize both public works and ordinary government outlays because most regular revenues were already pledged to debt servicing. Consequently, many Bolivians implored Kemmerer to introduce "scientific" fiscal procedures. They hoped his reforms would mitigate the vicious circle of deficits and debts, attracting foreign capital for more productive purposes. They expressed contradictory desires for lower taxes but more ample and reliable government revenues, for reduced expenditures but more fruitful development of credit and transportation facilities, and for Kemmerer's revision of the financial and fiscal system, but without imitation of foreign formulas.[20]

Bolivia faced its fiscal crisis during a period of unusual political stability under civilian rule. Contestation mainly occurred among the factions of two elite parties with virtually indistinguishable programs, the Liberals and the Republicans. Throughout the 1920s the latter group retained the presidency through fraudulent elections and army support.

Elected in December 1925 and inaugurated in January 1926, Hernando Siles, a member of the aristocracy from Sucre, presided over near bankruptcy. He fell into arrears on payment of salaries, to the dismay of bureaucrats and teachers. The military was calling for fiscal reorganization in the interest of national security. President Siles tried to feed the treasury by decreeing forced loans from the private banks. When Simón Patiño's Mercantile Bank balked, Siles seized its books and expressed his disgust with the existing financial system. To maintain order he declared a state of siege, which remained in effect after Kemmerer's arrival. Denouncing the La Paz political oligarchy, Siles staffed his administration with younger, middle-class technocrats. The traditional elites and Congress, however, blocked his economic reforms, so Siles looked to the Kemmerer mission. A believer in the laissez-faire gospel of the era, the embattled president shared the Money Doctor's vision of progress.[21]

The Kemmerer Mission

Immediately upon taking office Siles dispatched two government officials to assess Kemmerer's work in Chile. After receiving their positive report, the government heard doubts from the North American head of the Permanent Fiscal Commission. He argued that such a mission was unnecessary because Bolivia already possessed a healthy currency that had been rising in value since 1922, a strong central bank that only required small improvements to equal the Kemmerer model, a sound tax system that was already swelling government coffers, a revamped budgetary process that would soon bring accounts into balance, an excellent credit rating with foreign lenders, and U.S. fiscal monitors who did not need their functions usurped. Therefore the commissioners recommended that the administration simply adapt the Kemmerer laws already passed in Colombia and Chile. Nevertheless, Siles invited Kemmerer and a team of experts under his supervision. They were requested to make recommendations on currency and banking, taxation, customs, railroads, budget procedures and controls, and public credit and loan policies. Siles argued that Kemmerer would be able to refine, integrate, and augment the series of financial reforms already carried out by Bolivians. Moreover, he would add his "technical prestige" to those innovations and to other laws the administration had been unable to pass. His findings would allow Siles to blame the fiscal mess on the sins of his predecessors and to shore up his own political position. Above all, the strapped government expected the mission to enhance its ability to float further foreign loans, with or without the approval of the previous lenders represented in the Permanent Fiscal Commission.[22]

Following Siles's orders, the Bolivian consul general in New York contracted Kemmerer to bring his Ecuadorean team—Jefferson, Byrne, Vorfeld, Lockhart, Feely, and Fetter, along with an additional expert in railway finance—to Bolivia in March of 1927 for a three-month visit. The government agreed to pay the mission travel and living expenses, as well as $80,000. It also supplied local advisers, translators, and clerks.[23]

In contrast with the reception accorded some of his other missions, Bolivian commentators stressed Kemmerer's utility for solving fiscal problems rather than money and banking deficiencies. They deplored budgetary waste, inefficiency, corruption, and politicization. Opposition leaders warned the mission that recommendations for vigorous tax collections, strict accounting controls, and severe austerity measures would evoke unscrupulous resistance and subversion from bureaucrats, soldiers, congressmen, political bosses, provincial promoters of railroad projects, and mine owners. Complaining of overtaxation, businessmen questioned, "What use is it that the Kemmerer Mission advises a rigorous system of economies in State expenditures, if the commitments of the Government drag it down fatally in order to ingratiate itself with its friends and conquer or at least neutralize its adversaries at the cost of the budget?"[24]

Despite such doubts, most Bolivian leaders believed Kemmerer would be helpful because his scientific skills had already been demonstrated in other countries. They expected little new in his recommendations, but they placed hope in his international prestige and independence from local vested interests. With those credentials he might be able to compel the government to implement and obey laws which domestic experts had been unable to get accepted.[25]

Prior to and upon his arrival Kemmerer was hailed by the leaders of all factions of the Republicans and Liberals. Newspapers exulted that "the eminent magician of world finances" would lay "the foundation upon which will rest the entire economic edifice of the nation." Enthusiasts claimed that his unprecedented successes in South America had spawned a new verb—*kemmerizar*—and a new noun—*kemmerización*. They expected equivalent miracles from his mission in Bolivia: "Those guileless and tranquil professors, physicians of nations, surgeons of luxuriant financial foliage, they examine, palpate, and analyze everything, until they convert the problem most entangled by the incoherences of legislative routine into a simple scheme."[26]

Although Bolivians typically expressed high expectations, some entertained doubts. Opinionmakers suggested that Kemmerer's financial reforms would leave unscathed the nation's most serious economic problems, such as poorly developed transportation, industry, and human capital. Mine owners and other businessmen feared he would contribute little to them except higher taxes. The outlying provinces also complained of neglect from a mission that was too brief and too costly: "they have only carried out a trip of pure tourism, at the expense of the nation." Critics preferred European or Bolivian experts who knew something about the nation and who would not impose predetermined U.S. blueprints. One newspaper warned that Kemmerer's laws would never function properly because, "this is not a town in the United States. This is a mestizo democracy of indolent Indians and adventurous and blustering Spaniards. . . . We will give ourselves the expensive luxury of having paid a first-class financial mission, in order to give ourselves afterward the pleasure of continuing to do what we desire." Although some antiforeign sentiments cropped up, nationalistic resentments of the mission were seldom voiced during its visit.[27]

Government officials and the Permanent Fiscal Commission greeted Kemmerer upon his arrival on March 29, 1927. The U.S. ambassador offered to help in any way possible. To the irritation of some otherwise effusive newspapers, Kemmerer refused, per usual, to answer journalists' questions. He claimed that his proposals could not be discussed until the work was completed because the needs of each country were so different. The government assigned a former minister of finance, as well as national and provincial commissions, to work with the mission. The enormous difficulty encountered compiling the most basic financial figures inspired the creation of the first General Office of Statistics in 1928. Kemmerer also asked a special commission of Bolivian jurists to draw up legislation on corporations, negotiable instruments, and commercial and agricultural securities. He thus tried to avoid the improper translation of North American codes which had occurred during previous missions.[28]

To gather further information and win over elites, Kemmerer conducted closed-door interviews with government and private sector leaders, toured key provinces, and received suggestions from throughout the nation. During his inspection of the provinces, every special interest complained of government neglect. Mine owners called for lower import and export duties as well as railroad fares; bankers and merchants asked for greater monetary stability and foreign exchange availability; and landowners sought government protection and loans, although Kemmerer announced that he was not going to deal with agricultural problems. One newspaper even urged him to remedy alcoholism among Indian workers. Nearly all sectors expressed high hopes for his impending reforms and high praise for his operating methods. As in the other Andean countries, some commentators lauded his heavy work schedule as an example for allegedly lethargic local bureaucrats: "Only with this methodical, well-disciplined, scientifically distributed labor can one study and resolve in three months the economic and financial problems of a country. What Bolivia needs is this kemmerization in all work."[29]

The mission submitted recommendations on: a central bank, currency, general banking, the budget, the treasury, and a national comptroller; taxes on income, real estate, and mining; and the customs, the salt monopoly, railroads, and public credit. The government hailed these projects and the fact that Bolivia's economic "healing is in the hands of a man of science rather than our creole witchdoctors." After receiving doctor honoris-causa degrees from all the universities of Bolivia, Kemmerer departed in early July, stopping to pay a brief visit to Chile to evaluate the progress of his institutions there. Upon reaching the United States, he delivered confidential copies of all his Bolivian recommendations to the State Department. Kemmerer also gave the department a downcast assessment of a country with small economic potential, an overtaxed mining industry, a foreign debt beyond its means, and a weak and corrupt government, concluding "that he is almost as pessimistic about Bolivia as he is optimistic about Ecuador."[30]

Unlike countries which immediately rubber-stamped Kemmerer's projects, the Bolivian government appointed three commissions—on money and banking, taxes, and fiscal administration—to work with Congress to polish the wording and details of the laws. Commentators praised the administration for making sure that Kemmerer's standard reforms from other countries were adapted to national conditions. In the same breath they urged the rapid passage of his legislation intact, to save the nation from financial ruin. Those commissions took only a couple of months to pass on all the Kemmerer recommendations. Their main purpose was simply to emboss the laws with a national seal of approval. Following very minor revisions, his bills reached Congress in 1928. The Financial Commission of the Chamber of Deputies approved all the Kemmerer proposals in less than four days. They did not want to examine the details and have congressmen pick each bill apart.

Congress had rejected Siles's request for an enabling act, which would have permitted him to effectuate the reforms without submitting each one separately to the legislators. Now the government pressed the legislature for rapid action. Its principal reason was that consummation of a loan from Dillon, Read, and Company to help pay past debts hinged on implementation of the Kemmerer package. But mine owners, merchants, industrialists, and bankers—frightened by false rumors of heavy new taxes—cautioned against hasty enactment. Some business and congressional leaders warned that Kemmerer's proposals might be too rigid and foreign to fit smoothly with Bolivian conditions. When Congress resisted approving such monumental laws—especially those on taxes—without fuller consideration, the president denounced, censored, and exiled many of the opponents. According to the U.S. embassy, he justified those heavy-handed measures under the "ruse that subversive plots against the government were in course of preparation." Becoming a virtual dictator, Siles employed a state of siege and the army to ram almost all the Kemmerer laws through the legislature by July 1928. Thus, Colombia remained the only Andean country to approve a mission's proposals by democratic rather than authoritarian methods.[31]

Most of Kemmerer's Bolivian laws did not go into effect until 1929 because of delays by the government and the organizers of the central bank. Diversifying its foreign connections, the government then hired a French technical adviser to the minister of finance to help implement the legislation during 1930 and 1931. He later criticized Kemmerer's fiscal institutions as excellent in the abstract but unsuited to Bolivian laws, customs, and conditions in practice. Although most Bolivians and foreigners—including the Permanent Fiscal Commission—greeted Kemmerer's reforms as the greatest achievement by the Siles administration, those laws had virtually no time to work their wonders before the onslaught of the Great Depression. Nevertheless, that legislation did leave an institutional legacy for the future.[32]

Kemmerer's Money and Banking Reforms

Rather than having to install a central bank from scratch, Kemmerer merely had to make adjustments in the existing entity. Because of the small number of other financial institutions in Bolivia, some leaders of the bank and the business community expressed reluctance to see it stripped of its developmental role and converted into strictly a bank of banks, like the U.S. Federal Reserve. Most elites, however, welcomed its "scientific" modernization by Kemmerer.[33] They criticized the previous bank for failing to implement the long-promised gold standard, for reducing its hard-currency reserves from 42 percent of notes in circulation in 1923 to 33 percent in 1925, for competing with commercial banks, and for succumbing to government and foreign domination.[34]

All economic sectors hoped the new central bank would allot them more credits. As elsewhere in the Andes, landowners subsequently became disappointed and pressed the government to establish a separate agricultural credit institution. They also followed their counterparts elsewhere by reacting to reduced domestic credit sources with attempts to float mortgage bonds in U.S. financial markets. During the depression they finally persuaded the bank to supply farm loans at especially low interest rates and longer terms. Outside the farm sector, capitalists gave Kemmerer's creation higher marks. Mine owners did not oppose the central bank and its gold exchange standard in 1928. They believed that they only gained from an unstable currency when its value normally fell rather than rose. The new bank in 1929 also eliminated the requirement for mineral exporters to turn over a portion of their foreign exchange earnings for national currency. From its inception the bank followed Kemmerer's advice to give preference to industrial and commercial loans. Merchants—as well as foreign investors—were also pleased with exchange stabilization. Thus, once Kemmerer won the private bankers over, no elite group stood against his plan.[35]

Bolivian bankers were satisfied because the new central bank would be less competitive and would offer discount privileges. Most important, U.S. bankers urged passage of the Kemmerer bill. If Bolivia implemented that legislation, Dillon, Read, and Company offered to float a $23 million bond issue to help pay the public debt and capitalize the central bank. Thus Kemmerer's institution proved necessary to acquire foreign capital, which, in turn, helped fund and justify it. Indeed, President Siles had opposed replacing the Bank of the Bolivian Nation with Kemmerer's substitute until the Dillon, Read loan materialized contingent upon that legislation. During the congressional debate in 1928, the minister of finance reported that he had obtained the approval of both Bolivian and U.S. bankers for the Kemmerer project. He pressed for speedy passage of the law on the grounds that pleasing the U.S. bankers was imperative to bail out the treasury. The minister then tried to assuage national pride by adding, "I do not want to say with this that the approval of the project for the creation of the Central Bank takes effect with the exclusive objective of satisfying the demands of the foreign bankers, because if that occurred it would be, up to a certain point, denigrating."[36]

The government and Kemmerer had to convince the old as well as the new U.S. lenders to endorse the central bank. Kemmerer argued that the U.S. trustees of a majority of the Bank of the Bolivian Nation's stock should accept the new institution as a more solid guarantee of their interests. He convinced them to assent by agreeing to their demand to examine and approve all the statutes of his bank. He also affirmed their claim to designate four of the bank's eight directors in the event of a government default on the Nicolaus loan. They already had the power to name two of the directors by virtue of holding a majority of the stock, and they would, in case of default, take over the government's right to select two others.[37]

After promulgation of the law in July of 1928, preparation for the bank's opening took until July of 1929. The officers of the new institution visited Chile to study the organization of its central bank. Following Chile's example, the stipulation of the bank law, and Kemmerer's advice, they hired North American Abraham F. Lindberg as technical assessor of the bank for its first three years. Lindberg had previously supervised a U.S. loan in Nicaragua, worked with a Kemmerer mission, and been named by the U.S. trustees for the Nicolaus loan as chairman of the Permanent Fiscal Commission, with the approval of President Siles. Thus he enjoyed the confidence of both the foreign bankers and the host government. Now he helped the Bolivians set the bank in motion and then reinforced their determination to sustain the gold exchange standard during the initial onslaught of the depression.[38]

Kemmerer created a board of directors with less representation for the government and more for economic interest groups. The new central bank's eight directors would be chosen by the government (two), the subscribing commercial banks (two), the public stockholders (in effect, the U.S. trustees for the Nicolaus loan) (two), the Association of Mining Industries (one), and the national chambers of commerce (one). This composition reflected the economic and political weakness of industry, labor, and agriculture. Before the election of the first board, however, the bank added a seat to be filled by the agricultural associations.[39]

In contrast with its predecessor, Kemmerer's bank raised its legal reserve requirement from 40 percent to 50 percent of notes in circulation and deposits. Also, as elsewhere in the Andes, the Central Bank of Bolivia far exceeded that requirement. The reported reserve percentage rose from 37 percent in 1926, to 42 percent in 1927, 88 percent in 1928, 94 percent in 1929, and 87 percent in 1930. The Dillon, Read loan supplied part of that reserve increase. The bank placed most of its reserves in London—adhering to its historic economic ties there—until Kemmerer advised a massive switch to New York during the conference of central banks in Lima in 1931, following England's exit from the gold standard.

Because the bank's opening coincided with the arrival of the depression, its activities dismayed the economic elites. During its first six months the bank's capital rose from 22 million to 26 million bolivianos and its metallic reserve from 27 million to 36 million, while its deposits fell from 19.4 to 17.9 million, its deposits abroad from 32.3 to 20.7 million, its notes in circulation from 45 to 42.5 million, and its loans from 25.8 to 21.6 million. Although the nominal money supply had grown from the 38.7 million bolivianos circulated by the Bank of the Bolivian Nation in 1927, critics complained that reserves had shot up from that year's figure of 19.2 million, while deposits had declined from 20.1 million and loans from 47.7 million. Discontent proliferated as the central bank raised its discount rate from 8 percent in 1929 to 9 percent in 1930.[40]

The greatest fear among Bolivians was that voracious politicians would bleed the bank. In response, Kemmerer established the rule that loans to the government could not exceed 25 percent of paid capital and reserves, or 35 percent in emergencies. Although the Bank of the Bolivian Nation had had a legal ceiling of 20 percent, its extensions to the treasury had far exceeded that limit. During the new central bank's first year, that public debt had to be reduced to the new quota, but then a decree in October 1930 allowed additional credits to the government.[41]

Even while public and private finances withered, the bank boasted of succeeding at its primordial task of maintaining exchange stability. It followed Kemmerer's monetary law, the same qualified gold-exchange standard implanted elsewhere in the Andes. Bolivia had been off the gold standard since the suspension of convertibility in 1914. Most commentators welcomed Kemmerer's reform in the belief that it would benefit the nation at the expense of vested interests—especially mine owners—who had been profiting from exchange fluctuations. Other analysts feared that this instrumentality would exacerbate gold outflows and financial instability in an export economy dependent upon the erratic fortunes of one commodity. The elimination of the Exchange Control Commission and its claim to a share of the tin barons' hard currency aroused worries that they would ship all their earnings abroad, leaving little for import necessities. Congress shared some of those concerns and chafed at pressure to rush through the Kemmerer laws. Nevertheless, it approved his monetary legislation, without modifications, in one session.[42]

A small controversy swirled around the precise fixing of the new exchange rate. No significant debate over stabilization itself took place because, after violent swings from 1914 to 1925, the boliviano had been holding steady at approximately 2.90 to the dollar (see table 5.3). As Kemmerer himself observed, "Throughout the last twelve months exchange has been as stable as could have been expected under a real gold standard. In fact it has been more stable than it was during much of the period of the legal gold standard from 1909 to 1914." Thus the mission's only achievement in this area was settling the argument between those who wanted a slightly higher or lower fixed value. Kemmerer pegged the rate a notch below the existing value at 2.70 bolivianos to the dollar.[43]

The central bank upheld that official value from July 1928 until September 1931. Then the country returned to the pre-Kemmerer system of inconvertibility managed by the Exchange Control Commission. In vain Bolivians hoped that it could restore monetary stability, as it had during 1925–28. Given Bolivian accomplishments prior to Kemmerer's visit, the republic had little need for his money and banking reforms. Given their unfortunate timing, his innovations—except for their allure for foreign bankers—mainly made matters worse.[44]

Some Bolivians also argued that an elaborate general banking code and agency seemed unnecessary in a country with only three commercial banks and three small mortgage institutions. They pointed out that such legislation had been adopted in the United States to restrict and regulate the rapid proliferation of banks, whereas the problem in their country was to spur growth. They feared that Kemmerer's tight rules would drive some banks out of business or to much more cautious lending practices. His strict capital and operating requirements discouraged new banks and forced existing institutions to concentrate on short-term commercial loans. That posed special problems because the central bank absorbed the Bank of the Bolivian Nation, which in 1926 had accounted for 47 percent of the capital, 41 percent of the deposits, 51 percent of the current accounts, and 43 percent of the loans held by all Bolivian banks. Business executives complained that Kemmerer would create "a banking system in frank opposition with the necessities of the country . . . a law of banks highly prejudicial to the industrial development of the Republic."[45]

Other Bolivians believed that the mission's commercial banking law would make credit allocations more efficient, safe, and productive. Supporters contended that too many loans had been tied up in long-term commitments, especially mortgages, since banks preferred security to liquidity. Now it was hoped that lenders would concentrate more on profitable urban activities. After initial hesitation, Bolivian bankers themselves became the leading proponents of the reform, believing it would make their operations more "scientific" and sound. Those able to meet the requirements of the legislation also realized that it would concentrate financial power in their hands. Despite complaints from agriculturalists, industrialists, and mine owners, the bankers began constricting transactions to adjust to the new regulations even before their enactment.[46]

In Congress some representatives bridled at being rushed to approve such a complex law. They worried that it contradicted other national laws and even the Constitution, that it delegated excessive powers to the superintendent of banks, and that it would shrink credit availability. The government countered that the system would make more loans available by getting banks out of so many long-term obligations. Above all, the Siles administration carried the day with assurances from New York bankers that passage of the law, as part of the entire Kemmerer package, would open the door for U.S. banks to extend loans and establish branches in Bolivia. After inserting some minor wording changes, Congress voted into law the general banking bill and the central bank legislation on June 14, 1928.[47]

Following the law's requirement that the superintendent of banks be a foreign expert for the first three years, Bolivia accepted Kemmerer's recommendation of E. O. Detlefsen, who had worked on tax reforms for the mission, but had no experience in banking. Detlefsen found the local bankers very cooperative, but they found him incompetent. When the bankers requested another nominee, Kemmerer replied that he could not find anyone qualified in the United States who would accept the low salary paid in Bolivia. After Detlefsen's first year he was replaced briefly in 1930 by Lindberg from the central bank, and then in 1931 by a Bolivian.[48]

To conform with the Kemmerer law, local banks demanded payments on long overdue loans, eliminated noncommercial operations, and cut back the credit supply. Since that adjustment in 1928–29 coincided with the credit and currency shrinkage caused by the Great Depression, the other economic elites blamed Kemmerer's legislation for a "banking offensive" against all borrowers and capital-starved producers. At the same time the banking oligopoly consolidated. The largest commercial bank closed some of its weaker regional branches and absorbed one of the independent mortgage institutions. Not only did the Kemmerer system fail to entice new foreign banks into the country, but its minimum capital requirements compelled the Transatlantic German Bank to close down. His regulations and superintendency did, however, help the remaining domestic institutions weather the depression.[49]

Kemmerer's Fiscal Reforms

Whereas Bolivians really desired Kemmerer's money and banking reforms only to placate U.S. lenders, they exhibited more intrinsic interest in his fiscal recommendations. Although monetary and financial institutions actually functioned smoothly prior to his arrival, the government handled its economic affairs poorly. Many Bolivian elites feared that expansion, inefficiency, corruption, and indebtedness had brought the government to the brink of bankruptcy. That insolvency might force it to subvert the nation's monetary stability, banking solidity, and creditworthiness. Government employees, whose paychecks were in arrears, hoped Kemmerer could improve public management without endangering their jobs. Domestic taxpayers and foreign investors had despaired of any internally generated reform when the Siles administration broke its promise to reduce the budget and instead added more cronies to the public payroll.

Bolivians believed that Kemmerer had a better chance of success because "it is well known that Americans possess an essentially practical culture, free from fatuities and verbalism." Newspapers admonished the government to follow whatever recommendations the mission made and not to treat them like so many Bolivian laws, which "remain without any practical application and serve only for export." Since the government's main motivation was to impress the U.S. bankers, however, it did treat much of the Kemmerer legislation as "laws for export." It especially honored them in the breach, after the depression rendered many of their provisions inapplicable or counterproductive.[50]

Many of Kemmerer's suggestions were already being tried by the Permanent Fiscal Commission. From 1923 on those two North Americans and one Bolivian had carried out many of the functions of the subsequent superintendent of banks and comptroller general—monitoring, fiscalizing, reforming, and reporting on government financial operations. Kemmerer's reforms mandated the commission to assist his new agencies and amplified its role as an overseer of the new taxes and their collection. Although wielding vast powers, its rulings on income and property taxes could be appealed to the minister of finance or the Supreme Court.[51]

Kemmerer's standard budgetary law received rapid approval in April 1928, as did accompanying legislation to make the Office of the Treasurer more independent and free from conflicts with the comptroller. All three laws took effect, even though Kemmerer himself reported that his concentration of budgetary authority in the hands of the president and the comptroller probably violated the Constitution's delineation of congressional powers. He convinced the government, however, that establishing fiscal order and restraint under his system was too urgent to await a constitutional amendment.[52]

The government immediately implemented this Kemmerer law, preparing the 1929 budget in accord with its provisions. Nevertheless, deficits continued, partly because the international price of tin fell (though the total value of exports and imports still rose in 1929). At the same time Congress continued adding special expenditures, and the executive branch—including Kemmerer's new agencies—went on hiring new employees. When the government claimed to be imposing austerity by cashiering some bureaucrats, it was normally just making room for its own friends or relatives.

Critics bemoaned the swelling government's refusal to adhere to the diet recommended by Kemmerer: "By temperament, by custom, and by inheritance, we are a statist and bureaucratic people." Others complained that Kemmerer's law, although bringing greater precision to the budgetary process, "is not a perfect work and is resented, like almost all the legislation presented by Kemmerer, for obeying a single model applied with few variations to all the different countries where he has performed." But most observers blamed the Siles administration, rather than Kemmerer, for the failure to adjust and balance the budget in response to the arrival of the depression: "The coming to the country of the Kemmerer mission proved fruitless, not because his recommendations were erroneous or inappropriate for the country, but because neither those nor the laws that incorporated them could change the opinion of our statesmen who had elevated to the rank of a national institution the policy of chronic deficits and indebtedness. It was the men that Kemmerer needed to change." Of course, many Bolivian elites realized that what Kemmerer really could not change was the fragility of a state whose developmental and employment aspirations were surpassing its reliable financial resources.[53]

Kemmerer installed the Office of the Comptroller General to keep the government within prescribed budgetary boundaries. That agency replaced previous lax supervision by the Congress, the National Tribunal of Accounts, and the Permanent Fiscal Commission. The biggest innovation was the establishment of pre- instead of post-facto approval of expenditures. Kemmerer further recommended that a foreigner be named comptroller or at least technical adviser to the comptroller.

In addition to teaching the government businesslike financial practices, the comptroller, as Kemmerer told the U.S. State Department, helped maintain Bolivia's credit standing by making sure that it properly paid its debts. One official in the Division of Latin American Affairs was so impressed with Kemmerer's achievements and laws that he recommended to the secretary of state "the desirability of incorporating in our treaties the more important and fundamental principles upon which these reforms turn, seems more and more desirable and I think realizable. It is a matter at least which calls for serious consideration and would lend much greater security to American investments in Latin America than they now possess."[54]

Bolivian public opinion also warmed to the comptroller, even managed by a foreigner, since fiscal order was the main result desired from the Kemmerer mission. As with his other recommendations, this project also received approval with only minuscule modifications by the special commission of "notables," appointed by the minister of finance to review these laws before submission to Congress. Their glowing report took only two paragraphs, and their primary contribution was the addition of a statistical office. Despite the commission's imprimatur, nearly a majority in Congress opposed the comptroller proposal. They complained because it transferred budgetary control from them to a powerful, independent agency attached to the executive branch and because it clashed with certain constitutional provisions. Nevertheless, like the other Kemmerer recommendations, it passed into law in 1928 and took effect in 1929. One congressman concluded that "the series of financial laws projected by the North American technicians has been received with approbation and confidence, not precisely because one has compared the content of the dispositions or verified the efficacy of the experts, but because the reforms come from elements unattached to the country and who do not shelter anyone. Any Bolivian who had presented these projects, which . . . are absolutely the same ones that were prescribed in Mexico, Ecuador, Colombia, and Chile, would have been ridiculed, because in our country we have lost faith in our men."[55]

During its first year the comptroller encountered severe problems straightening out accounts, winning the cooperation of bureaucrats, and fending off attempts at emasculation or domination by the Congress and the president. The new official's complaints about improper authorizations and payments evoked angry denunciations from congressmen and the minister of finance. The government moved to weaken the comptroller and to pack the office with political loyalists, arousing criticism of "bureaucratic parasitism." The Siles administration also continued fueling illegal deficits and fighting attempts to audit public works contracts. In response, the U.S. technical adviser hired from the Kemmerer mission, Joseph Byrne, threatened to resign. Despite its neutral public policy, the U.S. embassy urged the State Department to back Byrne in his struggle to enforce the law, because "neither the Department nor the bankers would view with favor any modification of the present organic law nor any measure aimed at debilitating the Office of the Comptroller General." The embassy concluded that the Bolivian government was not using the comptroller to discipline its finances but only to add credibility to its quest for foreign loans.[56]

Hampered first by opposition from the government and then devastation from the depression, the comptroller was unable to bring the budget fully under control. Nevertheless, it did gradually achieve more efficient managing, tracking, and reporting of state finances. Soon inscribed in the Constitution, that office developed even greater fiscal powers than its counterpart in Chile. All those agencies began identically in the countries advised by Kemmerer but, over time, they acquired individualized features to suit local conditions. And, despite their early tribulations, they all endured as major public financial institutions.[57]

To further shore up government finances, Kemmerer recommended tax reforms similar to those advocated for many years by Bolivians and the Permanent Fiscal Commission. His biggest innovation was a mildly progressive income tax, simplified from the U.S. model to suit Bolivian administrative capacities. The income tax was to be supervised by the Permanent Fiscal Commission as part of the guarantees for repayment of the 1922 loan. The commission now became a permanent part of the Ministry of Finance, which angered Bolivians, who believed that the Kemmerer reforms should have subtracted powers from that agency of U.S. bankers. Although initially fearful of Kemmerer's recommendation, most economic elites applauded this tax. They accepted it as a corrective to excessive reliance on indirect imposts, which currently supplied a majority of state revenues.[58]

Kemmerer's proposal on real property also only slightly increased taxpayers' burdens. This reform mainly sought to regularize and equalize evaluation and collection of these property levies, also to be supervised by the Permanent Fiscal Commission. The same efficiency purpose underlay his mild revamping of the tax on mining capital, profits, and exports.[59]

Despite misgivings about ceding so much jurisdiction to the Permanent Fiscal Commission, the government accepted all these tax proposals verbatim. The Siles administration then raised the tax rates slightly and added the National Tax Collection Company. The minister of finance called for cursory analysis and quick action by Congress, as a patriotic "act of confidence in the government."

During the tax debate many representatives complained about stuffing the treasury further and about laws "formulated from an American and not from a Bolivian point of view." One congressman protested, "We are too rich in laws copied from other legislations . . . it is not possible to copy tax laws from other countries, because they will not give us the expected results. With tax laws does not occur the same thing as with other types, such as social laws . . . which can remain on the books since many of them do not have practical application and only serve for exportation." Despite such concerns, Congress, after restoring the rates recommended by Kemmerer, passed all the tax legislation overwhelmingly, on the same day they passed the bills on the budget, the treasury, and the comptroller.[60]

Kemmerer agreed with many Bolivians that what the country needed most was not more taxes but more effective tax collection. Therefore he endorsed the government's proposals for the National Tax Collection Company and for a salt monopoly. The new central collection agency would also have its operations audited by the Permanent Fiscal Commission.[61]

With the new taxes and collectors, government receipts mounted in 1929, to the dismay of merchants and industrialists. Resistance by the middle and upper classes to paying the income and property taxes prompted the government to escalate consumption and sales taxes, especially as receipts from tin exports declined at the end of the year. Confronted with a widening gap between their wages and the cost of living, some workers echoed businessmen in protesting that the people were being "taxed to exhaustion." Detlefsen wrote to Kemmerer that "there are at present very hard times in Bolivia, and the Kemmerer laws are getting the blame therefore."[62]

Kemmerer's legislation also responded to Bolivian complaints that customs collections were inefficient and dishonest. In a country with such a weak and porous government, Kemmerer concluded that a majority of goods probably slipped in illegally. That caused grave concern because import duties supplied more than half the customs revenues, which in turn furnished the majority of state income. The Kemmerer bill to create a more powerful and effective customs agency was drafted by Robert H. Vorfeld, who came from the U.S. Tariff Commission. He had previously reorganized customs and tariffs in Paraguay and in the Dominican Republic during the U.S. occupation, and had worked with Kemmerer in Ecuador. His Bolivian legislation preached against protectionism, but Siles went ahead with new tariffs desired by industrialists. After Congress finally approved Kemmerer's bill in April 1929, the Chamber of Commerce denounced its rigid regulations and severe penalties. The government immediately revised the law to suit the import merchants.[63]

The Siles administration tried to expand revenues mainly in order to repay past foreign credits and justify the acquisition of new ones. By 1927, however, the difficulty of meeting existing obligations made more and more Bolivians leery of contracting further external loans. Some feared that the guarantees extended to foreign lenders "compromise national sovereignty . . . making us into a type of economic colony." Therefore the hope was expressed that Kemmerer's fiscal housecleaning would curtail deficit spending and render escalating indebtedness unnecessary.[64]

Kemmerer tried to fulfill those hopes by cautioning against further indebtedness, especially involving any large amounts or pledged revenues. He conceded that the per capita public debt (estimated at $20 total, $16 external) was not huge by international standards. But he warned that it was excessive when the majority of the population, who were Indians who contributed virtually nothing to the national treasury, were subtracted. Worse, over one-third of the national budget each year went to service the public debt. Although potentially valuable in the long run, the public works projects funded by those loans offered little promise of producing revenues to help pay those debts in the foreseeable future. Neither the government nor U.S. bankers, however, heeded Kemmerer's warning that "the existing debt situation of the country would not make foreign financing advisable or profitable at the present time." Instead, Siles kept this report secret and used the existence of the Kemmerer mission to pry more dollars out of New York.[65]

The impending arrival of the mission in 1927 had helped Siles obtain a $14 million loan at 7 percent from Dillon, Read, and Company, who had numerous conversations with Kemmerer during preparations for his trip to Bolivia. The government assigned those dollars to railway and highway projects. Siles had secured that loan by pledging some of the revenues generated by the new taxes inaugurated in 1924. In 1928 the same firm offered to underwrite another $23 million if the government enacted the Kemmerer reforms. The company told the State Department that Kemmerer's legislation made them feel much more confident about floating a new loan, and so "we are using every opportunity to encourage the government in proceeding with the plans laid out by the Mission. With this purpose in mind our discussions with the Bolivian government have been based on the primary condition that before the loan is made, the government shall adopt in full the entire Kemmerer program." The U.S. Commerce Department doubted that Bolivia would adhere to Kemmerer's rules or that even such adherence could safeguard new investments. Aware that Kemmerer and the Permanent Fiscal Commission opposed further indebtedness, Commerce advised the State Department to discourage Dillon, Read. Kemmerer himself discussed the proposed loan and the condition of Bolivian finances with the Bolivian government, Dillon, Read, the Equitable Trust Company, and the State Department, telling the latter that

> he himself would buy no Bolivian bonds. The country is very weak financially owing largely to the insistent demands of various sections of the country for the construction of railroads which can hardly be expected to pay their way for some generations to come. It already had a heavy debt and the government would be under constant pressure to increase it. In reply to an inquiry as to the possibility of Bolivian capitalists supporting the government's credit, he stated that he did not believe a man like Patiño would support the government's finances

from patriotic reasons or except under the pressure of circumstances. There was no great patriotic feeling in Bolivia. Personally he doubted whether the country would eventually survive as a nation. He was not as optimistic about Bolivian finances as Dillon, Read, and Company appear to be. Probably if no new loan were floated Bolivian finances would soon crash; whether they would eventually pull through or how long before they would crash if the Dillon, Read project were realized, he was not prepared to estimate. His pessimism, however, regarded the longer future.

Although conceding that Latin American governments had many ways of skirting legal restrictions, Kemmerer averred that Bolivia was serious about his financial reforms and therefore more deserving of a foreign loan. He took "an absolutely impartial position" on the pending Dillon, Read contract. He did, however, oppose that firm's demand for a North American comptroller. After all, Kemmerer pointed out, U.S. citizens he had recommended were already serving as adviser to that office, as superintendent of banks, and as manager of the central bank.[66]

Apparently Kemmerer was torn by his roles as an adviser to the Bolivian government, to U.S. bankers, and to the U.S. government. The formal boundaries separating those spheres became especially blurred in the Bolivian case. Examples of crisscrossing included Lindberg being appointed first to the bankers' Permanent Fiscal Commission and then to the central bank, and Feely becoming the U.S. ambassador after serving with the Kemmerer mission. The State Department also faced countervailing pressures. Its economic adviser warned that the Bolivian government should shore up its finances and refrain from further borrowing: "The Department . . . should solicitously follow the course of Bolivian finances, since there is greater probability of default in the case of Bolivia than in the case of any other Latin American country. Professor Kemmerer is very pessimistic as to the future of Bolivia. He found there less general ability in financial matters than in the other Latin American countries which he has assisted, and he stated that he found also a spirit which is not conducive to constructive reform." Although State shared the bleak assessment of the Commerce Department and Kemmerer, it decided not to object to the Dillon, Read venture, partly because the State Department preferred to refrain from officially approving or disapproving foreign loans. The department also did not dissuade Dillon, Read because it knew Bolivia was also contacting British lenders. It did not want Bolivia to default on its previous obligations and thus endanger all Latin American credit connections with New York. Furthermore, it did not want to harm diplomatic relations with Latin America, especially when the United States was already suffering criticism for its policies in the

Caribbean and Central America. Dillon, Read consummated that loan contingent on implementation of the Kemmerer reforms, but with no contractual requirement that they be carried out. When the Bolivian government thereafter circumvented some of those laws and undermined the comptroller, the State Department expressed displeasure but did not interfere. The State Department concluded that U.S. bankers and investors had taken their own private risks.[67]

For its part, the Bolivian government announced the Dillon, Read loan to Congress as justification for passing the Kemmerer laws. It also touted that contract as proof of the Siles administration's efficacy and prestige. The minister of finance reported that, just prior to introduction of that legislation, U.S. bankers had declined to place a loan for $8 million, but now were willing to handle one three times as large. That loan at 7 percent would be guaranteed by a long list of pledged revenues. It drew support because it would be used for railroad construction, for overdue salaries, and for founding the central bank, by liquidating government debts to local commercial banks. According to Kemmerer's laws, those banks were now supposed to invest in commerce and industry instead of in the government, which was expected to rely on taxes and foreign lenders. Some Bolivians bristled at swallowing the Kemmerer laws under inducement of a U.S. loan, just as they had balked at the Permanent Fiscal Commission. Seething at "our economic dependence" on collusive foreign lenders and advisers, one nationalist contended:

> We should recognize the bitter reality that Bolivia has sold part of its sovereignty. The recent reforms recommended by Professor Kemmerer have been promulgated as laws more like an imposition from our latest lenders, attending primarily to the interests of those bankers before the particular needs of the country. We do not doubt that Professor Kemmerer himself will not fail to recognize that the laws recommended to Bolivia, so analogous to those recommended to Colombia, Chile, and Ecuador and so similar to the laws of the United States of North America, have not been the product of a thorough study of the very particular economic structure of our country. The grand financier has believed that it was easier to mold public needs to the laws.

Despite misgivings, Congress and most elites approved the interconnected loan and laws.[68]

Like previous loans, a significant portion of those Dillon, Read funds was earmarked for railway construction. Since World War I Bolivian administrations had promoted railroads as the key to knitting the country together, defending national territory, and energizing the economy. The main beneficiaries were the tin exporters and the political representatives of the provinces selected for new lines. Kemmerer criticized many of the projects as poorly planned, uneconomical, and politically motivated. He feared they jeopardized the government's ability to stabilize its finances, pay its debts, and sustain the gold standard, and recommended more profitable management of existing lines and curtailment of new endeavors. Since most Bolivians desired lower fares and expanded service subsidized by the government, however, it suppressed and ignored the mission's advice. "In a country where the popular support accorded the government is in direct proportion to the number of miles of roads and railways which the government constructs," Siles opted to carry forward his public works programs. As the depression stunted those efforts, the economic elites denounced the burdens of taxes, foreign debt, and his administration.[69]

Depression and War, 1929–32

The depression also quickly turned Bolivians against Kemmerer's laws, institutions, and U.S. appointees. Many lambasted his system for increasing their vulnerability to the international crisis. They also denounced his reforms for shrinking their currency and credit supplies and for raising their taxes, partly to pay the expensive directors of his new agencies. Both before and after the crash Kemmerer assured nervous Bolivians, as well as his other clients, that exports could never fall so low as to necessitate abandonment of the gold standard.[70]

After the peak year of 1929, foreign trade plummeted from 1930 until 1934. Although leading the plunge, tin continued to account for around three-fourths of the value of all exports. In 1931 the big mine owners reacted to falling prices by forming, with the support of the government, an international cartel with their Asian and African counterparts to cut back production. From 1929 to 1933 exports of Bolivian tin dropped from 47,000 to 15,000 tons and their value also fell by two-thirds. That trade also shifted away from such heavy reliance on the British market. During 1929–33 England accounted for an average of 68 percent of all Bolivian exports and 18 percent of imports, the United States for 10 percent and 30 percent, respectively; during 1934–40 England claimed 47 percent of exports and 8 percent of imports, and the United States 18 percent and 32 percent. In the throes of the depression, the government reimposed on the mining companies the obligatory deposit of a majority of their foreign exchange earnings. It had promised not to raise their taxes, however, in return for a loan from Patiño prior to the Kemmerer mission. Immediately following the advice of Kemmerer and the mine owners, the government had then reduced the tax on tin exports to promote sales abroad. Consequently, those revenues as a percentage of fiscal income shrank from 10 percent in 1927 to 8 percent in 1928, 6 percent in 1929, and 4 percent in 1930, thereafter rebounding to 7 percent in 1931 and 1932, 11 percent in 1933, and 10 percent in 1934.[71]

As the depression deepened in 1930–31, some mine owners called for devaluation. Their national association, however, supported the government's attempt to sustain the gold standard, foreign debt payments, and the Kemmerer system, until Great Britain jettisoned convertibility. Then they spearheaded the campaign for Bolivia to follow suit, excoriating the merchants who still defended exchange stability.[72]

Caught in the contradictions of the Kemmerer system they had applauded, the importers took irreconcilable positions. They praised the gold standard but deplored the credit constriction caused by that law and by the ones for the central bank and general banking. They attracted agricultural and industrial allies for their crusade to relax Kemmerer's restrictions on the founding and lending practices of banks. By 1931, however, the merchants ended up isolated in their defense of exchange stability. Manufacturers further undermined the Kemmerer system by calling for devaluation and tariffs to block competitive imports and by demanding more public works. Indeed, none of the economic sectors strongly supported the letter or spirit of the Kemmerer legislation once it no longer attracted foreign credits. Neither the decision to adopt nor to discard his model resulted from fierce struggles among domestic interest groups; rather, those policy choices mainly responded to shifting international currents.[73]

From 1930 to 1931 producers became incensed because the central bank's deposits fell from 15 million to 8 million bolivianos and its currency in circulation from 40 million to 27 million. The deposits and loans of the remaining two commercial banks shrank accordingly. The operations of the two mortgage institutions stagnated. Amidst voluble criticism for maintaining high reserves instead of loan activity, the central and commercial banks defended their penurious policies. In December 1930 the central bank even argued that the amount of money in circulation per capita was excessive because the large Indian population seldom used cash. The superintendent of banks pointed proudly to the fact that all the existing financial institutions had survived the depression. In 1932, however, the banks and the government succumbed to public pressure and revised Kemmerer's law to permit greater flexibility in commercial credit operations.[74]

During 1929–30 the deteriorating economic and fiscal situation also enflamed discontent with the government. The traditional elites had resented Siles's elevation of technocrats and politicians from the middle class and the provinces. Now those critics stepped up their criticisms of his economic incompetence. Opponents also berated Siles for "selling out" to foreign interests. They particularly complained about the bulging external debt, the imposition of the Kemmerer laws and appointees, and concessions to U.S. transportation and communication firms. Nationalists also condemned the maintenance of a German military expert as army chief of staff. Even louder protests erupted against Siles's dictatorial methods. From 1927 through 1930 he had imposed a state of siege—muzzling, jailing, and deporting opposition leaders. Then he postponed the 1930 presidential elections so that he could serve a second term. Whereas such usurpation of power had angered Siles's enemies before, now it united his economic and political opposition.

That final transgression prompted the army to demand the resignation of Siles and his German commander. A junta headed by General José Blanco Galindo took office in June 1930. The new rulers promised to restore economic order, sustain Kemmerer's institutions, and call new elections. Merchants and other businessmen cheered the officers, urging reductions in taxes and expenditures. Government officials labored in vain to bring the budget under control, since over 40 percent of revenues were committed to military expenditures and over 70 percent to the foreign debt. Reluctantly, they fell behind on meeting those external obligations in January 1931, ending decades of punctual payments. Deriding Kemmerer's legislation as "a closed bible which he shows us saying 'this is your faith,'" Daniel Salamanca won the presidential balloting of 1931, serving from then until 1934.[75]

After four futile months of trying to reduce the deficit by pruning employees or paying them in promissory notes, President Salamanca definitively defaulted on the foreign debt in July 1931. When England left the gold standard in September, Bolivia—still part of the sterling block—followed immediately. On the heels of that decree Salamanca prohibited exportation of gold, established inconvertible paper money, and installed exchange and price controls. He also authorized emergency credits from the central bank. Even then, many Bolivian elites hoped for a speedy return to monetary and financial orthodoxy. But the inflation which took hold in October 1931 accelerated thereafter, especially during the Chaco War. Deficit spending soared as government income jumped from 22 million bolivianos in 1931 to 26 in 1933, 43 in 1934, and 56 in 1935, while expenditures zoomed from 31 million, to 104, to 129, to 193. After sinking under the weight of the depression, the Kemmerer system drowned under the onslaught of war.[76]

The two key decisions which unhitched Bolivia from the Kemmerer harness were the scuttling of service on the foreign debt and the abandonment of the gold standard. By 1931 the public debt had reached 216 million bolivianos (173 external, 25 internal, and 18 floating). That foreign obligation equaled $63 million. It had become virtually impossible to pay that annual bill and maintain the solvency of the government and the central bank. By 1930–31 many opinion leaders clamored for a suspension or at least reduction of outflows to U.S.

creditors. Nevertheless, some elites, especially merchants, still argued for a maximum effort to honor the debt and thus retain creditworthiness. The government, in consultation with the U.S. ambassador, scrambled desperately to meet its obligations until finally overwhelmed by the continuing crisis.[77]

In late 1930 the government sent representatives to try to negotiate lower debt payments with the bankers in New York. There, those emissaries discovered that the bankers could not adjust the debt because it was not held by the banks, but by thousands of bondholders. The bankers urged the government to rein in expenditures, abandon hopes of new credits, and continue debt servicing. At the same time the bankers recognized that Bolivia could only be expected to make payments within its current economic and fiscal means. Following those fruitless discussions, Bolivia, in 1931, became the first Latin American country during the Great Depression to suspend payments on its foreign debt.[78]

U.S. bankers first expressed sympathy for Bolivia's plight. They noted that, so far, debt defaults were much less widespread in Latin America than in the United States. Bolivia assured the bankers that it intended to resume reasonable payments as soon as the international crisis abated. The creditors grew frustrated, however, in their efforts to convince the Bolivian government to pay at least a percentage of the interest charges. When they tried to get the U.S. government to intercede on their behalf, the State Department refused to become involved in "negotiations between the interested bankers and the Bolivian Government." After breaking the loan contracts, Bolivia also ejected the two North American representatives on the Permanent Fiscal Commission. The country did not resume partial payments on the foreign debt until a settlement was reached with the Foreign Bondholders' Protective Council in 1948. In the meantime the government compensated for the unavailability of external credits through internal borrowing, increasingly from the central bank.[79]

The accompanying decision to depart from the gold standard was taken more reluctantly. During 1930 and 1931 more and more Bolivians complained that Kemmerer had given them a system unsuited to an underdeveloped country highly dependent on the volatile export price of one commodity. According to critics, he should have been aware of the recurring crises caused by downward fluctuations, even though he could not have forecast the extreme plunge during the depression. They also chastised him for not realizing that the positive balance of trade disguised a normally negative balance of payments, which rendered maintenance of his monetary law unlikely. Its chances of success were further reduced by the enormity of the external debt, the fragility of government finances, and the control of most capital and foreign exchange by a tiny elite concentrated in the mercurial export sector. When a government confronted a customs house delivering falling revenues and a central bank constricting credits, it had nowhere to turn for fiscal survival. Many commentators scorned the model they had previously lauded, now that it could no longer attract foreign loans. By 1931 critics were calling for currency and credit expansion through relaxation of "the Kemmerer laws, which are iron bars that imprison to death any attempt at industrial development."[80]

Despite such disillusionment, the orthodoxy of the age and the hope of recovery sustained many defenders of the gold standard. Heated debate raged in the press until the final abandonment. Early on, some owners of small mines argued for devaluation. By contrast, the tin magnates, who relied heavily on imported capital goods and who sent many of their profits overseas in the form of dividends, staunchly defended stable money from 1929 to 1931. Although in agreement with merchants on that issue up to the debt default, thereafter exporters clashed with importers over the exchange rate. After the merchants lost that monetary battle they tried to salvage their businesses. In 1932 they convinced the government to reinstate the requirement for mine owners to turn in a share of their foreign exchange receipts to be apportioned among importers. However, the tin companies seldom honored that obligation until compelled to do so by the Chaco War. Moreover, the central bank compensated them with credits in anticipation of export earnings. The scarcity of credit for groups other than the mine owners and the military also damaged agriculturalists, many of whom lost their mortgaged lands to the banks. Rural elites also lost faith in the gold standard.[81]

Until its default the Bolivian government defended exchange stability. The state was very reluctant to see the boliviano cost of servicing foreign obligations and importing necessities skyrocket. The U.S. embassy also encouraged the government to stick to the gold standard, as did the central bank, the most zealous champion of the Kemmerer system.[82]

From 1929 through 1931 the central bank continued maintaining a reserve far in excess of the legally required 50 percent, and it contracted currency and credit in accord with the shrinkage of foreign exchange inflows. The bank resisted calls for loan expansion from the government and merchants, although it did set special lower interest rates for agriculturalists and industrialists. The directors obtained and published letters from Kemmerer supporting their belt-tightening policies. In December 1930 he urged the bank to uphold exchange stability and loan restrictions. In 1931 their letters to him became more desperate, as the Bolivians saw Ecuador and Chile easing away from his orthodoxy. They asked how the gold standard could be sustained when their only source of foreign exchange, tin exports, was running out. They inquired whether exchange controls, as proposed in Chile, might be an advisable emergency measure. Despite growing doubts, the officers of the central bank, reinforced by Kemmerer and by U.S. adviser Lindberg, clung to free convertibility during most of 1931.[83]

They tried to buttress their case further—and find solutions to the crisis—by convening a conference of Kemmerer's central banks and the U.S. Federal Reserve in Lima. Lindberg and the other officials of Bolivia's central bank hoped to forge a united front of Kemmerer's South American institutions. Their hidden agenda was to solicit emergency advances for two or three years from the reserve banks and other financial institutions in the United States. What they were seeking was an international lender of last resort to rescue countries during balance-of-payments crises and thus save the world system, much like the institutions founded after World War II. They made the case to Kemmerer that those credits to ease the crisis and increase production would ultimately benefit U.S. exporters and bankers. In August of 1931 Lindberg asserted that, without such assistance, the Latin Americans would be forced to reduce imports, debt payments, and free convertibility. The U.S. ambassador to Bolivia, Edward F. Feely (previously general secretary with the Kemmerer mission there), advised the State Department to support the project; he believed it would foster political and economic stability in Latin America and improve the region's worsening relations with the United States. Committed to laissez-faire, however, Washington refused.[84]

England devalued in September 1931, before the Lima conference met. As a result, the Bolivian central bank lost over 100,000 pounds on its reserve deposits. Britain's decision particularly damaged the mine owners, who made most of their sales there and who now opposed the merchants' campaign for exchange stability. That calamity finally convinced the central bank and public opinion to bow to the inflationary demands from the government, which had been gathering momentum since the debt default. In October 1931 the bank requested and received from Congress laws suspending the gold standard, adopting exchange controls, and authorizing emergency credits to mining enterprises. The legislature also tried to amplify credit availability by softening the regulations in Kemmerer's general banking law. The essence of his institutions had endured only two years.[85]

In December 1931 Kemmerer attended and endorsed the meeting convened in Lima by the Bolivians. He arrived as the representative of the Federal Reserve Bank of New York. All the central banks could do at that reunion was reaffirm his financial and fiscal principles. They reiterated their belief in the gold standard, although some advocated exchange controls. At least temporarily, that conference and their reencounter with Kemmerer convinced most of the central bankers to renew their dedication to his system.[86]

The Bolivian delegation's hope that their separation from the gold standard would be brief was crushed by the onset of the Chaco War with Paraguay (1932–35). Like the northern Andean countries, Bolivia reacted to the decline of exports during the depression by clashing with its neighbors over border resources. As that longstanding dispute with Paraguay exploded, the Bolivian government turned to the central bank for support. The bank immediately lowered its reserve requirement to 40 percent and its interest rates from 9 to 7 percent, and then massively expanded loans to the government for the war effort and public works. From 1932 on, the government's Exchange Control Commission—composed of its representatives along with mine owners, merchants, manufacturers, and bankers—tried to determine the plummeting currency values. They usually set a compromise official rate, in between the desires of exporters and importers. They soon imposed multiple exchange rates, giving birth to a thriving black market. From 1931 to 1935 the bank's reserve fell to 6 percent, while the money supply increased tenfold.

As a result of depression and war, what had been largely a private institution dedicated to exchange stability became a government-dominated bank committed to developmental lending. As the central bank explained its new role: "It is necessary to evolve from a rigid system of a central banking mechanism for the restriction and purification of credit to a more ample, more tolerant policy—perhaps riskier, from a certain point of view, but indispensable—in order to justify the title of axis of the Bolivian economy." While adopting far different practices than he would have approved, Kemmerer's creation continued providing valuable services to the nation during and after the ill-fated war.[87]

The patterns laid down during the depression and war persisted thereafter. The expanding state augmented its control over the central bank to funnel inflationary credits to the bureaucracy, public works, and producers. Given the narrow economic base of Bolivian politics, fiscal sustenance and growth had to rely on internal loans when external sources shut down. Consequently, the number of bolivianos in circulation ballooned from 27 million in 1931, to 146 million in 1935, 1,500 million in 1945, and 6,200 million in 1952, the time of the national revolution. Government deficits, the money supply, and domestic prices spiraled upward, with only brief interruptions, from the 1920s to the 1980s.[88]

Both before and after the crises of the 1930s, Bolivians not only accepted the tutelage of foreign institutions but also manipulated them in pursuit of their national interests. Kemmerer's dicta had little lasting effect. To the contrary, his institutions helped Bolivians thereafter devise and implement expansionary policies, at least partly of their own making. With or without external assistance, local elites continued their integration in the international market, their elaboration of domestic capitalism, and their amplification of the central government.

6 DICTATORS, DEBTS, AND DEPRESSION IN PERU, 1930–1933

During the eleven-year reign (*oncenio*) of President Augusto B. Leguía (1919–30), Peru had developed most of the features of a "Kemmererized" country without actually having entertained one of his missions. That quintessential Andean republic had shifted dramatically from the British to the North American orbit and relied extensively on U.S. trade, corporations, investors, institutions, and advisers prior to Kemmerer's visit. Embracing U.S. capital and concepts (including a central bank), Peru tried to invigorate not only the external sector but also domestic urban ventures. It did so partly by emulating Kemmerer's reforms elsewhere in the Andes. In the 1920s the expanding central government supported technocratic modernization by channeling foreign loans into amplification of the state and its infrastructure.

When the depression torpedoed Leguía and his model of debt-led development, his successors tried to salvage the system of dictatorship resting on foreign loans by bringing in the Money Doctor. U.S. bankers and government officials became deeply involved in that rescue mission. In 1931 Kemmerer strove to save not only Peru but also his other South American clients. As the depression spurred inflationary demands from landowners and other elites, however, his system soon buckled. In a reversal which dismayed the New York bankers, the Peruvian government used Kemmerer's visit to escape from its external obligations. Since his standard medicine could no longer attract foreign loans, a career, a creed, and an international economic era came to an end.

Foreign Factors in Peruvian Development

In the 1920s Peru shifted increasingly from reliance on agricultural exports mainly produced by local elites to mineral exports largely owned by foreign companies. Far less monocultural than the other Andean countries, agricultural exports from 1920 to 1930 decreased in value from 74 percent to 32 percent, accounted for by sugar, cotton, and wool; and mineral exports increased from

17 percent to 44 percent, claimed by petroleum, copper, and silver. Some of the agricultural commodities were also produced by foreign companies. Even when domestic growers predominated, they relied on foreign commercial firms for credit, marketing, and transportation. Although exports kept rising in the 1920s, aggregate returned value declined as capital flowed overseas. The extremely favorable balance of trade, estimated in table 6.1, did not reveal the huge outflow of funds, largely to foreign investors. As U.S. companies came to dominate those export commodities, the United States also surpassed Great Britain as Peru's leading trading partner and achieved a very favorable balance of trade there (see table 6.2).

In the 1920s the United States also overtook England as Peru's largest foreign investor. The U.S. Commerce, State, and Navy departments helped open contacts and markets for U.S. merchants, companies, banks, and transporters. Those government agencies believed that U.S. direct and indirect investments induced Peruvian purchases from and contracts with U.S. companies. From 1919 to 1929 U.S. and British direct investments rose from

Table 6.1   Value of Peruvian Trade, 1913–1933 (in rounded-off millions of gold soles)

Year	Exports	Imports	(Manufactured imports)
1913	91	61	(38)
1918	200	97	(62)
1919	269	122	(80)
1920	353	184	(101)
1921	167	167	(99)
1922	187	106	(66)
1923	240	141	(89)
1924	251	180	(110)
1925	218	183	(113)
1926	240	196	(117)
1927	312	194	(120)
1928	315	176	(110)
1929	335	190	(117)
1930	236	140	(97)
1931	197	102	(64)
1932	179	76	(48)
1933	257	107	(72)

Sources: Rosemary Thorp and Geoffrey Bertram, *Peru 1890–1977: Growth and Policy in an Open Economy* (New York, 1978), pp. 39–40, 114–15; Perú, Ministerio de Hacienda y Comercio, Dirección Nacional de Estadística, *Anuario Estadística del Peru, 1944–1945* (Lima, 1947), pp. 344–62; Great Britain, Department of Overseas Trade, *Report on the Economic Conditions in Peru* (London, 1931), pp. 72–78.

Table 6.2   Value of Peruvian Total Trade with the United States and Great Britain, 1900–1930 (by percentage)

Year	Exports to		Imports from	
	United States	Great Britain	United States	Great Britain
1900	21	46	9	47
1913	34	37	30	26
1918	47	32	54	16
1919	47	31	62	14
1920	46	36	55	15
1921	39	35	50	14
1922	35	35	40	19
1923	40	33	39	20
1924	33	38	39	19
1925	35	34	39	19
1926	35	29	46	16
1927	28	28	42	16
1928	29	24	41	16
1929	33	18	42	15
1930	39	14	37	16
1932	17	36	29	17
1933	16	36	27	18

Sources: Perú, Ministerio de Hacienda y Comercio, Dirección Nacional de Estadística, *Extracto Estadístico del Perú, 1931–1932–1933* (Lima, 1935), pp. 73–113.

approximately $161 million to $209 million, with U.S. capital comprising $143 million at the end of the decade. Over 80 percent of that U.S. share went into mining and petroleum. Increasingly in the 1920s, even moderate Peruvian commentators criticized those foreign firms for contributing very little in terms of foreign exchange, taxes, or wages, while exploiting the irreplaceable resources of the nation. From 1919 to 1931 the public external debt leapt from $12 to $124 million, principally acquired in New York. Peru suspended service on those national and municipal foreign obligations in March 1931, immediately after seeking Kemmerer's assistance to extract emergency credits.[1]

The U.S. State Department encouraged that mission, as it had previously encouraged the lenders. From 1912 on State had prodded U.S. bankers to float Peruvian public loans to "give stability to our business interests . . . and . . . place in the hands of American capitalists the financial future of the Republic," as opposed to European and British suitors. Despite adopting for Peru and all of Latin America the 1922 policy of not assuming direct responsibility for any specific transactions, the department continued promoting U.S. companies and smoothing their communications with the Peruvian government. Throughout the decade, "the race for loans, for concessions and contracts . . . between British and American interests on the one hand and between American interests on the other" became increasingly intense. In 1928 the New York firm of J. and W. Seligman and Company secured the last big bond contract by paying a huge commission, in effect a bribe, to Leguía's son.[2]

Although muffled by the dictatorship, some Peruvians in the 1920s began criticizing the size and terms of those external obligations. They complained that the bankers received high commissions and interest rates for loans delivered well below the average nominal value. Also in contrast with Colombia and Chile—partly because they had been inspected by Kemmerer—Peru had to pledge specific revenues before receiving foreign loans.

Peruvians also chafed at the U.S. supervision that accompanied those debts. The first New York loan in 1921 had required a report by an American commission on the government's handling of funds. It had also necessitated the appointment of North American W. W. Cumberland, upon recommendation of the State Department, as director of the customs service, adviser on the budget, and member of the Board of Directors of the Reserve Bank of Peru, a central bank proposed by the U.S. commission and Cumberland. He also convinced Leguía to institute other financial and fiscal reforms similar to those installed by Kemmerer elsewhere in the Andes. Those similarities were scarcely surprising, since Cumberland had been a Kemmerer student and a foreign-trade adviser in the State Department. Although soon regretting its unusual involvement, State intruded in these loan negotiations in hopes of keeping Peru away from British bankers. Leguía made Cumberland's appointment prior to the New York loan so that the two events would appear unconnected; the U.S. ambassador approved, since "this will obviate wounding sensibilities of those who, whether for political reasons or otherwise, may be sensitive about sovereignty." Not unlike Kemmerer appointees in other countries, Cumberland reported to the State Department in 1923 that Leguía did not really want him to reform public finances, but instead to serve as a magnet for loans through U.S. banks. Cumberland also found that Peruvians resented his advice, especially against incurring excessive debts abroad. At the end of 1923 he resigned to accept a State Department appointment as financial adviser to Haiti, which he found more receptive to his management.

As in Bolivia, a 1926 loan required creation of a body to supervise revenues collection. In Peru this was the Administrative Company of Revenues, directed by the U.S. bankers. This group was empowered to collect the property, sales, inheritance, patent, stamp, and surtaxes hypothecated as securities; the government also needed their permission to change those taxes during the life of the loans. To satisfy U.S. lenders in 1928, Leguía submitted to another study of

Peru's monetary and banking system, this time by a former vice president of Bankers' Trust Company. That inspector's analysis was amplified in 1929 by a finance professor from Columbia University, who reassured the New York bankers by revising portions of the fiscal and tax systems. Thus Kemmerer would become simply the last and most illustrious in a long line of U.S. advisers hired to placate U.S. creditors.

Most Peruvian elites welcomed foreign capital as a spur to economic growth. Nevertheless, they questioned the price the country was paying and the threat to its sovereignty. Some critics made ominous references to armed interventions in the Caribbean and Central America. As one author concluded in 1928, "it is preferable to renounce the material progress that American capital can bring us, if it is only possible to obtain by subjecting ourselves directly or indirectly to foreign financial and political tutelage." Others, inspired by the writings of economic nationalists José Carlos Mariátegui and Víctor Raúl Haya de la Torre, went further, denouncing Peru's "economic enslavement" to the United States. Those criticisms, which reached a crescendo when the depression struck and Leguía fell, also hammered away at the government's allegedly unproductive deployment of those external credits.[3]

Leguía used those foreign funds to repay old debts, to cover deficits in the balance of payments and in the national budget, to expand the bureaucracy, to fatten the army (which kept him in office), and to build public works. Construction boomed on highways, railroads, ports, irrigation, and sanitation facilities. While providing employment for the growing urban population, those projects were usually consigned to U.S. construction firms. In short, U.S. loans served to pay U.S. companies. Although infrastructure improved, U.S. financiers later charged that many of the projects turned out to be exorbitant, unnecessary, and insufficiently productive to repay the loans. Nevertheless, Leguía's foreign borrowing to fuel government expansion did stimulate domestic demand and growth when returns from exports slackened in the 1920s. Once the state could no longer issue bonds in the New York market, however, the Great Depression devastated Peru.[4]

Leguía's embrace of U.S. capitalists formed part of a broader welcome extended to all North American influences. He hitched Peruvian foreign policy to U.S. diplomacy and accepted U.S. arbitration and advice in border disputes with Chile, Colombia, and Ecuador; followed the United States out of the League of Nations; became the only Latin American chief executive to express support for the U.S. occupation of Nicaragua; staged a huge welcome for President Herbert Hoover's visit in 1928; hung a portrait of President James Monroe in the presidential palace; and declared July 4th a national holiday. He also made generous concessions to U.S. companies, balancing them with some British firms. He even told the U.S. embassy that he wanted "to put Peru into the hands of the United States," suggesting "something in the nature of a protectorate." In return, the U.S. ambassador nominated Leguía, "the Giant of the Pacific," for the Nobel Peace Prize; he claimed the president "has the courage of Caesar, the power of Napoleon, and the diplomacy of Richelieu" and "would go down in history as one of the world's greatest men."

Besides bringing in a series of U.S. financial experts culminating in the Kemmerer mission, in the 1920s Peru also hired U.S. advisers to revamp the educational system along North American lines, reorganize the navy, establish the School of Aviation, improve urban hygiene, direct traffic in Lima, manage the Agricultural Bank, recast the secret service, and plan irrigation. Leguía declared, "My hope is to put an American in charge of every branch of our government's activities." Peruvians complained that even the president's doctor and dentist were North Americans. Maintaining lines to Europe, Leguía also imported experts from Germany, Spain, and England; they reformed the post office and telegraph service, the national police, the army general staff, and the Ministry of Education. That 1920s pattern of extreme subservience to foreign powers—especially the United States—rendered the Kemmerer mission both a logical and a resented response to the Great Depression.[5]

Economic Sectors and Problems within Peru, 1920–30

In the 1920s the growing mineral and petroleum sectors flourished in foreign hands. Entering principally from the United States, the largest corporations were the Cerro de Pasco Copper Corporation and the International Petroleum Company. As the amount and value of mineral and oil exports slid from 1929 to 1930, those firms tried to cut back production and employment. They also resisted government demands for higher tax payments and emergency loans, intended to keep the state solvent and to service its external obligations.[6]

Domestic capitalists concentrated their holdings in agriculture, some for export but most for local consumption. Plummeting international prices for sugar, cotton, and wool gave the landowners new grievances against an administration they had long seen as favoring urban over rural interests. The National Agrarian Society cheered the ouster of Leguía, criticizing his big spending and debts for raising their tax burden. They pressed his successors and the Kemmerer mission for lower taxes, expanded credits, and tariff protection. They hoped that Kemmerer's recommendations for reductions in the bureaucracy would help them recapture a state cleansed of Leguía's *arrivistas*. Agro-exporters also believed that their economic dominance would be enhanced by Kemmerer's defense of laissez-faire. Since the Reserve Bank had not given them adequate loan privileges, the agriculturalists had persuaded the government in

1929 to create the Central Mortgage Bank, but it could no longer meet their needs either. Above all, the agrarian aristocrats hoped to take advantage of the fall of Leguía to recapture the exalted political and economic predominance they had enjoyed prior to the *oncenio*.[7]

Despite resentments expressed by the landed oligarchy, urban elites remained weak and vulnerable. Although receiving some tariff protection, domestic manufacturing interests also complained about insufficient attention from Leguía. Industrialists called for more state assistance when the depression struck. Production of previously imported consumer goods had blossomed from the 1890s onward, but that growth slowed in the 1920s. In that decade expansion took place mainly through the arrival of foreign firms, notably in textiles and construction. That latter sector outpaced any other industry, fueled by Leguía's externally funded public works extravaganza. By the time Kemmerer arrived, the Great Crash had aroused new interest in promoting local manufacturing.[8]

Like agriculturalists and industrialists, most merchants also applauded the overthrow of Leguía and the invitation to Kemmerer. As imports fell some 50 percent from 1929 to 1930, the Chamber of Commerce and the Association of Peruvian Merchants called for two main reforms: stabilization of the sinking value of the currency and reduction of the cost of government. They also desired reorganization of customs administration. Merchants vacillated on the foreign debt. Although they wanted to maintain payments in order to uphold Peru's credit standing abroad, they hated to see hard currency spent on foreign bondholders instead of imported goods. They also opposed raising taxes to allow the government to keep meeting its external obligations. Thus importers hoped the Kemmerer mission could slash government expenditures so drastically as to simultaneously continue debt servicing, reduce taxes, and preserve exchange stability.[9]

From 1900 to 1930 the number of credit institutions in Peru climbed from five to twelve. This financial growth mainly benefited the urban and governmental elites, as well as the coastal agro-exporters. Having enacted no Kemmerer banking legislation, Peru had not experienced the compression of institutions seen in the rest of the Andes in the 1920s. When the depression arrived, the seven national banks (including the Central Reserve Bank of Peru) far overshadowed the operations of the five foreign branches (two British, one Canadian, one North American, and one German). Like external bondholders, these bankers had extended vast credits to the Leguía government and feared for their repayment when Kemmerer arrived. The banks also feared for their own survival, since one of the two largest—the Bank of Peru and London—had failed in 1930.[10]

All these institutions subscribed with 10 percent of their capital to the

Reserve Bank of Peru. Created in 1922 as the exclusive bank of issue, it was modeled after the U.S. Federal Reserve system. That design followed the recommendations of Peruvian bankers and of the U.S. inspectors who visited Peru to certify its credibility for Leguía's first loan from New York. Pressure from those domestic and foreign bankers had convinced the government to replace plans for a national development bank with this blueprint for a bank of banks. Its charter and operations bore so many similarities to Kemmerer's offspring that it boasted of being the first such central bank in South America, preceding Colombia's by one year. Nationalists complained that even the bank building was constructed in the United States, and the pieces shipped to Peru for assembly.

The bank maintained a gold reserve equal to 50 percent of circulation and deposits. It provided discounts to member banks and especially low-interest loans to agriculture. The ten members on its board of directors were named by the government (three), the large member banks (two), the small member banks (two), the foreign member banks (two), and the overseas fiscal agent for the government (one). The bank's charter further stipulated that at least two of the three directors chosen by the government and three of the six selected by the banks had to be Peruvians, ensuring at least an even split between foreigners and nationals; moreover, only directors chosen by the government and of Peruvian nationality could be elected president and vice president. To secure a foreign loan the Peruvians had granted foreign representation in their central bank well in excess of any Kemmerer institution. The biggest contrast, however, was that the Reserve Bank did not sustain a convertible gold exchange standard.[11]

For Peruvians, neither the severity of monetary depreciation nor price inflation seemed to justify a Kemmerer-style mission during the 1920s (see table 6.3). From 1901 to 1914 Peru had maintained exchange stability under the gold standard. After the shock of World War I the country switched to inconvertibility. During the 1920s the dollar value of the sol suffered a fluctuating but persistent decline. That descent, however, was neither deep nor steep. Indeed, the Reserve Bank boasted of keeping official exchange values within narrow boundaries until the depression. Nevertheless, most Peruvian elites—exporters planning to send their capital abroad as well as importers, bankers, and government officials—continuously tried to restore the gold standard. Prior to the brief success under Kemmerer in 1931, the last vain attempt to convert to gold occurred in 1930, following a devaluation of nearly 20 percent. Thereafter the government created the Commission of Monetary Reform, headed by Reserve Bank President Manuel A. Olaechea. That commission made no progress, and so called upon Kemmerer to achieve stabilization through his central bank.[12]

Peruvians mainly expected the Money Doctor to reassure foreign lenders by stabilizing the currency and government finances. When the depression arrived, the fiscal system nearly collapsed. External loans had accounted for most of the spectacular budgetary growth in the 1920s. After nearly quadrupling from 1918 to 1929, central government expenditures fell by 50 percent from then until 1932. During 1930 and the beginning of 1931, the government scurried to slash domestic outlays and continue payments on the foreign debt.[13]

That growth in the cost, size, and activities of the state had taken place under the authoritarian rule of Leguía. State articulation responded to the increasing need to deal with foreign capital, economic growth, urbanization, and emergent middle and working classes. Like his counterparts in the other Andean presidential palaces in the 1920s, Leguía believed in a powerful central government, organized with the most modern techniques. According to Leguía: "The State is, day by day, the most efficacious agent for carrying out the

Table 6.3   Peruvian Currency and Prices, 1914–1934 (1914 = 100)

Year	Cost-of-living index	Value of U.S. dollars in soles per $1
1914	100	100
1915	108	105
1916	118	89
1917	137	85
1918	158	87
1919	181	95
1920	202	105
1921	191	124
1922	183	105
1923	173	109
1924	180	105
1925	192	111
1926	193	123
1927	187	113
1928	174	110
1929	170	110
1930	162	145
1931	151	157
1932	145	256
1933	141	199
1934	144	189

Sources: United Nations, Public Debt, 1914–1946 (Lake Success, 1948), p. 113; Banco Central de Reserva del Perú, Boletín Mensual, no. 3 (November 1931): 49. Also see note 12.

beautiful work of human solidarity." Thus it could supply the order, infrastructure, credit, employment, and leadership for the economy to catch up with more advanced Western nations. The number of public employees increased 545 percent from 1920 to 1931.

Leguía funded that government expansion and activism with external loans: "We are tribute payers to foreign capital, still indispensable to construct our railroads, to sanitize our cities, to irrigate our arid coasts; but this corresponds to a transitory stage of our progress which leads necessarily to future independence." To reassure those outside investors and to update key public and private financial institutions, Leguía installed new banking, budgetary, tax, and customs laws; new codes for commerce, mining, and agriculture; special credit institutions for landowners; and the Office of the Comptroller General. Many of these innovations were modeled after Kemmerer's legislation in neighboring countries. His New York bankers had urged Leguía to copy Kemmerer's Chilean fiscal reforms so that Peru might receive equally generous treatment from U.S. lenders. He intended his state expansion and debt-led "dance of the millions" to foster the formation of urban capital and enterprises, which were expected to lead national development in the future.[14]

Leguía embodied the new urban, educated, commercial, financial, industrial elites, to the ire of the traditional landed oligarchy and its political servants. Agriculturalists producing for domestic rather than foreign consumption felt especially slighted, as did those in the outlying provinces. He exiled some members and representatives of the nation's wealthiest, most aristocratic families. Expansion of the bureaucracy and public works broadened his base to include significant middle- and working-class elements. Leguía's "New Fatherland," however, mainly rested on replacement of the old ruling class with new plutocrats and British with North American investors.[15]

At the start of 1930 Leguía tried desperately to trim expenditures and to secure emergency credits from his New York bankers. They agreed to help him meet payments to the bondholders if he would rush through reforms to stabilize the budget, banking, and exchange—in other words, if he would implement a Kemmerer package. Initially, however, the U.S. embassy advised the State Department against a Kemmerer mission. The ambassador argued that it might undermine Leguía's politically potent image as a financial wizard, that U.S. experts had already carried out such studies in 1928 and 1929, and that it would be extremely expensive for an already hard-pressed government.

As the depression deepened, however, the U.S. legation became fearful that, without foreign advice, loans, and public works, Leguía's popularity would sink so low that not even repression could keep him in office. Leguía told the embassy that he urgently needed the "moral support of opinion of some well known financial authority with reference to stabilization of exchange," and requested a visit by Kemmerer. The State Department notified Kemmerer of the invitation. The embassy had become eager for Kemmerer to accept and to provide an "excuse" for or against stabilization. Still, the department preferred him to act as an independent agent. Apparently Leguía hoped to arrange a Kemmerer visit as a "trump card" to impress the U.S. bankers and to back up the austerity policies he was already pursuing by cutting the government budget, Reserve Bank loans and notes in circulation, and imports.

As protests mounted against the dictatorship in July of 1930, the embassy advised the State Department to look favorably on any U.S. bank loan which could salvage Leguía, since "Peruvian friendship toward the U.S. is in very large measure due to President Leguía's own personal attitude." Only a visit by Kemmerer seemed likely to save the government: "His opinion may well be crucial with respect to the availability of a further loan, as no doubt American bankers would be more apt to follow Dr. Kemmerer's findings. Should these be satisfactory, and a further loan be desired and obtained by the President, the present regime should have a new lease on life." Since Kemmerer was busy with his second visit to Colombia, however, he proved unable to come to Peru until after Leguía's downfall in August of 1930.[16]

From 1929 to 1930 opposition to Leguía's dictatorial methods and economic policies spread rapidly. Leaders of every economic sector called for reductions in government spending, debt payments, and taxes, and bemoaned the falling value of the currency. They denounced his favors to foreign companies, bankers, investors, and advisers. As Leguía loosened and then lost his grip on power, long-seething economic nationalism burst forth to blame the depression on U.S. penetration.

Anti-Americanism grew so fervent that the U.S. embassy pressed Leguía's successors for protection for U.S. banks and companies threatened by demonstrators. In late 1930 the U.S. ambassador warned the Peruvian government that the State Department would not use its "good offices" to help with the debt crisis until "agitators," at such firms as the National City Bank, the International Petroleum Company, and the Cerro de Pasco Copper Corporation were rounded up. At the same time the secretary of state told the Peruvian ambassador in Washington that his government should send in the entire army if necessary to halt labor disturbances at Cerro de Pasco. Otherwise, the secretary warned, those mines might have to close down, Peru's credit rating might suffer, and its government might not deserve recognition by the United States. After Leguía's ouster, North American businesses in Peru also feared forced loans and new taxes; some urged the embassy to call in a battleship to signal the revolutionaries to respect U.S. property.[17]

The leader of the successful rebellion against Leguía was Colonel Luis M.

Sánchez Cerro. His August 1930 manifesto expressed moralistic revulsion against Leguía's tyranny, corruption, and subordination to U.S. interests. The rebels criticized "the yoke of the foreign creditor," "placing us at the mercy of foreign lenders, thus mortgaging our economic independence, with imminent danger for our national sovereignty." Their economic grievances also included excessive concessions to U.S. companies, elevated taxes and customs duties, budgetary excesses, and currency depreciation. Beginning as a regional uprising against the centralization of power in Lima, that movement soon attracted broad popular support. Whatever his image or intentions, Sánchez Cerro's most important backing came from the traditional aristocrats—especially landowners—who had been shunted aside politically by Leguía. They rallied to Sánchez Cerro in an effort to recapture lost privileges and to fend off threats from new mass movements. As a result, the upper class, from 1930 on, relied on the army to defend its interests. After his initial takeover in August 1930, Sánchez Cerro ruled during most of the Kemmerer mission; he stepped down in March 1931 while provisional governments presided over elections, which returned him to power in December 1931. He governed as constitutional president from then until his assassination in April 1933 by an *aprista*, a partisan of the American Popular Revolutionary Alliance (APRA).[18]

If most of the oligarchic opponents of Leguía huddled behind Sánchez Cerro, most of the middle- and working-class adversaries stood with the APRA. In addition, some regional groups, especially in the depressed northern provinces, who had been displaced by new foreign and domestic capitalists during the *oncenio*, supported the *apristas*. Ironically, many former Leguía partisans also came to back that movement, whose leader, Haya de la Torre, had been exiled by the dictator.

Haya's party spearheaded the populist, nationalist, semisocialist alternative to Leguía, Sánchez Cerro, and "yankee imperialism," outbidding the Communists for that role. The revolutionary rhetoric of the *apristas* in the early thirties caused most Peruvian and North American capitalists to dread them as leftists. Sánchez Cerro attacked the APRA as a Marxist menace. Some observers, however, thought the *apristas'* nationalistic and socialistic orientations sprang from other ideological origins. In a confidential report to the Council on Foreign Relations in New York, Peruvian historian Jorge Basadre concluded that the supposedly "communistic . . . Haya de la Torre . . . perhaps can be compared with Hitler rather than Lenin." After meeting with Haya, "who so described his own party and his own aims as to make it a pure fascist rather than a communist organization," the U.S. ambassador reported in 1932 that the APRA's beliefs, "while they may be somewhat socialistic in character, verge towards the fascist ideals rather than the communistic." Whatever its principal philosophical-political inspiration, the APRA confronted Kemmerer with the first nationalist, populist, mass movement he had encountered in Latin America. Because of the APRA and the depression, he faced the harshest attacks ever in his South American ventures.[19]

The Kemmerer Mission to Peru

Since it took place during the crisis of the depression, the Kemmerer mission to Peru spotlighted with unusual intensity the conflicting and crosscutting forces—international and domestic, public and private, political and economic—at play behind, through, and around that advisory mechanism. As during his first mission to Bolivia and his second to Colombia, U.S. bankers provided the primary impetus for the invitation to the Money Doctor. Lionel Stahl, the local representative of Peru's New York banking fiscal agents (J. and W. Seligman and Company and National City Bank), labored to convince Leguía's successors to carry through with the dictator's earlier plan to invite Kemmerer. The bankers grew even more fearful about debt payments now that economic nationalism had erupted. They were also apprehensive because an inexperienced and unpredictable government had taken power.

Stahl reported to U.S. Ambassador Fred Morris Dearing on his private meeting with the new ruler about the economic situation in September 1930: "As the conversation continued, it became evident to Mr. Stahl and he thinks also to Colonel Sánchez Cerro himself, that the latter did not know what he was talking about." Nevertheless, Stahl tried to convince the colonel that "a comprehensive stabilization plan" to reduce government expenditures, to improve the management of the central bank and commercial banks, to solidify the currency, and thus maintain debt payments should be "worked out by professor Kemmerer or some other well known expert." Since Sánchez Cerro tried to get U.S. companies in Peru to make advances to the government to help service its loans, they also pressured him to adopt a Kemmerer-style austerity plan.[20]

The New York bankers gradually persuaded the Peruvian government to invite Kemmerer by suggesting that his influence might convince them to float a new loan. They argued "that Kemmerer's prestige was so great and he was thought to be so sound, that whatever he might recommend, even a moratorium, would very likely be agreed to by the bankers, if his plans were adopted by Peru." As Stahl explained to the U.S. ambassador, he was trying to arrange between the bankers and the government a solution like the one just reached in Colombia, for an emergency loan conditioned upon the acceptance of a Kemmerer mission. Acting as both a director of the national tax collection agency and a director of the central bank, Stahl also sold the idea to the president of the Reserve Bank, Manuel Olaechea. The latter proved quite receptive, since he was the Peruvian attorney for the fiscal agents and the National City Bank.

The Reserve Bank then led the campaign for Kemmerer. Offering to pay the costs of the mission, it secured the government's authorization to issue the formal invitation in November 1930. That helped the government assuage economic nationalists by maintaining some distance from the mission. Stahl also convinced the government to approve that invitation by enlisting heavy lobbying from the U.S. embassy.[21]

Ambassador Dearing pressed Sánchez Cerro to invite Kemmerer. Dearing hoped that the mission would stabilize the economic situation and convince the New York bankers to tide over the government with some assistance, which he saw as their "moral obligation." "The patient, Peru, has been ill for some time. He has just realized his condition. We are interested in him. He needs a doctor and should ask for one. We should give him enough food to keep him alive until the doctor arrives. He must be induced to tell the doctor frankly and fully what his troubles are and to do what the doctor says. We wish him to recover so he will consume our products and continue to do business with us and be a healthy and happy member of society." Dearing therefore wired the State Department to urge Kemmerer to come: "I know of nothing which will tend so much to quiet the situation here, to rectify past errors, to establish conditions enabling this country to go to work and go forward than the formulation of a plan by Dr. Kemmerer. It will save the country's credit and self-respect. It will win for us a good will, which has been somewhat waning, and it will undoubtedly make for beneficial and advantageous relationships between our two countries." Dearing told the minister of foreign affairs that only an invitation to Kemmerer would persuade the State Department to use its "good offices" to smooth a deal with the fiscal agents. He believed that Kemmerer would be able to extract more cooperation and reliable information out of the junta than could the resented fiscal agents. The latter would, in turn, have more confidence in him than in the de facto government. The State Department agreed with its ambassador and the New York bankers "that Kemmerer is the best bet because the government would be more likely to accept his suggestions than the suggestions of the bankers."[22]

The State Department insisted, however, on maintaining formal neutrality. It informed both its ambassador in Lima and his Peruvian counterpart in Washington that the U.S. government would not get involved directly in discussions between international debtors and creditors. The State Department also told the New York bankers that they would have to take the initiative in convincing the Peruvians to invite Kemmerer and also in convincing Kemmerer to accept. The department hoped the bankers could extend short-term assistance to the junta, so that Peruvians would not blame them for the economic disaster. The department did not want Peru to default and trigger similar defections throughout the hemisphere.

Beyond unofficial lobbying of the Peruvian government to invite Kemmerer, however, the department did virtually nothing to protect the U.S. bankers or to seal a deal between them and Sánchez Cerro. For example, it told the bankers it would not condition recognition of the junta upon Peru's meeting the bankers' demands. Indeed, the under secretary of state cautioned the assistant secretary of state for Latin American affairs that the department might have gone too far in the Peruvian case: "I rather object to this making business for Kemmerer by recommending him quite so strongly as our people do. We have nobody so good and I think we should always be glad to have him go, but I do not think we should be in the position of going out and saying that he is the Moses that leads you out of your difficulties every time."[23]

Sánchez Cerro still hesitated to bring in any foreign financial expert, especially a North American. Several members of the governments succeeding Leguía shared the public opinion that Kemmerer would be too much associated with the increasingly despised U.S. bankers. As the commercial attaché in the U.S. embassy observed, "I am sure if there were any way out, other than inviting more Yankee financial assistance, the present Peruvian government would have found it. But they are up against it." Stahl, Dearing, and Olaechea convinced the junta that, regardless of technical qualifications, "a German expert who was being considered would not have so much weight or authority with the New York bankers, that most of the Peruvian bonds were held in America, that the American market was the most advantageous to borrow in, and that it would be much better to have Dr. Kemmerer." Rumors that Brazil might invite him first also sped up the government's decision. While the government believed Kemmerer would convince its creditors to grant a loan or a moratorium, the U.S. bankers expected him to persuade the Peruvians to pay their debts.[24]

The announcement of the invitation to Kemmerer and the appointment of his most ardent promoter, Olaechea, as minister of finance, immediately heartened not only the U.S. bankers but also Peruvian economic elites. According to Ambassador Dearing, Peruvians were now "looking forward to the arrival of the Kemmerer Mission from which much is expected. In its present mood this nation would accept Dr. Kemmerer's advice no matter how difficult it might be to follow." In anticipation of his arrival, Olaechea began slashing the budget. He also convinced the junta to entertain sweeping financial and fiscal reforms from Kemmerer, not just the monetary and banking tinkering they had originally intended. The Reserve Bank contracted to pay his team $100,000 plus traveling and living expenses for three months' work, and Kemmerer agreed to arrive in December 1931.[25]

The mission included Joseph T. Byrne as an expert on budget and accounting matters; among other previous duties, he had served as chief examiner of government accounts in Puerto Rico in 1908–11, as a member of the U.S. financial commission to Peru in 1922 and then as general superintendent of the Peruvian customs service until 1925, as a member of the Kemmerer missions to Chile, Poland, and Bolivia, and as comptroller general of Bolivia during 1928–30. The banking specialist, Walter Van Deusen, had worked for U.S. banks in Latin America, on the first board of directors of Colombia's Bank of the Republic, and as technical adviser to Chile's central bank and Ministry of Finance. Paul Moody Atkins, the only non-Spanish-speaking member, handled public credit issues. He was an engineer and economist employed by a U.S. investment securities firm. William F. Roddy advised on customs, as he had before in the Philippines and Nicaragua during U.S. occupations, in Ecuador following the Kemmerer mission during 1927–30, and in Colombia in 1931. A Harvard graduate student of economics and taxation, John Philip Wernette had just finished accompanying Kemmerer to Colombia. The general secretary of the mission, Stokely W. Morgan, had worked his way up in the U.S. State Department to become chief of the Division of Latin American Affairs in 1927; thereafter he had signed on with the investment banking firm of Lehman Brothers. Finally, the assistant secretary, Philip Lindsley Dodd, had experience with the U.S. embassy and the national bank in Nicaragua; he had resigned from the latter, along with the rest of the North American managers, in 1929.[26]

Upon their arrival on January 12, 1931, they were greeted by all U.S. embassy personnel, the directorate of the Reserve Bank, and the heads of the other financial institutions. Government officials did not attend, since the junta tried to shield itself against nationalistic attacks by maintaining the fiction that Kemmerer was simply the guest of the central bank. The dean of Lima's newspapers and the Chamber of Commerce led the warm welcome for "those physicians expert in tropical diseases, who are those best suited to treat illnesses endemic in our latitudes." They exuded confidence in Kemmerer because of his enormous successes elsewhere. Although Peruvians knew he would recommend nothing unexpected, they hoped he would issue the usual dicta with enough authority to restore internal and external confidence in the economy. "He will be able to define with scientific criteria and with his recognized veracity the problems everyone knows but about whose solution exists a divergence of opinion among ourselves." They realized, as Albert Hirschman has argued, that an outside adviser served as a sort of random device to select among competing solutions. Kemmerer's supporters also defended him against allegations about his links with his financier compatriots, extolling his independence and his internationalism; they claimed that the money merchants of Wall Street were just as unpopular within the United States as in Peru and that a university professor was a "natural antagonist" of such bankers.[27]

Many Peruvians, however, harbored deep suspicions about the mission. A few issued vociferous denunciations of Kemmerer as the "Agent of American Shylocks." Some expressed regret that it was a "national humiliation" to rely on outsiders: "We are all children and must receive silently the lesson of the foreign experts." Others voiced rather mild complaints that Kemmerer paid little attention to local conditions and opinions, that he offered nothing new, and that he was expensive. Many moderate commentators simply saw little technical need for the mission: "The famous imperialist financier, Mr. Kemmerer, is now in Lima. As an economic physician, he belongs to the naturalist school. He mainly does not use heroic drugs or emergency treatments. Except for a loan. He advises diet. Sobriety. Frugality. Rest. . . . Our financial physicians are—or should be—just as able as Mister Kemmerer. But they are not graduated from the University of Wall Street. And that is all. With Mr. Kemmerer, it is not a matter of science. It is a matter of diploma." Other centrist commentators questioned the wisdom of seeking advice on paying the debt from "a lawyer for the other side." The most sustained and widespread attacks came from the APRA. That party argued that Peru should tax and nationalize U.S. enterprises rather than pay more North Americans for advice. The *apristas* chided Sánchez Cerro for accusing Leguía of being a servant of the North Americans while himself bowing down to two representatives of U.S. capitalists, Olaechea and Kemmerer. Influenced by the APRA and the Communist party (PC), the General Confederation of Workers also lashed Kemmerer as a lackey of imperialism who counseled the government to pay foreigners at the expense of Peruvian laborers. That stance reversed the position of most Andean labor unions vis-à-vis Kemmerer missions prior to the Great Depression. The most vitriolic demonstrations and denunciations against "the Yankee Hunger Maker" came from the tiny PC, who urged, "Out with Kemmerer, the bankers and agents of imperialism."[28]

Prior to his arrival in Peru, Kemmerer had acquired a great deal of information from the New York fiscal agents and the U.S. State Department. The ambassador in Lima worried when the bankers' representative, Stahl, told him, "confidentially Kemmerer is in frequent communication with fiscal agents. While logical, that might have effect here of making Peruvians think him beholden of the bankers and not the independent agent he is." When interviewed by the Peruvian press, Stahl recommended following whatever advice came from Kemmerer.[29]

As always, the U.S. embassy played a subdued role. While Kemmerer kept it informed, it worked behind the scenes to convince Peruvian elites and government officials to cooperate with the mission. As the U.S. ambassador explained, "I told Dr. Kemmerer that while he was here the Embassy would be quietly and watchfully in the background and would avoid seeming too familiar with the

Mission but that he could count upon us for any cooperation whatever as I felt that the scope of my duties included assistance in any constructive measures."[30]

Kemmerer also worked smoothly with Peruvian capitalists, especially merchants, industrialists, and bankers. The Chamber of Commerce formed a special committee of advisers, including both national and foreign firms. Bank managers assembled another group to assist the mission. And the minister of finance, Olaechea, named a consultative commission of diverse private sector leaders to cooperate with Kemmerer. They praised the junta, in contrast with Leguía, for taking their opinions into account.[31]

Kemmerer's relationship with the Peruvian government was more problematic. The junta sought to deflect charges by the APRA and the PC of catering to U.S. interests. It distanced itself from the mission, which worked in the Reserve Bank rather than government offices. Although resenting the mission, Sánchez Cerro gradually became more cooperative. Describing their first meeting to the U.S. ambassador, "Dr. Kemmerer spoke most enthusiastically about Colombia and the cooperation existing between Olaya, our legation, the State Department, and the Bank authorities and says he fears there will not be so much teamwork in Peru, meaning that Sánchez Cerro will be the chief obstacle." The degree of presidential cooperation in Colombia was unusual, however. Kemmerer typically worked mainly with the minister of finance, as he did in Peru with Olaechea, who served as a bridge between the government, the central bank, and the fiscal agents. Equally typical was the mission's and the government's difficulty pulling together basic economic data. Collaborating with the government also proved difficult because it frequently changed personnel in response to rebellions, uprisings, strikes, and protests. What Kemmerer said he found most unpleasant was the junta's determination to pressure him to "give the Peruvians an alibi for a moratorium," while paying minimal attention to his reform efforts.[32]

Despite his strained relationship with the government, Kemmerer took the usual position that he was working strictly for Peruvian officials. He claimed that he could say nothing to the public or press until his recommendations had been delivered to and acted upon by the administration. As Kemmerer told the leading newspaper, "My role is exactly the same as that of a physician: I give the prescription and the treatment. If the patient likes it, he accepts it and follows it; if not, he simply throws it out the window. . . . I am nothing more than that: an adviser."[33]

In April Kemmerer delivered to the Reserve Bank and the government—with confidential copies to the U.S. embassy—the predictable recommendations on: a central bank, a gold exchange-standard, a general banking law, a budgeting system, a reorganization of the national treasury, a reorganization of the Comptroller General of the Republic, a new tax code with taxes on income and land, a customs code, and the public credit of the nation. After receiving the central banking and monetary laws, the bank and the junta enacted them in one day without reading them.

Attending a meeting of the bank's board of directors, Kemmerer was told that such blind approval was justified because "we were the experts and they trusted us." He marveled, "This is the speediest action we have ever had." The U.S. ambassador reported, "I am informed by one of the directors of the Reserve Bank that so complete was the confidence of the entire Board in Dr. Kemmerer's recommendations that the decrees were issued without the recommendations even having been read. . . . The Junta was disposed to do whatever the Reserve Bank desires and the Reserve Bank wished only to follow Dr. Kemmerer's advice. I am told that Dr. Kemmerer is elated." Although some elites complained about the total absence of public information and discussion, most applauded the government's rapid action. As the ambassador argued, "The decrees give critics and the public a fait accompli, prevent speculation, and very likely represent the only method by which the Kemmerer recommendations could ever have been enacted into law. If wide discussion should have been had in the way desired, . . . it is doubtful whether agreement could ever have been reached and it is certain that selfish interests would have done everything possible to accomplish their own ends." The junta issued the law on commercial banking two weeks later.[34]

Those money and banking bills soon aroused such virulent criticism, however, that the government delayed action on his other legislation by referring it to a special Central Budget Commission. The rest of Kemmerer's laws continued to be analyzed in the Constituent Assembly, which began in 1931; it rejected most of his proposals, but incorporated parts into the Constitution of 1933. Basically, however, the Kemmerer reports received little attention once it was discovered that they could not elicit financial salvation from New York.[35]

As the mission finished its work, the U.S. embassy warned the State Department that the Peruvian government was losing interest in Kemmerer's recommendations as it became more evident that external debt servicing could not be maintained. The ambassador thought it was especially important to be sending the State Department confidential copies of Kemmerer's reports because "I am not sure that they will ever be given out in their entirety here, as they will by inference not only criticize the government but the Reserve Bank as well, and neither will be anxious to prove itself inept and at fault." The department telephoned Kemmerer upon his return from Peru to get his assessment of that political situation. He reported that the interim government was very fragile financially and politically. Although hesitant to make a recommendation on

U.S. recognition of the new Peruvian government, he cautioned against hasty action. All observers agreed that the only achievements of those unstable post-Leguía administrations were the Kemmerer laws.[36]

Kemmerer's Money and Banking Reforms

Although already modeled after the U.S. Federal Reserve system, the existing Reserve Bank needed some adjustments to duplicate Kemmerer's installations elsewhere. Its board was controlled by bankers and it dealt exclusively with them rather than the public, it operated only in Lima, and it did not enforce a gold-exchange standard. As in 1922, many Peruvians in 1931 preferred a national development bank to inflate credit rather than a bank of banks. Nevertheless, they welcomed Kemmerer's reform as an improvement on that latter type. The provinces expressed pleasure that they now got branches of the central bank, especially from a government that had arisen partly as a regional protest against overcentralization.

Nearly all economic sectors applauded exchange stabilization. Because of the depression, however, more elites than during any other Kemmerer mission questioned how long that controlled rate could last. Although hesitant to challenge orthodoxy, many commentators asked whether expansion of currency and credit might not be more in the best interest of producers. The APRA led the criticism of Kemmerer's laissez-faire system. It called instead for public credit institutions to develop national industry, mining, and agriculture. Like their counterparts elsewhere in the Andes, landowners expressed particular dissatisfaction with the bank's conservative monetary and credit policies.[37]

Overcoming such misgivings, the Central Reserve Bank quickly replaced the previous reserve bank on September 3, 1931. Its leading advocate, Olaechea, became its first president.[38] Kemmerer's bank directorate reduced the roles of bankers and foreigners: now three directors would be named by the president of the country, two by domestic banks, one by resident foreign banks, one by J. and W. Seligman and Company and the National City Bank of New York (as mandated by their contract with the government), one by the National Agrarian Society, one by the National Industrial Society, one by the chambers of commerce, and one by labor organizations. Before, six of the ten directors had been appointed by the banks, one by the foreign bankers serving as the country's fiscal agents, and three by the government. The New York agents joined the four resident foreign banks in criticizing Kemmerer for only giving foreign bankers the same number of slots as the three Peruvian banks; they claimed that was illogical, since those domestic institutions had less extensive business and since one of them, the International Bank of Peru, was 50 percent controlled by W. R. Grace and Company and therefore really also a foreign firm. Neither foreign nor Peruvian bankers felt adequately served by Kemmerer's formula.[39]

As elsewhere, Kemmerer took exceptional pride in the post for a labor representative. In a conversation with the U.S. ambassador, "Dr. Kemmerer pointed out that the work of the Mission had nearly always been supported by the left rather than by the right—by labor rather than by large landholders and the vested interests. . . . I told Dr. Kemmerer that I thought the President would be extremely interested in knowing how labor, the left, and people at large regarded the work of the Mission and that it might indeed bring him to have a more friendly feeling for it and we agreed that at some early opportunity I should speak to the President along these lines." Conservative newspapers hailed the concept as a step toward cooperation between labor and capital. It was believed that by defending the gold standard—to avoid a depreciating currency and a rising cost of living—workers would have less need to strike. Since unions remained weaker than in Chile, however, the bank only required that the seat be held by someone familiar with and sympathetic to labor.[40]

The new central bank followed Kemmerer's advice to deposit part of its legal reserve overseas. That allowed the bank to redeem its notes in gold drafts on demand, to tap foreign exchange for international commerce, to earn interest, and, theoretically, to obtain greater access to external credits. Fortunately, the bank escaped the risks of that strategy by switching those deposits from London to New York just before England left the gold standard.[41]

During its first year the Central Reserve Bank defended the gold exchange standard as its highest priority, haunted by previous unsuccessful efforts. In strictest confidence, Kemmerer showed that recommendation, along with all the others, to Ambassador Dearing before revealing it to the Peruvian government. That monetary legislation included:

> a plan whereby the considerable gold reserve in accordance with the figure at which the Sol is stabilized may be used to solve Peru's immediate difficulty, that of procuring ready money for current expenses. The plan depends upon the government's not resorting to inflation and would give the government from five to six million dollars, which with its other resources would probably carry it for about a year. Dr. Kemmerer admitted that if the government were faced with a question of self-preservation, it would be warranted in resorting to inflation as an alternative to annihilation and pointed to the fact that during the Great War nearly every nation in the world had done so. He also pointed out that the government would have to take some strenuous measures with its own moneyed and propertied citizens to carry out

his plan. But he thought this might be possible because it would mean the preservation of the gold standard, the preservation of the country's credit, stabilization of the currency, money for immediate needs, and probably a fairly rapid improvement in the general economic situation. Dr. Kemmerer in passing remarked that if he had revealed his plan to Sánchez Cerro before he stepped down for the presidential election, it might even have saved the day for him by showing him how to get ready money. He seemed to imply that he was not particularly interested in doing this. He has had an adverse opinion of Sánchez Cerro from the start.

Thus Kemmerer deviated at times from his normal code of not working intimately with the U.S. embassy, of not meddling in local politics, and of not conceding the plausibility of resorting to inflation.[42]

From the 20 percent devaluation of 1930 to the Kemmerer stabilization in March 1931, the sol lost another 30 percent of its value. The New York fiscal agents and most Peruvians hoped his gold-exchange standard would halt that disastrous decline. Importers favored his system, as opposed to a depreciating currency, which only helped exporters, and expressed relief that "we have the doctor in the house." Representatives of wage and salary earners, such as the communist-led General Confederation of Workers of Peru, also expected stabilization to shore up the value of their incomes. The Central Reserve Bank assured doubters that Kemmerer's solution would not deepen the depression. Other advocates, however, admitted that it would require severe austerity measures, at least in the short run.[43]

The critics were led by Haya de la Torre and the *apristas*, who denounced the gold standard as "the imperialist law of the banker Kemmerer." Because of Peru's large silver production, they preferred bimetallism. They warned that Kemmerer's system would only result in a massive outflow of gold and capital to the United States and a worsening of the depression in Peru: "We said and we respect that Kemmerer could not do anything but defend his own interests, those of his country, his bank, his system. It was natural and just on his part. But it was ingenuous and suicidal on our part to fall in the net. We sustain that the small peoples live in economic war against the large ones. Their interests are diverse, opposed. . . . Thus the poor families should not adopt the system of life of the rich unless they want to ruin themselves."[44]

Like the *apristas*, other commentators also complained about the adoption of that law with no public discussion. They argued that the deteriorating balance of payments rendered the gold standard unsustainable without extreme contraction of the domestic money supply. Instead of Kemmerer's system tied to foreign exchange, these critics called for internal expansion of currency and credit.

Thus they hoped to meet the national need for recuperation and growth, especially since foreign capital could not be attracted during the crisis. In light of the calamitous condition of the country's international commerce, domestic production, national budget, and public debt, some Peruvians concluded that, "Señor Kemmerer has not had time to come to know in depth the idiosyncrasy of our economic reality or our true necessities, and has applied to Peru his standard plan, which is inadequate for the nation in its present circumstances."[45]

Per usual, Kemmerer set the value of the new currency at the prevailing exchange rate. In this case he reduced the worth of the sol from 40 cents on the U.S. dollar to 28 cents.[46] Typically, it was this precise valuation which stirred the hottest debate, even though most economic elites accepted the pragmatism of his selection. Those especially pleased with the low rate chosen were exporters, both foreign and domestic producers. Discontented were Peruvian nationalists and importers, as well as employees and workers on fixed incomes.

In expectation of Kemmerer's devaluation of the sol, the government hoped that its internal debt would cost less, but feared that its external debt would cost more. To avoid that problem the government decreed a moratorium on paying those foreign obligations, just days before issuing the monetary law. Shrewdly, it used the need for resources to back up the exchange stabilization as a justification for suspending its servicing of the foreign debt. Thus Peru, rather than the U.S. bankers, managed to use the Kemmerer mission to achieve what it wanted on the debt issue.[47]

The gold-exchange standard lasted officially from April 1931 until May 1932. Following England's suspension of the gold standard, Kemmerer sent a message to his South American clients in September 1931, urging them to hold firm. Peru's Central Reserve Bank and economic elites welcomed his support for their steadfastness. They exuded pride that they were outlasting Great Britain, believing that their exchange stability would soon attract foreign investments. At the end of 1931 the conference of Kemmerer's central banks in Lima reinforced Peru's resolve.

During the year of that monetary system's reign, gold and capital flowed overseas. The central bank's legal reserves shrank from 63 million to 44 million gold soles (though remaining far in excess of the legally required 50 percent) and its currency in circulation from 55 million to 50 million. Thereafter the bank brought home its 17 million gold soles deposited in foreign banks. When the government declared inconvertibility and scuttled the gold standard in mid-1932, the sol plunged from 28 to 16 U.S. cents.[48]

The other major Kemmerer legislation passed immediately and without revision by the government was the general banking law. After its imposition in May 1931, that code experienced only minor modifications in ensuing years. It superseded a similar decree in February 1931, which had been copied from Kemmerer's other banking legislation in the Andes; it had aroused resistance by establishing higher reserve requirements for the banks and greater powers for the superintendent. The desirability of the superintendency was enhanced by the prior collapse of the most important national credit institution, the Banco del Peru y Londres. When Kemmerer arrived, the other commercial banks were maintaining their stability by cutting back activities; they favored his reform to guarantee their solidity and restore public confidence.[49]

Duplicated from his previous missions, that legislation created a superintendent to enforce state regulation of conservative banking practices. Kemmerer counseled that "economic laws and the fundamentals of banking are the same in Peru as in other countries." He expected all financial institutions to obey the same universal, rationalized rules, noting that "every effort has been made to put foreign banks and national banks on the same footing." He justified those provisions by arguing that "a country that needs to attract foreign capital cannot afford to put obstacles in its way by banking legislation inimical to the establishment of branches of foreign banks." For the first time, however, those foreign entities would now be subject to local governmental controls. Those regulations encouraged short-term loans to corporations rather than long-term credits to individuals or landowners. His system promoted more modern, urban, capitalist activities by both Peruvians and foreigners.[50]

During its first two years the Superintendency of Banks functioned smoothly and helped the remaining commercial institutions survive the depression. Following Kemmerer's advice, the superintendent made the disposition of the largest domestic entity, the Bank of Peru and London, his first task. After suspending payments in October 1930, that bank had been granted a moratorium by the government in hopes of salvaging the institution. The Chase National Bank and the National City Bank of New York preferred liquidation, so as to receive payment for their claims against the Banco del Peru y Londres. Despite opposition from many of that bank's employees and creditors, liquidation was carried out. The superintendent also heeded Kemmerer's recommendation to hire a foreign technician, obtaining written and personal advice from Van Deusen, counselor to the Central Bank of Chile.

By 1932, however, Peruvian officials proved fully capable of managing the agency by themselves. They adjusted Kemmerer's legislation to better suit national conditions; for example, reducing capital requirements for banks outside Lima. They also convinced the government to compensate landowners, starved for credit under the new regulations, by creating the Agricultural Bank of Peru in August 1931. During the depression the main complaints against Kemmerer's banking legislation were that it favored commerce and industry over agriculture and mining, that it constricted the supply of money and credit, and that it was an unsuitable import from a developed to a developing nation. However, most economic elites—especially bankers and merchants—praised the superintendency. In subsequent years banking prospered through additional state credit institutions for economic sectors like mining and industry, while retaining the Kemmerer system for commercial operations.[51]

Kemmerer's Fiscal Reforms

One of the government's motives for engaging Kemmerer was to obtain help with its ballooning budget deficits. It mainly hoped his mission could attract new foreign loans or justify suspension of payments on the old ones. He was also expected to improve tax collection. During 1930–31 the government pruned public works but it could not cut the bureaucracy. Vocally and effectively, those employees campaigned in opposition to paring their numbers and salaries and in favor of suspending debt payments. They argued, as did labor unions, that Kemmerer's devaluation had already drastically reduced their real incomes. Soldiers joined bureaucrats in urging Kemmerer and the government not to effect savings at their expense. Instead, the armed forces successfully called for budgetary increases.[52]

Kemmerer tried to encourage fiscal restraints and reductions with projects to reorganize budget making, the treasury, and the national comptroller.[53] Bowing to demands from his New York bankers for fiscal controls, Leguía had installed a comptroller general in 1929. He boasted that he had copied it from Kemmerer's models elsewhere but adapted it to national conditions. That institution was far less independent, powerful, and effective than its namesake in Chile. While some critics complained it was too weak, others feared Kemmerer's strengthened version in 1931 would interfere with the constitutional powers of the executive branch.[54]

The government resisted the Central Reserve Bank's urgings to enact the three Kemmerer budgetary laws. It did not want to anger bureaucrats, military officers, teachers, clergy, and numerous others dependent on state coffers. Stalling, it referred those projects to the specially appointed Central Commission on the Budget. That group also recommended passage, so as to demonstrate the government's determination to bring order to its finances and thus recapture foreign loans. When it became evident that no external credits were available, Peru archived those Kemmerer proposals.[55]

The same fate befell his tax legislation. Many Peruvian commentators agreed with his criticism of excessive reliance on indirect taxes, especially customs duties. But no one was willing to bear new burdens during the depression.

Government officials warned Kemmerer that "an attempt to increase revenues through direct taxes would be extremely unpopular and probably impossible of accomplishment." In a meeting with the Agrarian Society, he found agriculturalists hostile to his suggestion of a land tax. Nevertheless, he recommended higher internal taxes to facilitate further payment of the external debt and, eventually, less reliance on revenues from foreign loans and trade. Those proposals failed to win acceptance.[56]

Many Peruvians also wanted Kemmerer to rationalize customs administration, reducing incompetence, complexity, and corruption. They hoped he could raise those revenues, although agricultural exporters and merchant importers opposed the protectionist desires of industrialists. Kemmerer proposed lowering tariffs raised under Leguía, but the government ignored all his advice on customs.[57]

The public finance issue on which Peruvians most wanted Kemmerer's help was the question of external credit. By 1926 the total funded debt reached $62 million, of which external obligations accounted for $46 million, requiring annual service payments abroad of roughly $5.5 million (less than 15 percent of the government's ordinary revenues). Then J. and W. Seligman and Company, the National City Bank, and their associates in the United States issued loans for $15 million and $50 million in 1927 and for $25 million in 1928. As a result, those service payments consumed approximately 36 percent of government revenues by 1930. Foreign fiscal agents for the government constantly urged balanced budgets, reduced public works, and currency stabilization. Thus the bankers' objectives often conflicted with the desires of resident U.S. firms for low taxes and depreciating currency and of U.S. construction companies for additional contracts. As with the second Kemmerer visit to Colombia, the New York bankers extended a final emergency credit of $1.2 million in 1931, to help tide the government over during his Peruvian mission.[58]

U.S. and especially Peruvian critics of that indebtedness accused Leguía and his New York financiers of accumulating irresponsible, unrealistic obligations. They excoriated the president's relatives and friends for receiving commissions and profits on the foreign loans and public works contracts. During 1930 and 1931 Peru's leading newspaper argued that such extravagance and corruption under a dictatorship obliged the bankers to negotiate reduced debt payments for Peru; without such relief the country could not carry out the financial reforms that the bankers wanted Kemmerer to impose. These opinion leaders expected his mission to convince the fiscal agents to accept lower payments and extend emergency credits. If such a deal could not be struck, most economic elites contended that a moratorium was in order, though some leading businessmen in the Rotary Club urged continuation of the debt service.[59]

On the eve of Kemmerer's arrival, the South American representative of the Hanover Bank of New York observed that

> the ire of the people is directed chiefly against the government bankers and the more important foreign companies that obtained concessions or favors during the Leguía regime. There is not a single person of Peruvian nationality who does not advocate the revision of the foreign loan contracts signed between the late government and Messrs. J. & W. Seligman and Co. A vast majority feel that under the present circumstances the country is entitled to a moratorium on the debt service. One and all believe Dr. Kemmerer will recommend such a step; otherwise it is improbable that his services would have been contracted.[60]

Apristas and other more radical critics agreed with the need for a reduction or moratorium on debt payments but not with reliance on Kemmerer to effect such a solution. They thought Peru should set its own terms and raise taxes on U.S. corporations to cover debt obligations. According to the APRA, "Dr. Kemmerer is the instrument of foreign lenders."[61] Another nationalist warned against

> Señor Kemmerer, that professor of hackneyed economic policy, who so successfully tied South American finances to the interests of Wall Street, and who, in such a solemn tone and at such high prices, taught us the great discoveries he had made by penetrating the obscure jungle of economic sciences: "it is convenient to spend less than one brings in"—extraordinary novelty—and "pay your lenders (North Americans) punctually even though to do so you will have to take away the bread from the mouths of your children, because only thus will you encounter someone to lend to you again," stupendous maxim of renunciation which, perhaps for conflicting with human nature, is not practiced by the compatriots of señor Kemmerer, neither individually nor as sovereign states of the Union.[62]

A similar critic of the government's policies charged:

> The call to señor Kemmerer and the recognition of the credits claimed by the American bankers and the punctual payment of their interests have not been correct measures. They have given legitimacy to the process of economic conquest and of progressive absorption put in practice by the United States of North America in Peru; they have ratified contracts which should have been and should be revised for being injurious and prejudicial to national sovereignty; they turn over the fiscal and economic organization of Peru to a person who, above

all, is an American citizen and interested, therefore, in the success of the existing policy of his country and in the defense of American interests. The call to señor Kemmerer signifies, in sum, entrusting the solution of the question to the lawyer for the opposing side. . . . The American experts who have integrated the directorate of the Reserve Bank of Peru, who took over control and direction of the collection of our tax revenues and who informed the government about our fiscal and economic situation undoubtedly realized the alarming future of the country but also that the procedure followed was the way to absorb national finances and the economy and to convert Peru into practically a State dependent on the American State. The United States of North America, grand country which I admire profoundly for its perfect constitutional organization, for its solid financial structure, and for its grandiose industrial development, has utilized in Latin America the dollar like Spain utilized arms in the sixteenth century.[63]

Although Kemmerer tried to serve the needs of his hosts, it was true that he worked closely with U.S. interests before, during, and after his Peruvian visit. He described these connections in a letter to Lehman Brothers Investment Bankers, seeking one of their employees, Stokely Morgan, as a member of the mission:

As you know, the problems and interests involved in this Peruvian work are very important. Aside from the important fact that it involves the welfare of Peru's six million-odd population, there is the fact that something like $110,000,000 of Peruvian Government bonds are held by American investors, and the further fact that the large investments in Peru have been made by such American concerns as the Cerro de Pasco Corporation, W. R. Grace & Co., and important American oil interests. The National City Bank people, the W. R. Grace and Company people and the Seligman people are cooperating with me in every way possible in my effort to build up a Commission with a strong personnel.

During numerous meetings and correspondence, National City Bank and J. and W. Seligman urged Kemmerer to accept the Peruvians' invitation. They wanted him to convince his employers to adopt the gold standard, balance their budget, and pay their debts. In turn, Kemmerer asked the bankers to help persuade the Peruvian authorities to be receptive to his mission. At the same time he insisted on his loyalty to his employer. For example, he refused to give advice to a U.S. financial firm dealing in Peruvian bonds, on the grounds that he was under contract to the Peruvian government. Moreover, it would have been difficult for him to have simply served U.S. interests, because those clashed within Peru. While U.S. bankers and bondholders wanted that government to extract money from U.S. corporations to maintain order and service debts, the resident firms preferred Peru to forgo interest payments. Kemmerer was hard pressed to forge an acceptable compromise on sharing the costs of the crisis among Peruvian and North American contenders.[64]

The bankers told the U.S. State Department that they were "trying to hold Peru's hand until Kemmerer can report and Peru can make an offer to the bondholders." Although sympathetic to the bankers, State realized that the charges about bribing Leguía's son to consummate a loan contract were "unfortunately absolutely true" and that they had made imprudent loans to Peru. The department and its embassy hoped that Kemmerer could convince both the fiscal agents and the Peruvians to compromise on debt payments.[65]

Once in Peru, Kemmerer tried to mediate among the mutually suspicious government, fiscal agents, and embassy. His efforts were hampered by the departure as minister of finance of Olaechea, who had lobbied unsuccessfully for budget cuts to avert a moratorium on debt payments. He had been stymied by the army, who forced the government to borrow 1.5 million soles from the International Petroleum Company to pay soldiers' salary increases. Olaechea's replacement, Pedro Bustamante Santisteban, soon warmed to the mission, but then also resigned. His exit dismayed the bankers' representative in Lima: "Mr. Stahl felt confident that Bustamante Santisteban would have agreed to the plan of the Fiscal Agents and would have fallen in with Kemmerer's advice, which is virtually the same thing," bemoaned the U.S. ambassador.

Problems with political instability were compounded by the hostility of several government officials, especially Sánchez Cerro, toward U.S. interests. Kemmerer had to counter "the President's unshakable feeling that all bankers are crooks" and had to reassure him that the mission's meetings with them were purely to gather information. Keeping the embassy apprised of his progress, Kemmerer expressed disgust that Sánchez Cerro and his successors were inclined to make foreign bondholders, rather than Peruvian government employees, bear all the sacrifices for the economic adjustment. Kemmerer thought budget cuts were in order because the number of public employees had increased 20 percent and their total salaries 33 percent since 1926.

In their meetings Sánchez Cerro asked Kemmerer to help arrange a moratorium on the public debt with the U.S. bankers. Instead, Kemmerer recommended negotiations between the government and the private investors to whom the bankers had sold the bonds. But Sánchez Cerro replied that, "Peru could not pay this year one cent of her foreign debt. To ask her to do so would be like asking a starving man to give up food necessary for his life." Nevertheless, Kemmerer and Ambassador Dearing kept trying to persuade Sánchez Cerro and the successor interim government to make drastic budget cuts in order to maintain debt services and thus creditworthiness abroad. The fiscal agents' representative told the ambassador that they remained hopeful that Kemmerer could convince Peru to reach an accommodation with the bondholders: "Mr. Stahl thinks that Dr. Kemmerer has been doing exceedingly good work in the interest of sanity and soundness and in the interest of the American bondholders." Kemmerer also persuaded the bankers to be more sympathetic to Peru's plight and to help the government negotiate with the owners of the bonds.[66]

Kemmerer urged Peru to send a financial commission to deal with the U.S. bondholders, with the help of its fiscal agents. He also advised the bankers to tide the country over with a short-term loan, to be secured by pledging customs revenues. The mission further argued that the government should default on internal rather than external obligations. The U.S. advisers, bankers, and ambassador expressed optimism that this plan would be accepted by Peru and solve the crisis. Instead, on the same day Kemmerer's report was issued, the government suspended most foreign debt payments, ostensibly until further study of his recommendations and the situation.[67]

The government informed the New York fiscal agents that the depression made it impossible to continue full payments, pending implementation of Kemmerer's suggestions for expanding revenues and reducing expenditures. Thus Peru became the second South American nation, after Bolivia, to default on bonds held by North Americans. That early action soon facilitated relatively rapid recovery from the depression. The Peruvians, however, did not repudiate any of their obligations and, temporarily, maintained service on part of them. Merchants joined other economic elites in supporting the moratorium.[68]

Despite expressed desires to resume payments promptly, the government's dire situation caused it to lose interest quickly in Kemmerer's recommendations. The interim administration began favoring internal over external debt obligations, on the grounds that domestic creditors were poorer and might cause political turmoil. The minister of finance also issued a domestic loan; he pressured resident U.S. companies "that if they do not subscribe he cannot guarantee that communism will not break out and can not guarantee that the government can preserve law and order." At the same time he diverted funds earmarked for foreign debt service to general expenses. The outraged fiscal agents protested to both the Peruvian and U.S. authorities.[69]

Upon returning to the United States, Kemmerer informed Francis White at the State Department that he was still hopeful that the Peruvians, although in default currently, would soon try to follow his advice. He expected them to prune domestic expenditures and negotiate at least partial payments with their North American creditors. He also advised the New York bankers "to make the best settlement possible with the existing government," because the situation was likely to get worse. Prior to Kemmerer's return, the counsel for National City Bank had urged the United States, Chile, and Argentina to condition recognition of the Peruvian government "upon the adoption of the recommendations of Professor Kemmerer, who is now in Peru, and upon an agreement by Peru to pay within its capacity its present external obligations. This condition for recognition is in the national interest of the two countries since the improvement of Peruvian credit would immediately better Argentine and Chilean credit." He warned that, without such credit continuation, defaults and revolutionary movements were likely to sweep the hemisphere. After responding that the United States could not possibly make those bankers' terms a prerequisite for recognition, White sought Kemmerer's advice. Although reluctant to commit himself, Kemmerer suggested that the United States "go slow and let matters ride," since the interim government seemed too unstable to last. By contrast, Ambassador Dearing and the New York bankers recommended recognition after the default. They reasoned that it would help the government stabilize, negotiate with the bondholders, and resolve the debt issue.[70]

A month after the initial moratorium, however, Peru suspended payments on its entire public debt, internal as well as external. Since economic conditions failed to improve, the newly elected Sánchez Cerro government extended indefinitely the nonpayment of foreign obligations in January 1932. That same year Van Deusen became an adviser to the U.S. bondholders. He warned them, however, that the poor performance of Peruvian exports—partly due to U.S. tariffs against them—and the strapped government's need to make extraordinary military expenditures left no money for payments overseas. Peruvians also justified their continued default by referring to the extravagances of Leguía and his fiscal agents, unveiled by a U.S. Senate investigation. During the following decade, recurrent deficit spending, borrowing from the Central Reserve Bank, and currency depreciation kept Peru deaf to the pleas of U.S. bondholders.[71]

Kemmerer's last major effort to convince Peru and his other Andean clients of the virtues of adhering to his system occurred December 2–12, 1931, in Lima. At the instigation of the Central Bank of Bolivia, the leaders of Kemmerer's five Andean institutions convoked an emergency conference to discuss the economic crisis. He came as an informal representative of the U.S. Federal Reserve of New York. Although the U.S. State Department urged him to attend and favored limited central bank cooperation, it clung to the belief that the financial crisis could only be solved by private banks. Kemmerer recommended cleaving to the gold standard and high central bank reserves.

The Andean central banks hoped, in vain, that participation by Kemmerer and the Federal Reserve would help them obtain credits from the United States. They also convened to exchange information and forge cooperation on other problems, especially the foreign debt. Another burning issue was the insecurity of their overseas deposits in the wake of England's abandonment of the gold standard. At the time, gold backing held abroad represented 65 percent of the reserve for Chile, 28 percent for Colombia, 90 percent for Bolivia, 65 percent for Ecuador, and 36 percent for Peru, who luckily had deposited in New York rather than London. They also feared deficit spending as a threat to monetary stability. Furthermore, they debated exchange controls, which Bolivia, Colombia, and Chile had already adopted, but Ecuador and Peru opposed.[72]

While the central bankers and Peru's economic elites paid homage to Kemmerer and his ideas, the *apristas* and Communists denounced him as an agent of U.S. "imperialist corporations" and "financial domination." The PC called for a march against hunger, for minimum wages for unemployed as well as employed workers, and for free health care and lodging for displaced laborers. The Communist party complained:

> At the present time there is taking place in Lima a Latin American Financial Conference, presided over and headed by the Yankee pirate, Kemmerer. All the feudal lords and bourgeoisie of Latin America have sent their lackeys to find out how they are going to pay their debts to imperialism. At the moment when there are in this America four million people unemployed who are dying of hunger and need, those dogs are looking for a way to give away the gold that is left, to increase the taxes and to favor new sources of production. . . . We have nothing to eat and they plot to hand over our public finances—finances accumulated by our sweat and our blood—to the expert in colonization, Kemmerer, in order that he may fulfill his duty of increasing the capital of the National City Bank, of the Guaranty Trust and of Seligman and Company, represented by the Federal Reserve Bank of New York. . . . And all of these procedures are taking place in secret sessions. . . . Let us prevent this new robbery.

All other newspapers praised Kemmerer and the conference.[73]

The central bankers in attendance approved the following main resolutions: (1) maintain the gold standard; (2) demand guarantees of protection of the value of their reserves from foreign countries where they are deposited; (3) continue central bank control of the money supply free from political interference; and (4) insist that governments balance their budgets and avoid inflation. That act of faith proved incapable, however, of attracting new foreign loans or silencing domestic critics. Instead, the Kemmerer system collapsed under the weight of the relentless depression.[74]

Destruction by the Great Depression

The continuing contraction of the foreign sector deepened the depression during 1931–33. In response, anti-U.S. attitudes spread from the Communists and *apristas* through the Sánchez Cerro government and its supporters among the traditional economic elites. The administration capitalized on those sentiments to extract loans and taxes from resident U.S. corporations. Nationalistic attitudes reinforced the determination to withhold debt payments and undermined support for Kemmerer's other recommendations.[75]

Peru's export earnings plummeted 71 percent from 1928 to 1933, when recovery commenced. The proportion of Peru's exports generated by foreign companies dropped from over 60 percent at the end of the 1920s to under 30 percent by the end of the 1940s. One result was the partial and temporary revival of the pre-Leguía pattern of greater strength for agro-exporters and British importers. During the depression the United States remained Peru's primary supplier of imports, although Great Britain briefly recaptured the lead as consumer of exports.[76] As the significance of foreign trade and companies shrank, Peruvian elites temporarily turned against those outside forces. Many called for greater emphasis on domestic production, revised contracts and taxes for foreign firms, nonpayment of external debts, and introduction of exchange controls.[77]

In contrast with most exporters and agriculturalists, importers and other merchants staunchly defended the gold standard. They denounced demands for unbridled currency and credit expansion throughout the brief reign of the Kemmerer system. They also opposed successfully exchange controls and, unsuccessfully, deficit spending. Even some merchants complained, however, that Kemmerer's banking regulations strangled commerce during the depression, especially in the outlying provinces.[78]

As Kemmerer predicted, many indebted agriculturalists bemoaned his banking legislation's curbs on long-term loans to landowners. They draped their calls for special credit allocations in nationalistic rhetoric about the essentially agrarian character of the economy, about the predominance of domestic ownership of rural properties, and about the threat of foreign absorption of mortgaged estates. The greatest pressure for assistance from the Central Reserve Bank of Peru came from producers for external consumption. Although many agro-exporters increasingly favored monetary depreciation, most landed elites expressed the hope that the government could solve their credit shortage without scrapping the gold standard. They argued that the blame for its abandonment should fall on trade and budget deficits rather than on themselves. Nevertheless, they admitted great relief upon the declaration of inconvertibility in 1932. Since the traditional landed aristocracy had backed the overthrow of Leguía for courting urban interests, they expected and obtained better treatment from his successors.[79]

While the landowners still preferred—in theory—to combine exchange stability and credit expansion in 1931, they convinced the government to establish the Agricultural Bank immediately after Kemmerer's departure, to be modeled after similar public institutions in Chile, Ecuador, and Colombia. It compensated for the rigidity of the central bank's operations by diverting some of the parent institution's capital to agrarian needs. Most merchants and industrialists deplored this innovation in 1931 and the elimination of the gold standard in 1932 as inflationary subsidies for agro-exporters.[80]

As the depression crippled their businesses, industrialists complained that Kemmerer's banking legislation dried up their credit sources. Like agriculturalists, they called for longer-term credits to be supplied by a new government agency for their sector. Unlike farmers, manufacturers proved unable to obtain a public credit bank in 1931, although they received a weaker version for themselves in 1933. Above all, the National Industrial Society lobbied for tariff protection in the name of economic nationalism. They argued that import substitution would ease the balance-of-payments crisis and help sustain exchange stability. They claimed that local industrialization would fortify the nation's economic independence, like earlier self-sufficiency under the Incas. They also contended it would reduce spiraling unemployment, strikes, and radicalism among laborers. Both exporters and importers opposed their tariff campaign, which fared poorly.

Industrialists were also disappointed by the abandonment of the gold standard in May 1932. They had believed that system would prevent inflation and help them import raw materials and capital equipment. Manufacturers were weakened politically by the overthrow of Leguía and by the presence of some foreign capitalists in their ranks. Compared to their counterparts elsewhere in the Andes, Peruvian industrialists enjoyed less success at turning the depression to their advantage.[81]

From 1929 to 1933 government revenues declined steadily. In the 1931 presidential campaign between Sánchez Cerro and Haya de la Torre, the former called for a balanced budget and improvements in the Kemmerer laws to protect the shrinking supplies of gold, currency, and credit. Haya de la Torre also promised scientific budgets, stable money, and adjustments in the Kemmerer legislation.[82]

After taking office, however, Sánchez Cerro had to engage in deficit spending by tapping the Central Reserve Bank's reserves. He did so in order to pay the bureaucracy and the military, not in order to prime any Keynesian pump. Expenditures on the army soared during 1932–33, mainly as an emergency response to the Leticia border conflict with Colombia. Hostile toward the expansionary modernization policies of Leguía, his successors in the 1930s shied away from extended state activism, protection, and inflationary spending. Peruvians stopped short of the statist outbursts in the other Andean countries, especially Chile, Bolivia, and Ecuador.[83]

Critics of Sánchez Cerro's deficit spending complained that he was undermining the gold standard. The U.S. embassy and Kemmerer continued to urge its retention. The Chamber of Commerce and the nation's leading newspaper voiced the most ardent defense of Kemmerer's monetary system as it came under mounting attacks in early 1932. They pointed with horror at rising inflation and protectionism in Chile following its abandonment of convertibility. They applauded the central bank for its steadfastness, while excoriating exporters, agriculturalists, and speculators for the campaign in favor of devaluation and inconvertibility.[84]

Even Kemmerer's Central Reserve Bank and Superintendency of Banks, however, soon turned against the gold standard. They reluctantly stopped defending it as the central bank's gold reserves shrank by 48 percent, as the supply of currency and credit dwindled, as government deficits mushroomed, and as the depression worsened. Therefore both the bank and the superintendency advised Sánchez Cerro to suspend the gold-exchange standard. At the same time they expressed hopes that adoption of Kemmerer's fiscal reforms, reductions in government spending, and revival of international trade would allow restoration of convertibility in the near future. Peru's official decree of inconvertibility in May 1932 left Colombia as the first and last Andean country to adhere to Kemmerer's system.[85]

In the ensuing year the external value of the sol fell from 28 to 16 U.S. cents. Exporters welcomed their falling costs of production and their rising sales. Industrialists were pleased by the contraction of competitive imports, although disturbed by the high cost of foreign raw materials and capital goods. Although disappointed by depreciation, merchants and bankers expressed relief that the central bank continued to exert some restraint on the money supply and thus inflation. They also applauded the decision, recommended by Van Deusen, not to follow Chile's adoption of exchange controls. He argued that exchange controls helped Chile prevent foreign nitrate and copper exporters from obtaining an undue advantage from changing exchange rates at the expense of domestic consumers, but that free exchange was preferable in Peru because the main beneficiaries were native agro-exporters. Thus the coastal landowners, who had resented Leguía's concessions to foreign and urban capitalists, reaped rapid gains under his successors. Although all Peru's economic elites endorsed the idea that the suspension of the gold standard would be temporary, virtually none bemoaned its abandonment during the remainder of 1932.[86]

Thereafter the monetary system adjusted relatively smoothly to changes and growth in the Peruvian economy. After dropping from 85 million in 1931 to a low of 70 million in 1932, soles in circulation jumped to 110 million in 1933 and then rose gradually to 219 million by 1940. The index of the cost of living (with 1913 = 100) fell from 169 in 1930 to 147 in 1933 and subsequently crept up to 183 by 1940. After descending to 16 U.S. cents in 1932–33, the minimum value of the sol recovered to 22 cents in 1934, and then held fairly steady throughout the decade.[87]

While Peru scrapped Kemmerer's monetary system and never fully adopted his fiscal legislation, it preserved his banking institutions and the spirit of his orthodoxy. Some Peruvians criticized the Central Reserve Bank for not having unhitched from the gold standard sooner. Most commentators, however, praised its subsequent prudent management of the money supply. From 1932 on, it helped hold inflation in check and allowed less currency depreciation than exporters preferred. It continued to espouse Kemmerer's principles, resisting exchange fluctuations, denouncing government deficits, and advocating an eventual return to the gold standard.

At the same time the bank amplified the money supply more than Kemmerer would have approved. It lowered its reserves and expanded its loans to the government, especially during the border clash with Colombia. Agriculturalists joined public officials in leading the campaign for credit and currency expansion. Contrary to Kemmerer's intentions, the central bank became, increasingly, "the banker of the government." Peruvian critics of the apolitical, restrictive, automatic model he had recommended concluded that: "It is certain that it is easy for a wise man or monetary and financial expert to resolve these problems. He is not the one who has to struggle against the discontented mass of unemployed nor take responsibility for maintaining a sufficient volume of armaments. Nevertheless, it is incumbent on the responsible statesman to pay attention to the true causes of the illness. Otherwise the same thing could happen to him as to a physician when the patient dies of tuberculosis while being cured only of a cough."[88]

Since the original Kemmerer law had been promulgated without being read, the government easily justified minor revisions in the central bank's charter during 1932–33. That new legislation reduced capital and reserve requirements so that the bank could extend more loans to the state and agriculture. On the board of directors, another government representative was added, the seat for foreign creditors was deleted, and the slot for a labor spokesman was demoted to someone "knowledgeable about worker questions."[89]

At the same time the government recast the general banking law. It encouraged the establishment of more provincial institutions and the amplification of loans to the public and private sectors. When the highly independent superintendent of banks opposed these relaxations of Kemmerer's regulations, the government fired him, establishing more direct political control over the banking system. Agriculturalists and merchants supported these credit liberalization measures. For decades after these adjustments in their basic codes, both the Central Reserve Bank and the Superintendency of Banks continued to facilitate the financial development of Peru.[90]

Those reforms of Kemmerer's institutions helped economic recovery take hold in 1933. Agricultural exports, especially cotton and sugar, rebounded. Although government deficits persisted because of war preparations, tax receipts rose. That rapid resurrection from the depression, in turn, convinced Peruvians to cling to many essentials of Kemmerer's broader economic model. They abided by basically laissez-faire policies for many more years than their neighbors. Although Peru posed no barriers to foreign investments, it took time for U.S. capital to return. Within such an open economy, the growth of the state and urban enterprises also proceeded very gradually.[91]

That retention of key tenets of economic liberalism—despite the shock of the depression—resulted largely from the resiliency and diversity of Peruvian exports. Those sales abroad fortified the dominance of the traditional elites. For decades thereafter, they enlisted the armed forces to keep the APRA and its populist demands for more nationalist, statist, and redistributionist programs out of office. Those political and economic patterns derived not from the Kemmerer mission, but from the position of Peru's privileged groups in the international economy and in their own society. As elsewhere in the Andes, the impact and legacy of foreign advisers depended, above all, on their utility to the rulers of Peru.

7 FOREIGN ADVISERS AND THE POLITICS OF DEBT AND REFORM IN LATIN AMERICA

Few foreign advisers have ever had such far-reaching recommendations accepted so voluntarily, eagerly, and fully as Edwin Walter Kemmerer did in South America. Any present-day technocrat would be envious. In accord with the accepted thinking of his age, Kemmerer gave the Andean republics the advice they—and the United States—wanted, and he performed his task brilliantly. From that perspective, few could accuse the Money Doctor of malpractice.

The success of Kemmerer-style reform mongering can be judged at three levels: adoption, implementation, and effectuation. This chapter will assess the variables determining the operations and outcomes of such missions. Above all, the transnational politics of debt-led development will be analyzed. This chapter will then evaluate the general impact of Kemmerer's financial and fiscal legislation. In addition to the effects of specific reforms, broader consequences will be considered for the growth of external dependence, internal capitalism, and the central state, both in South America and elsewhere. The transformations wrought by the Great Depression in Kemmerer's institutions, policies, and legacies will be summarized and, finally, the long-run significance of this process will be addressed, as will parallels with more contemporary patterns.

Achievements of Kemmerer's Economic Missions

Adoption of Kemmerer's Reforms

Kemmerer's advisory teams experienced spectacular success in having their models adopted without serious revisions. In any era, in any country, the approval and installation of so many fundamental reforms in a few months would be a stunning political achievement. Kemmerer's record of legislative passage was especially impressive in the first three countries he advised (Colombia in 1923, Chile in 1925, and Ecuador in 1926–27), before soaring indebtedness and plummeting exports undercut his effectiveness in Bolivia (1927–28), Colombia

(1930), and Peru (1931). Why did so many diverse countries, with distinct problems and politics, enact the same laws in the same decade with such celerity? Above all, those nations wanted to improve their relations with and replicate the progress of the newly dominant international economic power, the United States. Almost regardless of technical knowledge and skill, the same mission coming from another country in another epoch could not have had the same success.

While Kemmerer viewed his major purpose as monetary stabilization, most Andean elites saw it as reassuring foreign investors. The Money Doctor himself understood that underlying motive as

> a . . . reason favorable to the appointment of American advisers, and one that undoubtedly has had much weight in the appointment of most American advisory commissions. It is the desire on the part of foreign governments through setting their financial houses in order, and through making thereby a favorable impression upon American bankers and investors, to facilitate the borrowing of money by the government in the American market and to encourage the flow of American capital to their shores for private enterprises. . . . A country that appoints American financial advisers and follows their advice in reorganizing its finances, along what American investors consider to be the most successful modern lines, increases its chances of appealing to the American investor and of obtaining from him capital on favorable terms.[1]

His reforms also met the desires of many local capitalists, especially in the urban sector. In most of his South American visits, Kemmerer arrived during a perceived economic crisis—banking collapse, fiscal bankruptcy, runaway inflation, export recession—and seemed to offer speedy relief.

It would be misleading to accept an image of such advisers succeeding because they parachuted into backward areas with surprisingly superior North American technology and dazzled the natives. There is no doubt that Kemmerer and his compatriots landed with some valuable innovations. But money doctors mainly helped local elites burnish and legitimize proposals they already expected, favored, and, in many cases, had initiated on their own. For example, all the countries had already laid the groundwork for a central bank before Kemmerer showed up. In most cases such missions merely incorporated and authenticated the orthodox institutions and ideas of the era. The transfer of new technology was quite small. After Kemmerer's 1923 expedition to Colombia, all the other countries read and knew the majority of his recommendations before his arrival. Hardly a word in his reports varied from Poland to Bolivia. In purely technical terms, he could have delivered most of his laws by mail.

The Andean governments also invited Kemmerer and accepted his legislation to improve their general political leverage at home. A mission's prestige attracted additional local as well as foreign support for governments and their proposals. Faith in foreign technocratic solutions to national problems—ranging from sanitation to stabilization—was widespread in that era. Teams from the Great Powers encountered few local experts or nationalists willing and able to challenge their recommendations. Most literate South Americans viewed outside experts as above local partisan divisions, as more trustworthy and talented than national elites, and therefore as able to discredit and override domestic opposition to authority and reforms. Host governments hoped, in particular, that Kemmerer's currency solidification and credit expansion would defuse rising discontent on the part of new urban economic elites, middle-income groups, and workers. The ability of foreigners to wield more influence than local leaders illustrated the jocular maxim: "An expert is anyone from out of town."[2]

In his 1926 address as president of the American Economic Association, Kemmerer himself gave the following explanation for governments hiring foreign advisers:

> The foreign economist can view the problems with absolute objectivity. He is disinterested. He has no political ambitions, and is therefore free from local political bias. He probably has no investments or business connections in the country, and he is therefore free from the bias of business interests. As a rule he has no relatives and few if any personal friends in the country whose interests are likely to warp his judgment. He goes abroad a free man without commitments and without local prejudices. It is chiefly for this reason that the public places so much confidence in the foreign economist, not because it believes that he has greater economic knowledge than its own nationals. As a matter of fact, if identically the same advice were given by their own economists it would have nothing like the chance of being adopted that it has when given by foreigners.[3]

Kemmerer's arrival usually coincided with the beginning of a fresh government willing and able to embark on sweeping reforms. The new leaders used Kemmerer's reports to blame previous administrations for mismanagement. They also took advantage of his administrative innovations to reshape and restaff bureaucracies more to their desires. Most were authoritarian but, whether dictators or, less commonly, democrats, those chief executives saw themselves as a new breed of businesslike, technocratic leaders. Their vision of orderly, planned, efficient, disciplined capitalist modernization harmonized with Kemmerer's. Like him, they believed in decisionmaking by trained professionals rather than by traditional politicians. Like many twentieth-century presidents, they adhered to the adage: "I am all in favor of government by experts—as long as they are my experts."[4]

In sum, hiring someone like Kemmerer could help these governments by: (1) focusing public attention on the problems the government wanted to solve; (2) choosing among competing solutions; (3) improving the details of reforms; (4) giving new programs a neopositivist aura of being purely technical and scientific, instead of "political"; (5) conquering domestic opposition to those initiatives and to the government in general; and (6) attracting foreign support. To a lesser extent such missions sometimes also introduced totally new ideas.[5]

At the same time, turning to such foreign assistance could entail risks and problems. Host governments had little choice but to implement the bulk of Kemmerer's recommendations after having invited this stellar mission with great fanfare, exposing their financial flaws to it, and staking their foreign credit rating and domestic political credibility on its success. Thus the negative repercussions of a Kemmerer-style overhaul could include: (1) revealing government errors and malpractices; (2) locking the government into undesired reforms, imposing exotic or utopian programs unsuited to local economic, political, social, or cultural conditions; (3) elevating certain ideas, institutions, groups, and individuals to sacred and untouchable positions of prestige and power; (4) impeding the open consideration of all national opinions and interests; and (5) creating the impression and, in some cases, reality of excessive governmental dependence on foreigners.

Kemmerer's missions' composition and procedures also contributed to their success. His ability to speak Spanish generated confidence among his hosts, as did his academic credentials. His teams contained experienced, distinguished, "scientific" specialists, who helped create the new "profession" of foreign economic advising. They were normally university economists, unconnected directly to U.S. agencies or companies. Before and after their missions, however, many of the members worked for U.S. departments and firms in Latin America. With or without collusion, their economic beliefs coincided with those of U.S. government and business leaders. Products of the Progressive Era, Kemmerer and his companions believed that scientific, technical advances in institutions managed by apolitical, public-spirited experts could bring about generalized economic and social improvements in any country. Their universal principles could be applied wherever leaders possessed sufficient wisdom, integrity, and willpower. Kemmerer was a true believer in his gold-standard system, not only as a practical mechanism but also as a moral virtue. Given the alleged certainty, efficacy, neutrality, and decency of such policies, they proved highly resistant to attacks from local politicians and vested interests.[6]

The mission's tactful and industrious behavior during their visit also generated local confidence in the reforms. Conducting selected private interviews with local political and economic elites served to sell the mission's preconceived programs more than to gather information. Dominated by Kemmerer and his diplomatic skills, the team avoided public discussion of their deliberations. Until the results of their labors were ready to unveil, the mission members maintained an aloof aura of scientific investigation and priestly secrecy, refusing to answer questions from the press. They claimed that any hint of their thinking would be premature until all their research and analysis had been completed behind closed doors, even though they knew most of their conclusions before arriving. Majestically handing down the projects from on high at the end of a few months of preparation inspired awe, averted constant debate along the way, and won approval for the legislation as an integrated package. They cast their interdependent proposals in rigorous, detailed, legislative form, ready to be passed into law virtually intact. Of course, those bills received the speediest enactment when simply decreed by dictators.[7]

Implementation of Kemmerer's Reforms

The missions naturally proved less successful in getting their laws properly carried out, although most of their institutions functioned quite well after their departure. Even when Kemmerer appointees stayed on as administrators, monitoring and following up to ensure that implementation adhered to legislative intent proved very difficult. Some of the missions' legislation never functioned as envisioned because it was drafted hastily, with little knowledge of the host country and scant participation by nationals. Immediately thereafter, local authorities usually rubber-stamped the recommendations with minimal adaptation to indigenous conditions. Consequently, the mission's influence sometimes faded quickly. One egregious example was the transference of Paraguay's customs law for international river commerce to Ecuador's internal waterway traffic. More typical was Colombia's deviation from Kemmerer's advice to exercise caution on public indebtedness and budgeting. Colombia became the only Andean country where he subsequently evaluated and revised his original reforms. His 1930 return visit there validated his oft-repeated warning that implementing the laws properly was far more important than writing them correctly.

Although some of Kemmerer's laws did work with universal predictability, others fit poorly with the legal, linguistic, cultural, political, and economic heritage of the Andean countries. For example, the Anglo-Saxon negotiable instruments legislation functioned inadequately because many of its terms translated badly and conflicted with older commercial codes. Open-market operations by the central bank proved ineffective in the absence of a viable market. A highly liquid commercial credit system provided little for farmers in countries far more agricultural than the United States. In export economies highly depen-

dent upon volatile external markets, monocultural products, and customs revenues, strict and nearly automatic mechanisms for managing money and the
national budget worked erratically. These countries also lacked sufficient financial and trained human resources to make all of Kemmerer's costly and complex
institutions operate properly.

At times his offspring did not perform as he expected because national
officials became more dedicated to his philosophy than was Kemmerer himself.
Although foreign advisers tried to design more perfect reforms in Latin America
than they could have at home, their converts in the host countries could become
even more perfectionist. Importing virtually unadulterated foreign institutions
and practices, those nations sometimes applied them too rigidly to less developed economies. For example, zealous central bankers, proving their mettle by
firm commitment to their patron's doctrines, maintained higher reserve percentages and more of those reserves in foreign banks than even the creator had
recommended. Such extreme loyalty by Kemmerer's annointed disciples proved
especially damaging during the Great Depression, when those countries should
have abandoned the gold standard and foreign debt payments earlier than they
did.[8]

In other cases implementation faltered because local political and economic
powers reshaped, distorted, and subverted Kemmerer's reforms after his exit.
His money and banking laws usually held up better than his fiscal renovations.
However technically sound, public financial institutions and their expert managers could not be insulated from politics anywhere in the world, let alone in
conflictual economies of scarcity with precarious governing systems based on
spoils. The technocratic fantasy of state or parastate agencies untainted by
private and partisan pressures bore no closer resemblance to reality in Latin
America than in the United States. For example, party, clientelistic, and regional demands undermined the comptroller's independence and puffed up budget
deficits.

Moreover, some of the countries had little interest in carrying through the
details of Kemmerer's reforms as ends in themselves. After passing his bills to
please foreign investors, host governments sometimes circumvented the spirit
and even letter of those laws to satisfy domestic political and economic pressure
groups. That tactic was similar to today's conduct of "demonstration elections"
in the Third World to mollify democratic dispensers of foreign aid; in both cases
the key audience resided in the United States, not in the host country. In the
Spanish-American colonial period officials in the New World told the crown "I
obey but do not execute," to avoid implementing royal decrees unacceptable to
local elites. In the nineteenth century Brazilians labeled behavior designed to
imitate and flatter powerful foreigners "for the English to see." In the 1920s

Bolivians called such legislation—concocted for foreigners to admire more than for citizens to obey—"laws for export."

Impacts of Kemmerer's Reforms

Kemmerer's profound reforms obviously made enormous contributions to the evolution of economic institutions in the hemisphere. When assessing developments in the era, however, it is difficult to weigh the impact of Kemmerer's laws as opposed to the larger impact of general economic trends. His missions clearly improved exchange stability, commercial prosperity, bank security, and fiscal health. However, overall economic growth in the twenties obviously affected such measures of success as swelling bank loans and government revenues. Those boom years rendered his reforms affordable, productive, and a bit more efficacious in appearance than in actuality, as the depression revealed when it wreaked havoc on those institutions. The following sections summarize the results of his innovations and accompanying forces in the Andes.

Financial reforms. Two decades ago, in an assessment of research in Latin American economic history, Miron Burgin suggested, "In the field of money and banking a study of central banks, particularly in countries where the Kemmerer mission was active in the first half of the interwar period, should prove highly instructive. It would be especially interesting to see how well were these establishments adapted to the requirements and potentialities of the economies they were intended to serve."[9] Those central banks became Kemmerer's most significant institutional contribution in the Andean countries.

Prior to their founding, most Latin American countries either maintained inconvertible money or an exchange office to handle transactions in gold and foreign currencies. All of Kemmerer's hosts paved the way for a central bank by transferring the right of monetary emissions from private banks to a government agency. In most cases Kemmerer merely had to revise central bank projects which were already being discussed or implemented by those governments. The groundwork for such initiatives had been laid by recommendations at international financial conferences in Brussels in 1920 and Genoa in 1922, which were convened to restore economic stability to the postwar world. Nonetheless, Kemmerer's impetus was also very important, as evidenced by the fact that only Mexico and Guatemala—also partly under his influence—joined the Andean republics in following the trend toward central banking in the 1920s.[10]

Kemmerer's model derived from the U.S. Federal Reserve system but he adapted it to fit the form of centralized government in primate cities in Latin America. His creations stood out in Latin America for their orthodox passivity toward money and credit, faithfully transmitting flows from the world economy. They were also distinctive for allowing government only minority control and for permitting direct, albeit limited, operations with the public. Many of their fundamental features followed standard guidelines still prevalent in most such banks of issue and central banks around the globe.

In all the Andean countries these central banks pleased bankers, merchants, and industrialists far more than landowners. Most agriculturalists preferred developmental institutions able to extend them long-term credits on generous terms. Therefore they convinced the governments to establish supplemental public banks for farmers. Despite their domination over land holding, these rural elites proved unable to dictate the policies of the premier national credit institution.

The composition of Kemmerer's banks' boards of directors reflected neither those representatives' rank in the national power structure nor their contributions to the institution's capital. Usually one-third of the seats went to government, one-third to banks, and one-third to private interest groups and shareholders. Most innovative were voting rights for labor unions and foreign bankers, although the latter were deleted over time. Despite widespread fears of political chicanery, these boards retained great independence from their governments until the Great Depression.

The central banks' capital came from the governments, the member banks, and private shareholders. They usually maintained legal reserves in excess of Kemmerer's 50 percent requirement. They also deposited a large share overseas, partly to the benefit of U.S. banks. Although those external deposits earned interest and smoothed transactions, they also increased vulnerability during the Great Crash. Moreover, many nationals argued for lower reserves and higher credit allocations for development. Although commercial bankers appreciated the security offered by central bank credits, other members of the private and public sectors complained about stringent loan policies. British disengagement from the gold standard in 1931 slashed the value of the foreign deposits of the central banks, which thereafter suspended convertibility and, in many cases, imposed exchange controls.

The devastation of the Great Depression was initially amplified by the procyclical reactions of the central bank. That calamity toppled Kemmerer's dicta, though not his institutions. Pressures from suffocating domestic elites forced the central bank to expand loans. It did so especially for government and for development banks, particularly for agriculture and import-substituting industries. The central bank became the government's mediator between more traditional agricultural and mineral export interests and newer industrial sectors. After abandonment of the gold standard, the government extended its influence over the central bank, hoping to adjust monetary policy to fiscal policy. Whereas the bank in the 1920s tried to subordinate the internal economy to external forces, in the 1930s it tried the opposite and became an instrument of inflationary growth. It relaxed its regulations to promote economic development, with exchange and monetary stability viewed merely as subcomponents of that broader national mission.[11]

After World War II, modifications in Latin America's central banks were also inspired by the International Monetary Fund, the U.S. Federal Reserve, the United Nations Economic Commission for Latin America, and local economists. Latin American governments began employing financial advisers from other countries in the region, as well as from the United States and Europe. While central banks in the hemisphere became more creative and less derivative, they continued to build upon the foundations laid by Kemmerer.[12]

He had designed his central banks, and the accompanying reforms, primarily to sustain the gold-exchange standard. It allowed central banks to use hard currencies and balances in New York and London as supplements to gold to form the legal reserves backing their notes in circulation and other liabilities. That automatic system was supposed to ensure exchange stability for the international movement of goods and capital. When a favorable balance of payments caused gold (or its equivalent) inflows to the central bank, that institution lowered discount rates and expanded the supply of money and credit to encourage imports and thus restore equilibrium. Conversely, when an unfavorable balance of payments triggered gold outflows from the bank, it raised discount rates and constricted the supply of money and credit to discourage imports. During such recessionary adjustments, foreign loans could ease the pain.[13]

Latin Americans accepted the gold standard for several reasons. With few dissensions, elites there adhered to the Western orthodoxy of the epoch. They shared U.S. desires for increased economic interaction and hoped to attract foreign capital. They also desired exchange stability and believed the gold standard could simultaneously curb domestic inflation, which exacerbated labor conflicts and jeopardized political stability.[14]

Within the Latin American countries the gold-exchange standard was most attractive to importers, debtors in foreign currency, bankers, and laborers. It seemed least attractive to exporters, debtors in domestic currency, and speculators. However, nearly all economic elites were willing to accept the system so long as it attracted foreign capital. Industrialists, for example, became willing to give up the protection afforded by depreciating currency in return for overseas investments. Once the depression eliminated funding from abroad, exporters and indebted agriculturalists usually spearheaded the drive to discard the gold standard.[15]

Most Latin American elites praised the gold system for facilitating economic growth in the 1920s, but they increasingly criticized its drawbacks: it removed monetary policy from the arsenal of state planning for development; it inhibited domestic credit expansion; and its procyclical automaticity could intensify inflation as well as deflation. Because the Latin American republics relied heavily on exporting a few primary products with mercurial sales and prices, reflexive domestic adjustments to maintain exchange stability were frequently disruptive and damaging. Monetary authorities lacked sufficient powers or money markets to counter or cushion jolts from overseas. The gold-exchange standard accentuated Andean dependence on fluctuating exports and foreign credits as determinants of national income and state revenues. Its transmission of those oscillations proved especially perturbing to economies wherein external commerce comprised a huge percentage of the gross national product. Trade slumps spawned frequent deficits in the balance of payments and in the national budget because customs revenues supplied most government income. Creditor countries could meet such balance-of-payments crises partly by lending less abroad, but debtor countries had to cover gold outflows by borrowing more overseas, which proved extremely difficult during recessions. By the end of the 1920s, falling export revenues and rising capital flight drove Andean elites to scuttle the gold-exchange standard.[16]

Given political realities, such a monetary system could only be sustained in one way—when "gold" normally flowed in. During an extended efflux of gold, governments turned against exchange stability because they needed emergency funding from the central bank. Their abandonment of the gold-exchange standard was encouraged by the export elites. Those producers were willing to see other sectors make gains when nearly everyone was progressing in the 1920s, but they were indisposed to suffer when sacrifices had to be endured. In poor export years they opted for a depreciating exchange rate.

Although more slowly and reluctantly than many of the non-Kemmererized countries in Latin America, the Andean republics soon joined most of the world in scrapping the gold standard. Argentina led the way in 1929, followed by a stampede after Great Britain disengaged in 1931. Kemmerer, however, never lost faith in his system as a defense against depreciation and inflation. Until his dying day he stood by this judgment expressed in 1934: "In general I may say that I have been from the beginning entirely out of sympathy with the Roosevelt Administration's monetary policy and I believe that the giving up of the gold standard and the devaluation of the dollar were both colossal blunders. In biblical language, I believe that the Administration sold the nation's monetary birthright for a mess of political pottage."[17]

Kemmerer's general banking legislation and superintendency continued serving the Andean countries well for many decades. Although those reforms concentrated banking in fewer hands, they also facilitated credit extension to urban enterprises. Despite local fears, few foreign banks took advantage of the doors opened by those laws. Indeed, Kemmerer's central and commercial banking legislation in some ways established checks on foreign banks and made domestic institutions stronger competitors. Those laws also helped prevent a rash of failures during the depression.

Fiscal reforms. In general, Kemmerer's financial reforms functioned more as expected than did his fiscal innovations. Local political and economic interests more quickly intruded in his fiscal institutions. His attempt to restrain the growth of the state proved futile. Nevertheless, some of his improvements in government financial management had a lasting impact. Indeed, many of the fiscal reforms advocated by the Alliance for Progress in the 1960s were foreshadowed by the Kemmerer missions in the 1920s.[18]

Like his rigid monetary law, his automatic budgetary system proved unsuitable for developing economies hitched to volatile foreign trade. Expansive governments beholden to local clienteles also violated his strictures against profligacy and deficits. Nevertheless, his strengthening of the executive branch and his introduction of more effective collection and accounting procedures enhanced the state's ability to amass and manage revenues. The central government became better prepared to play a more activist role in national development thereafter.[19]

Kemmerer's comptrollers labored in vain to enforce balanced budgets so that the Andean republics would neither drain their central banks nor default on their foreign debts. Those officials stumbled on bureaucratic resistance, political opposition, and resource and data inadequacies. As those institutions evolved, however, they significantly improved fiscal order and efficiency.

Like the comptroller, Kemmerer's recommendations for more streamlined, productive, and progressive taxes encountered numerous obstacles. Unlike his seemingly neutral financial system, those laws collided immediately with conflicting special interests, who frequently succeeded in vitiating his proposals. His attempt to reduce reliance on customs revenues enjoyed only minimal success. His income tax legislation did break new ground, however, and grew in importance in the years ahead.

Kemmerer's missions greatly helped these governments to attract more foreign loans on better terms. In a few cases he personally smoothed relations between debtors and creditors. But his Andean hosts did not heed his advice on prudence in contracting and spending those dollars. Cheered on by U.S. bankers, they incurred burdensome debts to fund extravagant public works projects. When those governments followed Kemmerer's advice to emphasize highways over railways, that redounded to the benefit of U.S. exporters, who sold more automobiles, as opposed to the British, who vended more railroads. Both railway and highway construction often produced more political than economic payoffs, at least in short-run terms of reproductive investments to help repay those debts. Whatever the cost or waste, those countries made major gains in attracting foreign capital and building domestic infrastructure for long-run growth.

Growth of dependence on the United States. Taken together, Kemmerer's financial and fiscal reforms accompanied and magnified three broad, continuing trends in the era: the growth of dependence on the United States, the growth of domestic urban capitalism, and the growth of the central state. The use of foreign economic advisers both resulted from and furthered those transformations. What do the Kemmerer missions reveal about that journey from debt-led development to debt-led disaster?

In 1931 Kemmerer was told that the "Pan American Society Executive Committee considered that I had done more for South America and more to cement the relations between U.S. and South America than any other man in the world."[20] He had certainly played an integral role in the enormous expansion of U.S. activities and leverage in the region. By the end of the 1920s, Andean trade with the United States far surpassed that with any single competitor. Both trade and direct investments were facilitated by the explosion of foreign loans from New York. Then that surging U.S. influence came to a halt—temporarily—when the Great Depression sparked defaults throughout the Andes.

The vast majority of countries defaulted because the continuing depression made a cost-benefit analysis of suspending debt payments compelling. By 1931 one estimate showed the amount needed for external debt service to be 73 percent of government revenues in Bolivia (the first Latin American country to default), 34 percent in Peru, and 32 percent in Chile and Colombia. As foreign exchange dried up, governments succumbed to domestic pressures, especially from exporters, landowners, and public employees, to declare a moratorium. Since those debts were sprinkled among thousands of bondholders, no comparable countervailing pressure or assistance could be supplied by the international banks. The U.S. government refused to intervene significantly. The 1931 attempt in Lima to achieve salvation through the U.S. Federal Reserve system came to naught. There was no powerful external creditor, government, or multilateral institution with whom to negotiate or from whom to receive emergency loans, despite small bailout efforts by U.S. banks in Colombia and Peru. As the contagion of default swept through the hemisphere, sanctions against isolated defectors also became ineffective. Even then these countries suspended debt servicing reluctantly and stopped short of repudiation. Default was a response to a crisis of resources rather than to any overwhelming wave of economic nationalism or ideological hostility against the system.[21]

Criticisms of such financial reliance on the United States emerged in the 1920s and gained momentum thereafter. One North American critic, who reflected the thinking of the indigenous, nationalist left in Latin America, leveled the following attack in the 1930s:

> Kemmerer was a gold-standard die-hard. He wanted currencies in Latin America kept high and stable as the rock of Gibraltar, regardless of the international trade situation, the price level, or anything else. This was, and is, our official desire. It enables Latin American countries to buy American goods and pay American debts. It helps prevent them develop an independent economy. In short, Mr. Kemmerer's sound financial ideas were tied to the apron strings of New York financial interests. He was the wizard of South American finance. He helped dictators put their abused revenue sources in order, so they could squeeze out more funds to pay more debts, buy more munitions, and pay their police forces to keep the people down and avoid revolution. He was hailed in Wall Street and he was hailed by the dictators of a continent and a half as a wonderworker. . . . Now, even the dictators are wiser, especially as the udders of American loans have gone dry.[22]

Later, more sophisticated interpretations stressed that the impact of investments and other foreign influences both shaped and was shaped by economic, social, and political structures within the recipient countries. In that framework the history of the Kemmerer missions sheds light on the process of integration into the world capitalist system. His experiences also revealed the reactions of domestic groups and institutions to that instrument and that process. For example, external loans could be harmful or beneficial to Latin American recipients, depending on their timing, on their terms, and on their usage by national decisionmakers. Local elites had some maneuvering room to adopt policies which could encourage debt-led development.[23]

In part, subordinate countries found space for bargaining, manipulating, and choosing because, as some Latin Americans learned to their surprise, the U.S. presence was not monolithic; U.S. interests and actors conflicted with each other. For example, exporters in the United States wanted Latin America's trade surplus spent on their products, while U.S. bankers desired that same foreign exchange to repay their loans. U.S. banks competed for loans; lenders preferred governments to pay debts with taxes on U.S. corporations; and resident U.S. exporters clashed with lenders and importers over exchange rates. When the leading exporters within a country were foreigners and the leading importers were nationals, Kemmerer's stabilization of a depreciating currency could favor Andean over resident U.S. elites, though exporters from the United States would also gain. Entangled in this diversity of interests, the Kemmerer missions became an instrument used by elites in both the center and the periphery. The former group tried to maximize U.S. penetration and profits, while the latter sought to take advantage of that envelopment and to compete for power and privilege domestically.

Studying the Kemmerer missions illuminates the surprising magnitude of U.S. penetration in the Andes in the 1920s. These countries imported from the United States not only goods, companies, and dollars, but also their major financial and fiscal institutions, sometimes managed by U.S. experts. The mirror image of the United States appointing an Ecuadorean, however well trained, to supervise its banking system is inconceivable. Increasingly, the fragile Andean economies and governments rose and fell along with the U.S. economy. In the 1920s their development depended, to a high degree, on external factors.

Like other recent studies, this investigation casts doubt on more extreme consequences hypothesized by some dependency theorists. Most important, it does not seem that mounting dependence inhibited the growth of the economy, industry, or the state. Structural change occurred within a dependent context. Openness to the world economy appeared largely beneficial during upswings in the 1920s and largely detrimental during downswings in the 1930s. The consequences of U.S. hegemony varied significantly with cycles in the world economy and with policies adopted by Latin American governments.[24]

Although the Andean economic and political elites became more beholden and submissive to the United States in the 1920s, they also proved capable of defying particular U.S. interests, especially in the 1930s. Even before the Great Depression slashed U.S. influence, South American governments used their dollars in ways contrary to the wishes of their U.S. lenders and advisers. Indeed, bowing to North American importunities, technocrats, and proctors was often a charade. After the crash Latin Americans suspended payments on the foreign debt, raised taxes on U.S. corporations, imposed tariffs on U.S. goods, and clamped restrictions on foreign exchange. Moreover, the institutions fostered by U.S. advisers in the 1920s helped Andean leaders carry out those policy initiatives in the 1930s. States heavily reliant on foreign models, advisers, and investors sometimes went to extreme lengths to placate those outsiders—for example in Colombia under President Olaya. At other times they engaged in relatively autonomous action to promote national development against the desires of external actors—for example in Chile after the fall of President Ibáñez.

The results flowed from evolving relationships among international capital, domestic elites, and state institutions. Within the host countries, foreign input lent dynamism to certain privileged sectors—especially urban capitalists and the central government—but rendered them quite susceptible to pressures and shocks from abroad. With varying success, national groups attempted to take advantage of those outside forces. They tried to minimize exploitation and concessions and to maximize gains vis-à-vis foreign and domestic competitors.

Their efforts constitute the political economy of these events within the Andean countries.

Growth of domestic capitalism and the state. The Kemmerer missions served the perceived interests of capitalist elites not only in the United States but also in the Andean republics. In South America such missions and their consequences were accepted because of the political calculations of competing interest groups. The interactions among those domestic actors and international forces determined the politics of those missions; that is, how and why those policy choices were made and carried out. Despite discrepancies and disagreements, those elites reached consensus that Kemmerer's reforms and the accompanying loans would accelerate internal economic growth, improve government efficiency, mollify emergent urban classes, and thus undergird political and social stability. When the Great Depression shattered that consensus and the influence of the United States, the Andean ruling groups broke away from the Kemmerer system.[25]

In the 1920s countries long dominated by agrarian and export elites faced mounting pressures for imports, credit, infrastructure, jobs, and government services. Those demands mainly came from expanding urban capitalist, middle sector, and working-class groups. Without dramatically raising taxes on the oligarchy, governments lacked sufficient resources to meet escalating expectations. To avoid hard choices among those competing claims, they increasingly incurred deficits in the budget and the balance of payments, inflation, and shortages of currency, credit, and foreign exchange. The resulting dissatisfaction fueled political crises. In response the ruling groups sought stabilization, sometimes under authoritarian regimes backed by the armed forces. To finance that stabilization without exacting sacrifices from domestic elites, they turned to debt-led growth. Foreign funds allowed for simultaneous exchange stabilization, economic expansion, and government activism. To reassure those foreign investors without blatantly ceding sovereignty, the state had to seek independent verification of its creditworthiness. Economic inspectors from the United States became the logical choice because of that country's ascendence as the world's banker.[26]

That strategy, however, relied on the powerful agricultural and export elites accepting greater relative gains for weaker urban capitalist interests. They proved willing to do that only so long as the international economy and foreign loans grew. Rural and urban elites could also reach agreement because they sometimes overlapped and shared investments. Any sharp economic downturn, however, produced a contrary coalition between the traditional dominant class and all those dependent upon the enlarged state. They reacted by calling for a cessation of the gold standard and of debt payments abroad. Despite recommendations for shrinkage of the bloated central government, that crisis generated further state expansion to compensate for the absence of foreign capital. Then inflationary currency and credit expansion was used to assuage all contenders as, in Albert Hirschman's phrase, "a substitute for civil war."[27]

In the 1920s a domestic coalition in favor of Kemmerer's promised currency stabilization was usually led by importers, other merchants, and consumers, who saw the cost of their goods spiraling upward. Normally, the military also opposed depreciation and inflation, which eroded their salaries, raised the price of their arms purchases, and provoked political and social unrest. Laborers falling behind the cost of living also tended to join coalitions in favor of Kemmerer. To overcome the natural and more powerful opponents of stabilization, these forces had to tip the balance by winning over divided or ambivalent groups, enticing the diehards with foreign loans, and adding external supporters to their camp. Broadening that support base became easiest during prosperous years, when stabilization did not require an acrimonious allocation of sacrifices because it was accompanied by foreign loans.

One ambivalent ally fairly easy to attract to the Kemmererian coalition was industrialists. Although depreciating currency provided them with protection against competitive imports, manufacturers also desired foreign capital and ingredients. Furthermore, they believed that stabilization would dampen labor protests. As creditors, bankers could also be enlisted in the pro-Kemmerer troops, once their anxieties about regulation and competition had been alleviated. Speculative and smaller banks, however, remained unlikely to be enthusiastic. The government and politicians were also torn. Easy money and credit, along with lax fiscal controls, allowed the state to spend freely for projects and clients and to reduce domestic debt burdens. The lure of foreign loans, hard currency to service external obligations, steady salaries for government employees, and sociopolitical calm, however, convinced the public sector of the virtues of Kemmerer's medicine.

The conversion of those ambivalent groups to the Kemmererian coalition helped pull over, or at least neutralize, the likely opponents, who traditionally wielded enormous power in the Andes. In economies crucially dependent on foreign trade, the export elites typically dominated policymaking, even though the state also made some relatively autonomous decisions. Whether foreign or domestic, agricultural or mineral, those producers for outside markets normally preferred flexible exchange rates so they could earn hard currency abroad but pay their workers with cheapened pesos. Especially during times of sharp fluctuations or declines, they opted for a depreciating value. During the general upswing of the 1920s, however, they acceded to a stable value in hopes of foreign credits. Other groups leery of Kemmerer's system included debtors in domestic currency, especially in the export and agricultural sectors. They were joined by speculators, who profited from exchange oscillations. Regional elites outside the capital core also feared that Kemmerer's reforms would accelerate the concentration of wealth and power.[28]

These potentially pro- or anti-Kemmerer alliances actually formed transnational coalitions, however tacit and informal. Although divided, U.S. interests mainly backed Kemmerer's reforms. Their support often proved decisive for the victory of a Kemmererian coalition and its transformation into nearly a nationwide consensus. The only U.S. group likely to enroll on the negative side was exporters residing in the Andean countries. On the positive side were exporters in the United States, U.S. investors, U.S. construction firms, and the U.S. government. Resident U.S. bankers hesitated over regulation but welcomed equal rights with domestic banks, stable exchange rates, and an emphasis on commercial banking, wherein they excelled.

Such transnational Kemmererian coalitions disintegrated during the Great Depression. As foreign funds and forces dwindled, the ambivalent domestic members of the stabilization coalition switched their allegiance to the side of most exporters, agriculturalists, and debtors. The majority of industrialists, bankers, military officers, the middle and working classes, and government officials became unwilling to pay the recessionary price of maintaining gold-exchange rates. The increasingly isolated import merchants lost their leverage during the downswing in the world economy, when nearly everyone called on the state for protection, money, and credit.

The growth of the state during the twenties had prepared it to become even more interventionist during and after the Great Depression. Kemmerer's fiscal reforms and the loans they attracted facilitated expansion of the central administration. That borrowing also enhanced U.S. leverage over Andean governments; for example, persuading them to grant concessions to U.S. investors or to offer positions to U.S. technocrats. The state followed Kemmerer's advice when it perceived advantages—for example on expanding revenues—but usually ignored him when the advice was against its perceived interests; for example, on reducing expenditures. Becoming more dependent on foreign capital, the state became less dependent on local capital, even establishing controls over the banking sector. The public sector became wealthier, larger, and more active, especially as an employer, a builder of infrastructure, and a manager of money and credit. Reliance on external financing, however, rendered those governments exceptionally vulnerable to the Great Crash. In the wake of that disaster, national capitalists, including exporters and agriculturalists, reasserted their domination over economic policymaking. Whereas governmental expansion in the 1920s had depended on foreign trade, loans, and advisers, the burgeoning state became an alternative to foreigners in the 1930s, supplying money, credit, and expertise.[29]

Beyond the Andes

The patterns traced above were unique to neither the Andean republics nor the Kemmerer missions. On his trips outside the Andes Kemmerer encountered similar conditions, delivered similar recommendations, served similar functions, and engendered similar results. For example, during the monetary chaos of the Mexican Revolution in 1917, that government asked Kemmerer to make a recommendation. He proposed the gold-exchange standard based on reserves deposited abroad to earn interest. The main advocates of that reform were foreign investors, domestic importers, labor representatives, and the government, which owed huge foreign debts in gold. Exporters, silver producers, and domestic manufacturers (who feared competitive imports) opposed the proposal. Because of continuing political instability, lasting currency reform had to await the founding of the Bank of Mexico in 1925.[30]

Persistent political upheavals also prevented Guatemala from acting on Kemmerer's 1919 recommendations for a gold standard maintained by a central bank, despite strong State Department support for the project. Again in 1924 Kemmerer tried unsuccessfully to consummate those reforms in conjunction with a loan contract. If that had come to fruition, one U.S. investment group promised Kemmerer a commission on the face value of the loan. He explained his role "as a sort of 'go between' for a group of American financiers and the Guatemalan government." On its own, Guatemala did establish in 1926 a central bank and a gold standard, modeled after Kemmerer's proposals.[31]

His mission to Poland in 1926 also illustrated the overlapping interests of U.S. advisers, financiers, and government officials. In order to float loans in New York, Poland—on the advice of Dillon, Read, and Company (its financial agent)—invited Kemmerer to study its finances. Poles viewed U.S. advisers as less politically biased than Europeans. According to one scholarly study of that Kemmerer mission: "The real interest of the Poles was the gaining of access to foreign financial markets with a minimum blow to their national pride and with the need to take unpopular internal measures reduced to the absolute minimum required to open those foreign markets." The vice president of the Bank of Poland even suggested that "the Kemmerer mission was merely a façade, made for the purpose of advertising Poland in the United States and that they never really expected any thoroughgoing reorganization as a result of it." At least on the surface, that government accepted a package of economic reforms devised by Kemmerer, the Federal Reserve Bank of New York, and the U.S. assistant secretary of the treasury. The Polish dictator, who seized power in 1926, then appointed that U.S. Treasury official as the country's chief economic adviser for the next three years. His presence secured a U.S. loan in 1927.[32]

In 1928 China invited Kemmerer to westernize its financial system and help attract foreign loans. Arthur N. Young, a member of that mission, stayed on from 1929 through the 1930s to assist with debt consolidation, loan negotiations, monetary reform, and budget management. He strengthened the Nationalist government and its ties with the United States. His recommendations for fiscal pruning, however, were swept aside by regional overlords and the 1937 Japanese attack.[33]

Other countries, including Brazil, Panama, Argentina, and Romania, also considered inviting Kemmerer missions but did not carry through.[34] Some of them, like Brazil, enacted similar monetary reforms without his presence. Other advisers spread the Kemmerer gospel elsewhere in Latin America and beyond. For example, Arthur Young, his former student and later a State Department official, was recommended by the department as an adviser to Honduras in 1920. Another Kemmerer student, William Wilson Cumberland, also served as economic adviser in the State Department and provided expertise to Armenia and Peru, again in tandem with loan negotiations with U.S. bankers. In 1922 in Peru, Cumberland encountered stiff resistance to his attempts to stabilize the currency, found a central bank, balance the budget, and streamline customs administration; he soon realized that his hosts wanted to use him as a magnet for foreign loans, not as an agent for sweeping reforms. A U.S. economic mission to Persia in the 1920s also discovered that its employers were far more interested in using their advisers to impress foreign lenders and consolidate a dictatorship than in adopting the substance of recommendations for fiscal renovations.[35]

The U.S. government pursued similar policies in Europe, using both semiprivate economic experts and cooperation among established central banks. In the 1920s Secretary of Commerce Herbert Hoover convinced Czechoslovakia, Poland, Yugoslavia, and Austria to hire U.S. technical missions and advisers to improve their access to U.S. bank loans and thus fortify good relations with the United States. The Federal Reserve Bank of New York collaborated with the existing central banks of England and Europe to promote loans to countries there which adopted the gold standard and balanced the budget. After a consortium of central banks issued a seal of approval by extending a stabilization credit, then private banks followed with private loans. The U.S. government encouraged these efforts, while emphasizing "private" rather than "public" agents of financial reform and expansion. Sending in ostensibly autonomous financial missions was preferable to collaboration among central banks because the former method was even further removed from any taint of formal governmental participation or responsibility. Because central bank cooperation also proved difficult to achieve even among industrialized countries, it was pursued only in Belgium, Italy, Poland, and Romania.[36]

Legacies from One Great Depression to Another, 1930s–1980s

The expanding global process of integration into Western capitalism through incorporation of U.S. advisers, institutions, investments, and trade was temporarily derailed by the Great Depression of the 1930s. The United States halted capital exports to Latin America and elevated tariff barriers against imports from Latin America. Those countries thus turned inward to generate recovery. In most cases recuperation came more quickly to those nations more willing to scuttle exchange and monetary stability, foreign debt payments, and balanced budgets—the heart of Kemmerer's orthodox system.

After initially resisting and slowing change, the institutions bequeathed by Kemmerer helped implement new countercyclical policies. During the crisis the Andean countries experimented without relying on foreign guidance. They built upon institutional innovations from the 1920s to add new public credit agencies in the 1930s. Government expenditures exceeded revenues in order to cope with the fiscal crisis; to assist exporters, landowners, and industrialists; to meet public payrolls; to respond to domestic upheavals; and to fight border conflicts inspired by scrambles for resources. Those expansionary policies responded to exigencies of the moment rather than to any coherent alternative to a Kemmererian model. Sudden and severe deficits in the balance of payments and the government budget propelled policy creativity. Nevertheless, that inadvertent Keynesianism fueled surprisingly rapid recovery from the depression. It also spawned structural changes, particularly in the growth of manufacturing. Import substitution occurred not only in industry but also in agriculture and services, including economic advice.[37]

In reaction to the depression most Andean leaders turned to exchange controls, currency devaluation, and direct or indirect central bank financing of government deficits and of credits for producers. As Kemmerer had feared, such credit liberalization fanned inflation. According to one estimate for 1931–40, cost-of-living indexes rose approximately 14 percent in Peru, 45 percent in Colombia, 100 percent in Chile, and 690 percent in Bolivia (mainly because of the Chaco War). Such reflationary measures facilitated recovery from the depression, as did diversification and revival of exports. Although costly, these new money, banking, and fiscal policies contributed to national development that was more insulated from external disturbances. While Kemmerer's policy prescriptions mainly fell by the wayside, his institutions continued serving the growth of national capitalism and the state.[38]

In later decades the linkages among foreign economic advisers, loans, domestic capitalists, and the state—highlighted by the Kemmerer experiences—reemerged. Although significant differences arose, some noteworthy continuities also appeared. After World War II thousands of economic experts, both individuals and teams, poured into Latin America. They wrote reports and recommendations for lending as well as borrowing governments, for unilateral as well as bilateral or multilateral agencies. Their analyses established conditions for the granting of billions of dollars in assistance from the "developed" to the "less developed" countries. Such economic advising became increasingly institutionalized and professionalized.[39]

Conditions in the 1970s came to resemble those in the 1920s, as loans to Latin American governments ballooned and came increasingly from private banks rather than public agencies. That influx of finance capital helped local elites escape from economic stagnation, a balance-of-payments squeeze, and a zero-sum political stalemate, exacerbated by rising demands from labor and the Left. To acquire those loans countries frequently had to obtain a passing grade from the International Monetary Fund. Its blessing usually required deflationary measures, such as reductions in budgets and wages, as well as exchange stabilization. Sometimes similar policies were adopted on the recommendation of private U.S. economists, often from the University of Chicago. Authoritarian governments proved most capable of carrying out those tough stabilization measures and thus receiving a flood of loans. In many countries the major beneficiaries became financiers and speculators. Soon, more open economies and more austerity measures became necessary to continue servicing the mushrooming debts. More international experts were brought in to report that the country was on the right track and therefore deserving of further credits. As a result, the Latin American debtors became extremely vulnerable to the international recession in the early 1980s.[40]

Just as the 1970s in Latin America echoed the 1920s, so the 1980s evoked comparisons with the 1930s. Once again many of those countries used free-market policies and foreign loans to follow the ups and downs of the global economy. During 1982–85 the hemisphere suffered the worst depression since the Great Crash. The stream of external financing slowed to a trickle. As in 1929–32, that economic catastrophe toppled many governments, especially military regimes.

Nevertheless, most countries in the eighties continued at least minimal service of their staggering foreign debts, even though those obligations loomed much larger—absolutely and relatively—than during the Great Depression. They used visits by the IMF, by the chairman of the U.S. Federal Reserve Board, and by U.S. academic economists to certify the rectitude of their policies. Thus they reasserted their worthiness to receive new public and private loans to maintain payments on their external obligations. Those outside experts also helped the governments to justify belt tightening to their citizens and lobby for leniency from their bankers. Equally important, they protected the investments of the foreign banks. These crisis managers served as intermediaries between international creditors and borrowers, as "third-party" observers, negotiators, or enforcers. Indeed, these economic authorities provided one linchpin holding the world economy together at fragile junctures.

Unlike Kemmerer's vain attempt to keep South America in line in Lima in 1931, the banks, international institutions, and, to a lesser extent, governments of the industrial superpowers successfully took the lead to keep the players in the game in the early eighties. Rather than being resolved by virtually universal default as in the 1930s, the debt crisis in the 1980s lingered on. It persisted mainly because the debts were owed to huge banking consortia instead of scattered individual investors, and these bankers could pressure, negotiate, and extend emergency credits. They could argue—in conjunction with their governments, multilateral agencies, and elites in the debtor countries—that full-fledged default threatened not simply an unfortunate collection of small bondholders but rather the entire international financial system.[41]

The disaster of the 1980s exhibited other contrasts as well as commonalities with the collapse of the 1930s. At least up to 1987, less protectionism took hold in the developed as well as the underdeveloped countries. Economic nationalism was restrained. Political changes in Latin America did not usher in drastically new economic policies. Governments labored mightily to sustain austerity and at least token debt payments. By the 1980s most of those countries had already gone through import-substituting industrialization and had become much more integrated into the world capitalist system. Any repudiation of its tenets would prove far more wrenching and explosive—ideologically as well as economically—than in 1930. Despite domestic pressures to renegotiate and recast the international rules of the game, most Latin American leaders shied away from any rupture with the global order.

By the mid-eighties it remained to be seen how long Latin America's governments could balance between external and internal demands. It became extremely difficult to harmonize the interests of foreign forces, domestic actors, and the state. One reason for Latin American leaders' patience, prudence, even timidity, was the absence of any coherent, compelling alternative model of development. As in the 1930s, policymakers groped for fresh recipes for growth, while old formulas fell into disrepute. They would have welcomed, perhaps, the remedies of a new "money doctor."

NOTES

I. Money Doctoring and the Diplomacy of the Dollar in Latin America

1. John H. Coatsworth, "Obstacles to Economic Growth in Nineteenth-Century Mexico," *American Historical Review* 83, no. 1 (February 1978): 80–100; Lauchlin Currie, *The Role of Economic Advisers in Developing Countries* (Westport, 1981), p. xiv. On the broader role of legal institutions, see Kenneth L. Karst and Keith S. Rosenn, *Law and Development in Latin America* (Berkeley, 1975).

2. Charles Lipson, *Standing Guard: Protecting Foreign Capital in the Nineteenth and Twentieth Centuries* (Berkeley, 1985).

3. Colombia, Contraloría General de la República, *Edwin Walter Kemmerer y su obra en Colombia* (Bogotá, 1945), esp. pp. 12–13.

4. Carlos Pantoja Revelo, *Saqueo, atraso y dependencia: De la piratería del siglo xvi al vampirismo del siglo xx* (Bogotá, 1974), p. 78; Carlos Alberto Clulow, *El oro yanqui en latinoamerica* (Montevideo, 1928).

5. For some of the most significant treatments of these complex issues, see Charles W. Bergquist, *Alternative Approaches to the Problem of Development: A Selected and Annotated Bibliography* (Durham, 1979); Heraldo Muñoz, *From Dependency to Development: Strategies to Overcome Underdevelopment and Inequality* (Boulder, 1981); Peter Evans, *Dependent Development: The Alliance of Multinational, State, and Local Capital in Brazil* (Princeton, 1979); idem, "After Dependency: Recent Studies of Class, State, and Industrialization," *Latin American Research Review* 20, no. 2 (1985): 149–60; Fernando Henrique Cardoso and Enzo Faletto, *Dependency and Development in Latin America* (Berkeley, 1979); Osvaldo Sunkel, *El subdesarrollo y la teoría del desarrollo* (Mexico, 1971); Andre Gunder Frank, *Capitalism and Underdevelopment in Latin America: Historical Studies of Chile and Brazil* (New York, 1967); James D. Cockcroft, Andre Gunder Frank, and Dale L. Johnson, *Dependence and Underdevelopment: Latin America's Political Economy* (Garden City, 1972).

6. J. H. Parry, *The Spanish Seaborne Empire* (New York, 1966); James Lockhart and Stuart B. Schwartz, *Early Latin America* (Cambridge, 1983).

7. William A. Williams, *The Tragedy of American Diplomacy*, rev. ed. (New York, 1962), esp. pp. 104–59; Federico G. Gil, *Latin American–United States Relations* (New York, 1971), esp. pp. 87–116; Scott Nearing and Joseph Freeman, *Dollar Diplomacy: A Study in American Imperial-*

271

ism (New York, 1925); Herbert Feis, *The Diplomacy of the Dollar, 1919–1932* (New York, 1950).

8. Rosemary Thorp and Laurence Whitehead, *Inflation and Stabilization in Latin America* (New York, 1979); Roberto Frenkel and Guillermo O'Donnell, "The 'Stabilization Programs' of the International Monetary Fund and Their Internal Impacts," in Richard R. Fagen, ed., *Capitalism and the State in U.S.–Latin American Relations* (Stanford, 1979), pp. 171–216; Barbara Stallings, "Peru and the U.S. Banks: Privatization of Financial Relations," in Fagen, *Capitalism and the State*, pp. 217–53; J. Keith Horsefield, *The International Monetary Fund, 1945–65*, 3 vols. (Washington, D.C., 1969); Margaret Garristen de Vries, *International Monetary Fund, 1966–71*, 2 vols. (Washington D.C., 1978); Cheryl Payer, *The Debt Trap: The International Monetary Fund and the Third World* (New York, 1974); Tony Killick, Graham Bird, Jennifer Sharpley, and Mary Sutton, *The Quest for Economic Stabilization: The IMF and the Third World* (London, 1984); Tony Killick et al., *The IMF and Stabilization: Developing Country Experiences* (London, 1984); Miguel S. Wionczek, *Politics and Economics of External Debt Crisis: The Latin American Experience* (Boulder, 1985).

9. Albert O. Hirschman, *Journeys toward Progress* (New York, 1963), pp. 175–210.

10. Robert N. Seidel, "American Reformers Abroad: The Kemmerer Missions in South America, 1923–1931," *Journal of Economic History* 32, no. 2 (June 1972): 520–45.

11. Bruce R. Dalgaard, "South Africa's Impact on Britain's Return to Gold, 1925" (Ph.D. diss., University of Illinois, 1976), pp. 68–70; Paul W. Drake, "Edwin Kemmerer," in John Eatwell, Murray Milgate, and Peter Newman, eds., *The New Palgrave: A Dictionary of Economic Theory and Doctrine* (London, 1987).

12. His principle writings include: Edwin Walter Kemmerer, *Money and Credit Instruments in Their Relation to General Prices* (New York, 1907); *Seasonal Variations in the Relative Demand for Money and Capital in the United States* (Washington, D.C., 1910); *Modern Currency Reforms* (New York, 1916); "A Proposal for Pan-American Monetary Unity," *Political Science Quarterly* 31 (March 1916): 66–80; *The ABC of the Federal Reserve System* (Princeton, 1918); *High Prices and Deflation* (Princeton, 1920); "Economic Advisory Work for Governments," *American Economic Review* 17, no. 1 (March 1927): 1–12; *The United States and the Gold Standard* (New York, 1932); *Money: The Principles of Money and Their Exemplification in Outstanding Chapters of Monetary History* (New York, 1935); *The ABC of Inflation* (New York, 1942); *Gold and the Gold Standard* (New York, 1944). Bruce R. Dalgaard, "E. W. Kemmerer: The Origins and Impact of the Money Doctor's Monetary Economics," in Bruce R. Dalgaard and Richard Vedder, eds., *Variations in Business and Economic History: Essays in Honor of Donald L. Kemmerer* (Greenwich, Conn., 1982), pp. 31–44; Joseph Dorfman, *The Economic Mind in American Civilization*, 5 vols. (New York, 1959), 4:308–12; John Kenneth Galbraith, *Money: Whence It Came, Where It Went* (Boston, 1975), p. 199; Edwin W. Kemmerer Papers, Princeton University Library (hereinafter cited as EWK), Box 3, letter from Kemmerer to A. Moncayo Andrade, February 14, 1933; Diary, May 1, 1931, p. 121.

13. Seidel, "American Reformers Abroad"; Kemmerer, "Economic Advisory."

14. Joseph S. Tulchin, *The Aftermath of War: World War I and United States Policy toward Latin America* (New York, 1971), pp. 3–4.

15. Melchior Palyi, *The Twilight of Gold, 1914–1936* (Chicago, 1972), pp. 78–87.

16. All figures on international investments must be treated with caution. Estimates vary due to data inadequacies, especially on direct investments. Despite disagreements over exact amounts, sources do concur on the general size and directions of these capital movements. See Max Winkler, *Investment of United States Capital in Latin America* (Boston, 1928), pp. 1–2, 39–53, 280–85; J. Fred Rippy, *British Investments in Latin America, 1822–1949* (Minneapolis, 1959);

John Michael Atkin, *British Overseas Investment, 1918–1931* (New York, 1977); Clarence Henry Haring, *South America Looks at the United States* (New York, 1928), pp. 80–88; Seidel, "American Reformers Abroad," p. 526.

17. David Joslin, *A Century of Banking in Latin America* (London, 1963).

18. J. F. Normano, *The Struggle for South America* (Boston and New York, 1931); J. Fred Rippy, *Latin America in World Politics* (New York, 1938); Michael J. Hogan, *Informal Entente: The Private Structure of Cooperation in Anglo-American Economic Diplomacy, 1918–1928* (Columbia, Mo., 1977); U.S. Department of State (hereinafter cited as USDOS), from Bogotá, September 2, 1930, 821.51A/50.

19. F. C. Schwedtman, "Lending Our Financial Machinery to Latin America," *American Political Science Review* 11 (May 1917): 239–251; Frederick M. Halsey, *Investments in Latin America and the British West Indies* (Washington, D.C., 1918); U.S. Chamber of Commerce, *Latin American Trade Relations* (n.p., 1927).

20. Robert N. Seidel, "Progressive Pan Americanism: Development and United States Policy toward South America, 1906–1931" (Ph.D. diss., Cornell University, 1973), pp. 215–46.

21. The best compilation on investments is Barbara Stallings, *Banker to the Third World: U.S. Portfolio Investment in Latin America, 1900–86* (Berkeley, 1987). Also see J. Fred Rippy, "Investments of Citizens of the United States in Latin America," *Journal of Business of the University of Chicago* 22, no. 1 (January 1949): 17–29; Cleona Lewis, *America's Stake in International Investments* (Washington, D.C., 1938); United Nations, Department of Economic and Social Affairs, *Foreign Capital in Latin America* (New York, 1955); idem, *External Financing in Latin America* (New York, 1965); Paul D. Dickens, *American Direct Investments in Foreign Countries* (Washington, D.C., 1930); idem, *A New Estimate of American Investments Abroad* (Washington, D.C., 1931); Mira Wilkins, *The Maturing of Multinational Enterprise: American Business Abroad from 1914 to 1970* (Cambridge, 1974); Joan Hoff Wilson, *American Business and Foreign Policy, 1920–1933* (Lexington, 1971), pp. 168–69; Henry Kittredge Norton, *The Coming of South America* (New York, 1932); William Manger, "Inversión de capitales extranjeros en las repúblicas americanas," Colombia, Banco de la República, *Revista del Banco de la República* 49 (November 1931): 385–425; U.S. Department of State, Francis White Papers (hereinafter cited as FW), Box 40, "U.S.–Latin American Financial Relations, 1928–1933: American Investments in Latin America"; Winkler, *Investment of United States Capital*; Seidel, "American Reformers Abroad."

22. Emily S. Rosenberg, "Foundations of United States International Financial Power: Gold Standard Diplomacy, 1900–1905," *Business History Review* 59 (Summer 1985): 169–202; Karl Polanyi, *The Great Transformation* (Boston, 1944).

23. FW, Box 3, "La General," memorandum, February 6, 1931; John T. Madden, Marcus Nadler, and Harry C. Sauvain, *America's Experience as a Creditor Nation* (New York, 1937); J. Fred Rippy, "A Bond-Selling Extravaganza of the 1920's," *Journal of Business of the University of Chicago* 23 (1950): 238–47; George W. Edwards, *American Dollars Abroad* (New York, 1928); Lewis, *America's Stake in International Investments*.

24. United Nations, *External Financing*, pp. 22–23; FW, Box 40, "U.S.–Latin American Financial Relations"; Winkler, *Investment of United States Capital*, pp. 42–43.

25. Rippy, "Bond-Selling Extravaganza"; United Nations, *External Financing*, pp. 23–30; FW, Box 40, "U.S.–Latin American Financial Relations, 1928–1933: Defaults in Interest Service on Dollar Bonds of Foreign Governments, Provinces, and Municipalities."

26. Madden, Nadler, and Sauvain, *America's Experience as a Creditor Nation*, pp. 111–25.

27. United Nations, *Foreign Capital*, pp. 7–11.

28. EWK, Diary, May 27, 1926, p. 147; November 11, 1927, p. 316; December 14, 1930, p. 348;

May 26, 1931, p. 146; interview with Frank Whitson Fetter, Hanover, N.H., July 29, 1976. In contrast with the general pattern in Kemmerer's personal diary, John Kenneth Galbraith charges that he served as a director of the investment trust of American Founders Group. Even if he did, that did not affect the public posture analyzed in this study. John Kenneth Galbraith, *The Great Crash* (Boston, 1979), p. 55.

29. For a small sample of Kemmerer's meetings with U.S. bankers, see EWK, Diary, October 4, 1928, p. 278; October 5, 1928, p. 279; October 11, 1928, p. 285; November 6, 1930, p. 310; Donald L. Kemmerer, "Comments to Staff of Central Bank of Bolivia, 1981," MS, 1981; idem, "How Dr. E. W. Kemmerer Worked and How He Directed the Work of His Advisory Commissions," MS, 1982; Emily S. Rosenberg, "American Foreign Financial Advising in Latin America Before the Great Depression: Form and Structure," MS, 1985.

30. Phelps, *The Foreign Expansion of American Banks*; Frank O'Malley, *Our South American Trade and Its Financing* (New York, 1920), p. 117; Miguel S. Wionczeck, *La banca extranjera en América latina* (Lima, 1969), pp. 3–15.

31. Normano, *Struggle for South America*, pp. 168–69; Rosenberg, "American Foreign Financial Advising," p. 1.

32. Merle Curti and Kendall Birr, *Prelude to Point Four: American Technical Missions Overseas, 1838–1938* (Madison, 1954); Frederick M. Nunn, *Yesterday's Soldiers: European Military Professionalism in South America, 1890–1940* (Lincoln, 1983); Jacques de Lauwe, *La América Ibérica* (Santiago, 1937), pp. 198–200.

33. Tulchin, *Aftermath of War*; Emily S. Rosenberg, *Spreading the American Dream: American Economic and Cultural Expansion, 1890–1945* (New York, 1982); Charles Evans Hughes, *Our Relations to the Nations of the Western Hemisphere* (Princeton, 1928); Samuel Guy Inman, "Imperialistic America," *Atlantic Monthly* (July 1924): 107–16; Sumner Welles, "Is America Imperialistic?" *Atlantic Monthly* (September 1924): 412–23.

34. Tulchin, *Aftermath of War*, pp. 241–46; Williams, *The Tragedy*; Kenneth J. Grieb, *The Latin American Policy of Warren G. Harding* (Fort Worth, 1976); Joseph Brandes, *Herbert Hoover and Economic Diplomacy* (Pittsburgh, 1962); Alexander DeConde, *Herbert Hoover's Latin American Policy* (Stanford, 1951); FW, Box 3, "Latin America General," memorandum, February 5, 1930.

35. Tulchin, *Aftermath of War*, pp. 104–243; Feis, *Diplomacy of the Dollar*; Hughes, *Our Relations*, pp. 54–72; Seidel, "Progressive Pan-Americanism," pp. 563–66; FW, Box 1, "Bolivia," memorandum of conversation with Mr. Chandler P. Anderson, Jr., Chase Securities Corp., November 5, 1930; Box 3, "Latin America General," memorandum, February 6, 1931; Box 40, "U.S.–Latin American Financial Relations, 1928–1933: The Department of State and Latin American Loans."

36. James W. Angell, *Financial Foreign Policy of the United States* (New York, 1933); Carlos G. Dávila, *North American Imperialism* (New York, 1930).

37. Duncan Snidal, "The Limits of Hegemonic Stability," *International Organization* 39, no. 4 (Autumn 1985): 579–614; Charles Kindleberger, *The World in Depression, 1929–1939* (London, 1973); idem, "Systems of International Economic Organization," in David Calleo, ed., *Money and the Coming World Order* (New York, 1976), pp. 15–40; idem, "Dominance and Leadership in the International Economy," *International Studies Quarterly* 25, no. 3 (1981): 242–54; Arthur A. Stein, "The Hegemon's Dilemma: Great Britain, the United States, and the International Economic Order," *International Organization* 38, no. 2 (Spring 1984): 355–86; James E. Alt, Randall L. Calvert, and Brian D. Humes, "Game Theory and Hegemonic Stability: The Role of Reputation and Uncertainty," MS, 1986.

38. Lipson, *Standing Guard*; Hogan, *Informal Entente*.

39. Rosenberg, "American Foreign Financial Advising." By the 1920s financial monitoring could also be carried out by the central banks in the industrial powers or by the League of Nations, but both were reluctant to get involved. The former only entered into a few European public loan negotiations, while the latter lacked significant funding, authority, or U.S. participation. Richard Hemmig Meyer, *Bankers' Diplomacy: Monetary Stabilization in the Twenties* (New York, 1970).

40. FW, Box 40, "U.S.–Latin American Financial Relations, 1928–1933: The Department of State and Latin American Loans."

41. Hughes, *Our Relations*, pp. 72–73.

42. Rosenberg, *Spreading the American Dream.*

43. Rosenberg, "American Foreign Financial Advising"; Kemmerer, *Modern Currency Reforms*; idem, "Economic Advisory"; EWK, Diary, November 15, 1930, p. 319. He also served as U.S. delegate to the Fourth Pan-American Commercial Conference in 1931, where the United States argued for apolitical central banks, stable currencies, and debt compliance. FW, Box 7, "Winston," letter to Garrard Winston, March 7, 1931; Box 21, "Fourth Pan-American Commercial Conference," October 5–13, 1931; interview with Fetter.

44. Rosenberg, "American Foreign Financial Advising"; Seidel, "American Reformers Abroad"; EWK, Diary, January 14, 1929, p. 14; November 4, 1930, p. 308.

45. Fredrick B. Pike, *The United States and the Andean Republics* (Cambridge, 1977).

2. Colombia's Dance of the Millions, 1923–1933

1. Alfonso Patiño Rosselli, *La prosperidad a debe y la gran crisis, 1925–1935* (Bogotá, 1981); William Paul McGreevey, *An Economic History of Colombia, 1845–1930* (Cambridge, 1971), pp. 11, 258; José Escorcia, *Historia económica y social de Colombia siglo xx* (Bogotá, 1978), pp. 87–88; Jorge Franco Holgúin, *Evolución de las instituciones financieras en Colombia* (Mexico, 1966), pp. 80–81.

2. Guillermo Torres García, *Historia de la moneda en Colombia* (Bogotá, 1945), pp. 360–62.

3. Estimates of national wealth varied widely but generally agreed on relative magnitudes. No precision is implied by the figures given. Climaco Villegas, *Vida económica y financiera de Colombia* (Bogotá, 1930), p. 4.

4. U.S. Department of Commerce, Bureau of Foreign and Domestic Commerce, Record Group 151 (hereinafter cited as USDOC), File no. 460, "Colombia," letter from Louis Domeratsky to Walter J. Donnelly, April 17, 1929.

5. Samuel Crowther, *The Romance and Rise of the American Tropics* (Garden City, N.Y., 1929), pp. 271–86.

6. USDOC, File no. 434, "Colombia," report from J. A. Montalvo, *Moody's Investors Service* 17, no. 96 (November 27, 1925): 391; Colombia, Departamento de Contraloría, *Anuario estadístico de Colombia, 1931* (Bogotá, 1932), pp. 270, 299, 306; McGreevey, *Economic History of Colombia*, pp. 11, 196; Torres García, *Historia de la moneda*, pp. 376–83; Escorcia, *Historia económica y social*, pp. 64–73, 89–91, 195–96.

7. Marco Palacios, *Coffee in Colombia, 1850–1970* (Cambridge, 1980), pp. 198–99; Stephen J. Randall, *The Diplomacy of Modernization: Colombian-American Relations, 1920–1940* (Toronto, 1978), pp. 30–32; McGreevey, *Economic History of Colombia*, pp. 11, 196; López C., *Estudio sobre la inflación*, pp. 39–43; Escorcia, *Historia económica y social*, pp. 65–91; Colombia, Departamento de Contraloría, *Anuario 1931*, pp. 283, 294.

8. On the general U.S. economic role in Colombia in these years, see Randall, *Diplomacy of*

Modernization; Oscar Rodríguez Salazar, *Efectos de la gran depresión sobre la industria colombiana* (Bogotá, 1973), pp. 34–35, tables A-1, A-2, A-3, A-8; P. L. Bell, *Colombia: A Commercial and Industrial Handbook* (Washington, D.C., 1921), pp. 16, 316; Colombia, Banco de la República, *Revista del Banco de la República* (hereinafter cited as *BR*) (May 1928), p. 205; López C., *Estudio sobre la inflación*, pp. 31–32; USDOC, File no. 460, "Colombia," Special Circular no. 179 (1925).

9. Randall, *Diplomacy of Modernization*, pp. 11, 56; McGreevey, *Economic History of Colombia*, pp. 207–13; E. Taylor Parks, *Colombia and the United States, 1765–1934* (Durham, 1935), pp. viii, 464–67; Centro de Estudios, "Anteo Quimbaya," *Formación del capitalismo en Colombia* (n.p., n.d.), pp. 41–54; Max Winkler, *Investments of United States Capital in Latin America* (Boston, 1928), pp. 118–31.

10. Bell, *Commercial and Industrial Handbook*, pp. 61, 354–55; U.S. Department of State, Record Group 59 (hereinafter cited as USDOS), from Bogotá, May 8, 1922, 821.00/501.

11. Bell, *Commercial and Industrial Handbook*, pp. 354–55; Parks, *Colombia and the United States*, p. 466; J. Fred Rippy, *The Capitalists and Colombia* (New York, 1931), pp. 174–75.

12. Parks, *Colombia and the United States*, pp. 440–71; Edwin W. Kemmerer Papers, Princeton University Library (hereinafter cited as EWK), Box 115, "Memorandum of Conversation with Mr. Van Dusen," March 20, 1923, p. 7; USDOS, from Bogotá, April 10, 1922, 821.00/499.

13. EWK, Box 115, "Memorandum with Van Dusen," pp. 1–20; Box 281, "Conference with Representatives from Department of Huila," April 25, 1923; "Memorandum of Conference Held with Enrique de Narváez," "Conference Held with Pedro A. López"; Luis Jiménez López, *El Banco de la República contra los intereses nacionales* (Bogotá, 1927), pp. 11–17.

14. EWK, Box 115, "Memorandum with Van Dusen," pp. 17–18; Box 281, letter from Parrish to Piles, August 2, 1923; Juan Claudio Morales C., *Régimen bancario* (Bogotá, 1969), pp. 8–12; USDOS, from Cali, October 30, 1929, 821.516/98; Bell, *Commercial and Industrial Handbook*, pp. 333–34.

15. Oliverio Rodríguez, *El Banco de la República y su influencia en la economía colombiana* (Bogotá, 1948), pp. 7–9; J. Osorio y Gil, *La moneda en Colombia* (Bogotá, 1937), pp. 6–9; Miguel Urrutia and Mario Arrubla, *Estadísticas históricas de Colombia* (Bogotá, 1970), pp. 158–59; José A. Andrade, *El Banco de la República* (Bogotá, 1927), pp. 9–10; Morales, *Régimen bancario*, pp. 10–11; Franco Holgúin, *Evolución*, p. 23.

16. Gustavo Otero Muñoz, *El Banco de la República, 1923–1948* (Bogotá, 1958), pp. 53–57; EWK, Box 93, "Notes on Colombian Currency," pp. 5–6.

17. Antonio José Uribe, *Crédito, moneda y bancos* (Bogotá, 1926), pp. vi–35; Rhys-Jenkins, *Report on Colombian Trade* (London, 1921), pp. 9–10; Otero, *El Banco de la República*, pp. 72–85; Andrade, *El Banco*, p. 130; Torres García, *Historia de la moneda*, pp. 332–37; EWK, Diary, May 16, 1923, p. 136.

18. Bell, *Commercial and Industrial Handbook*, pp. 51, 61–64, 312; Rodríguez Salazar, *Efectos de la gran depresión*, pp. 13–14; *El Colombiano*, July 28, 30, 31, 1923.

19. USDOS, from Bogotá, May 8, 1922, 821.00/501; Abel Cruz Santos, *Economía y hacienda pública*, 2 vols. (Bogotá, 1965), 2:167–73; Parks, *Colombia and the United States*, pp. 464–65.

20. Colombia, *Mensaje del Presidente de la República de Colombia al Congreso Nacional en las sesiones extraordinarias de 1923* (Bogotá, 1923), pp. 24, 39; Eugenio J. Gómez, *Ideas económicas y fiscales de Colombia* (Bogotá, 1949), pp. 242–43; Emily S. Rosenberg, "American Foreign Financial Advising in Latin America Before the Great Depression: Form and Structure," MS, 1985; USDOS, from Bogotá, September 30, 1922, 821.51A/2; October 16, 1922, 821.00/508; January 8, 1923, 821.00/514; from Washington, February 10, 1923, 821.51A/24.

21. *Administración Olaya Herrera* (Bogotá, 1935), p. 28; Edwin W. Kemmerer, *Address of Professor Edwin Walter Kemmerer of Princeton University, Chairman of the American Financial Commission to Colombia, at a Luncheon Given to the Commission by the Pan American Society of the United States, at the Bankers Club, New York City, November 24, 1923* (New York, 1923), p. 3. Other advisers considered by the State Department were William S. Culbertson and Sumner Welles. USDOS, from Washington, September 30, 1922, 821.51A/2; October 2, 1922, 821.51A/3; November 2, 1922, 821.51A/4; December 5, 1922, 821.51A/7; January 2, 1923, 821.51A/10; January 3, 1923, 821.51A/21.

22. USDOS, from Washington, February 13, 1923, 821.51A/19.

23. USDOS, from Washington, February 13, 1923, 821.51A/19; Kemmerer, *Address*, pp. 4–5.

24. Cruz Santos, *Economía*, 2:175–77; *El Espectador*, March 1, 10, 1923.

25. *El Diario Nacional*, March 23, 1923; Kemmerer, *Address*, p. 5; EWK, Diary, April 15, 1923, p. 105.

26. *El Espectador*, March–July, 1923; *El Diario Nacional*, March 21, 23, 1923; Kemmerer, *Address*, pp. 5–6; EWK, Diary, March 22–24, 1923, pp. 81–83.

27. EWK, Box 158, "Memorandum Concerning the Events Leading to the Establishment of the Bank of the Republic in Colombia," July 26, 1923; *El Espectador*, July 17, August 20, 1923; USDOS, from Bogotá, July 22, 1923, 832.516/49; July 23, 1923, 821.516/56; from Washington, July 30, 1923, 821.516/52.

28. Kemmerer, *Address*, pp. 13–14; EWK, Box 61, letter from Kemmerer to Lucas Caballero, February 10, 1926; *El Espectador*, August 19, 1923.

29. *El Tiempo*, July–August, 1923; *La Crónica*, March 13, 23, 18, 1923; *El Espectador*, March 10, 11, 16, July 2, 3, 10, August 14, 19, 29, September 13, 1923; *El Diario Nacional*, March 14, 21, July 17, 19, 24, 1923.

30. *El Espectador*, July 9, 11, August 14, 20, September 12, 13, 1923; USDOS, from Barranquilla, July 26, 1923, 821.516/53; Otero, *El Banco de la República*, p. 64.

31. Kemmerer, *Address*, pp. 6–9.

32. USDOS, from Bogotá, August 20, 1923, 821.516/60; *El Espectador*, August 14, 19, 20, 1923.

33. Kemmerer, *Address*, pp. 6–8; Uribe, *Crédito, moneda y bancos*, pp. vii–51.

34. Colombia, *Mensaje 1923*, esp. pp. 65–66, 114–16; Uribe, *Crédito, moneda y bancos*, p. 50.

35. *El Espectador*, July 2, August 14, 16, 1923; *La Crónica*, July 17, 1923.

36. *El Diario Nacional*, March 21, 1923.

37. *El Colombiano*, August 28, 1923; *El Diario Nacional*, September 8, 14, 1923; *El Tiempo*, September, 1923.

38. *El Diario Nacional*, September 13, 14, 1923; Jiménez, *El Banco de la República contra los intereses nacionales*, pp. 19–20, 63–65.

39. Esteban Jaramillo, *Memorandum for the Use of the Members of the International Economic Conference* (Geneva, 1926), p. 50.

40. Esteban Jaramillo, *Tratado de la ciencia de la hacienda pública*, 2 vols. (Bogotá, 1925), 1:xi–xiii.

41. *El Espectador*, August 6, 1923; *La Crónica*, July 31, 1923.

42. López C., *Estudio sobre la inflación*, pp. 101–2; USDOS, from Bogotá, May 8, 1922, 821.00/501; La Sociedad de Agricultores de Colombia, *Revista Nacional de Agricultura* (September–October 1923): 69–70; (November–December 1930): 255–56.

43. Jiménez, *El Banco de la República contra los intereses nacionales*, pp. vi–viii, 20–33, 45–65, 71–76, 116–34; *El Tiempo*, March 11, 1925, July 30, 1928; *El Espectador*, August 27–31, September 4, 14, 1923; *La Crónica*, July 31, 1923; *El Colombiano*, July–September, 1923.

44. Federación Nacional de Cafeteros, *Acuerdos, resoluciones y proposiciones de los congresos*

cafeteros (Bogotá, 1939), pp. 10, 39–89, 60–65, 78–106; Colombia, *Mensaje 1923*, pp. 58–64; Franco Holgúin, *Evolución*, p. 63; Otero, *El Banco de la República*, pp. 91, 123.

45. *El Colombiano*, August 3, September 4, 5, 1923; *El Tiempo*, June 7, 1923; USDOS, from Bogotá, April 10, 1922, 821.00/499; Luis Angel Arango, *Bancos de emisión* (Bogotá, 1924), pp. 106–7.

46. *BR* (August 1929): 238; Arango, *Bancos de emisión*, pp. 88–89.

47. *El Colombiano*, August 3, 1923; *El Tiempo*, June 7, 1923; *El Espectador*, July 2, 1923; Arango, *Bancos de emisión*, pp. 127–35.

48. Luis Ospina Vásquez, *Industria y protección en Colombia, 1810–1930* (Medellín, 1955); Escorcia, *Historia económica y social*, pp. 92–97.

49. EWK, Box 281, esp. "Conference . . . Huila"; Arango, *Bancos de emisión*, pp. 98–102; Otero, *El Banco de la República*, pp. 56–57, 63–64; Andrade, *El Banco*, pp. 46–59; *El Tiempo*, June 7, 1923; USDOS, from Bogotá, October 16, 1922, 821.00/508; July 2, 1923, 821.516/50; Colombia, *Leyes financieras presentadas al gobierno de Colombia por la misión de expertos americanos en los años de 1923 y 1930 y exposición de motivos de éstas* (Bogotá, 1931), pp. 34–92.

50. USDOS, from Barranquilla, July 26, 1923, 821.516/53; *El Espectador*, August 29, 1923; EWK, Box 281.

51. Otero, *El Banco de la República*, p. 113; Andrade, *El Banco*, pp. 35–36; Oscar Alviar, *Instrumentos de dirección monetaria en Colombia* (Bogotá, 1967), pp. 54–55.

52. Antonio José Restrepo, *Contra el cáncer de la úsura* (Bogotá, 1923), pp. 2–7; José del C. Gómez and A. Sandoval Mendoza, *Imperialismo y oligarquía en Colombia: el llamado Banco de la República—institución de la oligarquía nacional y extranjera* (Bogotá, n.d.); Escorcia, *Historia económica y social*, pp. 83–84; *El Espectador*, October 1, 1930.

53. Colombia, Banco de la República, *Primer informe anual presentado por el gerente a la junta directiva* (Bogotá, 1924), pp. 21–24.

54. EWK, Box 281; Gómez, *Ideas*, pp. 240–42; *El Colombiano*, August 9, 1923; *El Diario Nacional*, July 17, 19, 24, 1923; Bernardo Vélez, *Una campaña económica (1923–1929)* (Medellín, 1930), pp. 3–5.

55. Colombia, *Leyes financieras* (1931), pp. 41–72; EWK, Box 93, "Notes on Colombian Currency," p. 15; Box 281, "Conference . . . López"; "Memorandum . . . Narváez"; Andrade, *El Banco*, pp. 21–40; Arango, *Bancos de emisión*, pp. 91–117; Uribe, *Crédito, moneda y bancos*, pp. 28–30.

56. EWK, Box 158, "Memorandum Concerning the Events," p. 18.

57. *BR* (December 1927): 32; (August 1928): 283–84; *Primer informe*, esp. pp. 5–10.

58. Andrade, *El Banco*, pp. 22–23; Otero, *El Banco de la República*, pp. 95–97, 105, 111.

59. *BR* (August 1928): 277; (August 1929): 237; (January 1932): 5; Jiménez, *El Banco de la República contra los intereses nacionales*, pp. 74–94; Arango, *Bancos de emisión*, p. 103; *El Espectador*, October 1, 1930.

60. *BR* (August 1929): 238; *Primer informe*, pp. 20–21; Otero, *El Banco de la República*, pp. 73–74, 90–123; Arango, *Bancos de emisión*, p. 97; Jaramillo, *Memorandum*, pp. 34–36; USDOS, from Bogotá, September 16, 1929, 821.516/96.

61. *BR* (February 1929): 50; *Primer informe*, p. 14; Triffin, "La moneda y las instituciones bancarias en Colombia," *BR* (August 1944): 40.

62. Alviar, *Instrumentos de dirección*, pp. 10, 56–57, 63; Torres García, *Historia de la moneda*, pp. 344–47, 354–55; Bruce R. Dalgaard, "Monetary Reform, 1923–30: A Prelude to Colombia's Economic Development," *Journal of Economic History* 40 (1980): 98–104.

63. Hugo López C., *Estudio sobre la inflación en Colombia: el período de los años 20s* (Medellín,

1973), pp. 87, 150–54; Patiño, *La prosperidad*, pp. 73–99; Torres García, *Historia de la moneda*, pp. 352–62; Palacios, *Coffee in Colombia*, p. 208.

64. Triffin, "La moneda y las instituciones," pp. 14–15; Villegas, *Vida económica*, pp. 70–71, 136–37; Andrade, *El Banco*, pp. 97–103.

65. López C., *Estudio sobre la inflación*, pp. 78–182; Franco Holgúin, *Evolución*, pp. 61–63; *El Espectador*, August 26, October 28, November 5, 1930; *BR* (August 1930): 230; (May 1931): 160–61; (August 1931): 278; (February 1932): 39–40; EWK, Box 159, letter from Comité de Cafeteros de Fusagasugá; Esteban Jaramillo, *La carestía de la vida* (Bogotá, 1927), pp. 8–9.

66. Colombia, *Leyes financieras* (1931), pp. 187–267; Alejandro López, *Problemas colombianos* (Paris, 1927), pp. 85–93.

67. *La República* (Bogotá), June 19, 1923; *El Espectador*, June 22, August 1, 1923; *El Tiempo*, June 16, 1923; *La Crónica*, July 19, 1923; USDOS, from Bogotá, June 25, 1923, 821.51/242.

68. Colombia, Superintendencia Bancaria, *Informe presentado por el superintendente bancario al señor Ministro de Hacienda y Crédito Publico* (Bogotá, 1924), p. 18; idem, *Informe presentado por el superintendente bancario al señor Ministro de Hacienda y Crédito Publico* (Bogotá, 1925), pp. 23–45; idem, *Balances y consolidaciones* (Bogotá, 1925); *BR* (December 1930): 371; Jorge Ernesto Mesa Ospina, *El capital de los bancos extranjeros en Colombia* (Bogotá, 1969), pp. 18–19.

69. Colombia, *Leyes financieras* (1931), p. 259; Villegas, *Vida económica*, pp. 66, 80–81; Gómez, *Ideas*, p. 244; *BR* (January 1930): 15; Colombia, Superintendencia Bancaria, *Informe presentado por el superintendente bancario al señor Ministro de Hacienda y Crédito Publico* (Bogotá, 1934), pp. 16–36; Ligia Londoño Ocampo, *La industria bancaria en Colombia* (Bogotá, 1958), pp. 150–54.

70. Colombia, Ministerio de Hacienda y Crédito Publico, *Memoria de Hacienda* (Bogotá, 1931), no. 10; Andrade, *El Banco*, pp. 127–219; Otero, *El Banco de la República*, p. 87; Torres García, *Historia de la moneda*, p. 355; Franco Holgúin, *Evolución*, p. 68; Cruz Santos, *Economía*, 2:254; López C., *Estudio sobre la inflación*, p. 156.

71. *El Diario Nacional*, July 13, 1923; *El Colombiano*, July 5, 1923; *El Espectador*, August 1, 1923; Uribe, *Crédito, moneda y bancos*, pp. 8–10, 52–55.

72. USDOS, from Bogotá, November 15, 1923, 821.51A/30; May 12, 1924, 821.51A/34.

73. Colombia, *Leyes financieras* (1931), pp. 316–52; *El Espectador*, July 10, 1923; *El Colombiano*, July 19, 1923; *El Diario Nacional*, September 13, 14, 1923; Uribe, *Crédito, moneda y bancos*, pp. 20–23, 55–59; Cruz Santos, *Economía*, 2:195.

74. Manuel José González C., *La intervención del estado en Colombia* (Bogotá, 1945), pp. 97–98.

75. Colombia, *Leyes financieras* (1931), pp. 93–142.

76. Abel Cruz Santos, *El presupuesto colombiano* (Bogotá, 1937), pp. vi–viii, 22–25, 162–63; Leopoldo Lascarro, *La administración financiera y el control fiscal en Colombia* (Bogotá, 1941), pp. 207, 218, 240.

77. Cruz Santos, *El presupuesto*, pp. 23–25.

78. Jaramillo, *Memorandum*, p. 42; *El Espectador*, July 14, 1923; Cruz Santos, *El presupuesto*, pp. vi, 24–25, 58–59.

79. Lascarro, *La administración financiera*, pp. 40, 66–67, 218–43.

80. Cruz Santos, *Economía*, 2:204–6, 322; Colombia, Contraloría General de la República, *Informe financiero del Contralor General de la República de Colombia correspondiente al año fiscal de 1923* (Bogotá, 1924), pp. 7–8; USDOS, from Bogotá September 21, 1929, 821.51/545; November 20, 1929, 821.51/558; *La Crónica*, August 17, 1923; *El Colombiano*, September 2, 1930; Luis M. Arcila P., *Finanzas oficiales* (Manizales, 1926), pp. 12–13; Colombia, Minis-

terio de Hacienda y Crédito Publico, *Memoria y exposición ministerial al proyecto de ley de presupuesto de rentas y gastos ordinarios para el año de 1931* (Bogotá, 1930), pp. 56–68.

81. Colombia, *Leyes financieras* (1931), pp. 143–86; Lascarro, *La administración financiera*, pp. 14–15, 46–47, 214–17, 232–33; José Vicente Casas Galvis, *La contraloría en Colombia* (Bogotá, 1968), pp. 43–50; Augusto Ramírez Moreno, *Episodios* (Bogotá, 1930), p. 26.

82. Colombia, Contraloría, *Informe, 1923*; idem, *Informe, 1924*; USDOS, from Bogotá, October 19, 1923, 821.51A/28; November 12, 1923, 821.51/249; January 12, 1924, 821.51/254; August 6, 1924, 821.51/265; Robert N. Seidel, "American Reformers Abroad: The Kemmerer Missions in South America, 1923–1931," *Journal of Economic History* 32, no. 2 (June 1972): 520–45.

83. Casas, *La contraloría en Colombia*, pp. 53–55; Lascarro, *La administración financiera*, pp. 211–34; Colombia, Contraloría General de la República, *Codificación de la reglamentación dictada por la contraloría general de la República, 1924–54* (Bogotá, 1955), pp. 6–12; idem, *Edwin Walter Kemmerer y su obra en Colombia* (Bogotá, 1945), pp. 12–16.

84. EWK, Box 281, esp. "Conference . . . Huila."

85. *Anuario Colombia, 1927* (n.p., n.d), pp. 338–39.

86. USDOC, File no. 434, "Colombia," report from J. A. Montalvo, 1929; Colombia, Ministro de Hacienda, *Memoria* (1931), p. 105.

87. Colombia, *Leyes financieras* (1931), pp. 1–33; E. W. Kemmerer, Mission of Financial Advisors, *Proyecto de ley por la cual se establece el impuesto de pasajes* (Bogotá, 1923); *Informe sobre income tax* (Bogotá, 1923); *Recommendations on the Immediate Repeal of the Existing Provision of Law which Imposes an Ad Valorem Tax of 1% on the Exportation of Coined Gold* (Bogotá, 1923); EWK, esp. Box 125, "Memorandum relativo al impuesto sobre la renta"; Box 19, letter from Kemmerer to K. W. Williamson, July 13, 1930; Colombia, *Mensaje, 1923*, pp. 43–44; Cruz Santos, *Economía*, 2:163–64; *El Diario Nacional*, July 14, September 8, 1923; *El Espectador*, July 12, 15, 1923; *El Colombiano*, July 16, 18, 30, 1923.

88. Jaramillo, *Memorandum*, pp. 26–28; Cruz Santos, *Economía*, 2:202–13, 247–49; *El Espectador*, August 27, 28, 1923; E. W. Kemmerer, Mission of Financial Advisers, *Report on the Customs* (Bogotá, 1923).

89. Cruz Santos, *Economía*, 2:202–13; Vélez, *Una campaña económica*, pp. 16–17; Jaramillo, *La carestía*, pp. 13–14; López C., *Estudio sobre la inflación*, pp. 78–144; Rodríguez Salazar, *Efectos de la gran depresión*, pp. 43–48; *El Colombiano*, September 11, 15, 16, 29, 1930; Catherine LeGrand, *Frontier Expansion and Peasant Protest in Colombia, 1850–1936* (Albuquerque, 1986), pp. 89–97.

90. Triffin, "La moneda y las instituciones," p. 49; Emily S. Rosenberg, *Spreading the American Dream: American Economic and Cultural Expansion, 1890–1945* (New York, 1982), pp. 130–31; Ramón Gómez and Antonio Samper Uribe, *Colombia. Su deuda externa en 1925* (Bogotá, 1924), esp. pp. ix–xi, 42–47; Colombia, Ministerio de Hacienda y Crédito Publico, *Empréstitos externos nacionales* (Bogotá, 1932); *BR* (January 1928): 84–85; Central Union Trust Company of New York, *Financial and Economic Conditions in the Republic of Colombia* (New York, 1926), p. 6; *Anuario Colombia*, pp. 367–78; USDOS, from Bogotá, March 25, 1931, 821.51/905.

91. Colombia, *Leyes financieras* (1931), pp. 121–22; E. W. Kemmerer, Mission of Financial Advisers, *Sugestiones concernientes al programa de empréstitos para Colombia* (Bogotá, 1923); E. W. Kemmerer, Commission of Financial Advisers, *Report on Public Credit* (Bogotá, 1930); Esteban Jaramillo, *Informe sobre unificación de la deuda exterior* (Bogotá, 1924), pp. 7–9, 15–35; EWK, Box 281; USDOS, from Bogotá, June 17, 1928, 821.51/410; September 5, 1928, 821.51/417; Patiño, *La prosperidad*, pp. 33–35.

92. McGreevey, *Economic History of Colombia*, pp. 204–5; *Administración Olaya*, pp. 27–28; *BR* (March 1928): 123–24; (May 1928): 205; *Anuario Colombia*, pp. 420–21; Rippy, *Capitalists*, pp. 152–55.

93. Triffin, "La moneda y las instituciones," p. 49; Torres García, *Historia de la moneda*, p. 353; Winkler, *Investments of U.S. Capital*, pp. 129–31; Centro de Estudios, "Anteo Quimbaya," p. 58; Colombia, Ministerio de Hacienda, *Empréstitos*; Kemmerer, Commission, *Report on Public Credit*.

94. Randall, *Diplomacy of Modernization*, p. 56; Escorcia, *Historia económica y social*, p. 84; Colombia, Contraloría, *Informe, 1929*, p. 21; USDOS, from Washington, September 14, 1928, 821.51/420.

95. Jaramillo, *Memorandum*, p. 47.

96. *BR* (November 1928): 377; USDOC, File no. 434, "Colombia," report from J. A. Montalvo, 1929; Villegas, *Vida económica*, pp. 7–8, 16–19.

97. USDOS, from Bogotá, June 12, 1928, 821,51/410; July 20, 1928, 821.51/415; September 5, 1928, 821.51/417; Cruz Santos, *Economía*, 2:202–4.

98. Central Union Trust Co., *Financial and Economic Conditions*, p. 9; Kemmerer, *Address*, p. 14; Kemmerer, Commission, *Sugestiones*; Parks, *Colombia and the United States*, pp. 472–73; Francisco de Paula Pérez, *Cuestiones fiscales* (Bogotá, 1929), p. 20; Richard E. Hartwig, *Roads to Reason: Transportation, Administration, and Rationality in Colombia* (Pittsburgh, 1983).

99. Bell, *Commercial and Industrial Handbook*, pp. 308–9.

100. López C., *Estudio sobre la inflación*, pp. 50–54; Colombia, Contraloría, *Informe, 1931*, p. 88; USDOS, from Bogotá, April 28, 1930, 821.51/648.

101. *El Colombiano*, September 1, 1923.

102. Cruz Santos, *Economía*, 2:174–75; Diego Monsalve, *Colombia cafetera* (Barcelona, 1927), p. 828; José Raimundo Sojo, *El Comercio en la historia de Colombia* (Bogotá, 1970), pp. 170–76.

103. Central Union Trust Co., *Financial and Economic Conditions*, p. 9; Villegas, *Vida económica*, p. 19.

104. Monsalve, *Colombia cafetera*, pp. 828–936; López, *Problemas colombianos*, pp. 136–42; *BR* (December 1928): 404; López C., *Estudio sobre la inflación*, pp. 58–60, 95–96.

105. *El Diario Nacional*, August 16, 1930; *El Espectador*, October 4, 1930; *El Tiempo*, August 14, 1930; *El Gráfico*, August 23, 1930, pp. 839–40; Paula Pérez, *Cuestiones fiscales*, pp. 8–23; Gómez, *Ideas*, p. 330; *Administración Olaya*, pp. 15–30.

106. U.S. Department of State, Francis White Papers (hereinafter cited as FW), Box 16, letter from Garrard Winston to White, January 18, 1932; Palacios, *Coffee in Colombia*, pp. 201–9; Triffin, "La moneda y las instituciones," p. 15; José Antonio Ocampo, "The Colombian Economy in the 1930s," in Rosemary Thorp, ed., *Latin America in the 1930s: The Role of the Periphery in the World Crisis* (London, 1984), pp. 117–43; José Antonio Ocampo and Santiago Montenegro, "La crisis mundial de los años treinta en Colombia," *Desarrollo y Sociedad* 7 (January 1982): 37–96; Rosemary Thorp and Carlos Londoño, "The Effect of the Great Depression on the Economies of Peru and Colombia," in Thorp, *Latin America in the 1930s*, pp. 81–116.

107. Villegas, *Vida económica*, pp. 52–53, 75–76; Colombia, Ministerior de Industrias, *Boletín de Comercio e Industria* (April–May 1930): 4–5; (November 1930): 307; Colombia, Cámara de Representantes, *Proyecto de ley sobre poder liberatorio de la moneda* (Bogotá, 1932), pp. 14–15, 26–32.

108. Parks, *Colombia and the United States*, pp. 478–79.

109. Federación Nacional de Cafeteros, *Revista Cafetera de Colombia* (January 1931): 771.

110. Federación Nacional de Cafeteros, *Revista* (May–June 1932): 1403–4; *Acuerdos*, pp. 109–70.
111. La Sociedad de Agricultores de Colombia, *Revista* (July–August 1930): 151–71; *El Tiempo*, September 24, 1930; *Administración Olaya*, pp. 168–83, 398; Cruz Santos, *Economía*, 2:247–52.
112. Colombia, Ministerio de Industrias, *Revista de Industrias* (May 1930): 351–52; *Administración Olaya*, pp. 35, 411–13; *El Tiempo*, September 11, 1930; *El Espectador*, August 26, 1930.
113. Torres García, *Historia de la moneda*, pp. 398–403; Franco Holgúin, *Evolución*, pp. 55–59, 75–76; Cruz Santos, *Economía*, 2:253–59. *Administración Olaya*, pp. 68–70, 411–12.
114. *BR* (August 1930): 232; (August 1931): 277; Franco Holgúin, *Evolución*, pp. 75–76; *El Tiempo*, September 18, 1930.
115. *BR* (February 1930): 35–36; (September 1930): 260–61; (April 1931): 120–21; (August 1931): 271; USDOS, from Washington, November 25, 1929, 821.516/100.
116. Colombia, Contraloría, *Informe, 1931*, p. 89; USDOS, from Bogotá, November 20, 1929, 821.51/558; January 27, 1930, 821.51/572; March 6, 1930, 821.51/593; May 6, 1930, 821.51/660.
117. USDOS, from Bogotá, March 31, 1930, 821.51/603; August 28, 1930, 821.51/704; *El Tiempo*, January 15, September 2, 12, 1930; *El Espectador*, August 16, October 4, 1930.
118. *Administración Olaya*, pp. 61–76, 403–7; Torres García, *Historia de la moneda*, pp. 390–96.
119. Enrique Olaya Herrera, *Visita de Enrique Olaya Herrera a los Estados Unidos* (n.p., 1930), esp. pp. 7–21, 36; *Administración Olaya*, p. 35; Gabriel Castro, *La salvación de Colombia* (Medellín, 1930), pp. 187, 281–82.
120. FW, Box 3, memorandum to Mr. Carr, October 1, 1931; Box 9, "List of Cases When the Colombian Authorities Have Demonstrated a Favorable Attitude toward American Interests," pt. 2, April 9, 1933, p. 10; Box 10, "List of Cases," pt. 1, October 19, 1931, pp. 10–14.
121. FW, Box 9, letter from Jefferson Caffery to secretary of state, February 25, 1933; Box 3, memorandum to Mr. Carr; Box 9, "List of Cases," p. 1.
122. FW, Box 3, memorandum to Mr. Carr; Box 9, "List of Cases," pp. 31–36; Box 10, "List of Cases," pp. 18–20; Box 1, conversation with Mr. Curtis Calder, December 12, 1931; USDOS, from Bogotá, January 14, 1932, 821.51A/77; from Bogotá, March 17, 1931, 821.51/890.
123. USDOS, from Bogotá, November 6, 1931, 821.51/1220; February 3, 1932, 821.51A/80; Laureano Gómez, *Comentarios a un régimen*, 2d ed. (Bogotá, 1935), pp. 209–65; José de la Vega, *El buen vecino* (Bogotá, 1944), pp. 8–24, 192–93; José de la Vega, *El liberalismo en el gobierno, 1930–46*, 3 vols. (Bogotá, 1946), 1:36.
124. FW, Box 9, letter from Jefferson Caffery, October 10, 1929; *El Espectador*, October 11, 1930; Colombia, *Leyes financieras* (1931), pp. 509–39; Gómez, *Comentarios*, pp. 209–26; Vega, *El buen vecino*, pp. 192–93; idem, *Colombia* (Medellín), October 18, 1930. For the entire oil issue, see Randall, *Diplomacy of Modernization*, pp. 108–16.
125. *Administración Olaya*, pp. 32–33, 49–51, 404–7; *BR* (March 1931): 79–80; Parks, *Colombia and the United States*, pp. 474–77; FW, Box 1, dictation for hearings before Senate Finance Committee, January 11, 1932; Box 3, memorandum to Mr. Carr; Box 9, letter to Jefferson Caffery, March 5, 1931; Box 10, "List of Cases," pp. 1–8; Box 31, letter from Olaya, January 16, 1932; USDOS, from Bogotá, May 13, 1931, 821.51/952; from Washington, March 25, 1931, 821.51/899 & 1/2; February 21, 1933, 821.51/1579 & 1/2.
126. USDOS, from Bogotá, August 30, 1930, 821.51/712; March 17, 1931, 821.51/872; from Washington, February 21, 1933, 821.51/1579 and 1/2.
127. USDOS, from Washington, October 10, 1930, 821.51/752; from Bogotá, November 20, 1930, 821.51/799; EWK, Diary, June 24, 1930, p. 175.

128. USDOS, from Bogotá, May 13, 1931, 821.51/952; from Washington, March 9, 1931, 821.51/871 and 1/2; February 21, 1933, 821.51/1579 and 1/2.
129. USDOS, from Washington, October 10, 1930, 821.51/752; from Bogotá, January 6, 1930, 821.51/568; January 31, 1930, 821.51/576; September 19, 1930, 821.51/720; November 14, 1930, 821.51/789; March 12, 1931, 821.51/871; FW, Box 9, letter from White to Jefferson Caffery, October 27, 1930.
130. USDOS, from Bogotá, March 25, 1931, 821.51/908; October 4, 1931, 821.51/1101; FW, Box 1, telephone conversation with Mr. Garrard Winston, March 13, 1931; Box 31, letter from Olaya, January 16, 1932.
131. USDOS, from Bogotá, March 18, 1931, 821.51/891; October 10, 1930, 821.51/754; March 12, 1931, 821.51/871; October 4, 1931, 821.51/1101.
132. USDOS, from Bogotá, July 5, 1930, 821.51/682; November 20, 1930, 821.51/799; January 3, 1931, 821.51/832; March 17, 1931, 821.51/872; FW, Box 4, letter from Garrard Winston, March 6, 1931; EWK, Diary, September 30, 1930, p. 273; May 21, 1931, p. 141.
133. USDOS, from Bogotá, September 20, 1930, 821.51/736; September 26, 1930, 821.51/740; October 4, 1931, 821.51/1101; FW, Box 1, dictation for hearings.
134. Colombia, Ministerio de Hacienda, Memoria, 1931, pp. 37–41.
135. USDOS, from Bogotá, August 14, 1930, 821.51/696; October 23, 1930, 821.51/782; EWK, Diary, September 19, 1930, p. 262; October 16, 1930, p. 289.
136. Vélez, Una campaña económica; El Tiempo, September 29, 1930.
137. Castro, La salvación de Colombia, pp. 51–55, 187, 281–82; Administración Olaya, pp. 33–35; El Tiempo, September 16, 1930.
138. Cruz Santos, Economía, 2:166–67, 261–62; EWK, Diary, May 22, 1930, p. 142.
139. El Tiempo, September 1, 2, 16, 1930; USDOS, from Bogotá, September 5, 1930, 821.51A/51; EWK, Diary, August 31, 1930, p. 243.
140. Colombia, Leyes financieras (1931), Cámara de Fomento Industrial, Industria (La Paz) 1, no. 2 (August 1931): 62.
141. Ibid., pp. 454–97. BR (October 1930): 297.
142. USDOS, from Bogotá, September 29, 1930, 821.516/105; October 13, 1930, 821.51A Kemmerer Mission/9; 821.51/757; October 22, 1930, 821.51A Kemmerer Mission/13; Mundo al Día, September 12, October 8, 1930.
143. El Espectador, August 22, 29, 1930; El Tiempo, September 1, 21, October 5, 6, 8, 10, 18, 1930; USDOS, from Bogotá, September 12, 1931, 821.516/152; BR (April 1931): 124–27.
144. USDOS, from Bogotá, December 27, 1930, 821.516/112; April 6, 1931, 821.51/919; BR (October 1930): 293; (November 1930): 328–29.
145. Colombia, Leyes financieras (1931), pp. 285–315, 372–79; USDOS, from Bogotá, April 6, 1931, 821.51/919; El Espectador, October 2, 1930; EWK, Diary, September 3, 1930, p. 246.
146. Colombia, Contraloría, Informe, 1930, pp. xvii–xxii; Colombia, Leyes financieras (1931), pp. 359–71, 380–412; Colombia, Ministerio de Hacienda, Memoria, 1931, pp. 34–48; Cruz Santos, El presupuesto, pp. 25–29ff., 164–87; Richard C. Backus and Phanor J. Eder, A Guide to the Law and Legal Literature of Colombia (Washington, D.C., 1943), p. 67.
147. Edwin Walter Kemmerer, Commission of Financial Advisors, Proyecto de ley reformatoria de las leyes orgánicas de la contabilidad oficial de la nación y del departamento de contraloría (Bogotá, 1930); Cruz Santos, El presupuesto, pp. 200–207; Colombia, Contraloría, Edwin Walter Kemmerer y su obra en Colombia, pp. 4–5; idem, Informe, 1930, p. xxvii; idem, Informe, 1931, p. xxxv; Casas, La contraloría en Colombia, pp. 54–55.
148. USDOS, from Bogotá, June 2, 1932, 821.51A/87; Gómez, Comentarios, p. 213; Lascarro, La administración financiera, pp. 222–27.

149. Colombia, Contraloría, *Informe, 1931*, p. xxiv; Colombia, *Leyes financieras* (1931), pp. 413–53; Colombia, Ministerio de Hacienda, *Memoria, 1931*, pp. 49–53; Cruz Santos, *El presupuesto*, p. 111.
150. USDOS, from Bogotá, September 5, 1930, 821.51A/49.
151. EWK, Box 125, "Confidential Memorandum re Proposal to Place Export Tax on Bananas"; Diary, September 25, 1930, p. 268; USDOS, from Bogotá, September 10–24, 1930, 821.51A/52–55; May 9, 1931, 821.51/958; Randall, *Diplomacy of Modernization*, pp. 64–65.
152. Colombia, *Leyes financieras* (1931), pp. 353–58; USDOS, from Bogotá, December 22, 1930, 821.51A Kemmerer Mission/25; March 17, 1931, 821.51/890; Charles David Kepner and Jay Henry Soothill, *The Banana Empire. A Case Study in Economic Imperialism* (New York, 1935), pp. 291–93.
153. *BR* (October 1930): 295–96; *El Espectador*, August 19, 23, 1930; Kemmerer, Commission, *Proyecto de ley orgánica de aduanas* (Bogotá, 1930); Colombia, Ministerio de Hacienda, *Memoria, 1931*, pp. 44–46; idem, *Memoria, 1932*, pp. 110–15; Colombia, Contraloría, *Edwin Walter Kemmerer y su obra en Colombia*, pp. 7–8; USDOS, from Bogotá, March 10, 1932, 821.51A/84; May 5, 1932, 821.51A/85.
154. Colombia, Ministerio de Hacienda, *Memoria, 1931*, pp. 42–44; idem, *Régimen tributario y crédito público* (Bogotá, 1931); Cruz Santos, *Economía*, 2:262–65; USDOS, from Bogotá, July 24, 1931, 821.51A Kemmerer Mission/30; September 1, 1931, 821.51A Kemmerer Mission/31; Kemmerer, Commission, *Proyecto de ley por la cual se dispone la unificación de todos los gravamenes a que está sujeta la importación de mercancía* (Bogotá, 1930); idem, *Proyecto de ley por la cual se autoriza a las municipalidades para establecer el impuesto de valorización* (Bogotá, 1930); idem, *Proyecto de ley por la cual se modifican la ley 20 de 1923 y la 30 de 1929 relativas a la recaudación de timbres y derechos sobre documentos que se emplean en el despacho y en la importación de mercancías* (Bogotá, 1930); idem, *A Project of Law Creating a Public Debt Commission* (Bogotá, 1930); idem, *Project of Law Establishing Certain Provisions with Respect to the Indebtedness of the Departments and Municipalities of the Republic* (Bogotá, 1930); idem, *A Project of Law Authorizing the Issue of Treasury Certificates* (Bogotá, 1930); idem, *Project of Law Establishing upon Real Property a Compulsory Municipal and Departmental Tax and an Optional National Tax* (Bogotá, 1930); idem, *Report on the Tax on Successions and Donations* (Bogotá, 1930); idem, *A Project of Law Repealing All Laws Authorizing National Subsidies for Public Works and Improvements* (Bogotá, 1930); idem, *Project of Law Abolishing Participation and Establishing Other Provisions Relating to Indemnities* (Bogotá, 1930).
155. *El Espectador*, September 19, 1930, November 5, 1930, October 3, 28, 1931, February 25, 1932; Congreso Nacional de Cafeteros, *Informe* (Manizales, 1932), p. 11; *BR* (January 1931): 5; (October 1931): 343–48; (March 1932): 75–76; FW, Box 1, conversation with Mr. Neville Ford, December 11, 1931; Box 7, letter from White to Garrard Winston, December 21, 1931.
156. Torres García, *Historia de la moneda*, pp. 396–98.
157. Alviar, *Instrumentos de dirección*, pp. 63–67; Raimundo, *El Comercio en la historia de Colombia*, pp. 188–201; Urrutia and Arrubla, *Estadísticas históricas*, pp. 158–59; USDOS, from Bogotá, September 25, 1931, 821.51/1091; Miguel Urrutia, "Cincuenta años de desarrollo económico," MS, 1978, p. 1.
158. USDOS, from Bogotá, October 1, 1931, 821.51/1143; October 7, 1931, 821.51/1159; January 19, 1932, 821.51/1288; from Washington, February 19, 1932, 821.51/1328A; FW, Box 1, conversation with Mr. L. A. Crosby, April 5, 1933; Box 9, letter from Jefferson Caffery, March 29, 1933; *El Espectador*, September 11, October 4, 13, 1930; *El Nuevo Tiempo* (Bogotá), October 9, 1931; Colombia, Contraloría, *Informe, 1932*, pp. ix–x; Ocampo, "The Colombian Economy in the 1930s."

159. Franco Holgúin, *Evolución*, pp. 87–92; Triffin, "La moneda y las instituciones," pp. 19–28; Belisario Plata, *La crísis económica colombiana y sus probables remedios* (Bogotá, 1933), pp. 24–41.

160. Londoño, *La industria bancaria en Colombia*, pp. 53–63, 84–116; Raimundo, *El Comercio en la historia de Colombia*, pp. 188–215; Colombia, Contraloría, *Edwin Walter Kemmerer y su obra en Colombia*, esp. pp. 9–13; Triffin, "La moneda y las instituciones," pp. 19–22; Colombia, Superintendencia Bancaria, *Informe, 1934*, pp. 14–33, 149.

161. Cruz Santos, *Economía*, 2:19–20, 176–79, 197; Escorcia, *Historia económica y social*, pp. 195–98; Alviar, *Instrumentos de dirección*, pp. 27–28.

3. Eclipse of the Chilean *Papeleros*, 1925–1932

1. P. T. Ellsworth, *Chile, an Economy in Transition* (New York, 1945), pp. vii–16.

2. Charles A. Thomson, "Chile Struggles for National Recovery," *Foreign Policy Reports* 9, no. 25 (February 14, 1934): 282–92.

3. Great Britain, Department of Overseas Trade (hereinafter cited as GBDOT), *Report on the Industrial and Economic Conditions in Chile* (London, 1925), p. 9; GBDOT, *Report* (1926), pp. 8–9, 22; Adolfo Ruffat, *La política monetaria y el sector externo en Chile entre las dos guerras mundiales* (Santiago, 1969), pp. 50–51; Rolf Luders, "Chile 1926–1929: Estabilidad y las políticas del banco central en relación al padrón oro," *Cuadernos de Economía* 8, no. 25 (December 1971): 64–78.

4. Clarence F. Jones, *Commerce of South America* (Boston, 1928), pp. 186–87.

5. William Sherman, *The Diplomatic and Commercial Relations of the United States and Chile, 1820–1914* (Boston, 1926), p. 5.

6. Roberto Edwardson-Meeks Valdivieso, *Los impuestos internos en Chile* (Santiago, 1927), p. xxix.

7. GBDOT, *Report* (1926), pp. 16–17.

8. Edwardson-Meeks, *Los impuestos*, pp. xlii–xliii; Abraham R. Waissbluth, *La minería en la economía chilena* (Santiago, 1941), p. 15; Thomson, "Chile Struggles for National Recovery," pp. 282–92; Max Winkler, *Investments of U.S. Capital in Latin America* (Boston, 1929), pp. 94–99; *La Información* 10, no. 94 (June–July 1925): 179–80; Chile-American Association, *Reciprocal Resources of Chile and the United States* (New York, 1921); idem, *Mutual Trade and Resources of Chile and the United States* (New York, 1926), p. 57; idem, *Chile in 1930* (New York, 1930); Santiago Marín Vicuña, *La riqueza minera de Chile y su régimen tributario* (Santiago, 1924), pp. 18–31; Ricardo Latcham, *Chuquicamata, estado yankee* (Santiago, 1926), pp. 41–69; Santiago Macchiavello Varas, *El problema de la industria de cobre en Chile y sus proyecciones económicas y sociales* (Santiago, 1923); Markos Mamalakis, *The Growth and Structure of the Chilean Economy* (New Haven, 1976), pp. 41–43. For further information on foreign capital in mining, see F. Javier Cotapos Aldunate, *El aporte del capital extranjero en la industria minera de Chile* (n.p., n.d.).

9. GBDOT, *Report* (1930), pp. 33–35.

10. Cotapos, *El aporte del capital extranjero*, p. 75; J. Fred Rippy, *British Investments in Latin America, 1822–1949* (Minneapolis, 1959), pp. 133–38; idem, "A Century of British Investments in Chile," *Pacific Historical Review*, no. 21 (1952): 341; Sylvio Rostagno Macchi, *El capital extranjero en el desarrollo económico de América Latina, especialmente Argentina y Chile* (Santiago, 1947), pp. 21, 73.

11. Winkler, *Investments of U.S. Capital*, pp. 94–104; Thomson, "Chile Struggles for National

Recovery"; Rostagno, *El capital extranjero*, pp. 22–23, 74; Frederick M. Halsey and G. B. Sherwell, *Investments in Latin America. III. Chile* (Washington, D.C., 1926), pp. 5–8; Jones, *Commerce of South America*, pp. 188–90; Robert N. Seidel, "Progressive Pan Americanism: Development and United States Policy toward South America, 1906–1931" (Ph.D. diss., Cornell University, 1973), p. 317; Anibal Pinto, ed., *Antecedentes sobre el desarrollo de la economía chilena, 1925–1952* (Santiago, 1954), p. 78.

12.   Chile-American Assoc., *Mutual Trade and Resources*, pp. 6, 68.

13.   The total foreign debt held in U.S. hands was probably larger than official figures because North Americans acquired some sterling bonds. Halsey and Sherwell, *Investments in Latin America*, pp. 8–15; United Nations, Department of Economic Affairs, *Public Debt, 1914–1946* (Lake Success, 1948), pp. 38–41.

14.   Merle Curti and Kendall Birr, *Prelude to Point Four: American Technical Missions Overseas 1838–1938* (Madison, 1954), pp. 140–43, 156; Henry Clay Evans, Jr., *Chile and Its Relations with the United States* (Durham, 1927), p. 181.

15.   Marco A. Ballesteros and Tom E. Davis, "The Growth of Output and Employment in Basic Sectors of the Chilean Economy, 1908–1957," *Economic Development and Cultural Change*, no. 11 (1963): 152–76.

16.   The only significant foreign agricultural participation occurred with British and Argentine ranching enterprises in the far south, which exported wool and meat. Frank Whitson Fetter, *Monetary Inflation in Chile* (Princeton, 1931).

17.   Halsey and Sherwell, *Investments in Latin America*, pp. 22–23.

18.   Ballesteros and Davis, "The Growth of Output and Employment," p. 176.

19.   GBDOT, *Report* (1928), p. 51; Edwardson-Meeks, *Los impuestos*, pp. xxxvi–xxxviii.

20.   Henry W. Kirsch, *Industrial Development in a Traditional Society* (Gainesville, 1977), esp. pp. 82–91; Halsey and Sherwell, *Investments in Latin America*, pp. 3, 82–83.

21.   Pedro Luis González, *Chile. An Economic Survey* (Santiago, 1922), pp. 13–24.

22.   Halsey and Sherwell, *Investments in Latin America*, pp. 16–17; U.S. Department of State (hereinafter cited as USDOS), from Valparaíso, July 19, 1923, 825.516/32.

23.   Jorge Seco de la Cerda, *Proyecto económico y financiero* (Santiago, n.d.), pp. 3–8.

24.   Guillermo Subercaseaux, *Monetary and Banking Policy of Chile* (Oxford, 1922), pp. 128–35; Marcello Carmagnani, "Banques etrangeres et banques nationales au Chile, 1900–1920," *Caravelle*, no. 20 (1973): 31–52.

25.   Arturo Alessandri, *Mensaje leído por s.e. el presidente de la república en la apertura de las sesiones ordinarias del congreso nacional* (Santiago, 1921), p. 76.

26.   Fetter, *Monetary Inflation*; Enrique L. Marshall, "Régimen monetario actual de Chile y sus antecedentes históricos," *Revista Economía* 6, no. 14 (1945): 86–115. For a critical history of Chilean money and banking, see Agustín Ross, *Chile. 1851–1910* (Valparaíso, 1910). The four decades before and after Kemmerer are surveyed in P. S. Conoboy, "Money and Politics in Chile, 1878–1925" (Ph.D. diss., University of Southampton, 1977); and Rolf Luders, "A Monetary History of Chile: 1925–1968" (Ph.D. diss., University of Chicago, 1968).

27.   United Nations, *Public Debt*, pp. 38–39; Ballesteros and Davis, "The Growth of Output and Employment," p. 173. Another estimate of the annual rate of price inflation in Santiago shows a similar pattern, with a high of 22.7 percent in 1919, followed by a sharp decline to under 8 percent in the early 1920s, to less than 1 percent in the mid and late 1920s, and rising again to over 10 percent in 1931 (Mamalakis, *Historical Statistics of Chile*, 4:224).

28.   Albert O. Hirschman, *Journeys toward Progress* (Garden City, 1965), p. 160.

29.   The thesis of landowner villainy, later enshrined by Fetter, probably originated with Ross, *Chile. Semana de la moneda* (n.p., n.d.), pp. 69–80ff.

30. Ross, *Semana*, p. 402; Comité Pro-Estabilización de la Moneda, *Proyecto del memorial que se presentará al supremo gobierno para conseguir la estabilización de la moneda* (Valparaíso, 1925), p. 4; Edwin W. Kemmerer Papers, Princeton University Library (hereinafter cited as EWK), Box 190, interview with Alfred Houston of Braden Copper Company; César Araneda Encina, *Veinte años de historia monetaria de Chile. 1925–1945. Chile ante los convenios de Bretton Woods* (Santiago, 1945), p. 21; Thomas C. Wright, *Landowners and Reform in Chile: The Sociedad Nacional de Agricultura, 1919–40* (Urbana, 1981).

31. Edwin Walter Kemmerer, "Chile Returns to the Gold Standard," *Journal of Political Economy* 34 (June 1926): 265–73.

32. Fetter, *Monetary Inflation*.

33. Interview with Frank Whitson Fetter, July 29, 1976. For an attack on the Fetter thesis, see Mamalakis, *Growth and Structure*, pp. 47–49.

34. Sociedad Nacional de Agricultura, *Boletín de la Sociedad Nacional de Agricultura* 56, no. 7 (July 1925): 411–12; no. 10 (October 1925): 738–45; 57, no. 7 (July 1926): 412–23.

35. Hirschman, *Journeys*, pp. 161–75; Marshall, "Régimen monetario actual," pp. 109–12; Fetter, *Monetary Inflation*, pp. 146–47; Araneda, *Veinte años*, pp. 20–21; Kemmerer, "Chile"; Charles A. McQueen, *Chilean Currency and Exchange in 1921* (Washington, D.C., 1921), pp. 5–10; Alejandro Silva de la Fuente, *Asuntos económicos contemporáneos, 1925–1940*, 2 vols. (Santiago, 1944), 2:95–96; James O. Morris, *Elites, Intellectuals, and Consensus* (Ithaca, 1966), pp. 91–92.

36. Charles A. McQueen, *Foreign Exchange in Latin America* (Washington, D.C., 1925); Michael Monteón, *Chile in the Nitrate Era: The Evolution of Economic Dependence, 1880–1930* (Madison, 1982), esp. pp. 48–79.

37. McQueen, *Chilean Currency*, pp. 2–10; Edwardson-Meeks, *Los impuestos*, pp. xliv–xlv; Ross, *Semana*, pp. 355–71; USDOS, from Valparaíso, December 22, 1923, 825.515/13.

38. Kemmerer, "Chile," pp. 270–71; Guillermo Edwards Matte, *Errores financieros de actualidad* (Santiago, 1926).

39. *El Mercurio*, July 12, 1925; EWK, Box 280, "Fijemos el valor de la moneda," December 2, 1924; Fidel Muñoz Rodríguez, *Exposición sobre el estado de la hacienda pública* (Santiago, 1924), p. 21.

40. *La Nación*, July 13, 1925; EWK, Box 190, "Notes of Suggestions Made to the Kemmerer Mission by the Commission Named by the Central Chamber of Commerce"; Box 280, letter from Sociedad Unión Comercial de Santiago, July, 1925; Ross, *Semana*, pp. 48, 117–63, 342; Edwardson-Meeks, *Los impuestos*, p. liii; Macchiavello, *El problema*, pp. 122–25; Luis Guevara, *Cambio fijo a base de oro* (Valparaíso, 1921); idem, *El problema del cambio y las bolsas de valores* (Valparaíso, 1925).

41. Sociedad de Fomento Fabril, *Boletín de la Sociedad de Fomento Fabril* 42, no. 9 (September 1925): 587–88; *El Diario Ilustrado*, August 30, 1925; Ross, *Semana*, pp. 64–68, 555–57; McQueen, *Chilean Currency*, p. 5; Jorge Hormann, *Estudios sobre el cambio internacional y sobre el arancel aduanero* (Santiago, 1921), pp. 5–22.

42. *El Mercurio*, July 2, October 15, 1925; *La Nación*, July 22, 1925; *El Heraldo del Sur*, May 3, July 4, 1925; *El Obrero Industrial*, June 13, July 4, August 1, 15, 1925; Chile, Cámara de Senadores, *Boletín de las Sesiones Extraordinarias* (Santiago, 1924), pp. 96–97; Luis Lagarrigue, *Caja de emisión fiscal y estabilidad del cambio* (Santiago, 1924), pp. 10–26; Peter De Shazo, *Urban Workers and Labor Unions in Chile, 1902–1927* (Madison, 1983); Comité Pro-Estabilización, *Proyecto del memorial*, p. 3; Ross, *Semana*, pp. 18–21, 337, 402–3; Fetter, *Monetary Inflation*, pp. 125–62; interview with Donald Kemmerer, August 1981; EWK, Diary, June 27, 28, July 1–2, 1925, pp. 178, 179, 182, 183.

43. Arturo Alessandri, *Recuerdos de gobierno*, 3 vols. (Santiago, 1967), 2:297–322; *El Diario Ilustrado*, July 14, 1925; Fetter, *Monetary Inflation*, pp. 134–60.
44. For general coverage of the military in these years, see Frederick M. Nunn, *Chilean Politics, 1920–1931* (Albuquerque, 1970); Enrique Monreal, *Historia documentada del período revolucionario, 1924–1925* (Santiago, 1929); Agustín Ross, *Exposición presentada a s.e. el General don Luis Altamirano, presidente de la junta de gobierno, solicitando que se verifique la conversión a oro de la emisión fiscal de billetes en conformidad con el proyecto de ley que se acompana* (Valparaíso, n.d.); Ross, *Semana*, pp. 50–58; McQueen, *Foreign Exchange*, p. 37; *El Mercurio*, July 16, 1925.
45. Raúl Simón, "The Kemmerer Mission and the Chilean Central Bank Law," *Chile: A Monthly Survey of Chilean Affairs* 1, no. 1 (January 1926): 13–16, 19.
46. Hirschman, *Journeys*, pp. 174–77; Ross, *Semana*, pp. 355–99, 493–94; Fetter, *Monetary Inflation*, pp. 158–73; Subercaseaux, *Monetary and Banking Policy*, pp. 184–85; Comité Pro-Estabilización, *Proyecto del memorial*; Roberto Espinoza, *La balanza de cuentas internacionales* (Santiago, 1924), pp. 46–47, 85.
47. GBDOT, *Report* (1928), p. 70.
48. Silva de la Fuente, *Asuntos económicos*, 2:215.
49. Chile, Ministerio de Hacienda, *Memoria de la hacienda pública correspondiente al año 1927* (Santiago, 1928), pp. 53–54.
50. Ballesteros and Davis, "The Growth of Output and Employment," p. 176.
51. Germán Urzúa Valenzuela and Anamaría García Barzelatto, *Diagnóstico de la burocracia chilena (1818–1969)* (Santiago, 1971), pp. 44–52.
52. Chile, Misión de Consejeros Financieros, *Memorandum Relative to the Importance of Reorganizing the Bureau of Internal Taxes* (Santiago, 1925), p. 2.
53. Urzúa Valenzuela and García Barzelatto, *Diagnóstico de la burocracia*, pp. 44–52.
54. Charles A. McQueen, *Principal Features of Chilean Finances* (Washington, D.C., 1923), pp. 6–7; Edwardson-Meeks, *Los impuestos*, pp. xix–xxvi.
55. Santiago Macchiavello Varas, *Política económica nacional*, 2 vols. (Santiago, 1931), 1:148.
56. McQueen, *Principal Features*, pp. 7–8; Vítor R. Celis Maturana, *Los ingresos ordinarios del estado* (Santiago, 1922), pp. 461–64, 572–74.
57. Luis Alberto Canales, *El régimen económico del estado y la administración de la hacienda pública* (Santiago, 1923), pp. xi–30, 113–15; Muñoz Rodríguez, *Exposición sobre el estado*, pp. 19–22; Guillermo Edwards Matte, *Exposición sobre el estado de la hacienda pública* (Santiago, 1925); *El Diario Ilustrado*, August 30, 1925.
58. Canales, *El régimen económico*, pp. xi–30, 69, 113–17, 150–54, 212–13; Eugenia Puga Fisher, *La fiscalización de la administración financiera de Chile* (Santiago, 1917).
59. Arturo Alessandri, *Mensaje leído* (1921), pp. 53–80; (1922), pp. 74–76; (1923), pp. 79–80; (1924), pp. 102–12; idem, *El alma de Alessandri* (Santiago, 1925), pp. 111–13.
60. Arturo Prat, *Artículos económicos* (Santiago, 1933), pp. 4–11; Nunn, *Chilean Politics*.
61. USDOS, from Washington, March 23, 1925, 825.51A/6; *El Mercurio*, July 1, 1925; Fetter, *Monetary Inflation*, pp. 170–71; Seidel, "Progressive Pan Americanism," pp. 334–35; EWK Diary, April 4, May 22, 23, 1925, pp. 94, 142, 143.
62. Edwin Walter Kemmerer, "Work of the American Financial Commission in Chile," *American Bankers' Association Journal* (December 1925): 411–12, 460; *La Información* 10, no. 94 (June–July 1925): 127.
63. *El Mercurio*, July 3, 1925; Fetter, *Monetary Inflation*, p. 171.
64. *El Diario Ilustrado*, July 9, August 13, 21–23, 1925; *El Mercurio*, June 2, July 1, October 13, 1925; *La Información* 10, no. 94 (June–July 1925): 125–29; Hirschman, *Journeys*, p. 178.

65. Academia de Ciencias Económicas, *Acta de sus sesiones, años 1924, 1925 y 1926* (Santiago, 1927), p. 56.
66. *Los Tiempos*, July 2, 1925.
67. Interview with Fetter; USDOS, from Santiago, August 11, 1925, 825.51A/10; *La Nación*, July 4, 1925. Kemmerer also received a mysterious death threat, signed by "the red hand." EWK, Diary, July 6, 1925, p. 187.
68. *El Diario Ilustrado*, July 5, 8, September 8, 1925; Silva de la Fuente, *Asuntos económicos*, 1:178–79.
69. USDOS, from Santiago, August 11, 1925, 825.51A/10; EWK, Diary, August 9, 24, 1925, pp. 221, 236.
70. *El Heraldo del Sur*, July 12, 1925; *El Diario Ilustrado*, July 8, 1925.
71. *La Nación*, July 2, 3, 1925.
72. *El Diario Ilustrado*, July 18, 25, 1925; interview with Fetter; interview with Donald Kemmerer.
73. *La Nación*, July 3, 4, 1925; EWK, Box 61, letter from Fetter, October 23, 1925; Diary, August 15, 21, 1925, pp. 227, 233; interview with Fetter; Seidel, "Progressive Pan Americanism," p. 336; Donald L. Kemmerer, "The Central Bank of Chile during the Period 1925–1950," Banco Central de Chile, *Monetary Studies* 8 (April 1983): 11–28.
74. USDOS, from Santiago, August 11, 1925, 825.51A/10.
75. *El Mercurio*, July 2, 1925.
76. *Los Tiempos*, July 2, 1925; *El Diario Ilustrado*, July 18, 1925; *La Nación*, July 2, 1925; *El Mercurio*, July 2, 1925.
77. Academia de Ciencias Económicas, *Acta de sus sesiones*, pp. 56–57.
78. USDOS, from Santiago, October 6, 1925, 825.51A/16; *El Diario Ilustrado*, July 5, 1925.
79. EWK, esp. Book 105; Chile, *Legislación bancaria y monetaria* (Santiago, 1926); Chile, Misión de Consejeros Financieros, *Proyecto de reforma de los códigos de comercio, procedimiento y minas y ley de cuentas corrientes* (Santiago, 1925); *El Diario Ilustrado*, August 2, 1925.
80. EWK, esp. Box 196; Kemmerer, "Work," pp. 411–12, 460.
81. Simón, "The Kemmerer Mission," p. 16; Araneda, *Veinte años*, pp. 23–31.
82. Kemmerer, "Work," p. 412.
83. Academia de Ciencias Económicas, *Acta de sus sesiones*, pp. 49–50, 81–89; *El Mercurio*, September 5, 17, 1925; *El Diario Ilustrado*, August 24, 1925; EWK, Diary, August 22, 1925, p. 234.
84. Felipe Herrera Lane, *El banco central de Chile* (Santiago, 1945), pp. 55, 87, 189–91; Sociedad Nacional de Agricultura, *Boletín* 56, no. 9 (September 1925): 664.
85. *El Diario Ilustrado*, August 30, 1925.
86. Chile, Banco Central, *Monthly Bulletin*, no. 1 (January 1928): 1–2.
87. Silva de la Fuente, *Asuntos económicos*, 2:2.
88. *El Mercurio*, January 12, 1926; Academia de Ciencias Económicas, *Acta de sus sesiones*, pp. 84–86; Marcelo Morales and Leonardo Díaz, *Evolución de las reformas financieras en Chile* (n.p., 1971), p. 10.
89. Luis A. Iglesias Carrasco, *El banco central de Chile* (Santiago, 1938), pp. 36, 104.
90. Alessandri, *Mensaje leído* (1922), pp. 79–81; ibid. (1923), pp. 81–82; ibid. (1924), pp. 121–24; EWK, Box 280, letter from Augusto Villanueva, August 1, 1925; *Reportajes hechos al profesor E. W. Kemmerer y publicados por "La Nación" de Santiago de Chile en 30 y 31 de julio y 1 de agosto de 1927* (Bogotá, 1928), p. 6.
91. EWK, Box 190, interviews with Augusto Villanueva of Banco de Chile, Carlos Castro Ruiz of

Banco de Chile, and Agustín Edwards of Banco Edwards; Box 280, letter from Augusto Villanueva, August 1, 1925.

92. Silva de la Fuente, *Asuntos económicos*, 1:173.

93. W. M. Van Deusen, *Banco Central de Chile: sus funciones* (Santiago, 1927), pp. 29–30.

94. *El Mercurio*, August 3, 1925.

95. EWK, Box 78, letters from Van Deusen, esp. September 14, 1926; Van Deusen, *Banco Central de Chile*, p. 20.

96. Chile, *Legislación bancaria*, pp. 26–27, 178–79, 199–200.

97. EWK, Box 190, interviews with Wilhelm Hasse of Banco Alemán Transatlántico, Alfred Diekenmann of Banco de Chile y Alemania, Mr. Salmon of Anglo–South American Bank, and Mr. Little of National City Bank. The latter was not eager to have to join the central bank and forgo profits from exchange fluctuations. USDOS, from Valparaíso, August 26, 1925, 825.516/42; Chile-American Assoc., *Mutual Trade and Resources*, pp. 62–63; Banque Francaise et Italienne pour L'Amerique de Sud, *Le retour a l'etalon d'or au chili* (Santiago, 1925); Paride Mambretti, *El Sistema monetario de Chile* (Santiago, 1927), p. 7.

98. EWK, Box 190, "Notes of Suggestions"; Box 280, letter from Guillermo Subercaseaux, July 13, 1925; Kemmerer, "Work"; Comité Pro-Estabilización, *Proyecto del memorial*; Academia de Ciencias Económicas, *Acta de sus sesiones*, pp. 81–89; Ross, *Semana*, pp. 262–63; *La Nación*, July 28, 1925; *El Diario Ilustrado*, August 24, 1925; *La Información* 10, no. 94 (June–July 1925): 129–32; Alessandri, *Mensaje leído* (1921), pp. 77–79; ibid. (1922), pp. 79–81; ibid. (1923); ibid. (1924), pp. 121–24; Herrera, *El banco central de Chile*, pp. 39–43; Julio Pérez Canto, *Reforma del régimen monetario. El Banco central de Chile* (Santiago, 1921), esp. pp. 375–77, 565–71; Ricardo Onfray, *Silabario monetario chileno* (Valparaíso, 1924).

99. Chile, *Legislacion bancaria*, pp. 17–28, 64–68.

100. Silva de la Fuente, *Asuntos económicos*, 1:173, 180–82, 2:4; *El Mercurio*, August 23, 1925.

101. Chile, *Legislación bancaria*, pp. 18–20.

102. *El Mercurio*, August 3, 1925.

103. Iglesias, *El banco central de Chile*, pp. 45–47.

104. Interview with Fetter; EWK, Box 61, letter to Lucas Caballero, February 10, 1926.

105. *El Diario Ilustrado*, August 24, 1925; EWK, Box 20, letter from Consejo Obrero to Van Deusen, January 8, 1931.

106. *El Diario Ilustrado*, August 26, 27, October 4, 1925; Chile, *Legislación bancaria*, pp. 65–67; EWK, Diary, August 20, 1925, p. 232.

107. Herrera, *El banco central de Chile*, pp. 88–89.

108. EWK, Box 61, letters from Fetter, November 3, December 18, 1925; interview with Fetter.

109. Ibid.

110. EWK, Box 78, letters from Van Deusen, esp. September 14, 1926; Chile, Banco Central, *First Annual Report Presented to the Banking Superintendent. Year 1926* (Santiago, 1927), pp. 50–54.

111. Halsey and Sherwell, *Investments in Latin America*, p. 20; Iglesias, *El banco central de Chile*, pp. 50–53.

112. Van Deusen, *Banco Central de Chile*, pp. 14–24; Silva de la Fuente, *Asuntos económicos*, 2:6; Iglesias, *El banco central de Chile*, pp. 53, 84–91.

113. *El Mercurio*, August 30, 1925.

114. Chile, Superintendencia de Bancos, *Memoria de la Superintendencia de Bancos correspondiente a los años 1926 y 1927* (Santiago, 1928), pp. 33–34; Edwin Walter Kemmerer, *Funcionamiento de nuestra legislación bancaria y monetaria* (Santiago, 1927), pp. 8–16; Araneda, *Veinte años*, pp. 24–30.

115. Chile, Superintendencia de Bancos, *Memoria, 1927*, pp. 31–33; *El Diario Ilustrado*, August

23, 1925; *El Mercurio*, September 8, 1925, January 27, 1926; Rolf Luders, "Una historia monetaria de Chile," *Cuadernos de Economia* 7, no. 20 (April 1970): 4–28; idem, "Chile, 1926–1929," pp. 72–73.

116. Van Deusen, *Banco Central de Chile*, pp. 29–35; Chile, Superintendencia de Bancos, *Estadística bancaria. 1929* (Santiago, 1930), pp. 41–43.

117. Carlos Ibáñez del Campo, *Mensaje leído por s.e. el vicepresidente de la república en la apertura del congreso nacional, el 21 de mayo de 1927* (Santiago, 1927), pp. 21–22; Iglesias, *El banco central de Chile*, pp. 116–17.

118. Chile, Banco Central, *Second Annual Report Presented to the Banking Superintendent. Year 1927* (Santiago, 1928), pp. 10–13.

119. *El Diario Ilustrado*, August 24, 1925; *El Mercurio*, August 22, September 26, 1925; Iglesias, *El banco central de Chile*, pp. 35, 56–57, 106–7.

120. Chile, Misión de Consejeros Financieros, *Monetary Bill* (Santiago, 1925); Germán Max, "Diez años de historia monetaria de Chile," *Anexo al Boletín Mensual del Banco Central de Chile*, no. 94 (December 1935).

121. Kemmerer, "Chile," pp. 270–73.

122. GBDOT, *Report* (1926), p. 76; USDOS, from Chile-American Association in New York, November 16, 1925, 825.51A/20; Seco, *Proyecto económico y financiero*, pp. 3–8; Roberto Soto Vera, *La inflación monetaria en Chile* (Santiago, 1943), pp. 88–89.

123. Chile, Misión de Consejeros Financieros, *General Banking Bill* (Santiago, 1925); Kemmerer, "Work," p. 412; EWK, Diary, September 25, 1925, p. 268.

124. Sociedad de Fomento Fabril, *Boletín* 42, no. 10 (October 1925): 669–73; Pérez Canto, *Reforma*, pp. 180–88.

125. Francisco Langlois, *La nueva legislación bancaria* (Santiago, 1926), pp. 3–10; Soto Vera, *La inflación*, p. 89.

126. USDOS, from Santiago, August 2, 1926, 825.516/58; EWK, Box 61, letter from Fetter, December 18, 1925; Araneda, *Veinte años*, p. 27.

127. EWK, Box 78, letter from Van Deusen, April 10, 1926; Chile, Superintendencia de Bancos, *Circulares de bancos y consultas de los bancos* (Santiago, 1927), pp. xiii–xiv; idem, *Resumen de los estados de los bancos del país* (Santiago, 1927–32); idem, *Memoria de la Superintendencia de Bancos* (Santiago, 1928), pp. 1–6, 76; Chile, Banco Central, *Monthly Bulletin*, no. 2 (Santiago, 1926), pp. 3–10.

128. Chile, Superintendencia de Bancos, *Estadística bancaria* (1927–30); idem, *Resumen* (1927–31); idem, *Memoria* (1928).

129. Pérez Canto, *Reforma*, pp. 180–88; Iglesias, *El banco central de Chile*, p. 37.

130. Chile, Misión de Consejeros Financieros, *General Banking*; Chile, Superintendencia de Bancos, *Circulares*, pp. 237–43, 312–13.

131. EWK, Box 78, letters from Van Deusen, July 14, August 26, 1926.

132. EWK, Box 190, interview with Alfred Houston.

133. McQueen, *Principal Features*, pp. 8–9.

134. These figures are based on old pesos equivalent to eighteen pence and exclude railroad expenses and revenues. *La Información* 10, no. 93 (April–May 1925), p. 73; Enrique Correa, *La contraloría. El presupuesto del estado. Su control* (Santiago, 1928), pp. 26–30.

135. Ross, *Semana*, p. 263.

136. EWK, Box 280.

137. Asociación de Contadores de Chile, *Boletín de la Asociación de Contadores de Chile* 2, no. 5 (September 1925): 6.

138. *El Mercurio*, January 7, 1926.

139. *Los Tiempos*, July 2, 1925.

140. Chile, Misión de Consejeros Financieros, *Organic Budget Bill* (Santiago, 1925).

141. Silva de la Fuente, *Asuntos económicos*, 2:257–90.

142. *El Mercurio*, August 5, 1925; Correa, *La contraloría*, pp. 29–40.

143. *El Mercurio*, January 4, 1926; GBDOT, *Report* (1928), pp. 16–17.

144. Silva de la Fuente, *Asuntos económicos*, 2:235–36, 272–85; GBDOT, *Report* (1931), p. 85; Chile, Ministerio de Hacienda, *Memoria, 1927*, pp. 52–59; idem, *Memoria, 1928 y 1929*, pp. 3–4; idem, *Mensaje sobre proyecto del presupuesto ordinario correspondiente a 1928* (Santiago, 1927); idem, *Boletín de Hacienda* (Santiago, 1929); idem, *Presupuesto de entradas ordinarias correspondiente al año 1930* (Santiago, 1929); idem, *Exposición del Ministro de Hacienda sobre la situación de las finanzas públicas* (Santiago, 1931).

145. Chile, Ministerio de Hacienda, *Memoria, 1927*, pp. 51–53; Edwardson-Meeks, *El mundo y nosotros* (n.p., n.d.), p. 69.

146. Enrique Silva Cimma, *La contraloría general de la república* (Santiago, 1945), pp. 11–12, 79–80.

147. Chile, Misión de Consejeros Financieros, *Proyecto de ley para la reorganización de la contaduría e inspección fiscales, bajo la dirección de una oficina que se denominará contraloría* (Santiago, 1926); idem, *Project of Law Concerning the Reorganization of the Government Accounting and Auditing and the Creation of the Office of Accounting and Fiscal Control* (Santiago, 1925); idem, *Memorandum Concerning a Revised System of Accounting and Reporting for Treasury Department Offices* (Santiago, 1925); Chile, Contraloría General, *50 años de vida institucional. 435 de historia* (Santiago, 1977).

148. Sonia Pinto, Luz María Méndez, and Sergio Vergara, *Antecedentes históricos de la contraloría general de la república* (Santiago, 1977), p. 5; Chile, Banco Central, *Third Annual Report Presented to the Banking Superintendent. Year 1928* (Santiago, 1929), p. 12.

149. Ibáñez, *Mensaje, 1927*, p. 21.

150. EWK, Box 78, letter from Van Deusen, March 16, 1927; Pinto, Méndez, and Vergara, *Antecedentes históricos de la contraloría general*, p. 5–12.

151. Aníbal Jara Letelier and Manuel G. Muirhead, *Chile en Sevilla* (Santiago, 1929), pp. 149–52; Correa, *La contraloría*, pp. 18–19; USDOS, from Santiago, May 18, 1927, 825.51/253.

152. Chile, Contraloría General, *Primer informe anual de la contraloría general* (Santiago, 1929), pp. 19–25.

153. Correa, *La contraloría*, pp. 196–206; Silva de la Fuente, *Asuntos económicos*, 2:270–71.

154. USDOS, from Santiago, January 21, 1928, 825.51/271; Silva Cimma, *La contraloría general de la república*, pp. 81–88ff., 335; Chile, Contraloría General, *Memoria de la contraloría general correspondiente al ano 1932* (Santiago, 1933).

155. Alessandri, *Mensaje leído* (1923), p. 78; ibid. (1924), pp. 114–17; EWK, Box 194, "The Present Internal Tributary System in Chile."

156. EWK, Box 30, "Unofficial Commission from the Valparaíso Commerce," July 28, 1927; Box 194; Box 280, letter from Asociación de Productores de Salitre, July 24, 1925; *El Diario Ilustrado*, July 1, 8, 10, 13, October 14, 1925; *La Nación*, July 8, 10, 1925; *El Mercurio*, July 7, 1925; Sociedad de Fomento Fabril, *Boletín* 42, no. 6 (June 1925): 373–74; Prat, *Artículos económicos*, pp. 12–18; Canales, *El régimen económico*, pp. 8–17, 30–31, 113–15, 151–54, 276–78.

157. Academia de Ciencias Económicas, *Acta de sus sesiones*, pp. 53–54; Chile, Misión de Consejeros Financieros, *Project of Law for a Tax on Public Spectacles and Hippodromes*; idem, *Project of Law for a Tax on Membership Dues in Clubs and Other Organizations*; idem, *Project of*

Law for the Taxation of Tobacco; idem, *Draft of Project of Law for the Taxation of Real Property*; idem, *Project of a Stamp Tax Law*; idem, *Memorandum Relative to the Importance of Reorganizing the Bureau of Internal Taxes* (Santiago, 1925). These Kemmerer reports, like virtually all his recommendations, are also available in Spanish translations.

158. USDOS, from Santiago, November 4, 1929, 825.51/299.

159. Alessandri, *Mensaje leído*, (1923), p. 78; ibid. (1924), pp. 114–17; GBDOT, *Report* (1923), p. 10; *El Diario Ilustrado*, October 29, 1925; Edwardson-Meeks, *Los impuestos*, pp. xii–xxvi; Julio Undurraga Ovalle, *La riqueza mobilaria de Chile* (Santiago, 1923), pp. 518–19.

160. Chile, Misión de Consejeros Financieros, *Proyecto de ley de impuesto sobre la renta* (Santiago, 1925).

161. Chile, Presidente, *Mensaje leído por s.e. el presidente de la república en la apertura del congreso nacional el 21 de mayo de 1926* (Santiago, 1926), pp. 10–11.

162. Chile, Misión de Consejeros Financieros, *Project of Law for an Export Tax on Iron Ore* (Santiago, 1925); Macchiavello, *El problema*, pp. 116–20.

163. EWK, Box 280, letter from Alfred Houston, August 17, 1925; Markos Mamalakis and Clark Reynolds, *Essays on the Chilean Economy* (Homewood, 1965), pp. 227–28; Aída Vuskovic Bravo, *Participación del capital extranjero en la economía chilena* (Santiago, 1957), p. 87.

164. Sociedad de Fomento Fabril, *Boletín* 42, nos. 1–10 (January–October 1925); Sociedad Nacional de Agricultura, *Boletín* 56, nos. 2–9 (February–September 1925); EWK, Box 190, "Notes of Suggestions"; USDOS, from Chile-American Association in New York, November 16, 1925, 825.51A/20; *La Nación*, July 2, 1925; *El Mercurio*, January 20, 21, 1926; Pedro Cabezón, "Antecedentes históricos de las importaciones y de la política comercial de Chile," *Cuadernos de Economía* 8, no. 25 (December 1971), pp. 1–35.

165. *El Mercurio*, January 29, 1926.

166. Alfonso Ferrada Urzúa, *Historia comentada de la deuda externa de Chile* (Santiago, 1945), pp. 87–88; *La Información* 10, no. 93 (April–May 1925): 73.

167. Chile, Ministerio de Hacienda, *Valor de la deuda pública directa e indirecta de la república de Chile en 31 de diciembre de 1930* (Santiago, 1931); idem, *Memoria, 1927*, p. 61; Oscar Ilabaca León, *Breve estudio sobre los fundamentos económico-sociales de nuestros empréstitos externos* (Santiago, 1925), pp. 56–89.

168. *La Nación*, July 17, 18, 1925.

169. *El Diario Ilustrado*, July 1, 1925; GBDOT, *Report* (1926), pp. 14–15.

170. USDOS, from Santiago, October 2, 1925, 825.15/8.

171. Chile, Misión de Consejeros Financieros, *Report on the Public Debt Policy of Chile* (Santiago, 1925).

172. EWK, Box 61, letter to Chilean Ambassador Beltram Mathieu, December 8, 1925; Diary, December 3, 1925, p. 337.

173. USDOS, from Santiago, April 6, 1927, 825.51/249.

174. Luders, "Una historia monetaria de Chile," p. 18.

175. GBDOT, *Report* (1932), pp. 36–38; United Nations, *Public Debt*, pp. 38–41.

176. Price, Waterhouse, Faller, and Company, *Informe sobre el estado de la hacienda pública en 31 de diciembre de 1929* (Santiago, 1930); Chile, Contraloría General de la Republica, *Deuda fiscal en 30 de junio de 1929* (Santiago, 1929); Chile, Ministerio de Hacienda, *Valor, 1930*; idem, *Valor, 1928* (Santiago, 1929); Héctor Ríos Igualt, *Los empréstitos públicos* (Valparaíso, 1941), pp. 156–69.

177. Eugene Chevreaux, *Financial Developments in Latin America during 1929* (Washington, D.C., 1929), p. 8.

178. Chile, Ministerio de Hacienda, *Memoria, 1928 y 1929*, p. 39; USDOS, from Santiago, November 4, 1929, 825.51/299; Edwardson-Meeks, *El mundo*, p. 67; Ríos Igualt, *Los empréstitos públicos*, pp. 153–54.

179. Chile, Ministerio de Hacienda, *Memoria, 1927*, pp. 61–93; Ferrada, *Historia comentada de la deuda externa*, pp. 91–105.

180. Chile, Ministerio de Hacienda, *Memoria, 1928 y 1929*, p. 18.

181. USDOS, from Santiago, June 10, 1927, 825.51/254; Raúl Vera Vera, *Historia de la deuda externa de Chile* (Santiago, 1942), pp. 38–39, 70–92.

182. Carlos Keller, *La eterna crisis chilena* (Santiago, 1931), pp. 172–75; Luders, "Chile, 1926–1929," pp. 64–78.

183. USDOS, from Santiago, June 24, 1930, 625.4115/2; February 20, 1931, 625.4117/17; *El Mercurio*, January 20, 1926; Silva de la Fuente, *Asuntos económicos*, 1:185.

184. Augusto Santelices, *Esquema de una situación económica-social de Ibero-América* (Santiago, 1930), pp. 153–61.

185. Luders, "Chile, 1926–1929," pp. 66–67; Ellsworth, *Chile, an Economy in Transition*, p. 20.

186. Silva de la Fuente, *Asuntos económicos*, 2:272–80.

187. Leopoldo Arce G., *La crisis chilena* (Santiago, 1932), pp. 24–49; Oscar Alvarez Andrews, *Historia del desarrollo industrial de Chile* (Santiago, 1936), pp. 237–43.

188. *El Diario Ilustrado*, July 2, 25, August 1, 1925; *El Mercurio*, July 18, 1925; Halsey and Sherwell, *Investments in Latin America*, pp. 30–31; GBDOT, *Report* (1925), pp. 52–53; ibid. (1926), pp. 33–35; Sociedad Nacional de Minería, *Boletín Minero* 61, no. 315 (July 1925): 387–92; no. 319 (November 1925): 737.

189. GBDOT, *Report* (1928), pp. 52–53; Chile, Banco Central, *Monthly Bulletin*, no. 21 (September 1929): 1.

190. *Los Tiempos*, September 30, October 6, 1925.

191. Central Union Trust Company of New York, *Financial and Economic Conditions in the Republic of Chile* (New York, 1926); GBDOT, *Report* (1928), pp. 7–12.

192. Vuskovic, *Participación del capital extranjero*, pp. 41–58, 115; Pinto, Méndez, and Vergara, *Antecedentes históricos de la contraloría general*, pp. 39–43; Fernando Illáñez Benítez, *La economía chilena y el comercio exterior* (Santiago, 1944), p. 21.

193. Mamalakis, *Growth and Structure*, pp. 61–64.

194. Ibid.; *La Nación*, June 28, 1927; USDOS, from Santiago, July 27, 1927, 825.51/259.

195. Carlos Dávila, *North American Imperialism* (New York, 1930); Jara and Muirhead, *Chile en Sevilla*, p. 209.

196. GBDOT, *Report* (1928), pp. 7–8; Clarence Henry Haring, *South America Looks at the United States* (New York, 1928), pp. 217–22.

197. Santelices, *Esquema de una situación*, pp. 152–59; Macchiavello, *Política*, 1:134–36.

198. GBDOT, *Report* (1928), p. 11; ibid. (1931), pp. 32–33.

199. *Reportajes*; Chile, Banco Central, *Second Annual Report*, pp. 8–9, 33.

200. Ruffat, *La política monetaria*, pp. 33–57; Pinto, Méndez, and Vergara, *Antecedentes históricos de la contraloría general*, pp. 76–78, 86, 96.

201. GBDOT, *Report* (1928), pp. 10–11; ibid. (1931), pp. 90–91; Keller, *La eterna crisis chilena*, pp. 32–44, 176–78; René Montero Moreno, *La verdad sobre Ibáñez* (Buenos Aires, 1953), pp. 35–84.

202. Sociedad Nacional de Agricultura, *Boletín*, 1925–27; Arce, *La crisis chilena*, p. 45.

203. George M. McBride, *Chile: Land and Society* (New York, 1936), pp. 174–76; Silva de la Fuente, *Asuntos económicos*, 2:216–17; GBDOT, *Report* (1932), pp. 32–33.

204. Chile, Dirección General de Estadística, *Censo de la industria manufacturera y del comercio de*

1928 (n.p., n.d.). Although the precise figures in this rare census are open to question, the trends depicted are not. See Ellsworth, *Chile, an Economy in Transition*, p. 162; Silva de la Fuente, *Asuntos económicos*, 1:261–64; Gabriel Palma, "From an Export-led to an Import-substituting Economy: Chile 1914–39," in Rosemary Thorp, ed., *Latin America in the 1930's: The Role of the Periphery in the World Crisis* (London, 1984), pp. 50–74; Palma, "External Disequilibrium and Internal Industrialization: Chile, 1914–1935," in Christopher Abel and Colin M. Lewis, eds., *Latin America, Economic Imperialism, and the State: The Political Economy of the External Connection from Independence to the Present* (London, 1985), pp. 318–38.

205. Kirsch, *Industrial Development in a Traditional Society*, pp. 145–47.

206. Enzo Faletto, Eduardo Ruíz, and Hugo Zemelman, *Génesis histórica del proceso político chileno* (Santiago, 1971), pp. 55–71; Guillermo Viviani Contreras, *Sociología chilena* (Santiago, 1926), pp. 58–60, 116–17.

207. Jara and Muirhead, *Chile en Sevilla*, p. 513; GBDOT, *Report* (1932), p. 42.

208. Oscar Muñoz Goma, *Crecimiento industrial de Chile, 1941–1965* (Santiago, 1968), p. 194; Edwardson-Meeks, *El mundo*, p. 11.

209. Ellsworth, *Chile, an Economy in Transition*, esp. pp. 6–9, 50–53; Domingo Quintana Costa, *La crisis de 1929 y sus efectos* (Santiago, 1945); Pablo Macera, *La crisis de 1929 y las economías de Chile y el Peru* (Lima, 1974); Alvarez Andrews, *Historia del desarrollo industrial*, pp. 246–330; Carlos Keller, *Un país al garete* (Santiago, 1932), pp. 35–57, 98–99, 162–63; Eduardo Ortiz, *La gran depresión y su impacto en Chile, 1929–1933* (Santiago, 1982).

210. Ellsworth, *Chile, an Economy in Transition*, pp. 3–6; Mamalakis and Reynolds, *Essays on the Chilean Economy*, pp. 230–33; Thomson, "Chile Struggles for National Recovery," pp. 288–91; "Nitrogen," *Fortune* (August 1932): 43–70, 90–91.

211. Seidel, "Progressive Pan Americanism," pp. 609–14; U.S. Department of State, Francis White Papers (hereinafter cited as FW), Box 1, conversations with Garrard Winston, June 30, 1931, and April 19, 1932; with Harry Covington, June 14, 1932; with J. H. van Royen, October 22, 1931; and with Mr. Whepley, June 13 and 14, 1932; Box 3, memorandum to Mr. Carr, October 1, 1931.

212. Enrique Zañartu Prieto, *Hambre, miseria e ignorancia* (Santiago, 1938), pp. 152–53; Sociedad Nacional de Agricultura, *Memoria* (Santiago, 1932), pp. 5–25, 126–58; Jaime Larraín, *Orientación de nuestra política agraria* (Santiago, 1932); *El Mercurio*, December 27, 1931; Chile, Dirección General de Estadística, *Sinopsis geográfico-estadística de la república de Chile* (Santiago, 1933), pp. 154–57; Silva de la Fuente, *Asuntos económicos*, 2:48–50.

213. FW, Box 10, letter from William Culbertson, February 10, 1932; Keller, *Un país al garete*, pp. 157–58.

214. Ellsworth, *Chile, an Economy in Transition*, pp. 4–5; Chile, *Sinopsis*, pp. 214–71; Flavian Levine B., "Indices de producción física," *Economía* 5, nos. 10–11 (July 1944): 69–98.

215. USDOS, from Santiago, November 6, 1930, 625.003/127; November 20, 1930, 625.003/129; November 21, 1930, 625.003.128; January 27, 1932, 625.001/22.

216. Sociedad de Fomento Fabril, *Boletín* (1932); idem, *Plan de fomento de la producción* (Santiago, 1932); *El Mercurio*, December 24–26, 1931; *La Nación*, October 31, 1930; Silva de la Fuente, *Asuntos económicos*, 1:261–64; Alvarez Andrews, *Historia del desarrollo industrial*, pp. 322–30; Santiago Wilson Hernández, *Nuestra crisis económica y la desocupación obrera* (Santiago, 1933).

217. Ellsworth, *Chile, an Economy in Transition*, pp. 1–75, 128–29, 161–62; Mamalakis and Reynolds, *Essays on the Chilean Economy*, pp. 14–17, 54–55.

218. Chile, Superintendencia de Bancos, *Estadistica 1930*; idem, *Estadistica 1931*; idem, *Estadistica 1932*.

219. Ellsworth, *Chile, an Economy in Transition*, pp. 24–25; Chile, *Sinopsis*, pp. 317–27.
220. Ellsworth, *Chile, an Economy in Transition*, pp. 14–25; Alvarez Andrews, *Historia del desarrollo industrial*, pp. 223–25, 335–50; Clarence H. Haring, "The Chilean Revolution of 1931," *Hispanic American Historical Review* 13, no. 2 (May 1933): 197–203; Henry Grattan Doyle, "Chilean Dictatorship Overthrown," *Current History* 34 (September 1931): 918–22.
221. Ruffat, *La política monetaria*, pp. 61–71; Ellsworth, *Chile, an Economy in Transition*, pp. 4–35, 80–100; Chile, *Sinopsis*, pp. 114–18, 264–333; Keller, *La eterna crisis chilena*; idem, *Un país al garete*; Zañartu, *Hambre, miseria e ignorancia*, pp. 90–97; Alvarez Andrews, *Historia del desarrollo industrial*; Andre Siegfried, *Impressions of South America* (New York, 1933), pp. 81–87; Carlos Ibáñez del Campo, *Mensaje con que el presidente de la república da cuenta al congreso nacional* (Santiago, 1931); Antonio Cifuentes, *Evolución de la economía chilena desde la crisis hasta nuestros días* (Santiago, 1935); Julio Philippi, *Economía dirigida* (Santiago, 1933); Guillermo Subercaseaux, *La política social nacionalista moderna* (Santiago, 1932), esp. pp. 6–15.
222. None of these foreign debts were ever repudiated, and partial payments resumed in 1935. During 1927–31 approximately 41 percent of the government's foreign loans had gone into public works and at least 35 percent into payments on past debts. Vuskovic, *Participación del capital extranjero*, pp. 43–46; Ruffat, *La política monetaria*, pp. 65–67, 120; Ellsworth, *Chile, an Economy in Transition*, pp. 9–11; Chile, *Sinopsis*, pp. 299–305; GBDOT, *Report* (1932), pp. 36–38; José Carril Echevarri, *Nuestra deuda externa* (Santiago, 1944), pp. 11–14, 37–42, 89–95.
223. Carlos Keller, *Como salir de la crisis* (Santiago, 1932); Silva de la Fuente, *Asuntos económicos*, 1:265–67, 278, 2:33–45ff., 72.
224. There may have been some $20 million more in manufacturing and trading companies. United Nations, *Foreign Capital*, p. 63; Seidel, "Progressive Pan Americanism," p. 410; FW, Box 40, "United States and Latin America, 1929–1933," vol. 2, "Recent Problems in the Protection of American Interests in Chile"; USDOS, from Santiago, February 20, 1931, 625.4117/17; May 14, 1932, 625.003/152.
225. FW, Box 1, "Colombia," conversation with Mr. W. W. Lancaster of National City Bank, March 7, 1932; "Chile," conversation with Sir Ronald Lindsay, British ambassador, July 6, 1932.
226. Ibid.; Box 10, "William S. Culbertson," letter of November 18, 1931; conversation with Benjamin Cohen, May 19, 1933; Box 1, "Chile," conversation with Mr. Garrard Winston of National City Bank, June 30, 1931; Mr. J. H. van Royen, October 22, 1931; Seidel, "Progressive Pan Americanism," pp. 609–14; Juan E. Montero, *Mensaje del presidente de la república al congreso nacional* (Santiago, 1932).
227. Paul W. Drake, *Socialism and Populism in Chile, 1932–52* (Urbana, 1978), pp. 71–83; idem, *Partido Socialista, 4 de junio* (Santiago, 1933); FW, Box 6, "National City," telegram no. 89 to Mr. Hinson, June 15, 1932; letter to Floyd Blair, June 10, 1932; USDOS, from Santiago, June 4–16, 1932, 825.00 Revolutions/64–103.
228. The proposal to expropriate the banks' foreign currency deposits and compensate them at a very low peso rate would have cost U.S. interests about $800,000. Ibid.; USDOS, from Santiago, June 9–16, 1932, 825.516/126–151; FW, Box 1, "Chile," conversations with Sir Ronald Lindsay, British ambassador, June 11, 1932; Mr. R. F. Loree, June 9, 1932; Mr. R. F. Loree and Mr. W. J. Hoffman, June 13, 1932; Mr. Floyd Blair, June 13 and 14, 1932, and General Palmer E. Pierce, June 17, 1932; Box 6, letter from W. J. Hoffman, June 14, 1932; Ronald E. Raven, "El 4 de Junio: Birth of a Legend" (M.A. thesis, Wayne State University, 1973), pp. 4–61.

229. *El Mercurio*, June 20–26, July 1–27, August 16, 1932; *La Opinión*, June 18, 1932; *El Sol*, August 28, 1931; FW, Box 1, "Chile," conversations with Mr. Floyd Blair, July 18, 1932; Mr. Paul Claudel, July 28, 1932; F. D. G. Osborne, July 29 and August 27, 1932; USDOS, from Santiago, July 14, 1932, 825.00 Revolutions/157; July 15, 1932, 825.01/63; Zañartu, *Hambre, miseria e ignorancia*, pp. 30–143; Keller, *Un país al garete*, pp. 22–27; Cesar Salvatierra Leon, *Introducción al estudio de veinte años de historia monetaria en Chile, 1925–45* (Santiago, 1951), pp. 26–32.

230. Zañartu, *Hambre, miseria e ignorancia*, esp. pp. 90–132; Cifuentes, *Evolución de la economía chilena*, pp. 3–18; Araneda, *Veinte años*, pp. 37–47; Chile, Banco Central, *Cuarta Memoria Anual presentada a la Superintendencia de Bancos. Año 1929* (Santiago, 1930); idem, *Quinta Memoria Anual presentada a la Superintendencia de Bancos. Año 1930* (Santiago, 1931); Manuel Marfán, "Políticas reactivadoras y recesión externa: Chile 1929–1938," *Estudios Cieplán*, no. 12 (March 1984): 89–120; Ricardo Lagos E., "El precio de la ortodoxia," *Estudios Cieplán*, no. 12 (March 1984): 121–34; Patricio Mellar, "Elementos útiles e inútiles en la literatura económica sobre recesiones y depresiones," *Estudios Cieplán*, no. 12 (March 1984): 135–58.

231. Ibáñez, *Mensaje* (1931), pp. 13–16; Colombia, *Revista del Banco de la República*, (February 1931): 52–54; (April 1931): 132–34.

232. EWK, Box 30, letter to Van Deusen, August 17, 1931; Godofredo Vidal, *El crédito bancario* (Lima, 1941), pp. 35–36.

233. Chile, *Sinopsis*, pp. 310–16; Ellsworth, *Chile, an Economy in Transition*, pp. vii–35; Jorge Leiva Lavalle, *El sector externo, los grupos sociales y las políticas económicas en Chile, 1830–1940* (Santiago, n.d.), pp. 31–39.

234. Marshall, "Régimen monetario actual," p. 98.

235. Araneda, *Veinte años*, pp. 42–47; Perú, Banco Central de Reserva del Perú, *Boletín Mensual* (September 1932).

236. Cifuentes, *Evolución de la economía chilena*, pp. 11–18.

237. Ellsworth, *Chile, an Economy in Transition*, pp. 18–20, 35–43, 166; Araneda, *Veinte años*, pp. 45–58; Salvatierra, *Introducción al estudio de veinte años*, pp. 23–30; Cifuentes, *Evolución de la economía chilena*, pp. 8–11; Julio Pérez Canto, "El sistema monetario de Chile," Universidad Nacional de Córdoba, Escuela de Ciencias Económicas, *Sistemas monetarios latino-americanos* (Córdoba, 1943), pp. 229–59; Chile, Banco Central, *Sexta Memoria Anual presentada a la Superintendencia de Bancos. Año 1931* (Santiago, 1932); idem, *Séptima Memoria Anual presentada a la Superintendencia de Bancos. Año 1932* (Santiago, 1933).

238. Ellsworth, *Chile, an Economy in Transition*; Arturo Alessandri, *Mensaje leído por s.e. el presidente de la república* (Santiago, 1933); Chile, Banco Central, *Octava Memoria Anual presentada a la Superintendencia de Bancos. Año 1933* (Santiago, 1934); Mamalakis, *Growth and Structure*, p. 102.

239. Frank Whitson Fetter, *La inflación monetaria en Chile* (Santiago, 1937), pp. xvii–xxv; Carlos Keller, *Nuestro problema monetario* (Santiago, 1932); Guillermo Subercaseaux, *Los nuevos ideales sobre el valor de la moneda* (Santiago, 1930); idem, *Seis años de política monetaria (1933–38)* (Santiago, 1938), esp. pp. 5–6; Mario Antonioletti, *La moneda, el crédito y los bancos* (Santiago, 1934); Juan C. Bravo, *Proyecto de transformación monetaria* (Talca, 1933); Ruffat, *La política monetaria*, pp. 70–95; Arce, *La crisis chilena*, pp. 162–76; Prat, *Artículos económicos*, pp. 22–52.

240. Ellsworth, *Chile, an Economy in Transition*, pp. vii–32.

241. Subercaseaux, *Seis años de política monetaria*, esp. pp. 6–20; Araneda, *Veinte años*, pp. 55–65; Germán Max, *El sistema monetario de Chile y las condiciones de su funcionamiento* (Santiago, 1935).

242. Herrera, *El banco central de Chile*, pp. 11–13.
243. Chile, El Banco Central, *El Banco Central de Chile: reseña de su historia, funciones y organización* (Santiago, 1977); Milton Friedman, *Milton Friedman en Chile* (Santiago, 1975); Alejandro Foxley, *Latin American Experiments in Neo-Conservative Economics* (Berkeley, 1983).

4. Revolution and Regionalism in Ecuador, 1925–1933

1. Ecuador, Dirección General de Estadística, *Comercio exterior de la república del Ecuador en los años 1925 y 1926* (Quito, 1928), pp. 5–10, 692–96; Michael J. Meehan, *The Ecuadorian Market* (Washington, D.C., 1927), pp. 1–10.
2. Ecuador, Ministerio de Hacienda, *Resumen estadístico del comercio exterior de la república del Ecuador en el curso de la década 1911–1920* (Quito, 1923), pp. 7–8, 127; Luis E. Laso, *Contribución al estudio de la economía política ecuatoriana* (Quito, 1930), p. 19; Luis Guillermo Peñaherrera, *El problema económico de la república* (Quito, 1927), p. 19.
3. Víctor Emilio Estrada, *Ensayo sobre la balanza económica del Ecuador* (Guayaquil, 1922), esp. pp. 5–28, 56–60, 76–78, 90–91; Estrada, *La crisis de los cambios en el Ecuador* (Guayaquil, 1924), pp. 7–9. During 1914–21 the average cost of a kilogram of imports jumped from 21 to 54 centavos, while that of a kilogram of exports only inched up from 40 to 45 centavos.
4. Clarence F. Jones, *Commerce of South America* (Boston, 1928), pp. 444–45; Estrada, *Ensayo*, pp. 75–76; Luis Napoleon Dillon, *La crisis económica-financiera del Ecuador* (Quito, 1927), pp. 112–13; Ecuador, *Comercio 1925 y 1926*, p. 841.
5. Naciones Unidas, Comisión Económica para la América Latina, *El desarrollo económico del Ecuador* (Mexico, 1954), p. 18; Lois Crawford de Roberts, *El Ecuador en la época cacaotera* (Quito, 1980).
6. Ecuador, *Comercio 1925 y 1926*, pp. 688–91, 838–39; Ecuador, *Resumen*, pp. 115–20; Jones, *Commerce*, pp. 442–45; Meehan, *Ecuadorian Market*, pp. 14–21; J. R. McKey and H. S. Giusta, *United States Trade with Latin America in 1925. II. Southern Latin America* (Washington, D.C., 1926), pp. 28–29.
7. Max Winkler, *Investments of United States Capital in Latin America* (Boston, 1928), pp. 133–36.
8. United Nations, *Public Debt, 1914–1946* (Lake Success, 1948), pp. 56–57; Edwin W. Kemmerer Papers, Princeton University Library (hereinafter cited as EWK), Box 216, "Ecuador. Public Debt"; "Deudas garantizadas con rentas del estado"; *Resumen histórico de la deuda externa del Ecuador* (Quito, 1923); Eduardo Ríofrío Villagomez, *La deuda pública ecuatoriana* (Quito, 1938), esp. pp. 3–43.
9. Víctor Emilio Estrada, *Conferencia sobre empréstito* (Guayaquil, 1923), pp. 12–19; Ernesto Franco, *Conferencia sobre la crisis actual* (Quito, 1923), pp. 9–23; *El Día*, October 29, 1926, January 14, 1927.
10. Ecuador, *Resumen*, pp. 34–35, 115–18, 120–23; Ecuador, *Comercio 1925 y 1926*, pp. 686–87, 834–35; Estrada, *Ensayo*, pp. 69–75; Ricardo Salvatierra, *Al rededor de la crisis económica actual* (n.p., 1931), p. 13.
11. EWK, Box 133, "Agriculture in the Coastal Plain"; "Economic Recovery, Regeneration, or Tragedy," memorandum from N. Clemente Ponce; La Compañía de Crédito Agrícola e Industrial, *Boletín extraordinario de la Compañía de Crédito Agrícola e Industrial—dedicado a la Misión Kemmerer* (Quito, 1926), pp. 3–10; Estrada, *Ensayo*, pp. 85–91; Peñaherrera, *El problema económico*; *El Día*, October 23, 31, November 2, 5, 6, 1926.
12. Dillon, *La crisis*, pp. 296–98; Estrada, *Ensayo*, pp. 81–83; Naciones Unidas, *El desarrollo*, p.

110; *El Comercio*; February 10, 1927; EWK, Box 133, "Memorandum," from José Rodríguez Bonín; U.S. Department of State (hereinafter cited as USDOS), from Quito, May 15, 1927, 822.51/433. Industry probably employed no more than 2 percent of the active population. Osvaldo Hurtado, *El poder político en el Ecuador*, 2d ed. (Quito, 1977), p. 85; Rafael Quintero, *El mito del populismo en el Ecuador* (Quito, 1980), pp. 208–13.

13. Peñaherrera, *El problema económico*, p. 19; Quintero, *El mito del populismo*, pp. 188–93.

14. Luis Alberto Carbó, *Historia monetaria y cambiaria del Ecuador desde la época colonial* (Quito, 1953), pp. 102–17; Quintero, *El mito del populismo*, pp. 125–37.

15. Miguel Wionczek, *La banca extranjera en América latina* (Lima, 1969), pp. 31–33, 49.

16. Dillon, *La crisis*, pp. 90–91.

17. Laso, *Contribución*, pp. 7–41; idem, *Evolución de los sistemas monetarios y bancos centrales de América latina* (Guayaquil, 1972); Dillon, *La crisis*, pp. 64–67; Ernesto Franco, *Inundación de papeles inconvertibles* (Quito, 1923), pp. 1–17; *El Día*, October 17, 19, 1926; *El Telégrafo*, October 8, 1926.

18. Dillon, *La crisis*, pp. 18–20, 50–67; Peñaherrera, *El problema económico*, pp. 11–39; Víctor Emilio Estrada, *Moneda i bancos en el Ecuador* (n.p., 1925), pp. 40–63.

19. USDOS, from Quito, February 26, 1926, 822.516/27.

20. J. Ricardo Boada Y., *La situación bancaria del Ecuador* (Quito, n.d.), p. 12; La Compañía de Crédito Agrícola, *Boletín extraordinario*, pp. 7–9.

21. Carbó, *Historia monetaria y cambiaria*, pp. 116–17; USDOS, from Quito, July 31, 1925, 822.51/410.

22. Dillon, *La crisis*, pp. 49–55; Quintero, *El mito del populismo*, pp. 136–48; Oscar Efrén Reyes, *Los últimos siete años* (Quito, 1933), pp. 31–44; *El Comercio*, February 24, 1927.

23. Reyes, *Los últimos siete años*, pp. 30–38; Quintero, *El mito del populismo*, pp. 210–11; Hurtado, *El poder político*, pp. 164–66; Víctor Emilio Estrada, *Memorandum al Señor Presidente de la República y al Señor Ministro de Hacienda acerca de la cuestión de precios durante la incautación* (Guayaquil, 1923), pp. 3–12; Alberto Larrea Ch., *El encarecimiento de la vida y sus influencias en la economía del empleado público* (Quito, 1920), pp. 2–26.

24. Víctor Emilio Estrada, *La inconvertibilidad del billete bancario i su solución* (Guayaquil, 1923); Estrada, *Moratoria o conversión?* (Guayaquil, 1921); idem, *La crisis; Moneda i bancos*, esp. pp. 207–12, 363–74; Peñaherrera, *El problema económico*, pp. 20–37; Eduardo Ríofrío Villagomez, "El problema monetario y el problema fiscal en el Ecuador," *Anales de la Universidad Central* 36 (April–June 1926): 258–329; (July–September 1926): 145–57; (July–September 1927): 107–10; Eduardo Larrea S., *Ensayo sobre la moneda* (Quito, 1933), pp. 296–97; Alejandro Moreano, "Capitalismo y lucha de clases en la primera mitad del siglo XX," in Leonardo Mejía et al., eds., *Ecuador: pasado y presente* (Quito, 1975), pp. 137–224.

25. EWK, Box 216, "Ecuador. Public Debt."

26. Louis Baudin, *La estabilización de la moneda ecuatoriana* (Quito, 1928), pp. 6–7; Dillon, *La crisis*, pp. 8–12; Larrea Ch., *El encarecimiento*, p. 24. Also see Linda Alexander Rodríguez, "Ecuador's National Development: Government Finances and the Search for Public Policy, 1830–1940" (Ph.D. diss., University of California at Los Angeles, 1981), which provides extensive coverage of all these issues as well as the Kemmerer mission.

27. Franco, *Inundación*, pp. 6–9; Peñaherrera, *El problema económico*, pp. 10–35; Eduardo Ríofrío Villagomez, "El problema monetario y el problema fiscal en el Ecuador," *Anales de la Universidad Central* 36 (January–March 1926): 21–101; *El Universo*, April 30, 1972.

28. EWK, Box 216, "Ecuador. Public Debt"; "Deudas garantizadas."

29. Hurtado, *El poder político*, pp. 91–93, 119–49; Marcelo Ortíz Villacis, *La ideología burguesa en el Ecuador* (Quito, 1977), pp. 39–40, 66–78. For details on the July Revolution and

subsequent governments in the 1920s, see Luis Robalino Dávila, *El 9 de julio de 1925* (Quito, 1973).

30. Dillon, *La crisis*; Quintero, *El mito del populismo*, pp. 154–213.

31. *El Día*, July 12, 1927; Julio E. Moreno, *La revolución del 9 de julio y el gobierno de la dictadura* (Quito, n.d.), pp. 13–19, 56–76.

32. Reyes, *Los últimos siete años*, pp. 11–83; Hurtado, *El poder político*, pp. 119–31; Víctor Emilio Estrada, *El momento económico en el Ecuador* (Guayaquil, 1950), pp. 36–37; Dillon, *La crisis*; Dillon, *Conferencia sustentada por el Señor don Luis N. Dillon en el Teatro Sucre, el XXVI aniversario del 5 de junio de 1895* (Quito, 1921); *El Comercio*, January 8, 1927; *El Día*, October 23, December 11, 15, 1926.

33. *El Día*, July 9, 1927; Reyes, *Los últimos siete años*, pp. 44–80; Rodríguez, "Ecuador's National Development," pp. 190–91.

34. Ibid.; *El Comercio*, October 6, November 10, 28, 1926, February 21, 22, 1927; Platón, *Ante los hechos. Fragmentos de la historia* (Quito, 1927), pp. 13–17, 43–47; Ecuador, Junta de Gobierno Nacional, *Documentos relacionados con la transformación político-militar del 9 de julio de 1925* (Quito, n.d.), pp. 20–118.

35. Ibid.; Leonidas García, *Conferencia* (Quito, 1925); Kurt von Friede, *Crónicas fugaces (1925–30)* (Guayaquil, 1930), p. 398.

36. Moreano, "Capitalismo y lucha," p. 170; Dillon, *La crisis*, esp. pp. 162–208; García, *Conferencia*, pp. 20–26; La Compañía de Crédito Agrícola e Industrial, *Boletín extraordinario*, p. 15.

37. Moreano, "Capitalismo y lucha," pp. 6–20.

38. Dillon, *La crisis*, pp. 208–53; Reyes, *Los últimos siete años*, pp. 59–83; Ecuador, Ministerio de Hacienda, *Las instituciones de crédito del Ecuador en 1925. I. Banco Comercial y Agrícola (Guayaquil)* (Quito, 1926).

39. García, *Conferencia*, pp. 26–28; Ecuador, Junta, *Documentos*, esp. p. 118; Dillon, *La crisis*, pp. 221–308.

40. Ecuador, Ministerio de Hacienda, *Primera conferencia financiera de banqueros* (Quito, 1926); Ecuador, Conferencias Económicas, *Actas de las Sesiones* (Quito, 1926); Reyes, *Los últimos siete años*, pp. 20–129; La Compañía de Crédito Agrícola, *Boletín extraordinario*, pp. 11–16; *El Comercio*, January 16, March 13, May 1, 1927; Charles A. McQueen, *Latin American Monetary and Exchange Conditions* (Washington, D.C., 1926), pp. 33–35; Banco del Azuay, *Memorandum del Banco del Azuay a la Misión Kemmerer* (Cuenca, 1926); Banco del Pichincha, *Exposición que hace el Banco del Pichincha a la Comisión del Profesor Kemmerer y al pueblo ecuatoriano* (Quito, 1927); Banco de Descuento, *Facts about Ecuador* (Guayaquil, 1926), pp. 9–15; Víctor E. Estrada, *La Caja Central de Emisión y Amortización* (Guayaquil, 1926); *Actas de la Caja Central de Emisión y Amortización, 1926–27* (n.p., n.d.).

41. Ibid.; letter from V. E. Estrada to Humberto Albornoz, November 12, 1925; Banco del Pichincha, *Informes presentados por el directorio del Banco del Pichincha a las juntas generales de accionistas del 24 de enero de 1926 y 15 de enero de 1927, dedicados al estudio de la "Misión Kemmerer"* (Quito, 1927); La Previsora, Banco Comercial y de Ahorros, *Boletín Mensual de la Previsora* (Guayaquil, 1927); Banco del Ecuador, *Revista del Banco del Ecuador* 5, no. 63 (August 8, 1925): 3–5; idem, *Petición hecha por el intendente especial del Banco Comercial y Agrícola y presentada ante el honorable congreso de 1930* (Guayaquil, n.d.), pp. 7–11; EWK, Box 129, "El banco central es una verguenza nacional"; letter from Víctor E. Estrada to Kemmerer, November 11, 1927; USDOS, from Guayaquil, October 23, 1925, 822.516/18; *El Comercio*, October 19, November 10, December 4, 1926; *El Telégrafo*, November 1926, March–August 1927; *El Día*, October 23, December 11, 15, 1926, April 22, September 1,

1927; Platón, *Ante los hechos*, pp. 13–37; Estrada, *El momento*, pp. 42–44; Salvatierra, *Al rededor de la crisis*, pp. 5–13; Moreano, "Capitalismo y lucha," pp. 21–27.

42. Reyes, *Los últimos siete años*, pp. 136–57; Ortíz, *La ideología burguesa*, pp. 66–72; Moreano, "Capitalismo y lucha," pp. 24–26; *El Telégrafo*, May 29, 1927; *El Comercio*, October 5, November 18, 1926; USDOS, from Quito, April 12, 1926, 822.51/423; Isidro Ayora, *Mensaje del presidente provisional de la república a la asamblea nacional* (Quito, 1929), pp. 13–17.

43. Baudin, *La estabilización de la moneda*, pp. 8–9; *El Comercio*, November 28, 1926, February 21, 22, 1927.

44. USDOS, from Washington, September 7, 1923, 822.51A/8; from Quito, August 29, 1923, 822.51A/9; July 28, 1925, 822.51A/21; July 31, 1925, 822.51/410; Reyes, *Los últimos siete años*, pp. 80–83; Robert N. Seidel, "Progressive Pan Americanism: Development and United States Policy toward South America, 1906–1931" (Ph.D. diss., Cornell University, 1973), pp. 226–28; Rodríguez, "Ecuador's National Development," pp. 206–11.

45. USDOS, from Washington, December 18, 1925, 822.51A/23; from Quito, December 14, 1925, 822.516/23; March 2, 1926, 822.51A/24; March 6, 1926, 822.51A/26; March 25, 1926, 822.51A/25; March 30, 1926, 822.51A/30; EWK, Diary, October 10, 1924, p. 284; July 10, 1925, p. 191; Box 32, letter to Sr. Presidente de la República, June 23, 1925; Box 129, letter to Kemmerer from V. E. Estrada, April 5, 1925; Víctor E. Estrada, *El problema económico del Ecuador en 1934*, 2 vols. (Guayaquil, 1934), 2:13.

46. EWK, Box 2, letter from Kemmerer to O. C. Lockhart, May 21, 1926; Box 280, "Robert H. Vorfeld"; Diary, October 15, 1926, p. 288; USDOS, from Washington, October 4, 1926, 822.51A/34.

47. Hurtado, *El poder político*, pp. 129–31, 154–66; *El Comercio*, September 1926 through July 1927, esp. October 17, 19, 20, 21, 1926, February 23, 1927; *El Telégrafo*, December 1, 1926; *El Día*, October 1926 through June 1927, esp. October 21, 1926; EWK, Box 3, letter from Kemmerer to Arthur N. Young, March 24, 1927; Box 2, letter to Kemmerer from La Presidencia de la Sociedad Obrera, November 6, 1926.

48. *El Comercio*, October 21, 28, 1926.

49. *El Día*, October 21, 1926.

50. *El Comercio*, October 19, 1926, March 11, 1927; *El Día*, December 8, 1926; Reyes, *Los últimos siete años*, p. 159; Platón, *Ante los hechos*, p. 39.

51. *El Día*, December 8, 1926, June 16, 1927; *El Comercio*, October 19, 20, 23, 1926, January 18, February 9, 1927.

52. *El Comercio*, October 29, 1926; Banco de Descuento, *Facts about Ecuador*.

53. José Peralta, *La esclavitud de la América latina* (Cuenca, 1961), esp. pp. 11–23, 35–37, 49–52, 69–85.

54. Von Friede, *Crónicas fugaces*, pp. 14–15, 116–17, 331.

55. Ortíz, *La ideología burguesa*, pp. 39, 71–72.

56. Osvaldo Albornoz P., *Del crimen de El Ejido a la revolución del 9 de julio de 1925* (Guayaquil, 1969), pp. 150–52.

57. EWK, Box 2, letter from S. W. Morgan of the Department of State to Kemmerer, (no date).

58. USDOS, from Washington, October 4, 1926, 822.51A/34.

59. USDOS, from Quito, March 14, 1927, 822.51A/45; January 27, 1927, 822.51A/39.

60. EWK, letter from Kemmerer to Arthur N. Young, Department of State, March 24, 1927.

61. EWK, Box 3, letter from Kemmerer to J. Barberis, April 20, 1926.

62. EWK, Box 2; Box 3; Box 129, letters from V. E. Estrada to Kemmerer, November 11, 1927; October 6, 1925; April 5, 1925; *El Comercio*, October 14, 1926; April 5, 1927; *Los trabajos de la comisión Kemmerer* (Quito, 1927), pp. 5–15; Ecuador, *Informe aduanas* (1930), pp. 6–7;

Edwin Walter Kemmerer, Commission of Financial Advisers, *Graphic Charts Prepared in the Financial Survey of the Government by the Mission of Financial Advisers* (n.p., 1927).

63. USDOS, from Quito, October 23, 1926, 822.51A/36; January 27, 1927, 822.51A/39; February 22, 1927, 822.51A/44.

64. Ecuador, *Informe del Director General de Aduanas de la República del Ecuador correspondiente al primer semestre de 1930* (Guayaquil, 1930), p. 7.

65. USDOS, from Quito, February 11, 1927, 822.51A/41.

66. EWK, Box 3, letter from Kemmerer to Arthur N. Young, March 24, 1927.

67. USDOS, from Quito, January 27, 1927, 822.51A/39; February 22, 1937, 822.51A/44.

68. EWK, Book 52; *El Comercio*, March 15, 1927.

69. *Los trabajos*, pp. 2–15; *El Comercio*, March 14, 1927.

70. EWK, Box 3, letter from Kemmerer to Arthur N. Young, March 24, 1927; Moreano, "Capitalismo y lucha," pp. 25–39; Ayora, *Mensaje del presidente provisional*, pp. 17–19.

71. *El Día*, October 24, 1926; *El Comercio*, March 12, 27, 1927; *El Telégrafo*, April 25, 1927.

72. *El Universo*, May 5, 9, 1927.

73. *Actas de las sesiones de la Comisión Organizadora del Banco Central del Ecuador* (Quito, 1927); Ecuador, Departamento de Información, *El Banco Central del Ecuador* (Quito, 1927). For further information on the history of the Central Bank of Ecuador, see Banco Central del Ecuador, *Cincuenta años* (n.p., n.d.); Irving Iván Zapater, *Indices del Boletín del Banco Central del Ecuador, 1927–1976* (Quito, 1977).

74. Banco Central del Ecuador, Directorio, *Libro e actas*, 2 vols. (n.p., n.d.); *El Comercio*, March 11, May 10, 28, June 3, 1927; *Actas de las sesiones de la Comisión Organizadora*, pp. 5–6; USDOS, from Quito, July 27, 1927, 822.516/71.

75. EWK, Box 129, letters to Kemmerer from E. B. Schwulst, September 9, 29, 1927.

76. Banco Central, Directorio, *Libro*, 1:362–63, 2:120–22; *El Telégrafo*, May 16, June 23, 24, August, 1927; *El Comercio*, June 3, 19, 22, 25, 1927; *El Universo*, April 9, 16, 1927; Moreano, "Capitalismo y lucha," pp. 27–32.

77. Peñaherrera, *El problema económico*, esp. pp. 27–47; Estrada, *El problema 1934*, 2:25–44; EWK, Box 32, "Memoranda on the Conferences which the Kemmerer Commission held . . . Guayas," December, 1926.

78. *El Día*, July 5, August 2, September 28, 1947; Ecuador, Departamento de Información, *El Banco*, pp. 56–57; Ernesto Franco, *Nuestra crisis económica. Sus causas y remedios* (Quito, 1941), pp. 63–64.

79. EWK, Box 32, "Memoranda on the Conferences."

80. *El Telégrafo*, June 22, 1927; *El Comercio*, May 14, June 19, 1927.

81. *El Día*, June 21, 22, 1927; *El Comercio*, June 22, 23, 1927; *El Telégrafo*, April 3, June 21, 1927.

82. *Actas de la Caja Central*; Caja Central de Emisión y Amortización, *Informe 1926*; Ecuador, Conferencias, *Actas*, pp. 312–23, 419–20; Ecuador, Cámara de Diputados, *Cámara de Diputados, 1924*, no. 130, pp. 3–10; *El Telégrafo*, August 30, 1924; *El Comercio*, October 1, 1925; USDOS, from Guayaquil, October 23, 1925, 822.516/18; EWK, Box 129, letter to Kemmerer from V. E. Estrada, October 6, 1925; "Text of Spanish Chart Central Bank in Ecuador"; Ecuador, Commission of Financial Advisers, *Project of Law for the Creation of the Central Bank of Ecuador* (Quito, 1927).

83. *Actas de las sesiones de la Comisión Organizadora*; *El Comercio*, May 1, 6, 1927; *El Día*, November 2, 1926; EWK, Box 32, "Memoranda on the Conferences."

84. *El Comercio*, March 17, 18, May 9, 1927; *El Telégrafo*, December 1, 1926; *El Universo*, April 20, 22, 1927; *Actas de las sesiones de la Comisión Organizadora*, pp. 5–8; Ecuador, Banco

Central del Ecuador, *Segundo Informe Anual 1929*, pp. 8–9. Dillon was chosen as one of the initial directors of the bank by the Chamber of Commerce of Quito, but he died in 1929.

85. *El Universo*, May 14, 1927; *El Telégrafo*, May 28, June 5, 1927; Estrada, *El problema 1934*, 2:104–5.

86. *El Comercio*, October 1, 1925, February 18, 1927; Estrada, *El problema 1934*, 2:21–22; Estrada, *La Caja Central*, pp. 14–18; Ecuador, Banco Central del Ecuador, *Segundo Informe*, pp. 55–56.

87. Ecuador, Commission, *Project Central Bank*, pp. 24, 100–105; *Actas de la Caja Central*; Ecuador, Banco Central del Ecuador, *Segundo Informe*, pp. 43–47; Ríofrío, *La deuda*, pp. 55–56; Víctor E. Estrada, *A Recent Monetary Stabilization in South America: The Central Bank of Ecuador* (Guayaquil, 1928), pp. 3–8; *El Comercio*, March 8, 1927.

88. Ecuador, Banco Central del Ecuador, *Boletín Mensual del Banco Central del Ecuador* 1, no. 2 (September 1927): 33; 2, no. 16 (November 1928): 5; Víctor E. Estrada, *Un caso de estabilización previa a una deflación monetaria, 1927–31* (Guayaquil, 1934), pp. 12–22; idem, *Recent Monetary Stabilization*, pp. 10–11.

89. EWK, Box 32, "Memoranda on the Conferences."

90. Banco Central, Directorio, *Libro*, 1:366–67; idem, *Boletín* 3, no. 25 (August 1929): 34; Carbó, *Historia monetaria y cambiaria*, p. 165.

91. *El Universo*, May 7, 1927.

92. Ecuador, Banco Central, *Boletín* 2, no. 16 (November 1928): 5–7; idem, *Segundo Informe*, pp. 18–19; Ecuador, Banco Central del Ecuador, *Cuarto Informe*, p. 20; Alberto Larrea Ch., *Algunas opiniones del Profesor Kemmerer y mis puntos de vista* (Quito, 1931), pp. 25–28.

93. *El Comercio*, January 15, 1927; *El Día*, August 5, 1927; *Actas de las sesiones de la Comisión Organizadora*, pp. 3–7; Ecuador, Banco Central, Directorio, *Libro*, 2:24–32; idem, *Boletín* 1, no. 3 (October 1927): 5–11; Larrea S., *Ensayo sobre la moneda*, pp. 301–9; EWK, Box 129, letter to Kemmerer from V. E. Estrada, November 11, 1927.

94. Ríofrío, *La deuda*, p. 58.

95. Ecuador, Banco Central, *Boletín* 1, no. 8 (March 1928): 3–5; no. 11 (June 1928): 8; idem, *Segundo Informe*, p. 55; Carbó, *Historia monetaria y cambiaria*, pp. 164–67.

96. Ecuador, Conferencias, *Actas*, esp. pp. 7–52, 274–77; *El Comercio*, October 1, 1925; October 12, 1926; January 12, 14, February 7, 1927; Eduardo Ríofrío Villagomez, "El problema monetario y el problema fiscal en el Ecuador," *Anales de la Universidad Central* 36 (October–December 1926): 270–93; C. A. Alvarez, *Estudio teórico-práctico del cambio del dollar con respecto al sucre* (Quito, 1926).

97. Ecuador, Conferencias, *Actas*, pp. 272–304; Baudin, *La estabilización de la moneda*, pp. 9–13; Ecuador, Commission of Financial Advisers, *Project of a Monetary Law* (Quito, 1927); idem, *Supplement to the Report in Support of a Monetary Law* (Quito, 1927).

98. Estrada, *Un caso de estabilización*, pp. 3–16; EWK, Box 129, letter to Kemmerer from Minister of Finance P. L. Núñez, February 21, 1927.

99. Estrada, *Un caso de estabilización*, pp. 10–16; Eduardo Ríofrío Villagomez, *Manual de ciencia de hacienda*, 2 vols. (Quito, 1936, 1938), 1:60–67; Larrea S., *Ensayo sobre la moneda*, pp. 302–3; Luis Eduardo Laso, *La formación de un sistema nacional de crédito* (Quito, 1942), pp. 35–36.

100. Banco Comercial y Agrícola, *Informe* (Guayaquil, 1927); Banco de Descuento, *Facts about Ecuador*, pp. 8–10; Banco de Descuento, *Why Not Securities from Ecuador?* (Guayaquil, 1927); Banco del Pichincha, *Informes*, pp. 31–32.

101. Ecuador, La Superintendencia de Bancos, *Origen y funciónes del sistema en el Ecuador* (Quito, n.d.).

102. Ecuador, Conferencias, *Actas*, pp. 40–41, 333–49; EWK, Box 130, "Economic Conferences, Session of March 7, 1926."

103. Republic of Ecuador, Commission of Financial Advisers, *Project of a General Banking Law* (Quito, 1927); Laso, *La formación*, pp. 10–35; Larrea S., *Ensayo sobre la moneda*, p. 308; V. E. Estrada, *El Banco del Pichincha (1906–31)* (Quito, 1931), pp. 1–9; Ecuador, Superintendencia de Bancos, *Informe que el Superintendente presenta al Señor Ministro de Hacienda relativo a las labores del departamento en 1930* (Quito, 1931), p. 9.

104. Ecuador, Ministro de Hacienda, *Informe del Ministro de Hacienda don S. Sáenz de Tejada y D. a la H. Asamblea Nacional refutando el presentado por Harry L. Tompkins* (Quito, 1929); idem, *Comentarios acerca del informe presentado por el Superintendente de Bancos al Sr. Ministro de Hacienda* (Quito, 1929); *El Comercio*, February 10, 1927; *El Universo*, May 13, 1927; Von Friede, *Crónicas fugaces*, pp. 14–15.

105. Estrada, *El problema 1934*; EWK, Box 3, letter to Kemmerer from A. Moncayo Andrade, August 2, 1930; *Petición del Banco Comercial y Agrícola*.

106. Ecuador, Commission, *Project Banking*, pp. 42–44; Ecuador, *El Banco Hipotecario del Ecuador* (Quito, 1928).

107. Republic of Ecuador, Commission of Financial Advisers, *Project of a Law Governing Agricultural Security Contracts* (Quito, 1927).

108. Banco Central del Ecuador, *Boletín* 1, no. 5 (December 1927): 3–21.

109. Reyes, *Los últimos siete años*, esp. p. 166; Hurtado, *El poder político*, pp. 92–93; Fredrick B. Pike, *The United States and the Andean Republics: Peru, Bolivia, and Ecuador* (Cambridge, 1977), pp. 191–97; Carlos Rodríguez Peñaherrera, *Evolución y desarrollo del sistema administrativo ecuatoriano* (Quito, 1978), pp. 1–25.

110. Republic of Ecuador, Commission of Financial Advisers, *Project of an Organic Budget Law* (Quito, 1927); Ecuador, *La nueva ley de hacienda* (Quito, 1927); EWK, Diary, November 10, 1926, p. 314; *El Día*, October 20, December 10, 1926; *El Comercio*, December 7, 1926.

111. Ecuador, Departamento de Información, *El presupuesto del estado para 1928* (Quito, 1928), pp. 1–12.

112. Ecuador, Ministerio de Hacienda, *Ley orgánica de hacienda* (Quito, 1927).

113. *La Nación*, November 19, 1927.

114. Ríofrío, *Manual*, 1:20–21, 143–44; Larrea S., *Ensayo sobre la moneda*, pp. 299–300; Reyes, *Los últimos siete años*, pp. 171–80; Ernesto Franco, *Conferencia pública sobre la crisis económica y fiscal* (Quito, 1931), pp. 5–20.

115. EWK, Box 3, letter to Kemmerer from A. Moncayo Andrade, August 2, 1930; Ecuador, Dirección del Tesoro, *Informe de la Dirección del Tesoro* (Quito, 1931); Ecuador, *El presupuesto*; Ecuador, Ministerio de Hacienda, *Boletín de Hacienda* (Quito, 1928).

116. Ecuador, Contraloría General de la Nación, *Reseña histórica de la Contraloría General del Ecuador* (Quito, 1977); Ecuador, *La nueva ley de hacienda*, pp. 5–24; *El Comercio*, November 5, 6, 1926.

117. Republic of Ecuador, Commission of Financial Advisers, *Project of Law for the Reorganization of the Government Accounting and Auditing and the Creation of the Contraloría* (Quito, 1927).

118. EWK, Box 3, letter to Kemmerer from A. Moncayo Andrade, August 2, 1930, pp. 10–12; USDOS, from Quito, June 29, 1927, 822.51A/54; *El Comercio*, June 25, 1927; *El Día*, September 30, 1927; Peralta, *La esclavitud de la América latina*, pp. 83–84.

119. James H. Edwards, *Informe que el Señor James H. Edwards, Ex-Contralor General de la República del Ecuador, presenta a la Asamblea Nacional de 1928–1929* (Quito, 1929); Ecuador, Contraloría, *Reseña*; USDOS, from Quito, March 14, 1927, 822.51A/45.

120. Ecuador, Dirección del Tesoro, pp. 9–21.

121. Republic of Ecuador, Commission of Financial Advisers, *Report on the Organization of the Tax Administration Divisions of the Ministry of Finance* (Quito, 1927).

122. Republic of Ecuador, Commission of Financial Advisers, *Project of Law to be Substituted for the Present Law Imposing a Tax on Incomes* (Quito, 1927); Ecuador, Ministerio de Hacienda, *Lo que se dice y lo que es el impuesto a la renta* (Quito, 1930); idem, *Instrucciónes para la aplicación del impuesto a la renta* (Quito, 1930); Hurtado, *El poder político*, pp. 129–30; Estrada, *La crisis*, p. 23; Ríofrío, *Manual*, 1:345, 486–87.

123. Republic of Ecuador, Commission of Financial Advisers, *Report on the Stamp Tax* (Quito, 1927).

124. Republic of Ecuador, Commission of Financial Advisers, *Report on the Administration of the Government Alcohol Monopoly* (Quito, 1927).

125. Republic of Ecuador, Commission of Financial Advisers, *Project of Law for the Revision of the Present Tax on Rural Property* (Quito, 1927).

126. EWK, Box 133, "From the Review of the National Society of Agriculture," October, 1926; Box 3, letter to Kemmerer from Andrade, August 2, 1930, p. 16; Reyes, *Los últimos siete años*, pp. 90–91; *El Comercio*, December 2, 7, 1926.

127. EWK, Box 3, letter from Andrade, August 2, 1930, p. 14; Ecuador, Dirección del Tesoro, pp. 11–21; Larrea S., *Ensayo sobre la moneda*, p. 300.

128. Republic of Ecuador, Commission of Financial Advisers, *Project of Law Governing Customs Administration*; idem, *Project of a Customs Import Tariff* (Quito, 1927); idem, *Proposed Decree Governing Customs Documents Originating Abroad*; idem, *Project of Law for the Revision of the Present Export Duties on Ivory Nuts* (Quito, 1926); *El Comercio*, January 18, February 2, 1927.

129. EWK, Box 129, letter to Kemmerer from E. B. Schwulst, September 9, 1927; USDOS, from Quito, January 11, 1928, 822.51/450; December 5, 1929, 822.51A/86; *El Comercio*, April 2, 17, 1927; Ecuador, *Informe Aduanas*; Ecuador, Dirección del Tesoro, pp. 17–18.

130. Estrada, *Memorandum*, pp. 26–27; *El Día*, August 3, 7, 12, 1927.

131. Estrada, *El problema 1934*, 2:50–52; Larrea Ch., *Algunas opiniones*, pp. 29–31; Franco, *Conferencia pública*, pp. 9–22; Ríofrío, *Manual*, 2:301–2.

132. *El Día*, October 29, 1926, January 14, 1927; *El Comercio*, January 13, 14, 1927; Ríofrío, *La deuda*; Franco, *Nuestra crisis*, pp. 62–63; USDOS, from Quito, May 28, 1928, 822.51/474; Ecuador, *El presupuesto*, pp. 16–18.

133. Republic of Ecuador, Commission of Financial Advisers, *Report on Public Credit* (Quito, 1927); Estrada, *Un caso de estabilización*, pp. 5–6.

134. USDOS, from Washington, October 11, 1927, 822.51A/57; December 29, 1927, 822.51A/59; EWK, Diary, December 29, 1927, p. 364.

135. EWK, Diary, November 17, p. 322; December 2, p. 337; December 8, p. 343; December 14, p. 349; December 21, p. 356 (1927); USDOS, from Washington, November 10, 1927, 822.51/440; from Quito, January 27, 1928, 822.51/447; January 30, 193, 822.51/451; May 28, 1928, 822.51/474; September 12, 1928, 822.51/489; Francis White Papers, Box 4, Folder B, letter to Gerhard A. Bading, Quito, October 5, 1928; Box 1, "Ecuador," conversation with Juan Barberis, August 30, 1927; Von Friede, *Crónicas fugaces*, p. 331; Franco, *Nuestra crisis*.

136. República del Ecuador, *Ley y reglamento del estanco de fósforos* (Quito, 1928); EWK, Diary, October 27, 1927, p. 301; EWK Papers, Box 132; *El Universo*, May 16, 1927; Banco del Azuay, *Memorandum*.

137. Republic of Ecuador, Commission of Financial Advisers, *Report on the Construction of Public Works* (Quito, 1927); *El Universo*, April 14, 1927; Ecuador, *El presupuesto*, pp. 18–19.

138. Salvatierra, *Al rededor de la crisis*, pp. 13–14; Estrada, *El problema 1934*, 2:46–50; Ayora, *Mensaje del presidente provisional*, pp. 48–51; Great Britain, Department of Overseas Trade,

Economic and Financial Conditions in Ecuador (hereinafter cited as GBDOT) (1930), p. 12; Charles Cunningham, *Economic and Financial Conditions in Ecuador*, (Washington, D.C., 1931), pp. 26–27.

139. Republic of Ecuador, Commission of Financial Advisers, *Report on the Projected Quito-Esmeraldas Railway* (Quito, 1927); *El Comercio*, February 11, 14, 1927; Reyes, *Los últimos siete años*, pp. 164–65.

140. USDOS, from Washington, October 4, 1926, 822.51A/34; October 11, 1927, 822.51A/57.

141. Republic of Ecuador, Commission of Financial Advisers, *Memorandum on Functional Organization and Activities of the Administrative Branch of the Government*; idem, *Informe concerniente a la reforma de ciertos artículos de la constitución*; idem, *Proposed Amendments to the Code of Civil Procedure and the Organic Law of the Judiciary*; idem, *Project of Law Amending the Penal Code*; idem, *Report on Municipal Finances* (Quito, 1927).

142. *El Comercio*, November 18, 1926; Peralta, *La esclavitud de la América latina*, pp. 78–83.

143. *El Comercio*, February 10, 19, 20, 1927.

144. *El Día*, February 13, September 13, 1927; Peralta, *La esclavitud de la América latina*, pp. 83–84. For details on these episodes, see Rodríguez, "Ecuador's National Development," pp. 224–52.

145. Reyes, *Los últimos siete años*, pp. 167–68.

146. USDOS, from Quito, March 28, 1929, 822.51A/73; Ecuador, *Constitución política de la República del Ecuador dictada por la Asamblea Nacional Constituyente de 1928–29* (Quito, 1929).

147. USDOS, from Washington, January 31, 1928, 822.51A/61; Reyes, *Los últimos siete años*, pp. 168–69.

148. USDOS, from Quito, October 30, 1928, 822.51A/66; November 15, 1928, 822.51A/67.

149. USDOS, from Quito, June 26, 1929, 822.51A/79.

150. USDOS, from Quito, May 13, 1929, 822.51A/75; Edwards, *Informe*.

151. Reyes, *Los últimos siete años*, pp. 169–72.

152. During 1927–31 the relative standing of Ecuador's trading partners underwent no change, with the United States purchasing nearly 50 percent of exports and supplying approximately 40 percent of imports, thus remaining far ahead of second-place Great Britain and third-place Germany. GBDOT (1928), pp. 14–15; ibid. (1930), pp. 13–14; ibid. (1933), pp. 18–19; Ecuador, Banco Central del Ecuador, *Segundo Informe*, pp. 14–15; idem, *Boletín* 1, no. 12 (July 1928): 13–16; Cunningham, *Economic and Financial Conditions in Ecuador*, pp. 14–15.

153. Ecuador, Dirección del Tesoro, *Informe Anual* (1932), pp. 19–23; Víctor E. Estrada, *Memorandum relativo a la posición económica del Ecuador en 1930* (Guayaquil, 1930), pp. 11–12.

154. GBDOT (1933), pp. 18–20.

155. Cunningham, *Economic and Financial Conditions in Ecuador*; Ecuador, Banco Central del Ecuador, *Boletín* 3, no. 24 (October 1929): 15; no. 28 (November 1929): 11; EWK, Box 3, letter to Kemmerer from A. Moncayo Andrade, August 2, 1930, p. 4; Raimundo Flores Chiriboga, *Sugerencias que hace al Honorable Congreso Nacional, para remediar la crisis que aqueja a la República* (Quito, 1934).

156. Quintero, *El mito del populismo*, pp. 336–39.

157. Estrada, *Memorandum relativo a la posicion*, pp. 2–3, 37–39; EWK, Box 3, letter from V. E. Estrada to Kemmerer, May 30, 1931.

158. Ríofrío, *Manual*, 1:65; Quintero, *El mito del populismo*, p. 333; Cunningham, *Economic and Financial Conditions in Ecuador*, pp. 16–18; Ecuador, Banco Central del Ecuador, *Boletín* 4, no. 38 (September 1930): 5–26.

159. EWK, Box 3, letter to Kemmerer from Andrade, August 2, 1930; Ecuador, Banco Central del Ecuador, *Boletín* 4, no. 42 (January 1931): 3–6.

160. Larrea S., *Ensayo sobre la moneda*, pp. 323–24; Franco, *Conferencia pública*, pp. 7–13.

161. Franco, *Nuestra crisis*, pp. 38–45; Larrea Ch., *Algunas opiniones*, pp. 10–21.

162. Estrada, *Memorandum relativo a la posicion*, pp. 17–23; Salvatierra, *Al rededor de la crisis*, pp. 17–23; EWK, Box 3, letters to Kemmerer from A. Moncayo Andrade, August 2, 1930; October 30, 1931; January 6, 1933; GBDOT (1933), pp. 8–9; Larrea S., *Ensayo sobre la moneda*, pp. 273–74; Reyes, *Los últimos siete años*, pp. 159–63.

163. EWK, Box 3, letter from Kemmerer to A. Moncayo Andrade, February 14, 1933.

164. S. Sáenz de Tejada, *Acotaciones a los puntos de vista del Sr. Dr. D. Alberto Larrea Chiriboga, Superintendente de Bancos y Ex-Profesor de Economía de la Universidad Central* (Quito, 1931); Ecuador, Banco Central del Ecuador, *Boletín* 3 (1929–30); idem, *Segundo Informe*; idem, *Cuarto Informe*; EWK, Box 3, letter to Kemmerer from Cueva, December 16, 1930; "Puntos de vista y comentarios de los delegados del Banco Central del Ecuador al memorandum boliviano."

165. Carbó, *Historia monetaria y cambiaria*, pp. 180–90.

166. Larrea Ch., *Algunas opiniones*; Larrea S., *Ensayo sobre la moneda*, pp. 311–17; Moreano, "Capitalismo y lucha," pp. 175–91; Quintero, *El mito del populismo*, pp. 253–352; Ortiz, *La ideología burguesa*, pp. 78–111.

167. Ecuador, Banco Central del Ecuador, *Boletín* 3, no. 25 (August 1929): 18–20; idem, *Cuarto Informe*, p. 7; EWK, Box 3, "Proyecto de reformas a la ley orgánica del Banco Central del Ecuador"; letter from Kemmerer to Cueva, December 27, 1930.

168. Carbó, *Historia monetaria y cambiaria*, pp. 186–214; Larrea S., *Ensayo sobre la moneda*, pp. 329–40; Laso, *Evolución de los sistemas*, pp. 48–49.

169. Ríofrío, *La deuda*, pp. 59–60; Estrada, *El momento*, pp. 3–38.

170. Ecuador, Banco Central del Ecuador, *Boletín* 4, no. 40 (November 1930): 25; Ecuador, Director del Tesoro, *Informe Anual del Director del Tesoro* (Quito, 1931, 1932); GBDOT (1930), pp. 10–11; (1933), pp. 10–11; Cunningham, *Economic and Financial Conditions in Ecuador*, pp. 20–24; Rodríguez, "Ecuador's National Development," pp. 259–60.

171. GBDOT (1930), pp. 10–11; ibid. (1933), pp. 12–13; United Nations, *Public Debt*, pp. 56–57; Franco, *Conferencia pública*, pp. 32–33; Ríofrío, *La deuda*, pp. 32–43.

172. Quintero, *El mito del populismo*, pp. 253–352; Ortíz, *La ideología burguesa*, pp. 78–111; EWK, Box 3, letter to Kemmerer from A. Moncayo Andrade, January 6, 1933; Víctor Emilio Estrada, *La tragedia monetaria del Ecuador* (Guayaquil, 1940); Banco Central del Ecuador, *Cincuenta años.*

173. Rodríguez, "Ecuador's National Development."

5. Exporting Tin, Gold, and Laws from Bolivia, 1927–1932

1. For general information on the Bolivian economy, see Naciones Unidas, *El desarrollo económico de Bolivia* (Mexico, 1958); Carlos Harms Espejo, *Bolivia en sus diversas fases, principalmente económica* (Santiago, 1922); Julio Paz, *Historia económica de Bolivia* (La Paz, 1927); Ramon Piriz Coelho and Ernesto Barth, *Bolivia y sus riquezas* (La Paz, 1930); Augusto Guzmán, *Historia de Bolivia*, 4th ed. (La Paz, 1976); Herbert S. Klein, *Bolivia: The Evolution of a Multi-Ethnic Society* (New York, 1982); W. L. Schurz, *Bolivia: A Commercial and Industrial Handbook* (Washington, D.C., 1921).

2. Naciones Unidas, *Desarrollo económico de Bolivia*, pp. 7–27, 54–56; Bolivia, Ministerio de Hacienda e Industria, Sección Economía Social, *Boletín No. 1 B. El comercio internacional de Bolivia* (La Paz, 1927), pp. 1–18; Eduardo López Rivas, *Esquema de la historia económica de*

Bolivia (Oruro, 1955), pp. 56–68; Luis Peñaloza, *Historia económica de Bolivia*, 2 vols. (La Paz, 1954), 2:157–209.

3. Naciones Unidas, *Desarrollo económico de Bolivia*, pp. 8–9; René Gutiérrez Guerra, *Reorganización financiera de Bolivia* (Oruro, 1936), pp. 52–53.

4. Clarence Jones, *Commerce of South America* (Boston, 1928), pp. 412–13; Margaret Alexander Marsh, *The Bankers in Bolivia* (New York, 1928), p. 231; Robert W. Dunn, *American Foreign Investments* (New York, 1926), pp. 65–66; Frederick M. Halsey and James C. Corliss, *Investments in Latin America*, vol. 4. *Bolivia* (Washington, D.C., 1927), pp. 6–7; Laurence Whitehead, "El impacto de la gran depresión en Bolivia," *Desarrollo Económico* 12, no. 45 (April–June 1972): 49–80.

5. Marsh, *Bankers in Bolivia*; Jorge Palenque, *Estadística boliviana. Primera y segunda parte* (La Paz, 1933), pp. 14–25; Naciones Unidas, *Desarrollo económico de Bolivia*, pp. 11–13; Halsey and Corliss, *Investments in Latin America*, pp. 10–15; United Nations, *Public Debt, 1914–1946* (Lake Success, 1948), pp. 25–26; Charles A. McQueen, *The Bolivian Public Debt* (Washington, D.C., 1924); René Ballivián Calderón, *El concepto del enriquecimiento del estado* (La Paz, 1937), pp. 34, 129–31; Edmundo Vázquez, *Nociones de finanzas generales y hacienda pública de Bolivia* (La Paz, 1939), pp. 484–89.

6. Marsh, *Bankers in Bolivia*, esp. pp. 98–135; La Comisión Fiscal Permanente, *Primera Memoria presentada al Ministerio de Hacienda* (La Paz, 1924); idem, *Tercera Memoria presentada al Ministerio de Hacienda* (La Paz, 1926); Emily S. Rosenberg, "American Foreign Financial Advising in Latin America Before the Great Depression: Form and Structure," MS, 1985.

7. Marsh, *Bankers in Bolivia*, pp. 4–7, 106–27, 226–27; Vázquez, *Nociones*, pp. 328–329; *Bolivia Económica e Industrial* 1, no. 4 (July 1931): 308; Augusto Fajardo Rodríguez, *La deuda pública nacional* (La Paz, 1929), pp. 38–54.

8. José E. Rivera, *Los empréstitos extranjeros y la política americana* (La Paz, 1925), pp. 1–3, 71–99.

9. Marsh, *Bankers in Bolivia*, pp. 35–63; United Nations, *Foreign Capital in Latin America* (New York, 1955), p. 44.

10. *Boletín Comercial* 9, no. 320 (April 3, 1927): 9–33.

11. *El Diario*, March 22, June 14, 1927; Asociación de Industriales Mineros de Bolivia, *El porvenir del estaño en Bolivia* (La Paz, 1927); *Informes Especiales para los Socios* 1, no. 12 (January 30, 1927): 121–25; no. 13 (February 2, 1927): i–ix; *Boletín Nacional de Minería y Comercio* 1, no. 1 (September 18, 1928); Augusto Céspedes, *El dictador suicida (40 años de historia de Bolivia)* (Santiago, 1956), pp. 70–77; McQueen, *Bolivian Public Finance* (Washington, D.C., 1925), p. 9; Gutiérrez, *Reorganización*, pp. 25–27.

12. U.S. Department of State (hereinafter cited as USDOS), from La Paz, September 21, 1927, 824.51/435; Bolivia, Dirección General de Agricultura y Ganadería, *Revista de Agricultura y Ganadería* 1, no. 1 (May 1927): 3–5; no. 2 (November 1927): 5–18, 51; Arturo Taborga and Jesús Lozada, *Trabajos presentados a la Misión Kemmerer por los asesores de Cochabamba . . .* (Cochabamba, 1927), pp. 2–31; Máximo J. de Vacano, *Bolivia, su desarrollo y progreso, reflejos sobre su pasado, presente y porvenir* (Berlin, 1925), pp. 209–13; *El Diario*, March 30, April 3, 13, 1927; *El Republicano*, June 3, 1927; Halsey and Corliss, *Investments in Latin America*, pp. 46–47; Naciones Unidas, *Desarrollo económico de Bolivia*, p. 13.

13. Edwin W. Kemmerer Papers, Princeton University Library (herinafter cited as EWK), Box 88; *La Razón*, March 30, 1927.

14. EWK, Box 67, "Ligera reseña de los bancos de emisión, de préstamos, y casas bancarias"; René Gómez García and Rubén Darío Flores, *La banca nacional* (La Paz, 1962), pp. 39–58; Charles A. McQueen, *Currency, Exchange, and Banking in Bolivia* (Washington, D.C., 1924), pp. 12–

21; José Crespo G., *Bancos y sistemas bancarios en Bolivia* (La Paz, 1922); Francisco Belzu Muñoz, *Algunas notas históricas sobre el Banco Central de Bolivia* (La Paz, 1970).

15. Schurz, *Commercial and Industrial Handbook*, pp. 243–44; McQueen, *Bolivian Public Finance*, pp. 76–79.

16. Marsh, *Bankers in Bolivia*, pp. 110–13; Palenque, *Estadística boliviana*, p. 93; López Rivas, *Esquema de la historia*, pp. 61–71; Belzu, *Algunas notas históricas*, pp. 8–9; Crespo G., *Bancos y sistemas bancarios*, pp. 98–118; René Gutiérrez Guerra, *Al margen del sistema emisor boliviano* (n.p., 1920), pp. 5–17, 40–52; M. Mier y Leon, *Comentarios de la actualidad. A propósito de las reformas bancarias de la Misión Kemmerer* (Oruro, 1929).

17. USDOS, from La Paz, October 22, 1926, 824.51/391; EWK, Box 68, "Notes on Minutes of Junta Controladora de Cambio"; "El Cambio Internacional"; United Nations, *Public Debt*, p. 25; Palenque, *Estadística boliviana* p. 89; Peñaloza, *Historia económica de Bolivia*, p. 314; Charles A. McQueen, *Latin American Monetary and Exchange Conditions* (Washington, D.C., 1926), pp. 38–40; McQueen, *Bolivian Public Finance*, pp. 557–74; Casto Rojas, *La moneda de oro en Bolivia* (Lima, 1911); Julio Benavides Manzaneda, *Historia de la moneda en Bolivia* (La Paz, 1972).

18. Palenque, *Estadística boliviana*, pp. 41–73; Casto Rojas, *Historia financiera de Bolivia* (La Paz, 1916); Charles A. McQueen, *The Bolivian Fiscal System* (Washington, D.C., 1924); idem, *Bolivian Public Finance*.

19. René Gutiérrez Guerra, *Reforma tributaria en Bolivia* (La Paz, 1923); W. Jaime Molins, *El despertar de una nación (Bolivia)* (Buenos Aires, 1925); Rivera, *Los empréstitos*, pp. 74–84.

20. *El Diario*, March 30, April 28, 1927; *Industria y Comercio* 3, no. 149 (January 31, 1927): 1–2; EWK, Box 69, "Pledged and Specially Destined Revenues"; Oscar F. Montecinos, *Apuntes financieros* (La Paz, 1927); Vicente Mendoza López, *Las finanzas en Bolivia y la estrategia capitalista* (La Paz, 1940), pp. 45–49; Ballivián Calderón, *El concepto del enriquecimiento*, pp. 123–31; McQueen, *The Bolivian Fiscal System*, pp. 16–19; Fajardo, *La deuda pública*, pp. 102–4.

21. Céspedes, *El dictador suicida*, pp. 86–96; Hernando Siles, *Mensaje del presidente constitucional de la república al congreso nacional de 1926* (La Paz, 1926); Benigno Carrasco, *Hernando Siles* (La Paz, 1961); José E. Rivera, *Los factores de la producción y la defensa nacional* (La Paz, 1926), pp. 103–6; Ernest Galarza, "Debts, Dictatorship, and Revolution in Bolivia and Peru," *Foreign Policy Reports* 7, no. 5 (May 13, 1931): 101–18.

22. USDOS, from La Paz, January 6, 1926, 824.51/345; January 31, 1926, 824.51/349; Siles, *Mensaje del presidente constitucional*, p. 30; Frederick B. Pike, *The United States and the Andean Republics: Peru, Bolivia, and Ecuador* (Cambridge, 1977), p. 197.

23. EWK, Box 268, letter from Consul General Alberto Palacios, May 20, 1926; Gómez and Darío, *La banca nacional*, pp. 102–3ff.

24. *La Razón*, March 30, June 26, 1927; *El Diario*, April 5, March 31, 1927; *Industria y Comercio* 5, no. 166 (June 21, 1927): 8–9; Herbert Klein, *Politics and Political Change in Bolivia* (London, 1969), pp. 93–105.

25. *El País*, March 30, 1927; *El Diario*, March 29, April 3, 5, 1927; *La Razón*, April 9, 1927.

26. *El Diario*, March 31, April 14, May 13, 1927.

27. *La Razón*, March 30, April 1, July 22, 1927; *La Capital*, April 8, 1927; *Industria y Comercio* 5, no. 165 (June 11, 1927): 3; no. 166 (June 21, 1927): 8–9; Gómez and Darío, *La banca nacional*, p. 12; Marsh, *Bankers in Bolivia*, pp. 134–35.

28. *El Diario*, March 30, 31, April 9, 13, May 14, 1927; *La Razón*, March 30, April 1, 1927; Vázquez, *Nociones*, p. 326; EWK, Diary, March 29, p. 89; March 30, p. 90, 1927.

29. *El Diario*, April 14, June 14, 1927; *La Patria*, June 8, 1927; EWK, Box 268, "La Paz Confer-

ences"; Julio C. Alborta, *Los intereses creados frente a los intereses generales de la nación (breve estudio económico que el autor dedica a la Misión Kemmerer)* (La Paz, 1927); Taborga and Lozada, *Trabajos*, pp. 2–7.

30. For most of the Kemmerer legislation, see Francisco Mendoza, *La Misión Kemmerer en Bolivia* (La Paz, 1927). For a survey of the recommendations of the Kemmerer mission, see André Labrouquére, *La Bolivie nouvelle: ses problémes financiers* (Paris, 1933), esp. pp. 60–93; *El Diario*, July 5, 1927; USDOS, from Washington, October 11, 1927, 822.51A/57.

31. Bolivia, Legislatura Extraordinario de 1927–28, *Redactor de la H. Camara de Diputados* (La Paz, 1929), 8:456–542ff.; USDOS, from Washington, October 11, 1927, 822.51A/57; from La Paz, February 16, 1928, 824.51/447; July 9, 1928, 824.51D 581/34; *Industria y Comercio* 4, no. 198 (April 14, 1928): 1–3; *La Razón*, July 10, 29, 1927; *El Diario*, August 3, 4, 28, 1927; Klein, *Politics*, pp. 104–5; Gutiérrez, *Reorganización*, pp. 11–12; Eugene Chevreaux, *Latin American Financial Developments in 1928* (Washington, D.C., 1929), pp. 4–5.

32. Eugene Chevreaux, *Financial Developments in Latin America during 1929* (Washington, D.C., 1929), pp. 4–5; Bolivia, Comisión Fiscal Permanente, *Quinta Memoria Presentada al Ministerio de Hacienda, 1927* (La Paz, 1928); Labrouquére, *La Bolivie nouvelle*, pp. x, 106–11.

33. Banco Central de Bolivia, *El Banco Central de Bolivia durante la guerra del Chaco* (La Paz, 1936), pp. 23–29; Peñaloza, *Historia económica de Bolivia*, p. 39; Mendoza López, *Las finanzas en Bolivia*, pp. 127–29; Gómez and Darío, *La banca nacional*, pp. 59–70; *El Diario*, March 30, August 5, 1927; *La Razón*, March 30, 1927.

34. EWK, Box 68, J. L. Tejada S., "El Plan Kemmerer para la reorganización del Banco de la Nación Boliviana"; Box 268, letter from J. L. Tejada S., April 8, 1927; Mendoza, *La Misión*, pp. 138–39ff.

35. Bolivia, *Redactor Diputados*, 9:26–49; Banco Central de Bolivia, *El Banco durante la guerra del Chaco*, p. 34; Benavides, *Historia de la moneda en Bolivia*, pp. 153–55; Mier y Leon, *Comentarios de la actualidad*, pp. 26–27.

36. Bolivia, *Redactor Diputados*, 9:26–27; *El Diario*, June 10, 1928; USDOS, from La Paz, December 19, 1927, 824.516/44.

37. Mendoza, *La Misión*, pp. 144–57; EWK, Box 66, "Memorandum re Republic of Bolivia Trust Contract Dated May 31, 1922," June 13, 1928; Diary, June 11, p. 163, June 1929, p. 181, 1928.

38. Bolivia, *Ley de 20 de julio de 1928 que crea el Banco Central de Bolivia, reformada por el decreto—ley de 23 de octubre de 1930* (n.p., n.d.); Bolivia, Banco de la Nación Boliviana, *Vigésima Segunda Memoria Semestral* (La Paz, 1927); idem, *Vigésima Tercera Memoria Semestral* (La Paz, 1928); idem, *Vigésima Cuarta Memoria Semestral* (La Paz, 1928); idem, *Vigésima Quinta Memoria Semestral* (La Paz, 1929); Chile, Banco Central de Chile, *Third Annual Report Presented to the Banking Superintendent. Year 1928* (Santiago, 1929), p. 33; Gómez and Darío, *La banca nacional*, pp. 127–29; Benavides, *Historia de la moneda en Bolivia*, pp. 130–31.

39. Mendoza, *La Misión*, pp. 146–225; EWK, Box 68, Tejada, "El Plan."

40. Mendoza, *La Misión*, pp. 147, 152–53, 190–98; Bolivia, Banco Central de Bolivia, *Primera Memoria* (La Paz, 1929), p. 65; idem, *Revista de Economía y Finanzas* 1, no. 1 (September 1931): 29; 2, no. 9 (April 1932): 22; Chevreaux, *Financial Developments*, pp. 4–5; López Rivas, *Esquema de la historia*, pp. 61–72.

41. Gómez and Darío, *La banca nacional*, pp. 128–29, 181–82; Mendoza, *La Misión*, pp. 144–45, 174–76.

42. Republic of Bolivia, Commission of Financial Advisers, *Project of a Monetary Law* (La Paz, 1927); *El Diario*, July 29, 1927; *Industria y Comercio* 6, no. 207 (June 29, 1928): 1–2; EWK, Box

268, letter from Tejada, April 8, 1927; Alborta, *Los intereses creados*; Bolivia, *Redactor Diputados*, 9:41–49, 164–78.

43. Bolivia, Commission, *Project of a Monetary Law*, pp. 1–15; EWK, Box 68, Tejada, "El Plan," pp. 23–35; López Rivas, *Esquema de la historia*, pp. 62–73.

44. *Revista de Economía y Finanzas* 2, no. 8 (March 1932): 26–27; Benavides, *Historia de la moneda en Bolivia*, pp. 126–53; Mendoza López, *Las finanzas en Bolivia*, pp. 131–33; Peñaloza, *Historia económica de Bolivia*, pp. 207–9.

45. *Industria y Comercio* 6, no. 187 (December 26, 1927): 1–10; Mendoza López, *Las finanzas en Bolivia*, pp. 123–25; Jorge Palenque, *Estadística bancaria* (La Paz, 1927), pp. 31–72.

46. *El Diario*, March 31, 1927; Mier y Leon, *Comentarios de la actualidad*, pp. 9–34; Humberto Cuenca, *Memorias de un banquero* (La Paz, 1972), pp. 64–66.

47. Bolivia, *Redactor Diputados*, 1:466–69, 9:32–38, 123–62, 329–85; Mendoza López, *La finanzas en Bolivia*, pp. 123–26; Republic of Bolivia, Commission of Financial Advisers, *Project of a General Banking Law* (La Paz, 1927).

48. EWK, Box 268, letter from E. O. Detlefsen, October 31, 1929; Bolivia, Banco Central de Bolivia, *Segunda Memoria* (La Paz, 1930), p. 45; Cuenca, *Memorias*, pp. 66–67.

49. *El Banco Nacional de Bolivia en sus setenta y cinco años* (Buenos Aires, n.d.), pp. 135–37; Mier Y Leon, *Comentarios de la actualidad*, pp. 10–45; Gómez and Darío, *La banca nacional*, pp. 49–71; Mendoza López, *Las finanzas en Bolivia*, p. 126; *Industria y Comercio* 6, no. 184 (November 30, 1927): 1–2.

50. *La Razón*, July 2, 1927; *El Diario*, March 30, April 20, May 19, 27, 1927; *Industria y Comercio* 5, no. 169 (July 11, 1927): 1–2; Mendoza López, *Las finanzas en Bolivia*, pp. 44–58; Bolivia, Contraloría General de la República, *Primer Informe de la Contraloría de la República* (La Paz, 1929), p. 3. For details on all the government agencies organized or reorganized as a result of Kemmerer's visit, see Bolivia, Oficina Nacional de Estadística Financiera, *Esquema de la organización de las entidades públicas y los regímenes económico administrativos de Bolivia*, vol. 1 (La Paz, 1929).

51. Bolivia, Comisión Fiscal Permanente, *Sexta Memoria Presentada al Ministerio de Hacienda* (La Paz, 1929); idem, *Octava Memoria Presentada al Ministerio de Hacienda* (La Paz, 1932); Vázquez, *Nociones*, pp. 328–31.

52. Mendoza, *La Misión*, pp. 353–400; USDOS, from Washington, May 1, 1929, 824.51/512; Edmundo Vázquez and Jorge Palenque, *La hacienda nacional* (La Paz, 1928), pp. 162–69.

53. Bolivia, Oficina Técnica de Ministerio de Hacienda, *Cálculo de las entradas ordinarias relativas al presupuesto nacional correspondiente a 1929* (La Paz, n.d.); Bolivia, Oficina Nacional de Estadística Financiera, *Anuario 1929: Economía y Finanzas* (La Paz, 1930); Bolivia, Banco Central de Bolivia, *Primera Memoria*, p. 46; *Revista de Economía y Finanzas* 2, no. 9 (April 1932): 2–8; *Bolivia Económica e Industrial* 2, no. 12 (February 1932): 18–20; Gutiérrez, *Reorganización*, pp. 12–14; Fajardo, *La deuda pública*, pp. 112–13.

54. USDOS, from Washington, May 1, 1929, 824.51/512; Mendoza, *La Misión*, pp. 401–37.

55. *La Razón*, July 14, 1927; Montecinos, *Apuntes financieros*, pp. 71–77; Mendoza López, *Las finanzas en Bolivia*, pp. 61–91.

56. USDOS, from La Paz, April 18, 1929, 824.51/511; June 14, 1929, 824.51/518; *Revista de Economía y Finanzas* 2, no. 9 (April 1932): 8; Bolivia, Contraloría, *Primer Informe*, p. 3; Hernando Siles, *Mensaje del presidente constitucional de la república al congreso nacional de 1929* (La Paz, n.d.), pp. 42–44.

57. Bolivia, Banco Central de Bolivia, *Primera Memoria*, pp. 49–51; Enrique Silva Cimma, *La Contraloría General de la República* (Santiago, 1945), pp. 276, 294–300.

58. Gutiérrez, *Reforma*; Mendoza, *La Misión*, pp. 285–320; *El Diario*, March 30, May 24, 1927; May 30, 1928.

59. Mendoza, *La Misión*, pp. 253–84; Republic of Bolivia, Commission of Financial Advisers, *Report on Mining Taxation* (La Paz, 1927); *El Diario*, April 6, 1927; *La Razón*, June 8, 1927; *Revista de Economía y Finanzas* 2, no. 10 (May 1932): 15–16.

60. Bolivia, *Redactor Diputados*, 8:542–73, 758–59; *La Razón*, July 10, 1927; Vázquez, *Nociones*, pp. 370–98; Vázquez and Palenque, *La hacienda nacional*, pp. 142–53; Galarza, "Debts, Dictatorship, and Revolution," p. 107.

61. *La Prensa*, June 7, 1927; *El Diario*, June 7, 1927; Republic of Bolivia, Commission of Financial Advisers, *Letter of E. W. Kemmerer to Finance Minister with Reference to the Proposal for the Establishment of a Monopoly in Bolivia for Refining and Sale of Salt* (La Paz, 1927); Vázquez and Palenque, *La hacienda nacional*, pp. 157–62; Mier y Leon *Comentarios de la actualidad*, p. 19.

62. EWK, Box 268, letter from E. O. Detlefsen, October 31, 1929; Bolivia, Banco Central de Bolivia, *Primera Memoria*, pp. 46–47; Galarza, "Debts, Dictatorship, and Revolution," p. 107.

63. Republic of Bolivia, Commission of Financial Advisers, *Proyecto de Ley Orgánica de Administración Aduanera* (La Paz, 1927); idem, *Proyecto de Arancel Aduanero de Importaciones* (La Paz, 1927); EWK, Box 280, "Robert H. Vorfeld: Summary of Service"; Siles, *Mensaje del presidente constitucional, 1929*, pp. 40–41; *El Diario*, April 8, July 21, 1927; Vázquez, *Nociones*, pp. 446–48.

64. EWK, Book 15, "Crédito Público de Bolivia"; Box 16, "La Deuda Externa de Bolivia"; *La Rázon*, May 23, 1927; Fajardo, *La deuda pública*, pp. ii–101; Peñaloza, *Historia económica de Bolivia*, 2:312–31.

65. Republic of Bolivia, Commission of Financial Advisers, *Report on Public Credit* (La Paz, 1927); *New York American*, January 13, 1932.

66. USDOS, from Washington, June 5, 1928, 824.51D581/4; July 20, 1928, 824.51D58/8; from La Paz, June 12, 1928, 824.51/453; from Dillon, Read, and Company, June 13, 1928, 824.51D581/7; from Department of Commerce, June 23, 1928, 824.51D581/26; Palenque, *Estadística boliviana*, pp. 23–24; EWK, Diary, March 25, 1926, p. 84; May 27, 1926, p. 147; October 3, 1927, p. 277; October 11, 1927, p. 285; January 7, 1928, p. 7; January 18, 1928, p. 18; April 5, 1928, p. 96; July 10, 1928, p. 192; September 11, 1928, p. 255.

67. USDOS, from Washington, May 8, 1928, 824.51/449; May 9, 1928, 824.51/449; April 23, 1929, 824.51/508; Robert N. Seidel, "Progressive Pan Americanism: Development and United States Policy toward South America, 1906–1931" (Ph.D. diss., Cornell University, 1973), pp. 559–66.

68. Explaining the Dillon, Read loan to Congress, President Siles said that, "the contract ratifies the express recommendation that the plan of reforms which the Kemmerer Mission proposed had to be adopted within the legislative mechanism of the country." Siles, *Mensaje del presidente constitucional, 1929*, p. 35; Bolivia, *Redactor Diputados*, 9:23–25; USDOS, from La Paz, July 9, 1928, 824.51D581/34; from Washington, July 20, 1928, 824.51D 58/8; Galarza, "Debts, Dictatorship, and Revolution," pp. 106–7; *Industria y Comercio* 7, no. 213 (August 22, 1928): 3–4; no. 217 (October 31, 1928): 1–2; Fajardo, *La deuda pública*, pp. 108–10.

69. Republic of Bolivia, Commission of Financial Advisers, *Report on Condition and Organization of Certain Bolivian Railway Lines* (La Paz, 1927); idem, *Project of Law Amending the Present Law Governing Applications for and Approval of Rates, Fares, Charges, and Other Regulations of Rail, Water and Other Carriers Operating in Bolivia, Also Certain Increases in Such Charges* (La Paz, 1927); idem, *Informe sobre el Ferrocarril Cochabamba–Santa Cruz* (La Paz, 1927); idem, *Report on Public Credit*, pp. 28–29; EWK, Box 65, letter from Kemmerer to President Siles,

June 24, 1927; *El Diario*, June 26, 1927; *La Razón*, June 17, July 12, 1927; Marsh, *Bankers in Bolivia*, pp. 77–89; Galarza, "Debts, Dictatorship, and Revolution," pp. 104–5; Manuel Mendieta S., *Tierra rica, pueblo pobre* (Sucre, 1928); Edward F. Feely, "Bolivia and the Kemmerer Commission," *International Investor* 4 (January 16, 1928): 48–50.

70. Mier y Leon, *Comentarios de la actualidad*, pp. 35–36; *Industria y Comercio* 7, no. 226 (January 28, 1929): 9–12.

71. Merwin L. Bohan, *Informe económico de Bohan*, 3 vols. (La Paz, 1943), 3:86–91; Naciones Unidas, *Desarrollo económico de Bolivia*, pp. 12–31; López Rivas, *Esquema de la historia*, pp. 69–84; Mendoza López, *Las finanzas en Bolivia*, pp. 355–59; Whitehead, "El impacto de la gran depresión," pp. 68–72; José E. Rivera, *Incertidumbres nacionales. Nuevas sombras sobre el negocio minero* (La Paz, 1928); Asociación de Industriales Mineros de Bolivia, *Informes Especiales para los Socios* 2, no. 9 (October 30, 1928).

72. Asociación de Industriales Mineros de Bolivia, *Informes Especiales para los Socios* 4, no. 1 (September 1930): 2–15; *Cambio Internacional* (La Paz, 1931); Bolivia, Banco Central de Bolivia, *Primera Memoria*, pp. 56–59; Gutiérrez, *Reorganización*, pp. 27–29; Edmundo Vázquez, *La economía y las finanzas de Bolivia* (La Paz, 1931); Vázquez, *Nociones*.

73. *Comercio y Minas* 3, no. 122 (March 18, 1930); Vázquez, *La economía*; idem, *Nociones*; Gustavo Adolfo Otero, *Notas sobre el comercio boliviano* (Barcelona, 1929), pp. 35–39; La Camara de Fomento Industrial, *Industria* 1, no.1 (July 1931); no. 2 (August 1931); *Bolivia Económica e Industrial* 2, no. 12 (February 1931), pp. 41–46.

74. Bolivia, Banco Central de Bolivia, *Boletín*, no. 17 (December 15, 1930): 8–12; Jorge Palenque, *Reseña sobre la organización bancaria nacional y su situación* (La Paz, 1931), pp. 1–18; idem, *Estadística boliviana*, pp. 49–75; Labrouquére, *La Bolivie nouvelle*, pp. 104–6; Cuenca, *Memorias*, pp. 67–79.

75. Vázquez, *La economia*; Henry Kittredge Norton, *The Coming of South America* (New York, 1932), pp. 65–72; Céspedes, *El dictador suicida*, pp. 88–115; Galarza, "Debts, Dictatorship, and Revolution," pp. 108–10; *Comercio y Minas* 3, no. 129 (July 21, 1930).

76. Klein, *Politics*, pp. 133–41; Bohan, *Informe económico*, 3:1.

77. Bolivia, Banco Central de Bolivia, *Segunda Memoria*, pp. 64–71; idem, *Tercera Memoria*, p. 66; U.S. Department of State, Records of Francis White, Assistant Secretary of State for Latin American Affairs, 1921–33 (hereinafter cited as FW), Box 11, letter from Edward F. Feely, November 24, 1930; *La Razón*, October 11, 12, 15, 1930; Vázquez, *La economia*; Vázquez, *Nociones*; Gutiérrez, *Reorganización*, pp. 3–10; Manuel Sofovich, *La tragedia boliviana* (Buenos Aires, 1932), pp. 38–43.

78. Whitehead, "El impacto de la gran depresión," p. 61; *Bolivia Económica e Industrial* 1, no. 3 (May 1931): 217–20; EWK, Diary, December 19, 1930, p. 353.

79. FW, Box 1, "Memo of Conversation with Mr. Robert O. Haywood, Dillon, Read, and Co.," March 28, 1931; "Memo of Conversation with Mr. Lawrence Bennett and Mr. Adam Geiger of the Chase Securities Co.," July 30, 1931; "Telephone Conversation with Mr. Adam Geiger, Chase National Bank," February 5, 1932; Bolivia, Banco Central de Bolivia, *Cuarta Memoria*, p. 63; United Nations, *Foreign Capital*, p. 43.

80. *Revista de Economía y Finanzas* 1, no. 3 (November 1931): 25–40; 2, no. 7 (February 1932): 5–9; *Bolivia Económica e Industrial* 1, no. 1 (January 1931): 23–24; *La Razón*, October 5, 14, 1930; Gómez and Darío, *La banca nacional*, pp. 132–37; Fajardo, *La deuda pública*; Luis Cabezas Villa, *La moneda en Bolivia* (Potosi, n.d.); Humberto Fossati, *Estudios económicos* (La Paz, 1937); Humberto Cuenca, *Reorganización del Banco Central de Bolivia y creación del Banco de la República* (La Paz, 1944), pp. 21–22.

81. Whitehead, "El impacto de la gran depresión," pp. 57–80; Cabezas, *La moneda en Bolivia*, pp.

90–95; Belzu, *Algunas notas históricas*, p. 13; Vázquez, *La economía*; Vázquez, *Nociones*; J. L. Tejada S., *La unión aduanera continental. La situación del cambio internacional en Bolivia* (La Paz, 1931), pp. 25–27; *Revista de Economía y Finanzas* I, no. 4 (December 1931): 5–6; *Bolivia Económica e Industrial* I, no. 1 (January 1931): 5–21; no. 2 (April 1931): 111–61.

82. While lobbying to keep the Bolivian government loyal to the gold standard, the U.S. ambassador also visited Argentina in 1931: "While there I came near selling the government a Kemmerer Commission, and it may come yet although there is much opposition to foreign intervention." EWK, Box 18, letter from Edward F. Feely, April 1, 1931; Box 268, letter from Edward F. Feely, December 9, 1930.

83. EWK, Box 268, letters to Kemmerer from Carlos Guachalla, Banco Central de Bolivia, November 26, 1930; September 9, 1931; Bolivia, Banco Central de Bolivia, *Boletín*, nos. 8–20 (April 1, 1930–March 31, 1931); *Bolivia Económica e Industrial* I, no. 1 (January 1931): 51–60; Gutiérrez, *Reorganización*, pp. 23–25.

84. EWK, Box 268, letter from Alberto Palacios, Banco Central de Bolivia, August 26, 1931; letter from A. F. Lindberg, August 20, 1931; letter from Guachalla, September 9, 1931; letter from Edward F. Feely, September 8, 1931.

85. Demetrio Canales, *La cuestión del cambio en Bolivia* (La Paz, n.d.), pp. 3–10; Gutiérrez, *Reorganización*, pp. 25–94; Gómez and Darío, *La banca nacional*, pp. 136–41; *Revista de Economía y Finanzas* 2, no. 6 (January 1932): 7–9.

86. Bolivia, Banco Central de Bolivia, *Tercera Memoria*; Mendoza López, *Las finanzas en Bolivia*, pp. 133–43.

87. Bolivia, Banco Central de Bolivia, *Tercera Memoria*; idem, *Cuarta Memoria*; idem, *El Banco durante la guerra del Chaco*; *Revista de Economía y Finanzas* 2, no. 6 (January 1932); no. 7 (February 1932); Gómez and Darío, *La banca nacional*, pp. 142–55, 296; Mendoza López, *Las finanzas en Bolivia*, pp. 147–58; López Rivas, *Esquema de la historia*, pp. 87–95; Bautista Saavedra, *La moneda boliviana* (Arica, 1936).

88. Naciones Unidas, *Desarrollo económico de Bolivia*, pp. 57–60; Belzu, *Algunas notas históricas*; Benavides, *Historia de la moneda en Bolivia*; Cuenca, *Reorganización*; Franklin Antezana Paz, *Misión de los bancos centrales* (La Paz, 1941); Franklin Antezana Paz, *Moneda, crédito, cambios extranjeros y estabilización* (Mexico, 1957); Víctor Paz Estenssoro, "Bolivia," in Luis Roque Gondra et al., eds., *El pensamiento económico latino-americano* (Mexico, 1945), pp. 36–69; Guillermo Alborta Velasco, *El flagelo de la inflación monetaria en Bolivia, país monoproductor* (Madrid, 1963); George Jackson Eder, *Inflation and Development in Latin America: A Case History of Inflation and Stabilization in Bolivia* (Ann Arbor, 1968).

6. Dictators, Debts, and Depression in Peru, 1930–1933

1. James C. Carey, *Peru and the United States, 1900–1962* (Notre Dame, 1964), pp. 33–77ff.; United Nations, *Foreign Capital in Latin America* (New York, 1955), pp. 133–34; idem, *Public Debt, 1914–1946* (Lake Success, 1948), pp. 113–15; Aníbal Quijano, *Imperialismo, clases sociales y estado en el Perú, 1890–1930* (Lima, 1978), pp. 89–92ff.; Carlos Malpica S. S., *El mito de la ayuda exterior*, 3d ed. (Lima, 1977); Heraclio Bonilla, "The Emergence of U.S. Control of the Peruvian Economy: 1850–1930," in Joseph S. Tulchin, ed., *Hemispheric Perspectives on the United States* (Westport, 1975), pp. 325–54; Rosemary Thorp and Geoffrey Bertram, *Peru 1890–1977: Growth and Policy in an Open Economy* (New York, 1978), pp. 338–39; Max Winkler, *Investments of United States Capital in Latin America* (Boston, 1928), pp. 145–51.

2. U.S. Department of State (hereinafter cited as USDOS), from Washington, August 4, 1933, 823.51/567-1/2; U.S. Department of State, Records of Francis White, Assistant Secretary of State for Latin American Affairs, 1921–33 (hereinafter cited as FW), Box 10, "Fred Morris Dearing," letter to Edwin V. Morgan, June 4, 1931; Frank Hindes MacKaman, "United States Loan Policy, 1920–1930: Diplomatic Assumptions, Governmental Politics, and Conditions in Peru and Mexico," 2 vols. (Ph.D. diss., University of Missouri, 1977).

3. Manuel Yrigoyen P., *Bosquejo sobre empréstitos contemporáneos del Perú* (Lima, 1928), Ernest Galarza, "Debts, Dictatorship, and Revolution in Bolivia and Peru," *Foreign Policy Reports 7*, no. 5 (May 13, 1931): 101–18; J. M. Ramírez Gastón, *Medio siglo de la política económica y financiera del Perú, 1915–64* (Lima, 1964), pp. 93–97ff.; Manuel E. de los Ríos, *El Perú libre* (Lima, 1922); idem, *La verdadera democracia* (Lima, 1925); Dora Mayer de Zulén, *El oncenio de Leguía* (Callao, n.d.); Pedro Ugarteche, *La política internacional peruana durante la dictadura de Leguía* (Lima, 1930), pp. 38–40; Emily S. Rosenberg, "American Foreign Financial Advising in Latin America Before the Great Depression: Form and Structure," MS, 1985; Joseph S. Tulchin, *The Aftermath of War: World War I and United States Policy toward Latin America* (New York, 1971), pp. 200–204; William Bollinger, "The Rise of United States Influence in the Peruvian Economy" (Ph.D. diss., University of California, Los Angeles, 1972); Geoffrey Bertram, "Development Problems in an Export Economy: A Study of Domestic Capitalists, Foreign Firms, and Government in Peru, 1919–1930" (Ph.D. diss., Oxford University, 1974); USDOS, from Lima, June 5, 1923, 825.516/28; Carey, *Peru and the United States*, pp. 71–72; MacKaman, "U.S. Loan Policy," 2:594–633.

4. Thorp and Bertram, *Peru 1890–1977*, pp. 114–15; FW, Box 2, "Peru," memorandum dated March 9, 1931; José E. Bonilla, *El siglo de Leguía* (Lima, 1928); Augusto B. Leguía, *Discursos, mensajes y programas*, 3 vols. (Lima, 1924–26); Augusto B. Leguía, *Mensaje* (Lima, 1928; 1929; 1930); Augusto B. Leguía, *Yo tirano, yo ladrón* (n.p., n.d.); José Reano García, *Historia del leguiismo, sus hombres y sus obras* (Lima, 1928); Perú, Ministerio de Fomento, *The New Country of Peru* (Lima, 1928).

5. USDOS, from Lima, May 13, 1931, 823.01A/2; Carey, *Peru and the United States*, pp. 54–55, 82–88; Mayer de Zulén, *El oncenio de Leguía*, pp. 19, 46–88; Galarza, "Debts, Dictatorship, and Revolution," p. 117; Ugarteche, *La política*, pp. 14–44; Jesús Víctor Fajardo, *Para la historia* (La Paz, 1921); Abelardo Solis, *Once años* (Lima, 1934), p. 112; Steve Stein, *Populism in Peru* (Madison, 1980), pp. 53–55; Kenneth Grieb, *The Latin American Policy of Warren G. Harding* (Fort Worth, 1976), pp. 158–59.

6. Perú, Ministerio de Fomento, Dirección de Minas y Petroleo, *Estado del padrón general de minas* (Lima, 1931); *Boletín Oficial* (December 1932).

7. Sociedad Nacional Agraria, *La Vida Agrícola 7*, no. 83 (October 1, 1930): 743–49; no. 84 (November 1, 1930): 835–80; 8, no. 86 (January 1, 1931): 1–3; no. 89 (April 1, 1931): 299–300; no. 90 (May 1, 1931): 309–11; Edwin W. Kemmerer Papers, Princeton University Library (hereinafter cited as EWK), Box 483, "Inspección Fiscal de Bancos Hipotecarios"; Baltazar Caravedo Molinari, *Clases, lucha política, y gobierno en el Perú (1919–1933)* (Lima, 1977).

8. Thorp and Bertram, *Peru 1890–1977*, pp. 118–29, 348–50; Baltazar Caravedo Molinari, *Burguesía e industria en el Perú, 1933–1945* (Lima, 1976); W. E. Dunn, *Peru, a Commercial and Industrial Handbook* (Washington, D.C., 1925), esp. p. 243.

9. La Camara de Comercio de Lima, *Boletín Mensual 3*, nos. 19–22 (January–April 1931); EWK, Box 483, letter from Asociación de Comerciantes del Peru, January 31, 1931.

10. Carlos Camprubí Alcázar, *Historia de los bancos en el Perú* (Lima, 1957); Alfonso Walter Quiroz, "Financial Institutions in Peruvian Export Economy and Society, 1884–1930" (Ph.D.

diss., Columbia University, 1986); Banco del Perú y Londres, *Breve reseña histórica de la fundación y desarrollo del Banco del Perú y Londres al cumplirse el cincuentenario de su establecimiento* (Lima, 1927); Luis Alberto Sánchez, *Principios de economía política aplicada al Perú* (Lima, 1934), pp. 109–10; Perú, La Inspección Fiscal de Bancos, *Noveno Informe Correspondiente al año 1929* (Lima, n.d.), pp. 6–7; Great Britain, Department of Overseas Trade (hereinafter cited as GBDOT), *Report on the Economic Conditions in Peru* (London, 1921); GBDOT, *Report* (1926); Perú, Ministerio de Hacienda y Comercio, Dirección Nacional de Estadística, *Extracto Estadístico del Perú, 1931–1932–1933* (Lima, 1935), pp. 60–61; EWK, Box 483; USDOS, from Lima, March 24, 1931, 823.51/622.

11. Banco de Reserva del Perú, *Proyecto* (n.p., n.d.); idem, *Estatutos* (Lima, 1922); idem, *Ley No. 4,500* (Lima, 1922); Banco Central de Reserva del Perú, *Banco Central de Reserva del Perú, 1922–1972* (Lima, 1972); idem, *Banquete al Presidente de la República* (Lima, 1929); Emilio Romero, *Historia económica del Perú*, 2d ed., 2 vols. (Lima, n.d.), 2:224; Ríos, *La verdadera*, pp. 490–91; *El Comercio*, January 1, 1931.

12. Dunn, *Peru*, pp. 249–53; Romero, *Historia económica del Perú*, 2:220–222ff.; Thorp and Bertram, *Peru 1890–1977*, pp. 128–38; Charles A. McQueen, *Peruvian Public Finance* (Washington, D.C., 1926); Gianfranco Bardella, *Setenta y cinco años de vida económica del Perú, 1889–1964* (Lima, 1964), pp. 88–141; Rómulo A. Ferrero, *La historia monetaria del Perú en el presente siglo* (Lima, 1953), esp. pp. 5–6; Bruno Moll and Emilio G. Barreto, "El sistema monetario del Perú," in Universidad Nacional de Cordoba, *Sistemas monetarios latino-americanos* (Cordoba, 1943), 1:141–226; Ricardo Martínez de la Torre, *Apuntes para una interpretación marxista de historia social del Perú*, 2d ed. (Lima, 1947), 1:16–19, 76; Perú, Ministerio de Hacienda, *Extracto Estadístico, 1931*, pp. 28–59; A. M. Rodríguez Dulanto, "La restauración del patrón de oro en el Perú," *Revista Económica y Financiera* (June 1929): 3–27.

13. Perú, Ministero de Hacienda, *Extracto Estadístico 1931*, pp. 228–33; EWK, Box 483, letter from J. and W. Seligman and Co., December 12, 1930; Mayer de Zulén, *El oncenio de Leguía*, pp. 32–48; Víctor Andrés Belaúnde, *La crisis presente, 1914–1939* (Lima, 1940), p. 129.

14. Augusto B. Leguía, *Leguía* (Lima, 1927), esp. pp. 49–53; Leguía, *Mensaje* (1929); Solis, *Once años*; Guillermo Forero Franco, *Entre dos dictaduras* (Bogotá, 1934), pp. 146–215ff.; Stein, *Populism in Peru*, pp. 39–81. For further information on the Leguía period, see Alejandro Rabanal, "La economía peruana en la decada del 20," in Heraclio Bonilla, ed., *Las crisis económicas en la historia del Perú* (Lima, 1986), pp. 189–210; Howard Lawrence Karno, "Augusto B. Leguía: The Oligarchy and the Modernization of Peru, 1870–1930" (Ph.D. diss., University of California, Los Angeles, 1970); and Gary Richard Garret, "The Oncenio of Augusto B. Leguía" (Ph.D. diss., University of New Mexico, 1973).

15. *La evolución del Perú en el quinquenio 1919–1924* (Lima, 1924); Clemente Palma, *Había una vez un hombre . . .* (Lima, 1935); Carlos Miró Quesada Laos, *Autopsia de los partidos políticos* (Lima, 1961), pp. 448–65; Manuel Burga and Alberto Flores-Galindo, *Apogeo y crisis de la república aristocrática* (Lima, 1979), pp. 136–40; Quijano, *Imperialismo*, pp. 92–96; Caravedo, *Clases*.

16. USDOS, from Lima, January 3, 1930, 823.516/67; February 25, 1930, 823.516/75; May 15, 1930, 823.00/580; June 20, 1930, 823.51A/15; June 21, 1930, 823.51A/16; July 18, 1930, 823.51/489; 823.51A/19; EWK, Box 18, letter to C. S. Calvin, November 10, 1930; Box 268, letter from Edward F. Feely, November 14, 1930; Diary, March 24, 25, 1927, pp. 84–85; June 24, 1930, p. 175. Leguía had previously discussed the possibility of a mission when Kemmerer had visited him in Lima in 1927.

17. USDOS, from Washington, October 30, 1930, 823.00 Revolutions/267; from Santiago, December 23, 1930, 823.51/557; from Lima, September 17, 1930, 823.51/500; October 23, 1930,

823.51/524; October 30, 1930, 823.5045/54; November 22, 1930, 823.002/134; February 21, 1931, 823.51/578; February 27, 1931, 823.51/587; March 6, 1931, 823.00 Revolutions/181; FW, Box 2, "Peru," conversation with Don Manuel de Freyre y Santander, Peruvian ambassador, October 23, 1930; Box 3, "LA General," memorandum to Mr. Carr, October 1, 1931; GBDOT, *Report* (1931), p. 9; La Cámara de Comercio de Lima, *Boletín* 2, no. 15 (September 1930): 647–50; Sociedad Nacional Agraria, *La Vida Agrícola* 8, no. 88 (March 1, 1931): 163–64; Carey, *Peru and the United States*, pp. 62–64; Benjamín Chirinos Pacheco, *Hacia un Perú nuevo* (Arequipa, 1932).

18. Luis M. Sánchez Cerro, *Manifiesto a la nación* (Lima, 1930); Diego Camacho, *La revolución de agosto de 1930* (n.p., n.d.); Samuel Ramírez Castilla, *La tiranía se desencadena* (Lima, 1932); Luis E. Heysen, *El comandante del Oropesa* (n.p., 1931); Tomás Escajadillo, *La revolución universitaria de 1930* (Lima, n.d.); Quijano, *Imperialismo*, pp. 97–124. For details on the Sánchez Cerro years, see Orazio A. Ciccarelli, "The Sánchez Cerro Regimes in Peru, 1930–1933" (Ph.D. diss., University of Florida, 1969); Caravedo, *Clases*.

19. EWK, Box 168, "Letter from Peru," Dr. Jorge Basadre, June 27, 1932; USDOS, from Lima, January 6, 1932, 823.00B/66; Manuel Seoane, *Nuestros fines* (Buenos Aires, 1931); idem, *Páginas polémicas* (Lima, 1931); Carlos Manuel Cox, *En torno al imperialismo* (Lima, 1933); Pedro E. Muñiz, *Penetración imperialista* (Santiago, 1935); Víctor Raúl Haya de la Torre, *Teoría y táctica del aprismo* (Lima, 1931); Partido Aprista Peruano, *Programa mínimo o plan de acción inmediata* (Lima, 1931); Peter F. Klaren, *Modernization, Dislocation, and Aprismo: Origins of the Peruvian Aprista Party, 1870–1932* (Austin, 1973).

20. USDOS, from Lima, September 20, 1930, 823.51/503; FW, Box 3, "LA General," telephone conversation with Mr. W. W. Lancaster, National City Bank, June 25, 1931.

21. USDOS, from Lima, October 6, 1930, 823.51/509; October 15, 1930, 823.51/508; November 1, 1930, 823.51/530; November 7, 1930, 823.51/534.

22. USDOS, from Lima, October 16, 1930, 823.51/514; October 18, 1930, 823.51/517; October 24, 1930, 823.51/516; from Washington, October 27, 1930, 823.51/536.

23. FW, Box 2, "Peru," memorandum to under secretary and secretary of state, October 27, 1930; telephone conversation with Mr. Henry C. Breck, J. and W. Seligman and Co., October 27, 1930; Box 4, "Caffery," letter from Garrard Winston, counsel for National City Bank, March 6, 1931; Box 7, "Winston," letter to Garrard Winston, March 7, 1931; USDOS, from Lima, October 27, 1930, 823.51/520; from Washington, November 1, 1930, 823.51/516.

24. USDOS, from Lima, October 24, 1930, 823.51/516; November 1, 1930, 823.51/530; November 4, 1930, 823.51/526; November 7, 1930, 823.51/534.

25. USDOS, from Lima, November 6, 1930, 823.52/531; November 21, 1930, 823.51/540; December 4, 1930, 823.51/544; EWK, Box 18, cable from Olaechea, November 6, 1930; letter from W. W. Cumberland, December 19, 1930.

26. EWK, Box 18; Box 483.

27. *El Comercio*, October 27, 1930; January 1, 12, 13, 14, April 21, 1931; *El Perú*, January 16, April 17, 20, 21, 1931; La Cámara de Comercio de Lima, *Boletín Mensual* 3, no. 19 (January 1931): 2–13; EWK, Box 483, "Concerning the Kemmerer Mission"; Diary, January 12, 1931, p. 12; Lizardo Alzamora Silva, *La situación económica y fiscal del Perú* (Lima, 1931), pp. 3–10; Albert O. Hirschman, *Journeys toward Progress* (Garden City, 1965).

28. *La Prensa*, October 30, 1930; *La Libertad*, March 29, 1931; *La Noche*, February 4, 1931; *La Hora*, January 20, 1931; *Revista Semanal* 5, no. 175 (January 8, 1931): 5–6; no. 176 (January 15, 1931): 1; EWK, Box 168, "Communist Party of Peru"; Box 483, letter to Ambassador Dearing, January 30, 1931; USDOS, from Lima, January 19, 1931, 823.51A Kemmerer Mission/11; January 22, 1931, 823.51A Kemmerer Mission/16; January 29, 1931, 823.00B/25;

May 7, 1931, 823.00B/43; Seoane, *Nuestros fines*, p. 39; Víctor Raúl Haya de la Torre, *El plan del aprismo* (n.p., n.d.), p. 58; Magda Portal, *América latina frente al imperialismo y defensa de la revolución mexicana* (Lima, 1931), p. 41; Carlos Manuel Cox, *Ideas económicas del aprismo* (Lima, 1934).

29. USDOS, from Lima, December 4, 1930, 823.51/544; December 6, 1930, 823.51/542; EWK, Box 18, esp. letter from Gordon Rentschler, president of National City Bank, November 13, 1930; *El Comercio*, January 30, 1931.

30. USDOS, from Lima, January 18, 1931, 823.51A Kemmerer Mission/10; January 19, 1931, 823.51A Kemmerer Mission/11; January 31, 1931, 823.51/574.

31. La Cámara de Comercio de Lima, *Boletín Mensual* 3, no. 20 (February 1931): 65–66; *El Comercio*, January 14, 15, 17, 1931.

32. USDOS, from Lima, January 16, 1931, 823.51/566; January 18, 1931, 823.51A Kemmerer Mission/10; January 19, 1931, 825.51A Kemmerer Mission/ll; January 31, 823.51/574.

33. *El Comercio*, January 13, February 18, March 18, 1931; EWK, Diary, March 17, 1931, p. 76.

34. *El Comercio*, April 11, 17, 19, May 25, 26, 1931; USDOS, from Lima, April 22, 1931, 823.51/660; April 28, 1931, 823.50/5; May 25, 1931, 823.51/680; EWK, Diary, April 18, 1931, p. 108.

35. Perú, *Constitución política del Perú, sancionada por el congreso constituyente de 1931, promulgada el 9 de Abril de 1933* (Lima, 1933).

36. USDOS, from Lima, April 2, 1931, 823.51/637; FW, Box 2, "Peru," telephone conversation with Professor E. W. Kemmerer, May 6, 1931.

37. Reserve Bank of Peru, Commission of Financial Advisers on Finances of National Government of Peru, *Project of Law for the Creation of the Central Reserve Bank of Peru, Together with a Report in Support Thereof* (Lima, 1931); EWK, Box 483, "The Reserve Bank of Peru," December 31, 1930; "Memorandum," January 20, 1931; *El Comercio*, May 18, September 6, 1931; La Cámara de Comercio de Lima, *Boletín Mensual* 3, no. 23 (May 1931): 272–73; USDOS, from Lima, May 11, 1931, 823.516/126; Banco Central de Reserva del Perú (1972); Cox, *Ideas*, p. 21.

38. USDOS, from Lima, September 18, 1931, 823.51/735; Banco Central de Reserva del Perú, *Decretos leyes de su creación* (Lima, 1931).

39. Reserve Bank of Peru, *Project of Law*; Banco Central de Reserva del Perú, *Boletín Mensual* (September 1931): 3–6; USDOS, from Lima, May 11, 1931, 823.516/126.

40. USDOS, from Lima, January 19, 1931, 823.51A Kemmerer Mission/11; *El Comercio*, January 28, 1931; Banco Central de Reserva del Perú, *Boletín Mensual* (July 1932): 257–59.

41. Reserve Bank of Peru, *Project of Law*, pp. 84–85; USDOS, from Lima, October 20, 1931, 823.516/154; Alzamora, *La situación*, pp. 180–84.

42. Reserve Bank of Peru, Commission of Financial Advisors on Finances of National Government of Peru, *Project of a Monetary Law Together with a Report in Support Thereof* (Lima, 1931); USDOS, from Lima, March 4, 1931, 823.51/605; Bardella, *Setenta y cinco años*, pp. 152–56.

43. La Cámara de Comercio de Lima, *Boletín Mensual* 2, no. 14 (August 1930): 584; 3, no. 20 (February 1931): 62–65; *El Pueblo*, November 8, 1930; USDOS, from Lima, February 24, 1931, 823.00 Revolutions/143; Banco de Reserva del Perú, *Boletín Mensual* (August 1931): 3–4; Ignacio Meller, *Patrón de oro o bimetalismo* (Lima, 1932); Enrique Echecopar García, *Moneda estable* (Lima, 1931).

44. Cox, *Ideas*, pp. 22–47; Víctor Raúl Haya de la Torre, *Discurso programa de 1931* (Lima, 1963), pp. 36–37; idem, *Manifiesto a la nación* (Trujillo, 1933); Magda Portal, *Frente al imperialismo yanqui* (Lima, 1931).

45. Lizardo Alzamora Silva, *Sobre el plan Kemmerer* (Lima, 1931), pp. 1–37; Oscar F. Arrús, *La estabilización de nuestra moneda* (Lima, 1931); F. Mario Bazán, *El proceso económico del Perú* (Buenos Aires, 1954), pp. 24–76; Moll and Barreto, "El sistema monetario del Perú," pp. 171–75.

46. GBDOT, *Report* (1931), pp. 6–12.

47. *El Comercio*, January 13, February 13, 14, April 19, 20 22, 23, 1931; *El Perú*, April 22, 1931; *La Prensa*, April 20, 21, 1931; *La Tribuna*, May 17, 1931; *Revista Semanal* 5, no. 190 (April 23, 1931): 1; La Cámara de Comercio de Lima, *Boletín Mensual* 3, no. 21 (March 1931): p. 124; USDOS, from Lima, December 6, 1930, 823.51/545; April 22, 1931, 823.51/660; April 24, 1931, 823.516/118; April 28, 1931, 823.50/5; May 6, 1931; from Washington, May 6, 1931, 823.00/677; EWK, Box 483, letter from Liga General de Comercio y Economía, February 10, 1931; Arrús, *La estabilización de nuestra moneda*; W. C. de Blois Leach, *Conferencia sobre teoría de cambios* (Lima, 1931).

48. Perú, Ministerio de Hacienda, *Extracto Estadístico, 1931*, pp. 26–29; Banco Central de Reserva del Perú, *Boletín Mensual*, (September 1931); *El Comercio*, October 7, 1931; *Economista Peruano*, no. 1 (October 1932): 4–10; Oscar Miró Quesada, *Vulgarizaciones económicas. La moneda y el cambio* (Lima, 1932), pp. 140–42, 221–26; USDOS, from Lima, January 14, 1932, 823.515/135.

49. Godofredo Vidal, *El crédito bancario* (Lima, 1941).

50. Reserve Bank of Peru, Commission of Financial Advisers on Finances of National Government of Peru, *Project of a General Banking Law Together with a Report in Support Thereof* (Lima, 1931); Perú, Superintendencia de Bancos, *Ley de bancos*, 3d ed. (Lima, 1944); La Cámara de Comercio de Lima, *Boletín Mensual* 3, no. 21 (March 1931): 133–38; 4, no. 33 (March 1932): 137–38; *El Comercio*, March 1, 1931.

51. Perú, Superintendencia de Bancos, *Memoria* (Lima, 1932, 1933); idem, *Situación de las empresas bancarias del Perú al 28 de octubre de 1931* (Lima, 1931); idem, *Perú en Cifras (1944–45)* (Lima, 1945), pp. 433–35; USDOS, from Washington, May 23, 1931, 823.516/134; from Lima, May 26, 1931, 823.516/137; EWK, Box 483; *El Comercio*, March 22, 1932; Alzamora, *Sobre el plan Kemmerer*, pp. 32–36; Bardella, *Setenta y cinco años*, pp. 159–62.

52. EWK, Box 161, "Memorandum. Conversation between Dr. Kemmerer, Dr. Olaechea"; Box 483, letter from "Soldados," January 16, 1931; USDOS, from Lima, July 12, 1931, 823.51/715; November 29, 1931, 823.504/39; *Economista Peruano* (January 1930): 2454–62; Perú, Contraloría General de la República, *Balance y cuenta general de la república. Año 1931* (Lima, 1932).

53. Reserve Bank of Peru, Commission of Financial Advisers on Finances of National Government of Peru, *Project of Law for the Reorganization of the National Treasury, Together with a Report in Support Thereof*; idem, *Project of an Organic Budget Law, Together with a Report in Support Thereof* (Lima, 1931); Joaquín Ortega Zegarra, *Digesto de hacienda del Perú (1821–1933)*, 2 vols. (Lima, 1929, 1934).

54. Leguía, *Mensaje* (1930), pp. 64–66; Solis, *Once años*, pp. 73–74; EWK, Box 483, "Ministerio de Hacienda—Contraloría General"; Enrique Silva Cimma, *La contraloría general de la república* (Santiago, 1945), pp. 327–29; Manuel Seoane, *Autopsia del presupuesto civilista, como derrocha una casta los dineros del pueblo* (Buenos Aires, 1936).

55. USDOS, from Lima, November 7, 1930, 823.51/534; April 28, 1931, 823.50/5; August 18, 1931, 823.51/726.

56. Reserve Bank of Peru, Commission of Financial Advisers on Finances of National Government of Peru, *Report on the Taxation Policy of Peru*; idem, *Project of an Income Tax Law Together with a Report in Support Thereof*; idem, *Project of Law Authorizing Provincial and District*

Councils to Impose a Real Property Tax Together with a Report in Support Thereof (Lima, April 1, 1931); idem, *Ultimas Noticias*, January 18, 1931; USDOS, from Lima, April 1, 1931, 823.51/634; October 19, 1933, 823.032/167; EWK, Box 161, "Memorandum. Conversation between Dr. Kemmerer, Dr. Olaechea"; Box 164, "Chief Peruvian Taxes"; Cox, *Ideas*, pp. 24–25; Romero, *Historia económica del Perú*, 2:240–41.

57. Reserve Bank of Peru, Commission of Financial Advisers on Finances of National Government of Peru, *Project of an Organic Customs Law Together with a Report in Support Thereof* (Lima, 1931); EWK, Box 483, "Aduana"; La Cámara de Comercio de Lima, *Boletín Mensual* 3, no. 21 (March 1931): 128; *El Comercio*, March 29, 1931; *La Crónica*, October 26, 1931.

58. USDOS, from Lima, April 8, 1932, 823.51/822; La Cámara de Comercio de Lima, *Boletín Mensual* 4, no. 32 (February 1932): 72.

59. Lawrence Dennis, "What Overthrew Leguía," *New Republic*, September 17, 1930, pp. 117–20; *El Comercio*, January 1, 13, 19, March 16, 1931; *La Prensa*, February 6, 1931.

60. USDOS, from Lima, September 17, 1930, 823.51/500; from Santiago, December 23, 1930, 823.51/557; EWK, Box 18, letter from Van Deusen, November 28, 1930.

61. USDOS, from Lima, March 16, 1931, 823.51/614; May 7, 1931, 823.00B/43; Seoane, *Nuestros fines*, pp. 35–38; *La Hora*, January 27, February 3, 1931.

62. Ferrero, *La historia monetaria del Perú*, p. 205.

63. Alzamora, *La situación*, pp. 5, 10–11, 16–43.

64. EWK, Box 18, letter from Frederick Strauss, J. and W. Seligman and Co., November 6, 1930; letter to Gordon S. Rentschler, National City Bank, November 7, 1930; "Memorandum," November 21, 1930; letter from Kemmerer to Arthur Lehman, November 21, 1930; Box 483, letters between J. R. Edwards and Co. and Kemmerer, February 19, March 19, 1931; Diary, November 14, 20, December 26, 27, 1930, pp. 318, 324, 360, 361; USDOS, from Lima, March 27, 1931, 823.51/625.

65. USDOS, from Lima, October 24, 1930, 823.51/516; January 16, 1931, 823.51/566; FW, Box 2, "Peru," telephone conversation with Mr. Henry C. Breck, J. and W. Seligman and Co., April 10, 1931; telephone conversation with Mr. Robert H. Patchin, W. R. Grace and Co., April 17, 1931; Box 4, "Dearing," letter from White to Ambassador Fred Morris Dearing, January 28, 1931.

66. USDOS, from Lima, January 31, 1931, 823.51/574; February 2, 1931, 823.51/570; February 3, 1931, 823.51/575; February 5, 1931, 823.51/576; February 8, 1931, 823.52/577; February 21, 1931, 823.51/594; March 15, 1931, 823.51/603; March 19, 1931, 823.51/619; EWK, Box 161, "Memorandum of a Conversation between the President and Dr. Kemmerer"; Diary, January 30, February 5, 6, March 16, 1931, pp. 30, 36, 37, 85; *El Comercio*, February 1, 1931.

67. Reserve Bank of Peru, Commission of Financial Advisers on Finances of National Government of Peru, *Report on the Public Credit of Peru* (Lima, 1931); USDOS, from Lima, March 16, 1931, 823.51/614; March 19, 1931, 823.51/619; Alejandro Revoredo, *Apuntes de historia política y financiera* (Lima, 1974).

68. Carey, *Peru and the United States*, pp. 77–80; *El Comercio*, March 28, May 25, 28, 30, 1931; La Cámara de Comercio de Lima, *Boletín Mensual* 3, no. 22 (April 1931): 200–205.

69. USDOS, from Lima, April 2, 1931; FW, Box 2, "Peru," conversation with Mr. Henry C. Breck, J. and W. Seligman and Co., April 15, 1931.

70. USDOS, from Lima, April 22, 1931, 823.51/660; from Washington, March 3, 1931; FW, Box 2, "Peru," memorandum to the secretary from White, May 4, 1931; telephone conversation with Professor E. W. Kemmerer, May 6, 1931; EWK, Diary, May 5, 7, 1931, pp. 125, 127.

71. USDOS, from Lima, June 8, 1931, 823.51/701; January 5, 1933, 823.51/936; March 2, 1933, 823.51/950; May 22, 1933, 823.51/966; from Washington, December 13, 1932, 823.51/940;

William H. Wynne, *State Insolvency and Foreign Bondholders*, 2 vols. (New Haven, 1951), 2:188–94.

72. *El Comercio*, November 14, December 1, 2, 13, 14, 15, 1931; Banco Central de Reserva del Perú, *Boletín Mensual* (December 1931): 57–63; Robert Seidel, "Progressive Pan Americanism: Development and United States Policy toward South America, 1906–1931" (Ph.D. diss., Cornell University, 1973), pp. 627–34.

73. EWK, Box 168, "Communist Party"; *La Tribuna*, October 7, 1931; USDOS, from Lima, November 20, 1931, 823.50/7; December 10, 1931, 823.51/757.

74. Colombia, Banco de la República, *Revista del Banco de la República* (January 1932): 8–10.

75. USDOS, from Lima, December 20, 1931, 823.51/758; December 24, 1931, 823.51/762; April 28, 1932, 823.504/55; May 6, 1932, 823.51/837; FW, Box 2, "Peru," telephone conversation with Mr. C. V. Drew, Cerro de Pasco Copper Corporation, February 17, 1933; GBDOT, *Report* (1931), p. 9.

76. Thorp and Bertram, *Peru 1890–1977*, pp. 151–53; Quijano, *Imperialismo*, pp. 108–12.

77. *El Comercio*, January 6, May 31, 1931; *Economista Peruano*, no. 10 (September 1933): 121–22.

78. Jorge Basadre, *Historia de la república del Perú*, 5th ed., 10 vols. (Lima, 1961–64), 10:352–53; Jorge Basadre and Rómulo Ferrero, *Historia de la Cámara de Comercio de Lima* (Lima, 1963), pp. 160–67; La Cámara de Comercio de Lima, *Boletín Mensual* 4, no. 31 (January 1932): 2–7; no. 33 (March 1932): 134; no. 34 (April 1932): 215; *El Comercio*, May 6, 1932.

79. Sociedad Nacional Agraria, *La Vida Agrícola* 8, no. 91 (June 1, 1931): 382–419; no. 94 (September 1, 1931): 596; 9, no. 102 (May 1, 1932): 265; no. 103 (June 1, 1932): 299–302; Sociedad Nacional Agraria, *Memorial* (Lima, 1932); *El Comercio*, May 3, 1931; USDOS, from Lima, January 18, 1931, 823.51A Kemmerer Mission/10; January 22, 1932, 823.5151/26; 823.61/10; August 19, 1932, 823.515/151; Luis Ponce, "La crisis mundial de 1929 y la agricultura de la costa nor central," in Bonilla, ed., *Las crisis económicas en la historia del Perú* (Lima, 1986), pp. 211–30.

80. Perú, Ministerio de Hacienda, *Memoria* (Lima, 1931), pp. 326–27ff.; *El Comercio*, January 1, 1931; USDOS, from Lima, August 20, 1931, 823.516/149.

81. Sociedad Nacional de Industrias, *Industria Peruana* 1, no. 1 (July 1931); no. 2 (November 1931); 2, no. 3 (August 1932); *Revista Semanal* 5, no. 174 (January 1, 1931): 9; *La Hora*, January 20, 1931; Caravedo, *Burguesía*.

82. USDOS, from Lima, August 26, 1931, 823.00/736; September 2, 1931, 823.00/737; Luis M. Sánchez Cerro, *Programa de gobierno* (Lima, 1931); Partido Aprista Peruano, *Programa mínimo*.

83. Thorp and Bertram, *Peru 1890–1977*, pp. 182, 185; Víctor Villanueva, *Ejército peruano: del caudillaje anárquico al militarismo reformista* (Lima, 1973), pp. 200–211; USDOS, from Lima, June 1, 1932, 823.00/894; December 13, 1932, 823.51/940; February 16, 1933, 823.51/945.

84. La Cámara de Comercio de Lima, *Boletín Mensual* 4, no. 35 (May 1932): 286–92; *El Comercio*, May 3, 5, 6, 16, 1932; USDOS, from Lima, January 22, 1932, 823.51/773.

85. Basadre and Ferrero, *Historia de la Cámara*, 10:350–60; Perú, Superintendencia de Bancos, *Memoria* (1933), pp. 14–17, 72–76; USDOS, from Lima, May 16, 1932, 823.5151/35; May 17, 1932, 823.51/844.

86. *El Comercio*, May 19, 20, 1932; La Cámara de Comercio de Lima, *Boletín Mensual* 4, no. 42 (December 1932): 771; Asociación de Comercio e Industrias de Arequipa, *Revista* 1, no. 2 (April 1936): 55–56; USDOS, from Lima, September 8, 1932, 823.5151/37; Roxanne Cheesman, "Políticas de reactivación económica en la crisis de 1929," in Bonilla, ed., *Las crisis económicas en la historia del Perú* (Lima, 1986), pp. 263–98.

87. Ferrero, *La historia monetaria del Perú*, pp. 8–21; Bardella, *Setenta y cinco años*, pp. 163–73.

88. Moll and Barreto, "El sistema monetario del Perú," pp. 172–204; Seoane, *Autopsia*, pp. 139–40.

89. Banco Central de Reserva del Perú, *Boletín Mensual* (July 1932): 253–59; idem, *Banco Central de Reserva del Perú, 1922–1972*; USDOS, from Lima, June 30, 1932, 823.516/197; July 18, 1932, 823.516/201; September 5, 1932, 823.516/213; October 10, 1938, 823.516/246.

90. Perú, Superintendencia de Bancos, *Memoria* (Lima, 1934), pp. 65–69; USDOS, from Lima, January 14, 1932, 823.516/169; February 19, 1932, 823.516/177; January 23, 1933, 823.516/227; March 26, 1935, 823.516/236; from Washington, September, 1935, 823.50/20.

91. Thorp and Bertram, *Peru 1890–1977*; Rosemary Thorp and Carlos Londoño, "The Effect of the Great Depression on the Economies of Peru and Colombia," in Rosemary Thorp, ed., *Latin America in the 1930's: The Role of the Periphery in the World Crisis* (London, 1984), pp. 81–116; GBDOT, *Report* (1934); EWK, Box 168, Walter M. Van Deusen, "Letter from Peru," February 15, 1933.

7. Foreign Advisers and the Politics of Debt and Reform in Latin America

1. Edwin W. Kemmerer, "Economic Advisory Work for Governments," *Economic Review* 17, no. 1 (March 1927): 1–12.

2. Arthur Bloch, *Murphy's Law. Book Two* (Los Angeles, 1983), p. 48.

3. E. Kemmerer, "Economic Advisory," p. 2.

4. Thomas A. Krueger and William Glidden, "The New Deal Intellectual Elite: A Collective Portrait," in Frederic Cople Jaher, ed., *The Rich, the Well Born, and the Powerful* (Urbana, 1973), pp. 338–74; Fredrick B. Pike, *The United States and the Andean Republics* (Cambridge, 1977), p. 197.

5. Albert O. Hirschman, *Journeys toward Progress* (Garden City, 1965), pp. 175–281.

6. Emily S. Rosenberg, *Spreading the American Dream: American Economic and Cultural Expansion, 1890–1945* (New York, 1982), pp. 86, 154–59; idem, "American Foreign Financial Advising in Latin America Before the Great Depression: Form and Structure," MS, 1985.

7. E. Kemmerer, "Economic Advisory"; Donald L. Kemmerer, "Como trabaja el professor E. W. Kemmerer y como dirigia las labores de sus misiones asesoras," *Cultura* 7, no. 19 (May–August 1984): 477–79; interviews with Donald L. Kemmerer, Urbana, Ill., 1980–83; interview with Frank Whitson Fetter, Hanover, N.H., July 29, 1976.

8. Hirschman, *Journeys toward Progress*, pp. 217–384.

9. Miron Burgin, "Research in Latin American Economics and Economic History," in Howard F. Cline, ed., *Latin American History*, 2 vols. (Austin, 1967), 2:466–76.

10. Robert Triffin, "Central Banking and Monetary Management in Latin America," in Seymour Harris, ed., *Economic Problems of Latin America* (New York, 1944), pp. 93–116; Robert N. Seidel, "American Reformers Abroad: The Kemmerer Missions in South America, 1923–1931," *Journal of Economic History* 32, no. 2 (June 1972): 520–45; Luis Eduardo Laso, *Evolución de los sistemas monetarios y bancos centrales de América latina* (Guayaquil, 1972), pp. 6–8; Frank Tamagna, *La banca central en América latina* (Mexico, 1963); Maria-Renata Manassewitsch, *Los bancos centrales hispano-americanos* (Caracas, 1945).

11. Seidel, "American Reformers Abroad," p. 535; Triffin, "Central Banking and Monetary Management," pp. 96–98; Laso, *Evolución*, pp. 7–13; Tamagna, *La banca central*; Oscar Pedro Ballen, *Los bancos centrales* (Montevideo, 1937), pp. 91–104.

12. Tamagna, *La banca central*; Mario Rietti, *Money and Banking in Latin America* (New York, 1979), pp. 174–80.

13. Melchior Palyi, *The Twilight of Gold, 1914–1936* (Chicago, 1972).

14. Dean E. Traynor, *International Monetary and Financial Conferences in the Interwar Period* (Washington, D.C., 1949); League of Nations, Secretariat, Financial and Transit Department, *International Currency Experience: Lessons of the Inter-War Period* (Princeton, 1944).

15. For example, when the United States introduced the gold standard in Puerto Rico at the turn of the century, sugar planters complained because they had been selling their crops for gold while paying their workers in depreciating local currency. Emily S. Rosenberg, "Foundations of United States International Financial Power: Gold Standard Diplomacy, 1900–1905," *Business History Review* 59 (Summer 1985): 169–202.

16. Palyi, *Twilight of Gold*; A. G. Ford, *The Gold Standard, 1880–1914: Britain and Argentina* (Oxford, 1962); Raúl Prebisch, *El patrón oro y la vulnerabilidad económica de nuestros países* (Mexico, n.d.).

17. EWK, Box 17, letter from E. W. Kemmerer to Fred Morris Dearing, July 20, 1934.

18. William P. Glade, *The Latin American Economies: A Study of Their Institutional Evolution* (New York, 1969); Jerome Levinson and Juan de Onis, *The Alliance that Lost Its Way: A Critical Report on the Alliance for Progress* (Chicago, 1970).

19. Henry C. Wallich, "Fiscal Policy and the Budget," in Seymour Harris, ed., *Economic Problems of Latin America*, pp. 117–40.

20. EWK, Diary, May 7, 1931, p. 127.

21. Barbara Stallings, "Default vs. Refinancing: Peruvian Debt Crises, 1826–1983," MS, 1983; Max Winkler and Maxwell S. Stewart, "Recent Defaults of Government Loans," *Foreign Policy Reports* 7, no. 22 (January 6, 1932): 395–408; John T. Madden, Marcus Nadler, and Harry C. Sauvain, *America's Experience as a Creditor Nation* (New York 1937).

22. Carleton Beals, *The Coming Struggle for Latin America* (Philadelphia, 1938), pp. 198–99.

23. Charles W. Bergquist, *Alternative Approaches to the Problem of Development: A Selected and Annotated Bibliography* (Durham, 1979); Charles W. Bergquist, *Labor in Latin America: Comparative Essays on Chile, Argentina, Venezuela, and Colombia* (Stanford, 1986); Heraldo Muñoz, *From Dependency to Development: Strategies to Overcome Underdevelopment and Inequality* (Boulder, 1981); Fernando Henrique Cardoso and Enzo Faletto, *Dependency and Development in Latin America* (Berkeley, 1979); Osvaldo Sunkel, *El subdesarrollo y la teoría del desarrollo* (Mexico, 1971); Peter Evans, *Dependent Development: The Alliance of Multinational, State, and Local Capital in Brazil* (Princeton, 1979); Peter Evans, "After Dependency: Recent Studies of Class, State, and Industrialization," *Latin American Research Review* 20, no. 2 (1985): 149–60.

24. Andre Gunder Frank, *Capitalism and Underdevelopment in Latin America* (New York, 1966); idem, *Latin America: Underdevelopment or Revolution* (New York, 1969); James D. Cockcroft, Andre Gunder Frank, and Dale L. Johnson, *Dependence and Underdevelopment* (New York, 1972); Theotonio Dos Santos, *Dependencia y cambio social* (Santiago, 1972); Frank Bonilla and Robert Girling, *Structures of Dependency* (Stanford, 1973); Immanuel Wallerstein, "The Rise and Future Demise of the World Capitalist System: Concepts for Comparative Analysis," *Comparative Studies in Society and History*, no. 4 (September 1974): 387–415; Christopher Abel and Colin M. Lewis, *Latin America, Economic Imperialism, and the State: The Political Economy of the External Connection from Independence to the Present* (London, 1985).

25. For an analysis of comparable issues in Europe and the United States, stressing the interplay between shifting external forces and internal coalitions, see Peter Gourevitch, *Politics in Hard Times: Comparative Responses to International Economic Crises* (Ithaca, 1986).

26. Pike, *The United States and the Andean Republics*, pp. 177–78.

27. Hirschman, *Journeys toward Progress*, pp. 294–95.

28. Andean agricultural and export elites were not unique. In the decades prior to 1930 the supposedly all-powerful Brazilian agro-exporters also frequently failed to obtain the easy money and credit policies they desired from the national government, which preferred exchange stability to satisfy foreign investors and urban consumers. There, too, the relatively autonomous state could sometimes choose independent policies when internal and external elites were divided. Steven Topik, "The State's Contribution to the Development of Brazil's Internal Economy, 1850–1930," *Hispanic American Historical Review* 65, no. 2 (May 1985): 203–28.

29. E. V. K. Fitzgerald, "Foreign Finance and Capital Accumulation in Latin America: A Critical Approach," in Abel and Lewis, eds., *Latin America, Economic Imperialism, and the State*, pp. 451–71.

30. Edwin Walter Kemmerer, *Monetary System of Mexico: Proposed Reforms* (Mexico, 1917); idem, *Modern Currency Reforms* (New York, 1916); idem, *Inflation and Revolution: Mexico's Experience of 1912–1917* (Princeton, 1940); Cirpiano Bueno, *Juicio crítico del estudio monetario de México y reformas propuestas, por el Sr. E. W. Kemmerer* (Querétaro, 1918).

31. Donald L. Kemmerer and Bruce R. Dalgaard, "Inflation, Intrigue, and Monetary Reform in Guatemala, 1919–1926," *Historian*, no. 66 (November 1983): 21–38; Joseph S. Tulchin, *The Aftermath of War: World War I and United States Policy toward Latin America* (New York, 1971), pp. 190–98.

32. Rosenberg, *Spreading the American Dream*, pp. 154–55; Richard Hemmig Meyer, *Banker's Diplomacy: Monetary Stabilization in the Twenties* (New York, 1970), pp. 63–99.

33. Merle Curti and Kendall Birr, *Prelude to Point Four: American Technical Missions Overseas* (Madison, 1954), pp. 176–83.

34. EWK, Diary, December 11, 1925, pp. 344–45; May 25, 1927, p. 146; June 27, 1927, p. 179; Winston Fritsch, "Aspects of Brazilian Economic Policy Under the First Republic (1889–1930)" (D. Phil. diss., Cambridge University, 1983), p. 193. I am grateful to Joseph Love for this citation.

35. Curti and Birr, *Prelude to Point Four*, pp. 160–88, 207; Rosenberg, "American Foreign Financial Advising."

36. Rosenberg, *Spreading the American Dream*, pp. 77–78, 152–59; Meyer, *Banker's Diplomacy*, pp. 2–3, 111, 138.

37. See Rosemary Thorp, ed., *Latin America in the 1930s: The Role of the Periphery in the World Crisis* (London, 1984), and especially Carlos F. Diaz Alejandro, "Latin America in the 1930s," pp. 17–49, therein.

38. "Monetary Developments in Latin America," *Federal Reserves Bulletin* 31, no. 6 (June 1945): 519–31.

39. Lauchlin Currie, *The Role of Economic Advisers in Developing Countries* (Westport, 1981).

40. Barbara Stallings, *Banker to the Third World: U.S. Portfolio Investments in Latin America, 1900–86* (Berkeley, 1987); idem, "Peru and the U.S. Banks: Who Has the Upper Hand?" MS, 1978; idem, "Peru and the U.S. Banks: Privatization of Financial Relations," in Richard R. Fagen, ed., *Capitalism and the State in U.S.–Latin American Relations* (Stanford, 1979), pp. 217–53; Roberto Frenkel and Guillermo O'Donnell, "The 'Stabilization Programs' of the International Monetary Fund and Their Internal Impacts," in Fagen, ed., *Capitalism and the State*, pp. 171–216; Milton Friedman, *Milton Friedman en Chile* (Santiago, 1975); Charles Lipson, *Standing Guard: Protecting Foreign Capital in the Nineteenth and Twentieth Centuries* (Berkeley, 1985), pp. 85–139.

41. Charles P. Kindleberger, "The 1929 World Depression in Latin America—from the Outside," in Thorp, ed., *Latin America in the 1930s*, pp. 315–30. Among countless publications on the

debt crisis of the 1980s, three good books to begin with (in addition to the monograph by Stallings) are Richard E. Feinberg and Valeriana Kallab, *Adjustment Crisis in the Third World* (New Brunswick, 1984); Miguel S. Wionczek, *Politics and Economics of External Debt Crisis: The Latin American Experience* (Boulder, 1985); and Miles Kahler, *The Politics of International Debt* (Ithaca, 1986).

INDEX

Abadía Mendez, Miguel, 53, 56, 63, 65, 68, 70
Academy of Economic Sciences (Chile), 90
Academy of Lawyers (Ecuador), 165
Administrative Company of Revenues (Peru), 215
Africa, 127, 205
Agricultural Bank of Peru, 217, 235, 245
Agriculturalists, 28, 33, 253, 256, 257, 260, 263–65, 268, 323 n.15, 324 n.28; in Bolivia, 175, 182, 190, 192, 194, 196, 206, 209; in Chile, 78, 80, 83–85, 88, 90, 93, 97–99, 101, 106, 109, 112–13, 115–17, 121–23, 245, 286 n.16; in Colombia, 33, 35, 42–43, 47–48, 50, 55–56, 59–62, 69–70, 73–75, 245; in Ecuador, 129, 132, 135, 142, 149–57, 160, 164, 168, 171, 172, 174, 245; in Peru, 212–13, 217–19, 221, 223, 231, 232, 235, 237, 244–48
Alessandri Palma, Arturo, 81, 86, 88–93, 96, 104–6, 116, 120, 122
All American Cables, 119
Alliance for Progress, 259
American and Foreign Power Company, 119
American Economic Association, 9, 251
American Economic Bulletin, 9
American Economic Review, 9
American Popular Revolutionary Alliance (APRA), 111, 223–24, 228, 229, 231, 233, 238, 243, 248
Anaconda, 119
Anglo South American Bank, 130
Antioquia, Colombia, 37, 38, 39, 43, 44, 47, 49–50
Aramayo company, 181

Argentina, 10, 11, 12, 16, 19, 30, 31, 36, 37, 56, 57, 59, 77, 83, 108, 142, 242, 258, 267, 286 n.16, 314 n.82
Armenia, 267
Asia, 205
Association of Accountants of Chile, 101
Association of Agriculturalists of Ecuador, 132
Association of Employees of Ecuador, 132
Association of Mining Industries of Bolivia, 194
Association of Nitrate Producers of Chile, 95
Association of Peruvian Merchants, 218
Atkins, Paul Moody, 227
Australia, 106
Austria, 95, 267
Authoritarianism, 17, 251, 253, 261, 263, 266, 267, 269; in Bolivia, 188, 191, 207; in Chile, 87, 88, 90, 93, 99, 114, 123–24; in Colombia, 70; in Ecuador, 139, 140, 146–49, 163; in Peru, 212, 215, 220, 222, 223, 237
Ayora, Isidro, 36, 138–40, 147, 149, 157–59, 163, 165, 168, 170, 171, 172, 173

Bananas, 14, 32, 59, 64, 71–72
Banco Central Hipotecario (Colombia), 61
Banco Comercial y Agrícola (Ecuador), 131–32, 136–39, 141, 156
Banco de Chile, 94
Banco de Colombia, 63
Banco de Descuento de Guayaquil, 143
Banco del Pichincha, 155
Banco Francés e Italiano, 35
Bankers, 27, 28, 256, 257–59, 264–65; Boli-

ABOUT THE AUTHOR

Paul W. Drake is Institute of the Americas Professor of Political Science and History and Director, Center for Iberian and Latin American Studies, University of California, San Diego.